The Carolingians and the written word

The Carolingians and the written word

ROSAMOND McKITTERICK

Lecturer in History, University of Cambridge,
and Fellow of Newnham College

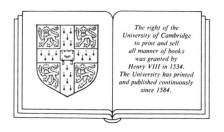

The right of the
University of Cambridge
to print and sell
all manner of books
was granted by
Henry VIII in 1534.
The University has printed
and published continuously
since 1584.

CAMBRIDGE UNIVERSITY PRESS

Cambridge
New York   Port Chester
Melbourne   Sydney

Published by the Press Syndicate of the University of Cambridge
The Pitt Building, Trumpington Street, Cambridge CB2 1RP
40 West 20th Street, New York, NY 10011, USA
10 Stamford Road, Oakleigh, Melbourne 3166, Australia

First published 1989
Reprinted 1990

Printed in Great Britain by the University Press, Cambridge

British Library cataloguing in publication data

McKitterick, Rosamond
The Carolingians and the written word.
1. Carolingian Empire. Literacy
I. Title
302.2′0944

Library of Congress cataloguing in publication data

McKitterick, Rosamond
The Carolingians and the written word/Rosamond McKitterick.
p.   cm.
Bibliography.
Includes indexes.
ISBN 0 521 30539 X.   ISBN 0 521 31565 4 (pbk.)
1. Written communication – Europe – History.   2. Carlovingians.
I. Title.
P211.3.E85M35 1989
001.54′3′094 – dc19   88-29232   CIP

ISBN 0 521 30539 X hardback
ISBN 0 521 31565 4 paperback

60 0361 4042

UP

IN MEMORIAM
John Henry Bernard McKitterick
1910–1987

Fodere quam vites melius scribere libros:
Ille suo ventri serviet, iste animae.

Alcuin, *MGH Poet.* I, p. 320

Contents

Maps

Tables

Preface

Much of this book has been presented in the form of papers and lectures over the past seven years in the Universities of Chicago, Cornell, Columbia, Harvard, Illinois and Notre Dame in the United States of America, of Heidelberg and Münster in West Germany, in the University of Western Australia, in Cambridge, Durham, Edinburgh, London and Oxford in Britain, in University College, Dublin, in Ampleforth College, Yorkshire, and in the Leys School, Cambridge. I am indebted to my hosts, especially the late Julian Brown and the late Peter Classen, Hugh Amory, Isobel Durack, Donald Eddy, Stephen Gersh, Michael Hoeflich, Ralph McInerny, Peter Johanek, Karl Morrison, the organizers of the Antiquary Lecture in Edinburgh and, above all, David Rollason, who first encouraged me to put together my thoughts on literacy in Charlemagne's Europe. I benefited much from the comments, criticisms and reactions of my various audiences and wish to record my heartfelt thanks to them all.

For assistance during my visit to St Gall and accommodation to my needs, I am grateful to the Stiftsarchivar, Werner Vogler, and the Stiftsbibliothekar, Peter Ochsenbein and their staff. I should like also to thank the librarians and staff of the following libraries: the Bibliothèque Nationale, Paris, the Bibliothèque Municipale, Valenciennes, the Bamberg Staatliche Bibliothek, the British Library in London, Cambridge University Library, Corpus Christi College Library, Cambridge, the Bodleian Library, Oxford, the Pierpont Morgan Library, New York, the Beineke Library in Yale and the Biblioteca Apostolica in the Vatican. For their expert guidance in programming and sorting the St Gall charter material I am grateful to John Dawson and his staff at the Literary and Linguistic Computing Centre in Cambridge University.

Many friends and colleagues have given me much help and encouragement while I have been working on this book, whether by feeding me references or by reading what I made of them. Without the efforts, and candour, of Michael Clanchy, Sarah Foot, Don MacKenzie and Janet Nelson, who between them read the entire text, it would have been very much less presentable. But I am also grateful to Stuart Airlie, Michel

Banniard, Michael Borgolte, Edward Booth, Peter Brown, John Contreni, Simon Coupland, David Dumville, David Ganz, Hans-Werner Goetz, Michael Gorman, Susan Kelly, Simon Keynes, Michael Lapidge, Vivien Law, Douglas Lee, John Lonsdale, Paul Needham, Thomas Noble, Andrew Palmer, Jonathan Shepard, Julia Smith, Peter Stein, Ian Wood and all my students over the past seven years, who have read sections, asked and answered questions on specific points or provided me with timely encouragement. I owe much too to Martin Shepherd of the Hambledon Press. I am particularly indebted to Bernhard Bischoff for furnishing me with priceless information about important manuscripts, and in particular for his verification of dates and origins of most of the codices listed in Table A. None of the aforementioned, of course, is in any way responsible for the interpretations advanced in this book.

For invaluable help with the production of the final typescript my thanks are due to Lorraine Ostler and Elizabeth Murray of the History Faculty Office, Cambridge University, and, for seeing the book through the press, to William Davies and the staff of Cambridge University Press. Newnham College has continued to offer an excellent working environment and I wish in particular to thank Mary Beard, Margaret Spufford and Gillian Sutherland for fruitful conversations about literacy, and the Principal and Fellows for the financial help afforded me for my visit to Switzerland.

In presenting the text I have referred to manuscripts in an abbreviated form by their present location and shelfmark (thus: 'Autun 3' rather than Autun, Bibliothèque Municipale Manuscript 3). Full details of libraries and shelfmarks can be found in the Index of Manuscripts at the end of the book. Wherever possible I have cited Latin texts in English translation with reference to existing published translations (as well as to the Latin edition) so that those with little Latin who wish to do so may look up the context of the extracts I have quoted. I wish here to record my special thanks to David King for his permission to quote from his translations of Charlemagne's capitularies in P. D. King, *Charlemagne. Translated Sources* (Lambrigg, Kendal, 1987). Personal names have been standardized as much as possible, and modern forms used when these are widely accepted. For the names of scribes and witnesses in chapter 3, the problem of erratic and inconsistent spelling was particularly acute. Different forms have been retained when these clearly indicate different men, but when the same person is concerned one of the variants has been selected and thus standardized.

My last thanks are due to my daughter Lucy for demonstrating how literate skills are acquired, and, as always, to my parents and to my husband David for their unfailing support and faith in the enterprise.

Cambridge, 29 February 1988

Acknowledgements

The illustration on the cover is the scribe from the early ninth century manuscript in the Universitätsbibliothek Düsseldorf MS A 14, fo. 119v. The manuscript is a Leihgabe der Stadt Düsseldorf an die Universitätsbibliothek Düsseldorf. I am grateful to the Direktor of the Universitätsbibliothek Düsseldorf, for permission to reproduce the drawing from this book.

Abbreviations

AA SS	*Acta Sanctorum* (Antwerp, 1643–)
Annales E.S.C.	*Annales: Economies, Sociétés, Civilisations*
BEC	*Bibliothèque de l'Ecole des Chartes*
Bischoff, *Lorsch*	Bernhard Bischoff, *Lorsch im Spiegel seiner Handschriften*, Münchener Beiträge zur Mediävistik und Renaissance Forschung Beiheft (Munich, 1974)
Bischoff, *MS* I, II, III	Bernhard Bischoff, *Mittelalterliche Studien* I (Stuttgart, 1966) II (Stuttgart, 1967) III (Stuttgart, 1981)
Bischoff, *Schreibschulen* I, II	Bernhard Bischoff, *Die sudostdeutschen Schreibschulen und Bibliotheken in der Karolingerzeit* I *Die Bayerischen Diözesen* (3rd edn, Wiesbaden, 1974) II *Die Vorwiegend Osterreichischen Diözesen* (Wiesbaden, 1980)
BL	British Library, London
BN	Bibliothèque Nationale, Paris
Bruckner, *Scriptoria* II, III	Albert Bruckner, *Scriptoria Medii Aevi Helvetica. Denkmäler schweizerischer Schreibkunst des Mittelalters* II *Schreibschulen der Diözese Konstanz. St Gallen I* (Geneva, 1936) III *Schreibschulen der Diözese Konstanz. St Gallen II* (Geneva, 1938)
ChLA	Albert Bruckner and Robert Marichal, *Chartae Latinae Antiquiores. Facsimile Edition of the Latin Charters prior to the Ninth Century* I– (Olten, Lausanne, 1954–)

CLA	Elias Avery Lowe, *Codices Latini Antiquiores. A Palaeographical Guide to Latin Manuscripts prior to the Ninth Century* I–XI plus Supplement (Oxford, 1935–71)
Clm	Codices latini monacenses, Bayerische Staatsbibliothek, Munich
DA	*Deutsches Archiv für die Erforschung des Mittelalters*
EHR	*English Historical Review*
IRMA	*Ius Romanum Medii Aevi* (Milan, 1961–)
JTS	*Journal of Theological Studies*
Lehmann, *Mittelalterliche Bibliothekskataloge*	Paul Lehmann, ed., *Mittelalterliche Bibliothekskataloge Deutschlands und der Schweiz I Die Diözesen Konstanz und Chur* (Munich, 1918)
McKitterick, *Frankish Church*	R. McKitterick, *The Frankish Church and the Carolingian Reforms 789–895* (London, 1977)
McKitterick, *Frankish Kingdoms*	R. McKitterick, *The Frankish Kingdoms under the Carolingians, 751–987* (London, 1983)
MA	*Le Moyen Age*
MGH	*Monumenta Germaniae Historica*
Cap.	*Capitularia*
Conc.	*Concilia*
Epp.	*Epistulae*
Formulae	*Formulae Merovingici et Karolini Aevi, Leges Sectio* V
Leges Germ.	*Leges nationum Germanicarum*
Poet.	*Poetae aevi Karolini*
SS	*Scriptores*
SS i.u.s.	*Scriptores in usum scholarum*
SS rer. merov.	*Scriptores rerum merovingicarum*
MIÖG	*Mitteilungen des Instituts für Österreichische Geschichtsforschung*
PL	J. P. Migne, ed., *Patrologiae cursus completus series Latina* (Paris, 1844–55)
RB	*Revue Bénédictine*
RHEF	*Revue d'Histoire de l'Eglise de France*

Settimane	*Settimane di Studio del Centro Italiano di Studi sull'alto Medioevo* 1– (Spoleto, 1954–)
TRHS	*Transactions of the Royal Historical Society*
Vat.	Biblioteca Apostolica Vaticana, Rome
W.	H. Wartmann, *Urkundenbuch der Abtei St Gallen* I and II (700–920) (Zurich, 1863)
ZSSR	*Zeitschrift der Savigny Stiftung für Rechtsgeschichte*
GA	*Germanistische Abteilung*
KA	*Kanonistische Abteilung*

1 ✺ *The spoken and the written word*

I INTRODUCTION

Literacy and the use of the written word in the early middle ages have hitherto been thought to have been confined to a clerical elite, while society at large conducted its affairs orally. Many, indeed, have seen the beginning of 'good things' at the millennium, with a 'rebirth' of literacy in the eleventh and twelfth centuries,[1] as if brand new awakenings and skills appeared in the wake of Halley's Comet to an awed Europe. But if such great changes were taking place in the eleventh century, from what were they a change?

Rather than a sudden enlightenment, are we not observing in the history of western Europe after about 1000 an increase, extension and diversification of literate skills, the next stage in a continuous pattern from late antiquity to the early Germanic kingdoms? We also need to establish the possible functions of literacy, both private and public, in relation to a particular society's needs; as those needs change so do the particular contexts in which literate modes are required. Above all, the early Germanic kingdoms were not only Rome's heirs, they were Christian. In societies whose religion was one of the Book, and whose government and legal practice were founded, to a greater or lesser extent, on the written word, it cannot be maintained that they were purely oral societies.[2] The

---

[1] The most stimulating discussions of mediaeval literacy after *c.* 1000 are the now classic studies by Michael Clanchy, *From Memory to Written Record 1066–1307* (London, 1979); H. Grundmann, 'Litteratus–illiteratus. Der Wandel einer Bildungsnorm vom Altertum zum Mittelalter', *Archiv für Kulturgeschichte* 40 (1958) 1–66, and his earlier 'Die Frauen und die Literatur im Mittelalter', *Archiv für Kulturgeschichte* 26 (1936) 129–61; and J. W. Thompson, *The Literacy of the Laity in the Middle Ages* (New York and London, 1939 and 1960). New perspectives have been offered by Franz H. Bauml, 'Varieties and consequences of medieval literacy and illiteracy', *Speculum* 55 (1980) 237–65, and Brian Stock, *The Implications of Literacy. Written Language and Models of Interpretation in the Eleventh and Twelfth Centuries* (Princeton, 1983). It is Stock who goes so far as to speak of a 'rebirth of literacy' *c.* 1000. His forthcoming *Studies in Literacy, Rationality and Society in the Middle Ages* (Cambridge) will also concentrate on the eleventh century onwards.

[2] I accept Walter Ong's definition of a primary oral culture, that is, a culture totally untouched by any knowledge of writing or print, and maintain that neither Carolingian

written word had a function in early mediaeval society and it is for us to determine precisely what that function was.[3]

There was undoubtedly some continuity and much change in the functions of writing and possession of literate skills from the late Roman to the Carolingian periods; there is certainly sufficient evidence to dispose of any Pirenne-like thesis of the decline in literacy outside a clerical elite by the eighth century and a rebirth of literacy in the eleventh century. The Franks in particular increased their resort to literate modes for legal and administrative business from the mid-eighth century. The written word became a fundamental element of Carolingian culture, and Frankish society in the Carolingian period was transformed into one largely dependent on the written word for its religion, law, government and learning. The purpose of this book is to demonstrate how it was so transformed, and how this manifests itself in our sources.

Past studies of early mediaeval Frankish culture, such as those of Pirenne or Riché, invaluable in documenting strands of Roman survival, have measured early mediaeval developments by the yardstick of classical culture.[4] Preoccupation with cultural 'decline' or the degree of survival of classical culture, however, is tangential to a study of Carolingian culture. It is not simply a matter of whether or not Roman literary culture and education survived, but what kind of culture existed and the degree to which the written word was an element of that culture. If it was an element, why was it, and from what source was its use continued and promoted? The most remarkable legacy of Roman civilization to Frankish Gaul was not in fact its content but its form. In the pursuit of lingering traces of the content our awareness of the form is in danger of being blunted. It was the written word which was the most vital vehicle of continuity, a continuity about which there is now a growing consensus.[5]

culture nor that of the early middle ages generally can be understood as an oral culture, even if both preserved, in Ong's terms, 'much of the mind-set of primary orality': Walter Ong, *Orality and Literacy. The Technologizing of the Word* (London, 1982), p. 11.

[3] The studies contained in R. McKitterick, ed., *The Uses of Literacy in Early Mediaeval Europe* (Cambridge, forthcoming), will concentrate on this issue in a selection of early mediaeval societies, from Ireland to Byzantium and the Jewish communities of the Mediterranean region before the eleventh century.

[4] Henri Pirenne, 'De l'état de l'instruction des laiques à l'époque mérovingienne', *RB* 46 (1934) 165–77, and P. Riché, *Education et culture dans l'occident barbare VIᵉ–VIIIᵉ siècles* (Paris, 1962), Eng. trans. J. J. Contreni (Columbia, South Carolina, 1976); but compare the position adopted in Riché's more recent *Ecoles et enseignement dans le Haut Moyen Age* (Paris, 1979), especially pp. 285–313.

[5] See, for example, the illuminating comments and assessments in Edith M. Wightman, *Gallia Belgica* (London, 1985), pp. 239–56, and Michael McCormick, *Eternal Victory. Triumphal Rulership in Late Antiquity, Byzantium and the Early Medieval West* (Cambridge and Paris, 1986), especially pp. 6–7. For some sense of the trends of opinion in the older literature see P. E. Hübinger, ed., *Kulturbruch oder Kulturkontinuität im Übergang von der Antike zum Mittelalter* (Darmstadt, 1968).

What was transmitted from late Roman Gaul to the Frankish kingdom that succeeded it was the use of literate modes, the structure of the law and written instruments, the pattern of administration and its dependence, at least to some extent, on the written word and the Latin language. It is on the role of the written word in Carolingian society, therefore, that this study concentrates.

This book is also in some ways a reaction against the preoccupation with the later middle ages of most recent studies of mediaeval literacy. It is based on the conviction that the roots of later mediaeval developments are to be sought in the centuries immediately succeeding the period of Roman rule. It is only with reference to the transformations of these years that the changes documented in the eleventh and twelfth centuries and later, now attracting an increasing amount of attention and interest from a variety of perspectives, can be interpreted.

The questions of Frankish literacy and the function of writing in Frankish society can be reduced to the purely quantitative. What proportion of the population possessed literate skills or employed literate modes in their social organization? Was that proportion further differentiated by function? Was literacy only possessed by a particular group within society or was it more widespread? Is the number of people possessing literate skills, employing literate modes and participating in literacy statistically significant enough for Frankish society in the eighth and ninth centuries as a whole to be regarded as literate in the pragmatic sense, that is, literate for practical purposes rather than, or, as well as, learned ones?[6] Given that Frankish society cannot be described as a purely oral culture, may we call it a literate one?

Such quantitative questions, however, inevitably depend on qualitative ones. The study of the place of the written word in any society cannot confine itself to literacy and its uses alone. Some attempt must be made to study the relationship between orality and literacy, and the operations of literacy in Frankish society. It will be argued that in the prodigious output of the written word at every level of Carolingian society we are observing essential phases in the development of a literate culture, with new ideals and definitions of education and knowledge dependent on a written tradition. The consequences are to be seen in an impulse to the recording of the past in writing, in the exploitation of the written word in government and administration and in a marked impact on the character of aristocratic and lay culture in general. It is my hope that this study may

---

[6] On the notion of pragmatic literacy I follow Malcolm Parkes, 'The literacy of the laity', in D. Daiches and A. K. Thorlby, eds., *Literature and Western Civilization. The Mediaeval World* (London, 1973), pp. 555–77, especially p. 555.

prompt other investigations, particularly concerning the degree to which the foundations for the developments I describe were laid down in the Merovingian period.

The role of the written word in Carolingian society has to be demonstrated rather than asserted. An arresting image in Carolingian manuscript illumination is of the Book from John the Divine's apocalyptic vision. As interpreted by patristic and Frankish exegetes, the Book represented the gift of the written law of God in the Old and New Testaments. The implication of this iconography and the explanation of the written words on which it is based is that possession and use of writing were, for the Franks, the keys to faith, knowledge and power. The iconography and symbolic meaning of the Book, moreover, are to be linked with the theology of the Word, the *Logos* of St John's Gospel, for it was a connection not lost on Carolingian commentators on this text.[7] A manuscript such as the Trier Apocalypse is the expression of a highly sophisticated understanding of the functions of word and image; but the Franks' pragmatic understanding of the use of the written word is the essential context in which such symbolic interpretations are to be understood. The largely pragmatic contexts and manifestations of the use of the written word on which I have chosen to concentrate in this book are thus only some among many on which it would be possible to dwell. My aim is to expose the essential foundations of the uses of the written word, the many manifestations of literacy in the eighth and ninth centuries and the degree to which they are either innovative or a result of steady evolution from the fifth century.

The first consideration has to be the degree to which Latin can be or was regarded either as a foreign language or even exclusively as the language of literacy in the eighth and ninth centuries. I therefore rehearse the arguments concerning the development of Romance, and the survival of Latin as a spoken language, in the remainder of this chapter. One spectacular demonstration of the vigour of Latin in the early barbarian kingdoms as a whole was the redaction of their customary laws in Latin. Law and the use of the written word thus form the subject of my second

[7] See, for example, the Trier Apocalypse, Trier 31 *passim* and the commentary with facsimile, in R. Laufner and Peter K. Klein, eds., *Trierer Apokalypse* (Graz, 1975); compare the frontispieces to the Apocalypse or Book of Revelation in the bibles of Charles the Bald: BN lat. 1, fo. 415v, San Paolo fuori le Mura Bible, fo. 331v, and also the Moutier-Grandval bible, BL Add. 10546, fo. 449r. The context of this iconography and the general relationship between text and image in Carolingian painting will be discussed in R. McKitterick, 'Text and image in the Carolingian world', in McKitterick, ed., *Uses of Literacy*. For Carolingian exegesis on St John see, for example, Alcuin, 'Commentaria in sancti Johannis Evangelium', *PL* 100, col. 745.

chapter. I discuss there the status of law, the significance of the recommendations for recourse to the written word in legal transactions and the implications of legislation from the Carolingian period, which assumes a widespread ability to communicate by means of the written word in the process of administration and government. The third chapter narrows the focus of the discussion of the law by examining a large group of charters. These documents provide crucial information concerning the conduct and record of a society's methods of gift, endowment and exchange, and the status of the written word within a community at a lower level than is usually appreciated. They also reveal participation in literacy and actual use of literate modes by members of the lay population as well as by the clergy and monks in their midst.

The second half of the book broadens the enquiry to embrace various manifestations of the written word in Carolingian society and how these can be interpreted to reveal attitudes towards writing and books. It demonstrates how in both social and intellectual contexts the written word and the particular forms it took were the embodiment of a written Romano-Christian tradition, defined and refined by the Carolingians in their turn, and passed on to their successors. I consider the social status of the book and the written word in economic terms and how members of a warrior society were able to adapt their code of values to rank the possession and production of books with their greatest treasures, an adaptation with crucial and far-reaching consequences for western European society. I take up the compilation of inventories of this book-formed wealth, and show how in the intellectual sphere, methods were employed to systematize the enumeration of items of the golden hoard of words, with the effect of providing a canon of texts to form the basis of both contemporary knowledge and future libraries. This canon is in itself, in a real sense, one of the consequences of literacy; it shaped intellectual development and spiritual understanding of the Christian faith in a particular and distinctive way, and influenced the forms and expressions of both clerical and lay piety. These chapters have implications indeed for the extent of both clerical and lay literacy and show the Carolingian period as one in which fundamental transformations and adjustments concerning the function and future of the written word took place. But at a more practical level the hints in the evidence concerning the laity need fuller investigation. The last chapter therefore examines the questions of the education of the laity and the degree to which the 'lay aristocracy', and especially the women, can be regarded as literate. It is based on a wide variety of different types of evidence, some of it not usually considered in

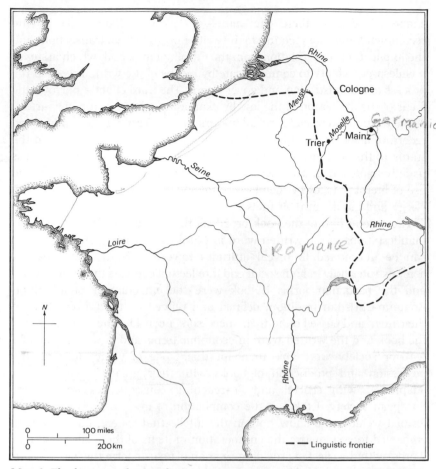

Map 1 The linguistic frontier between 'Romance' and 'Germanic' in the eighth
century

Source: based on Werner König, *dtv-Atlas zur deutschen Sprache* (Munich, 1978), p. 70

this context, but which, as I argue, has much to tell us about the use and
functions of the written word in Carolingian society, and thus in a vital
and formative period in the history of western Europe.[8]

[8] I have assumed a general familiarity with the main discussions of literacy. For those who
are new to the subject the following, in addition to the studies cited in nn. 1, 2 and 6, may
serve as useful introductions to the wide variety of interpretations and perspectives:
Harvey J. Graff, *Literacy in History. An Interdisciplinary Research Bibliography* (New York
and London, 1981); Brian V. Street, *Literacy in Theory and Practice* (Cambridge, 1984),
especially pp. 95–125; Jack Goody, *Literacy in Traditional Societies* (Cambridge, 1968);
idem, *The Domestication of the Savage Mind* (Cambridge, 1977); idem, *The Logic of Writing
and the Organization of Society* (Cambridge, 1986); Eric A. Havelock, *Origins of Western
Literacy* (Toronto, 1976); Carlo Cipolla *Literacy and Development in the West* (Harmondsworth, 1969); R. Pattison, *On Literacy. The Politics of the Word from Homer to the
Age of Rock* (Oxford, 1982).

II THE QUESTION OF LANGUAGE

In 844, Lupus of Ferrières wrote to Abbot Marcward of Prüm, asking him whether he could send him three young men – his nephew, son of Guago, and two others – for instruction in the German language. Marcward was clearly willing to receive them, for three years later, Lupus thanked him for giving the boys an understanding of the German language, the need for which Lupus regarded as important at that time.[9]

The passage highlights the linguistic complexity of the Frankish kingdoms in the ninth century. Broadly speaking, the regions from the Rhineland eastwards were Germanic-speaking areas, and those west of the Rhineland were Latin-based or Romance-speaking areas. But there was a great diversity of dialects in both east and west; many areas, for example, the northern Moselle region, were essentially mixed language regions and many 'pockets of Romance' have been posited in Germanic areas.[10] Although a map (such as that provided, Map 1) can give a rough idea of the language areas, it is totally inadequate as far as informing us what language or languages a person in any one region could speak or understand, let alone which languages he or she could read. Given the great diversity of dialects, the possession by the church and lay individuals of lands in both eastern and western portions of the Carolingian realm, the intermarriage between men and women within the Frankish kingdoms, the intellectual and spiritual links between monasteries on either side of the Rhine (evinced by such exchanges as Lupus sending boys to Prüm, Lupus himself having studied at Fulda, and the German Hraban Maur going to Tours) and the enormous stress on the essential unity of the Frankish kingdoms, it is hardly likely that monolingualism was the norm except among particularly isolated social groups or in remote areas with no contact with people in another community speaking a different language or dialect. The whole process of Germanic settlement in the late Roman Empire must have created great linguistic diversity in all areas once part of the Roman Empire. A process of assimilation and adaptation in social spheres undoubtedly had an impact on language patterns as well. We may, therefore, throughout the early mediaeval period in the areas

[9] Lupus of Ferrières, ed. Léon Levillain, *Loup de Ferrières. Correspondance* (Paris, 1964), Epp. 35 and 70, and see also Epp. 58 and 65, Eng. trans. Graydon W. Regenos, *The Letters of Lupus of Ferrières* (The Hague, 1966), from Levillain's edition.

[10] A useful study of a linguistic 'frontier region' between Romance and German is that of A. Joris, 'On the edge of two worlds in the heart of the new Empire: the Romance regions of northern Gaul during the Merovingian period', *Studies in Mediaeval and Renaissance History* 3.3 (1966) 1–52. I addressed some of the problems of the vernacular and discussed the older literature in *Frankish Church*, though I concentrated on the German vernaculars. Work since then on Late Latin and Romance has necessitated modification of some of the views I there expressed, and I would now lay more stress on the continuity of the Latin language.

dominated by the Franks, be dealing with a largely bilingual or even polylingual population as far as the spoken word is concerned. A modern parallel could be made with the situation in present-day Switzerland.

The type of spoken word is relatively easy to determine in the Germanic-speaking areas, for the dialects within Old High German have been largely agreed by modern scholars and we are fortunate in the possession of written witnesses to the language from the end of the eighth century onwards.[11] As far as either Romance or Latin is concerned, however, there is no agreement, not even on the proper broad linguistic categories.[12] The problem is exacerbated, from the historian's point of view, by a lack of written records of the spoken Romance forms in any quantity until the end of the tenth century, though glosses and some short texts survive from the first half of the ninth century onwards.[13] The debate concerning the nature of the spoken word in Frankish Gaul has sometimes formulated the problem under the heading 'When did Latin cease to be spoken in Gaul?', and has more recently been reformulated as 'When did Latin cease to be understood in Gaul?'.[14] The key questions at issue therefore are as follows: did the Franks adopt Latin as their native speech, and to what extent did they introduce their own language habits into it? To what degree was the Latin encountered by the Franks in the fourth century already modified and changing? Did Latin gradually evolve into 'Romance' and when did it do so? It is the last of these which is the most relevant for determining the language of the Carolingians.

Let us consider the situation in the so-called Romance regions. It used to be the general view that it was during the period between 600 and 800 that 'Latin', until then the language of the Franks in Gaul (as far as we can gather from the written Latin texts which survive) became Romance, that Latin remained the written language, while the spoken language,

---

[11] The most useful guide to Old High German is J. Knight Bostock, *A Handbook on Old High German Literature*, 2nd edn revised by K. C. King and D. R. McLintock (Oxford, 1976).

[12] For an excellent survey of recent work on Late Latin and proto-Romance, with full bibliography, see Marc van Uytfanghe, 'Histoire du Latin, protohistoire des langues romanes et histoire de la communication. A propos d'un recueil d'études, et avec quelques observations préliminaires sur le débat intellectuel entre pensée structurale et pensée historique', *Francia* 11 (1983) 579–613. His reflections constitute a response to Reinhold Kontzi's two collections of essays by various scholars on the history of the Romance languages: *Zur Entstehung der romanischen Sprachen* (Darmstadt, 1978) and *Substrate und Superstrate in den romanischen Sprachen* (Darmstadt, 1982). See also Mario Pei, *The story of Latin and the Romance Languages* (New York, San Francisco and London, 1976), especially pp. 67–77.

[13] Henry F. Muller, 'When did Latin cease to be a spoken language in France?', *The Romanic Review* 12 (1921) 318–24, and Ferdinand Lot, 'A quelle époque a-t-on cessé de parler Latin?' *Archivum Latinitatis Medii Aevi* VI *Bulletin du Cange* (1931) 97–159.

[14] For example, by Michael Richter, 'A quelle époque a-t-on cessé de parler Latin en Gaule? A propos d'une question mal posée', *Annales E.S.C.* 38 (1983) 439–48.

Romance, moved steadily away from it. We are apprised of communication problems in the canons of the reform councils of 813, with their reference to the need to *transferre* sermons into *rusticam Romanam linguam aut theotiscam*. Whether *transferre* actually means 'translate' in this context has been disputed.[15] Further, the Strasbourg oaths of 842 provide the texts of the oaths sworn by the eastern and western Frankish followers of the sons of Louis the Pious in 'Romance' and 'German'.[16] An important consideration in estimating the nature and use of the vernacular, of course, is that we only become aware of it in the literary evidence, and this is inevitably some time after the main developments in the formation of the mediaeval Romance idiom have presumably taken place. It is generally agreed, moreover, that the emergence of written Romance was very gradual.

The socio-linguistic perspectives of such scholars as Richter, Banniard and Itkonen, however, have considerably altered our understanding of late and mediaeval Latin and the early history of the Romance languages. They have, for example, retarded considerably the emergence of Romance languages perceived as different from Latin by hearers and speakers, and they have indicated that a prolonging of the organic connection between written and spoken languages far into the ninth century is now far more likely. The search for proto-Romance is moving to the Carolingian and even post-Carolingian eras.[17]

---

[15] *MGH Conc.* II. 1, p. 288, and see the discussion of the meaning of *transferre* by Roger Wright, 'Late Latin and early Romance: Alcuin's *De Orthographia* and the Council of Tours (813 A.D.)', *Papers of the Liverpool Latin Seminar* 3 (1981) 343–61, at 355–8.

[16] Nithard, *Histoire des Fils de Louis le Pieux*, ed. P. Lauer (Paris, 1926), p. 104, and Eng. trans. Bernard Scholz, *Carolingian Chronicles* (Ann Arbor, 1970), p. 162.

[17] Michael Richter: 'A socio-linguistic approach to the Latin middle ages', *Studies in Church History* 11 (1975) 69–82; 'Kommunikationsprobleme im lateinischen Mittelalter', *Historische Zeitschrift* 222 (1976) 43–80; 'Urbanitas–rusticitas: linguistic aspects of a mediaeval dichotomy', *Studies in Church History* 16 (1979) 149–57; *Sprache und Gesellschaft im Mittelalter. Untersuchungen zur mündlichen Kommunikation in England von der Mitte des elften bis zum Beginn des 14 Jarhhunderts*, Monographien zur Geschichte des Mittelalters 18 (Stuttgart, 1979). Michel Banniard: 'Le Lecteur en Espagne wisigothique d'après Isidore de Seville: de ses fonctions à l'état de la langue', *Revue des Etudes Augustiniennes* 21 (1975) 112–44; *Le Haut Moyen Age occidental*, Que sais-je?, 1807 (Paris, 1980), pp. 104–12, and see his references on pp. 126–7; 'Géographie linguistique et linguistique diachronique. Essai d'analyse analogique en occitano-roman et en latin tardif', *Via Domitia* 24 (1980–2) 9–43; 'Vox egrestis: quelques problèmes d'élocution de Cassiodore à Alcuin', in *Trames. Etudes antiques* (Limoges, 1985), pp. 195–208; 'Iuxta uniuscuiusque qualitatem. L'écriture médiatrice chez Gregoire le Grand' in *Gregoire le Grand*, Colloques Internationaux du C.N.R.S. (Paris, 1986), pp. 477–88; 'Théorie et pratique de la langue et du style chez Alcuin: rusticité feinte et rusticité masquée', *Francia* 13 (1985) 579–601; *Communication écrite et communication orale du IVe au IXe siècle en occident latin* (forthcoming). E. Itkonen, *The Significance of Merovingian Latin to Linguistic Theory. Four Linguistic Studies in Classical Languages* (Helsinki, 1978); 'Un conflit entre facteurs phonétiques et facteurs fonctionnels dans un texte en Latin mérovingien', *Neuphilologische Mitteilungen* 70 (1969) 471–84.

One of the most interesting contributions to the debate about the idea of written Latin and spoken Romance has been that of Roger Wright whose thesis is still being digested by the philologists. Wright challenges the view of written Latin and spoken Romance as two separate languages coexisting before 800. He argues that late Latin was early Romance, that there was no difference between spoken and written Latin until the Carolingians created it, not just with their emphasis on correct Latin, but by introducing new, and reviving old, rules for the pronunciation of written Latin. This made Latin virtually unintelligible to those used only to speaking it. Those already used to writing it would simply have had to learn the new Latin pronunciation instead of the old Romance one. In Romance communities before 800, everyone would have learnt automatically to speak the local vernacular when young, while when, and if, he learnt to read later, he would have learnt to spell the old-fashioned correct way, that is, Latin. When the Strasbourg oaths were recorded in 842, because Latin pronunciation had been changing, a spelling reform to represent the spoken Latin/Romance phonetically was thought necessary for the first time.[18]

After all, the concept of a general lack of correspondence between spelling and pronunciation, that is, a non-phonetic orthography, should not astonish English native speakers, as it is something to which we have long been accustomed. Absurdities such as the eight different pronunciations of 'ough' – though, thorough, bough, through, rough, lough, cough and hiccough – and the sound changes wrought by the addition of a final 't' do not disturb us at all. Nor, generally, do the varieties in accent and pronunciation among the different English-speaking groups, all of them represented by the same group of letters. Other modern analogies are the distinctions between Dutch and Flemish, or the regional pronunciations of Chinese, which rely on the same written characters. Writing, when all is said and done, is but a sign language, and there is perhaps an inevitable discrepancy between graphic representation and the sound of words, even in the apparently most phonetically transliterated of languages. Letters are a mnemonic device; they form a written code, similar in function, as far as the reader is concerned, to musical notation, for they give a guide to sounds. But the degree to which they record and preserve oral delivery is dependent also on the understanding accorded the letters and the sounds they represent. They do not necessarily, therefore, represent a sound precisely. The knowledge and exploitation of writing

[18] Roger Wright, *Late Latin and Early Romance in Spain and Carolingian France* (Liverpool, 1982). My brief summary does less than justice to but a portion of Wright's important book.

may have suggested deliberate variations of spelling in an attempt to represent sound, much as modern novelists try and render sound by a particular sequence of letters when reporting rustic or colloquial speech. If a particular convention of written language as far as spelling and even syntax is followed, and insisted upon, then its relation to speech may not be close. If the written convention had become somewhat etiolated, but steps were taken to restore old rules and impose uniform spelling and grammar in the written language (because, presumably, the more colloquial forms were felt to be too local to be generally acceptable, as seems to have been the case with the Carolingians and their deliberate promotion of purer Latinity), the pronunciation of the spoken language would not necessarily have been affected; its written forms simply accorded with stricter universal conventions.

Wright argues that the Carolingians not only sought to reimpose stricter conventions on the written language as far as spelling was concerned, but that a pronunciation reform was instigated as well. This he attributes to the influence of Alcuin of York who came from Anglo-Saxon England, a country where the vernacular was a totally different language from the Latin of the church and where Latin when pronounced was phonetic and based on traditional Latin spelling. This view raises a number of questions. Did the English in Anglo-Saxon England have a system of writing symbols that provided a faithful guide to the pronunciation of the vernacular?[19] Were the English taught to pronounce Latin phonetically by the seventh-century Italian and Irish missionaries who presumably introduced them to the language for the first time, not to mention the Franks with whom they were in contact? That is, was Latin in England pronounced as if the letters or combinations of letters in the words represented invariable sounds, with a strict correspondence always between sound and letter? Why should the late sixth- and early seventh-century Italian and Greek clerics, the Irish missionaries or the Frankish bishops and chaplains have been speaking Latin phonetically? Might they not also have been speaking forms of Late Latin? The notion of Alcuin speaking phonetically exact Latin because he had learnt it, as it were, from a book is a nice tidy one, but one fears that it may have been more complicated than that. Although an eighth-century Italian could understand the speech of an eighth-century Spaniard, Boniface the Englishman had problems in the early eighth century making himself understood when speaking Latin in Rome; all only became crystal clear when he wrote his views down in formal written Latin for the Pope

[19] On some aspects of Latin and Old English literacy in Anglo-Saxon England, see Susan Kelly, 'Anglo-Saxon lay society and the written word' in McKitterick, ed., *Uses of Literacy.*

to read.[20] Were the difficulties due to Boniface using a phonetic pronunciation or an artificially preserved archaic British, Irish or Italian one? Wright envisages Alcuin arriving in the Frankish kingdom of Charlemagne and being much struck, not to say taken aback, by the different pronunciation of Latin prevailing there. With his *De Orthographia*, he set about reforming Frankish Latin pronunciation and 'mediaeval Latin was invented'.[21] But this vision is based on what may be false assumptions about the sounds made by Englishmen in the eighth century when they spoke Latin.

Wright's arguments, fully backed up by a wealth of linguistic evidence, are, apart from my quibble about Alcuin, of great interest and constitute one of the most stimulating and convincing contributions to the debate about spoken and written Latin in the Carolingian period, with those of van Uytfanghe and Banniard, to appear for some time. The relationship between oral discourse and written texts is one that has been explored fruitfully in relation to the Merovingian saints' lives by van Uytfanghe, for example, and Banniard's work on communication, the perceptions of linguistic change and the status of writing as a representation of sound in the crucial period from the sixth to the ninth centuries are of the utmost importance.[22] Wright, moreover, is surely correct to envisage our Latin texts as written representations of a spoken language that may have sounded very different from what we think.

It is also quite clear from the evidence that the Carolingians promoted correct written Latin closer to classical norms with great success, and it may be that a new pronunciation on what were understood to be classical principles was also advocated to such an extent that the written forms became unacceptably distant from the spoken forms and new spelling had to be devised, that is, Romance spelling, in order to cater for it. There is, however, a danger in too hasty an acceptance of the speed of this so-called pronunciation reform (quite apart from its supposed progenitor!). Indeed, it is noticeable with what relief many Romance philologists reach the early ninth century, as if the insistence on correct Latin by the Carolingians effected an instant transformation at this point, it becomes safe to talk about 'Romance', confine 'Latin' to a clerical elite, and all major problems

[20] The Italian Firmadus in relation to the Spaniard is mentioned in Rudolf of Fulda's *Vita Leobae, MGH SS XV*, pp. 121–31, at p. 131. Boniface's written profession of faith is described in Willibald's *Vita Bonifacii* c.6, ed. R. Rau, on the basis of the edition by Michael Tangl and Wilhelm Levison, *Bonifatii Epistolae. Willibaldi Vita Bonifacii* (Darmstadt, 1968), p. 491.

[21] See, for example, Wright, *Late Latin and Early Romance*, p. 104, with the chapter heading 'Carolingian France: the invention of mediaeval Latin'.

[22] Note the assessment of Wright by van Uytfanghe, 'Histoire du Latin', Postscriptum II, 611–13. For Banniard's work, see above, n. 17.

fade away. On the contrary, as far as what people spoke and could read is concerned, it is in the early ninth century that the problems really begin. Is the definitive emergence of Romance in fact set too early? In the past, it has been asserted that 'Romance' emerged in the ninth century but there is now a growing feeling among philologists themselves that the real changes may indeed have occurred in the late ninth or even early tenth centuries.[23] Certainly, as mentioned above, the written examples of Romance are exceedingly, even suspiciously, sparse before the tenth century. It may be that instead of dismissing the huge bulk of written material in Latin as evidence of the use of a learned, or a religious, language, by a small, clerical elite, one could regard these Latin texts and books (many of them, as will be argued in subsequent chapters of this book, used by the laity) simply as instances of the written language of the people (whatever it may have sounded like). In other words, Latin may not have been the foreign or learned second language of the Franks, but their native tongue in its regularized and conventionalized written representation.

Of further assistance in assessing the degree to which Latin of a kind was the first language of the Franks in the Carolingian period, possessing both spoken and more formal written forms, as distinct from the learned second language of a small clerical elite, is the evidence from the teaching of grammar. Although we only observe grammar teaching in a learned context, there is a distinctiveness in the type of grammars in use in the Frankish kingdoms in the eighth and ninth centuries, in contrast to the type used in a society where Latin was undoubtedly a second language, namely England and Ireland, that is highly significant in its implications.

The reception of Latin grammar in the barbarian kingdoms of the early middle ages was far from straightforward. The classical grammars, such as those of Donatus and Priscian, by far the most widely known and used in later centuries, and the less popular works, such as those of Pompeius, Consentius, Sergius, Charisius, Diomedes, Eutyches, Phocas or Martianus Capella, were designed for pupils at schools in a Latin-speaking milieu and for a curriculum in which rhetoric and dialectic were the main objects of study, and in which knowledge of the Latin language could be taken for granted.[24] These classical grammars were discussions of the language and its principal characteristics, rather than manuals designed to assist one to learn it. One could not learn Latin from the classical grammars, though

---

[23] See van Uytfanghe *ibid.* 608, and the important suggestions of Jacques Fontaine, 'De la pluralité à l'unité dans le latin carolingien', *Settimane* 27 (1979), II, 765–805.

[24] An excellent summary of the works of the classical grammarians is provided by Vivien Law in her pioneering study, *The Insular Latin Grammarians* (Woodbridge, 1982), pp. 11–30. It will be clear from what follows how indebted I am to Dr Law's work.

one could learn much about its structure and peculiarities. A modern analogy might be trying to learn English from Fowler's *The King's English*.

The *Ars Minor* of Aelius Donatus, fourth-century Roman grammarian and teacher of Jerome, for example, dealt only with the parts of speech and was by no means a comprehensive account of Latin accidence. Instead of demonstrating nouns from each declension, Donatus chose examples from each gender (*magister* (m), *musa* (f), *scamnum* (n)), nouns common of two genders (*sacerdos*) and nouns common of three (*felix*). His *Ars Maior* added to the more elementary material of the *Ars Minor* in dealing with topics related to rhetoric, metrics and theoretical linguistics, but again offered little help with fundamental word formation and declensions. Book II of the *Ars Maior* on the parts of speech, for instance, included no paradigms. The whole work is, above all, a discussion of general linguistic categories.[25] Yet the structure and range of topics provided by Donatus furnished a framework for subsequent grammarians and commentators. Both the *Ars Minor* and the *Ars Maior* dominated grammatical studies until the mid-ninth century when they were ousted by Priscian.

The *Institutiones Grammaticae* of Priscian, the sixth-century Byzantine grammarian, prepared for an audience with knowledge of Greek and Latin, was not widely known in western Europe before the ninth century.[26] From the early ninth century, however, Priscian became increasingly popular. His short summary of key features of the inflecting parts of speech, on the other hand, the *Institutio de nomine et pronomine et verbo*, which provided an exposition of the classification of nouns by declension (in contrast to that of Donatus by gender) was among the best-known grammatical works in the seventh and eighth centuries, especially among insular scholars.[27] Priscian told his pupils the form of nouns and verbs and what they were, but he did not set them out or provide rules for forming them.

If one encounters these classical grammarians still being preferred in the ninth century in the so-called Romance regions, the implication is that their essential approach, aimed at the Latin speaker, is still considered appropriate, or appropriate enough not to make an alternative necessary.

[25] Donatus, ed. Heinrich Keil, *Grammatici Latini* IV (Leipzig, 1968), pp. 354–66 (*Ars Minor*) and pp. 367–402 (*Ars Maior*). The best study of Donatus is Louis Holtz, *Donat et la tradition de l'enseignement grammatical* (Paris, 1981), but compare the review by Vivien Law in *Beiträge zur Geschichte der deutschen Sprache und Literatur* 108 (1986) 101–9.

[26] Priscian, ed. Heinrich Keil, *Grammatici Latini* II and III (Leipzig, 1855–9). Present knowledge of the transmission of Priscian is inadequate but Margaret Gibson, 'Priscian, "Institutiones Grammaticae": a handlist of manuscripts', *Scriptorium* 26 (1972) 105–24, is a useful beginning.

[27] On the insular use of the *Institutio de nomine*, see Law, *Insular Grammarians*, p. 21.

If they were not, one would expect in a non-Latin-speaking environment that the traditional classical grammars would be adapted to new needs, abandoned altogether in favour of new elementary grammars designed as introductions to a foreign language and collections of paradigms, or amalgamated into new form-based schemes. A preliminary adaptation of the presentation of grammar for the benefit of Christian readers of Latin had been made in the course of the fifth and sixth centuries, even though the theoretical basis of the Latin grammars remained unchanged. Grammatical education became oriented to the needs of Christian students and the consequences can be observed in the work of Cassiodorus and Isidore of Seville, and above all in the Christianized version of the *Ars Minor* of Donatus.[28] This 'Christian *Ars Minor*', probably produced in the sixth century, was drawn on by the compiler of the *Ars Asporii*, a text more comprehensive in its provision of paradigms and emphatically Christian in tone. The *Ars Asporii* apparently enjoyed considerable popularity on the Continent until the mid-ninth century. Asporius added paradigms of nouns conjugated in full, but there is no conceptual framework and no idea of declension. Law suggests an early seventh-century or even sixth-century date, and the possibility of a Burgundian provenance. She also points out that one section at least of the *Ars Asporii* indicates a Latin-speaking milieu, for the remarks Asporius makes about nouns, their orthography and the correct formation of the plural, draw attention to typical 'faults' of Late Latin and 'mistakes' which a foreigner who depended on grammars and written texts for his knowledge of Latin was unlikely to make.[29]

  Further adaptations of the traditional grammars, which tackled to some extent the theoretical basis as well as the presentation of the classical grammars, were made in the seventh and eighth centuries for the benefit of Old English and Irish speakers.[30] Latin was encountered in the British Isles in the context of conversion to Christianity and was associated with the church. The vernacular culture (not necessarily illiterate, as is clear from ogam and runic inscriptions)[31] was confronted with a written literary language, Latin, and a defined canon of texts that were the fundamental articles of belief for that religion. The contrast between the vernacular and Latin constituted a pedagogical problem, for there was no tradition in England or Ireland for teaching a foreign language. There were no books

---

[28] *Ibid.*, p. 33.   [29] *Ibid.*, pp. 35–41.   [30] *Ibid.*, pp. 42–97.
[31] On early literacy in England and Ireland see Kelly, 'Anglo-Saxon lay society'; Jane Stevenson, 'Literacy in Ireland: the evidence of the Patrick dossier in the Book of Armagh', in McKitterick, ed., *Uses of Literacy*; Anthony Harvey, 'Early literacy in Ireland: the evidence from ogam', *Cambridge Mediaeval Celtic Studies* 14 (1988) 1–15; and Jane Stevenson, 'The beginning of literacy in Ireland' (forthcoming).

specifically designed for it; the grammatical books available were the
classical grammars designed for Latin native speakers. The English and
Irish tried to solve the problem by devising elementary grammars which
concentrated on form and structure rather than semantic categories.
Grammars such as the *Ars Tatuini*, the *Ars Bonifacii* and the works of
Diomedes, Virgilius Maro Grammaticus, Malsachanus and the anonymous
author of the *Quae sunt quae* were specifically designed to cater for those
learning Latin as a foreign language.[32]

If the contrast between Latin and the vernacular had been strong in the
Frankish kingdoms one might expect to find Carolingian grammars similar
in type to the elementary insular grammars, or else a wide dissemination
of insular grammars on the Continent. One does not find the former, and
with the latter there are difficulties which emerge on closer examination.

In the first place, the undoubtedly Continental emphasis in the
dissemination of insular grammars has definite limits. It is true that insular
grammars rarely survive in insular manuscripts but almost exclusively in
Carolingian copies of the first half of the ninth century. The surviving
manuscripts of the *Declinationes nominum*, for example, are all preserved in
manuscripts of the ninth century or later (apart from Berne 611).[33] But the
distribution and nature of these grammatical codices fail to fulfil any
expectations that the Franks received the insular elementary grammars as
a godsend in their supposed predicament. The grammatical manuscripts
fall into two categories. The first group comprises manuscripts either from
insular centres on the Continent, where Anglo-Saxon and Irish men and
women ventured in the wake of Willibrord and Boniface or as part of their
own individual self-imposed exile or *peregrinatio* for the love of God, or they
come from centres known to have insular connections. That is, these
insular texts were not necessarily used by Franks but by people brought up
in a somewhat different educational and linguistic tradition. The
concentration of elementary insular grammars is in fact in the Romance-
speaking areas rather than in the Germanic-speaking areas east of the
Rhine, where one might have supposed that they would be more
appropriate.

The second category, which constitutes the bulk of the surviving copies,
relates not to a context of elementary schooling but to a very specific,
professional, pedagogic and intellectual interest in which the court circle
of Charlemagne himself is an important common link. Angilbert of St

[32] Law, *Insular Grammarians*, pp. 42–97.
[33] *Ibid.*, pp. 120–4. Law has signalled the need for work to trace the transmission of Late
Latin grammars to distinguish, where possible, insular from Continental branches of the
manuscript tradition, just as she was able to do for the 'Christian *Ars Minor*'.

Riquier, a prominent member of the court circle, for example, who possessed copies of both the *Ars Tatuini* and the *Ars Bonifacii*, may have encountered the grammar of Tatwine at the royal court, for it appears to have started its Continental career at a north Frankish centre, probably the palace scriptorium itself.[34] The texts of the insular grammars, moreover, usually form part of grammatical miscellanies such as Naples IV.A. 34, Berne 207, St Gall 876, BN lat. 13025 and Berlin Diez B. Sant. 66.[35] The last codex indeed reflects the grammatical preoccupations of the court circle and it is in this manuscript that the famous list of some of the books in Charlemagne's library is preserved.[36] These composite grammatical volumes thus witness to a preoccupation with teaching grammar and an interest in different approaches to a discussion of the main characteristics of the Latin language. They suggest an alertness to different presentations of grammatical material and the wish to assemble as many texts as possible relevant to the teaching of grammar. The insular grammars are cheek by jowl in these codices with the Late Latin and early mediaeval compilations designed for Christian Latin native speakers. Their position is thus entirely consistent with a concern for improvement and reform of a formal written language and does not enhance in any significant way at all the notion of Latin as an essentially foreign language. In other words, I disagree with the notion that Hiberno- and Anglo-Latin grammars were widely circulated on the Continent because they were regarded as no less suitable for 'speakers of the Frankish dialect' than for their original audience.[37] These grammatical miscellanies reflect an

[34] The wider context and significance of this is discussed briefly in R. McKitterick, 'The diffusion of insular culture in Neustria between 650 and 850: the implications of the manuscript evidence', in Hartmut Atsma, ed., *La Neustrie. Les pays au nord de la Loire, 650 à 850, Beihefte der Francia* 16/1 and 16/2 (Sigmaringen, 2 vols., 1988), vol. 16/2, pp. 395–432. On the transmission of Tatwine see V. Law, 'The transmission of the *Ars Bonifacii* and *Ars Tatuini*', *Revue d'Histoire des Textes* 9 (1979) 281–9.

[35] Naples IV.A.34, for example includes excerpts on grammar from Isidore's *Etymologiae*, Bede's *De Orthographia*, Consentius, Servius, Diomedes and Eutyches on the verb, Victorinus on parts of speech, Phocas, Asper, Alcuin, Virgilius Maro, Servius' commentary on Donatus, a tract on prosody, etc.; Berne 207 also contains various alphabets, a tract on declensions, the *Ars Maior* of Donatus, Servius, Asper, commentaries on Donatus and extracts from Isidore's *Etymologiae* on grammar; St Gall 876 includes the *Ars Minor* of Donatus put into dialogue form, a commentary on Donatus based on 'Augustine, Servius and Comminianus', extracts from Isidore's *Etymologiae* on grammar, Donatus' *Ars Minor* and *Ars Maior*, Diomedes, Bede's *De arte metrica*, Pompeius' commentary on Donatus and a collection of alphabets, etc.; BN lat. 13025 also contains Servius and Asper; Berlin Diez B. Sant. 66 also includes Donatus, Servius, Pompeius, a tract entitled *De litteris* and extracts from Isidore's *Etymologiae* on grammar, etc.

[36] *CLA* VIII, 1044, discussed by Bernhard Bischoff, 'Die Hofbibliothek Karls des Grossen', *MS* III, pp. 149–69. The manuscript has been published in facsimile: Bernhard Bischoff, ed., *Sammelhandschrift Diez B. Sant. 66, Grammatici Latini et Catalogus librorum*, Codices selecti phototypice impressi 42 (Graz, 1973).

[37] Law, *Insular Grammarians*, p. 101.

interest in Latin grammar of a specialized linguistic kind rather than a concern to cope with a problem of teaching Latin as a foreign language.

Did the Carolingians themselves, however, adapt existing Late Latin and early Christian grammars in such a way as to throw light on their linguistic situation? Insufficient work has been completed on this, but the indications so far are that the grammars written by members of the court circle continued the insular tradition of Latin grammars only to a limited extent. The *Ars Donati quam Paulus Diaconus exposuit* follows insular precedent in adding much more material on the inflecting parts of speech and a tract on declensions.[38] The grammar of Clemens Scottus conforms closely to insular patterns. Peter of Pisa's grammar, on the other hand, while it follows insular models in its general selection of paradigms set out by declensions, terminations and genders, is nevertheless more reminiscent of late classical commentators.[39] None of these authors in any case was a Frank. Alcuin himself, paradoxically enough, departed completely from the insular tradition and relied in his work on Donatus, Priscian and other Late Latin grammarians.[40] From the beginning of the ninth century the tendency to return to the classical grammarians became increasingly marked; *florilegia*, or collections of excerpts from the classical grammars, and abbreviated versions of the work of a single traditional grammarian were produced. Priscian's *Institutiones Grammaticae* became ever more popular and gave rise in its turn to the compilation of excerpts on particular aspects of grammar, such as Hraban Maur's *Excerptio de arte grammatica Prisciani* and Walafrid Strabo in his personal compilation in St Gall 878.[41] Further commentaries on grammar such as those by Sedulius Scottus and Remigius of Auxerre, or Gottschalk of Orbais, move still further away from insular models.[42] Law has posited a turn away from the insular tradition of exegetical grammars in the second half of the ninth century on the Continent, with scholars showing greater interest in seeking alternative and more detailed presentations of grammatical doctrine. By the mid-ninth century, indeed, direct insular influence on the grammatical studies on the Continent had virtually ceased.[43]

---

[38] *Ibid.*, pp. 101–2, and see also Vivien Law, 'Linguistics in the earlier Middle Ages: the Insular and Carolingian grammarians', *Transactions of the Philological Society* (1985) 171–93.   [39] Law, *Insular Grammarians*, p. 102.

[40] *Ibid.*, p. 103. Law discusses the *Dialogus Franconis et Saxonis de octo partibus orationis*, structured in question and answer form.

[41] Hraban Maur, *PL* 111, cols. 613–70. On Walafrid's compilation, see Bernhard Bischoff, 'Eine Sammelhandschrift Walahfrid Strabos (Cod. Sangall. 878)', *MS* II, pp. 34–51.

[42] Law, *Insular Grammarians*, p. 105. On Gottschalk, see C. Lambot, *Oeuvres théologiques et grammaticales de Godescalc d'Orbais*, Spicilegium Sacrum Lovaniense 20 (Louvain, 1945), and Jean Jolivet, 'L'Enjeu de la grammaire pour Godescalc', in *Jean Scot Erigène et l'histoire de la philosophie*, Colloques Internationaux du C.N.R.S. No. 561 (Paris, 1977), pp. 59–67.   [43] Law, *Insular Grammarians*, p. 105.

The wide dissemination of the grammars of Donatus and Priscian within the Frankish realm on the other hand suggests that the traditional grammars designed for native Latin speakers remained the most widely used among the Franks. But it is important to consider the specific location of these grammar manuscripts before drawing any conclusions. The distribution of Donatus, for example, shows a concentration in the Loire valley and the St Gall–Reichenau area, both regions with clusters of important monasteries where classical studies flourished.[44] There is also a small concentration in Picardy and the Paris basin. Elsewhere the distribution suggests pockets of production of grammatical texts in particular centres in Austrasia (presumably linked with the court of Charlemagne), in Regensburg, in central Italy and in northern Spain. What this distribution tells us is where the manuscripts were produced, not necessarily where they were used, nor where they were thought appropriate. Palaeographical research on Carolingian schools and scriptoria, however, has demonstrated that there is a close correlation throughout the ninth century between books produced and books used in particular centres, though the exchange and export of books were also common.[45] It becomes possible, therefore, to think in terms of these concentrations of grammar production as also being those of grammatical study.

That the Carolingians used Donatus and Priscian rather than elementary grammars of the insular type may of course be an illusion presented by a lopsided manuscript tradition which has preserved only those works used by the learned who could benefit from the relatively advanced treatment. In other words, these grammar codices may reflect the efforts of the scholars of the Carolingian Renaissance to pursue higher studies of the Latin language, and may be entirely irrelevant in any consideration of what language the Franks understood or could read. It is certainly the case that the concentration of grammar books, especially that in the Loire valley and at Corbie, is in precisely those centres where the study of classical authors was most avid, and which were responsible for the bulk of the classical manuscripts copied in, and preserved from, the Carolingian period.[46] Yet this formal teaching of Latin is the only evidence

---

[44] I base my comments here on the study of the manuscript tradition of Donatus outlined by Holtz, *Donat*, pp. 352–423.

[45] Bernhard Bischoff, 'Die Bibliothek im Dienste der Schule', *MS II*, pp. 213–33.

[46] See R. McKitterick, 'Manuscripts and scriptoria in the reign of Charles the Bald, 840–877', in E. Menesto and C. Leonardi, eds., *Giovanni Scoto nel suo tempo. L'organizzazione del sapere in eta' Carolingia* (Todi and Perugia, 1989). Of relevance is the manuscript transmission of Bede's and Alcuin's works on orthography: see Carlotta Dionisotti, 'On Bede, Grammars, and Greek', *RB* 92 (1982) 111–41.

we have for the teaching of a reading knowledge of the language in the Frankish realms. There is not a trace of the promotion of a reading knowledge of the vernacular in the Romance regions of the Frankish kingdoms such as we have in the case of Old English in Alfred's England.[47] The most concerted effort to promote the German vernacular did not occur until the late tenth century, at St Gall.[48] The indications from such manuscripts as Aberystwyth 21553 of the late ninth century, moreover, are that Donatus was the basis for instruction in the schools.[49] This could only have been so if Latin represented the formal version of the native tongue.

Given the Carolingians' efforts to establish the use of correct Latin, evidenced in such texts as the *De litteris colendis* and the *Admonitio Generalis*, it makes good sense to see these manuscripts as being the outward and visible sign of the work to promote the study of Latin grammar as part of the formalization and reform of a native tongue; the study of Latin was used to improve the use of a known language, not to learn it as a new one.[50] There is no hint in any of the statements on the need for education or improved style that anything but the more correct use of a native tongue was being proposed. It is ironic that these same efforts to formalize and correct the language led, in the end, to too great a disparity between the written and spoken forms of the Franks' native tongue, and in due course 'Romance' or 'Old French' became recognizably distinct. Nevertheless, the continued use of Latin as an administrative language had the decided advantage of providing a common tongue in an increasingly disparate realm.

[47] The best discussion is that of Donald Bullough, 'The educational tradition in England from Alfred to Aelfric: teaching *utriusque linguae*', *Settimane* 19 (1972), II, 453–94. Indeed, a complete contrast to the Frankish attitudes towards Latin is presented by such English sources as Bede's letter to Egbert c.5, ed. Charles Plummer, *Venerablis Baedae Opera Historica* I (Oxford, 1896), pp. 408–9, Eng. trans. Dorothy Whitelock, *English Historical Documents* I *ca. 500–1042* (London, 1979), p. 801; Asser's *Life of King Alfred* c.77, ed. W. H. Stevenson, *Asser's Life of King Alfred* (Oxford, 1904), Eng. trans. Simon Keynes and Michael Lapidge, *Alfred the Great* (Harmondsworth, 1983), pp. 90–1; and Alfred's Preface to his translation of Gregory's *Cura Pastoralis*, ed. Henry Sweet, *King Alfred's West-Saxon Version of Gregory's Pastoral Care*, Early English Texts Society, original series 45 (London, 1871–2), Eng. trans. Keynes and Lapidge, *Alfred the Great*, pp. 125–6.

[48] On Notker and his translations into Old High German for use in the school at St Gall see E. H. Sehrt, T. Starck, J. C. King and P. W. Tax, *Die Werke Notkers des Deutschen* (Tübingen, 1972); H. Backes, *Die Hochzeit Merkurs und die Philologie. Studien zu Notkers Martian-Übersetzung* (Sigmaringen, 1981); and I. Schrobler, *Notker III von St Gallen als Übersetzer und Kommentator von Boethius' 'De consolatione philosophiae'* (Tübingen, 1953).

[49] R. McKitterick, 'A ninth-century school book from the Loire valley: Phillipps 16308', *Scriptorium* 30 (1976) 225–31.

[50] *MGH Cap.* I, No. 22, c.72, pp. 59–60; Paul Lehmann, 'Fuldaer Studien', *Sitzungsberichte der Bayerischen Akademie der Wissenschaften, phil. hist. Klasse* (Munich, 1925) 4–13; and *MGH Cap.* I, No. 29, p. 79.

The linguistic unity created by the use of Latin was undoubtedly appreciated and promoted by the Carolingians. There is much to be said for applying the notion of *diglossia* to the linguistic situation in the Carolingian realm.[51] That is, we can see the spoken and written forms of Latin not as two distinct languages but as two registers or levels of the same language which differ from each other less phonetically than lexically and in morphology and syntax. The spoken form was the spontaneous language of everyday discourse, and the written form was the 'higher' text language. Each level, despite internal differences, had its proper function, but intercomprehension remained assured. This notion differs from that of a standard language with regional dialects in that it is differentiated not geographically but by function. But there was a dynamic manifestation of *diglossia* in the Carolingian period in that it was not passive but actively and consciously promoted by pressure for a nationally understood and correct language in its written or high form, by the need for maintaining communication in the sphere of government, and by the requirements of the Christian church and learning. That the formal written language had such an illustrious past and historical significance, moreover, considerably enhanced the continued use of Latin in its written form throughout the Carolingian world in every sphere of activity.[52] The Frankish kingdoms under the Carolingians thus represent a unique blend of linguistic factors in which the status of Latin as the primary means of communication in writing was maintained.

Latin, therefore, was in no sense a second or foreign language in the western regions of the Frankish kingdoms in the Carolingian period. It continued to be understood. The extant texts represent the high, formal level of the current language of the people. In the eastern regions of the Frankish kingdoms, where Germanic regional dialects were the native speech, we are faced with a more complex set of linguistic relationships, in which Latin was a different language, but one that had long been accepted as the language of law and religion and of written texts. Use of written

[51] *Diglossia*, defined by C. A. Ferguson, 'Diglossia', *Word* 15 (1959) 325–40. H. Lüdke, 'Die Entstehung romanischer Schriftsprachen', *Vox Romanica* 23 (1964) 3–12 (reprinted in Kontzi, ed., *Zur Entstehung*, pp. 386–409), is the best discussion of how *diglossia* might be applied to the problem of Late Latin and Romance, though not all linguistic historians are convinced of its appropriateness to the eighth and ninth centuries. Compare, for example, Banniard, 'L'écriture médiatrice', and van Uytfanghe, 'Histoire du Latin', and note the discussion between them at the end of Banniard, 'L'écriture médiatrice', p. 488. See also C. Drettas, 'La Diglossia: un pèlerinage aux sources', *Bulletin de la Société Linguistique de Paris* 76 (1981) 61–98.

[52] On aspects of the function of Latin as a unifying factor in the divers regions of the Frankish kingdoms and the reform of Latin see Anita Guerreau-Jalabert, 'La "Renaissance Carolingienne": modèles culturels, usages linguistiques et structures sociales', *BEC* 139 (1981) 5–35.

vernacular forms in the east Frankish regions was primarily in the context
of translation; it was limited, and markedly self-conscious. Bilingualism on
the part of those involved in public life at every level would have been
required. The linguistic situation with regard to Latin would have been
somewhat similar to that prevailing in many modern African states (for
example, English vis-à-vis Kiswahili),[53] in India or at one time in Malaya,
or in many schools in present-day Wales, with respect to English and the
native vernacular languages. The interchangeability between English,
French and Latin in post-Conquest England, for example, has been fully
elucidated by Michael Clanchy. He comments that 'the language of record
depended on the status of the persons concerned and the nature of the
document, and not on the language actually spoken on the occasion [of
the transaction recorded]'.[54] In the Frankish kingdoms in the eighth and
ninth centuries a man or woman would have spoken a 'Romance' dialect
or an Old High German one, or both, but would have read Latin and used
Latin in court and in church. This interchange between High and Low
forms of the same language, or between two and three different languages,
one of which is the language of record, has many parallels, both mediaeval
and modern, with the linguistic situation prevailing in the Frankish
kingdoms under the Carolingians.

What then are the implications of the Carolingian linguistic situation for
Frankish literacy? It becomes quite simply the question of how easy it was
to learn to read. We should not exaggerate the difficulties that the diversity
of languages would create, for they had a common written norm, that
which we recognize as Latin. When one learnt to read, one learnt to read
in Latin. In the Latin regions one was learning to read the formal written
version of one's native language; in the German-speaking areas one was
learning the written form of a language encountered at every level of
public life and worship. Latin was, therefore, not the obstacle to literacy
that it has hitherto appeared in the minds of historians of literacy in the
early middle ages.[55] Above all, the acquisition of the ability to read Latin
has to be seen in the context of the purposes for which literacy was
required, and the degree to which social and political organization
assumed literate skills on the part of the population with whom it joined
in ruling the country, apart from the clergy serving the church. Let us
turn, therefore, to the evidence provided by the practice of Carolingian
government and its use of the written word.

[53] See, for example, W. H. Whitely, *Swahili: The Rise of a National Language in Tanzania*
(London, 1969).
[54] Clanchy, *From Memory to Written Record*, p. 160.
[55] Thompson, *Literacy of the Laity*.

2 ❧ Law and the written word

There was an enormous increase in both the quality and the quantity of legal and administrative documentation in the Carolingian period. How is one to account for this? It is due partly to the strands of continuity maintained from the Roman and through the Merovingian periods. In the political development of the Frankish kingdoms from the fifth century, a striking feature is the integration of writing into the legal process. It is the most obvious inheritance from the Roman past. Thus the written word was accommodated within Frankish society not only through the influence of the Christian church and its promotion of a 'religion of the book', but also through the secular law and administration. If it be correct to understand Frankish society before the late fifth century as pre-literate, the process of expansion, political assertion and social integration in sub-Roman and Merovingian Gaul meant that legal norms gradually ceased to reside in the memory of each man in the community, but instead were recorded in writing and preserved, and thus given a new character. This is evident in the legacy of the Roman imperial and the sub-Roman legal tradition to the successor kingdoms of western Europe in the fifth and sixth centuries,[1] in the survival of elements of Roman or sub-Roman law in the

[1] The best assessment of research on the germanic law codes is the lucid exposition by C. Schott, 'Der Stand der *Leges* Forschung', *Frühmittelalterliche Studien* 13 (1979) 29–55, covering the problems of transmission and sources, continuity, the idea of law, effectiveness, the social structure the laws reveal, the language of the laws and methodology; see especially 43–6 on Roman law and his references. An older, still useful, guide is R. Buchner, *Die Rechtsquellen*, Beiheft to W. Wattenbach and W. Levison, *Deutschlands Geschichtsquellen im Mittelalter* (Weimar, 1953). The classic studies are E. Levy, 'Reflections on the first "Reception" of Roman law in Germanic states', *American Historical Review* 48 (1942) 20–9; idem, *West Roman Vulgar Law. The Law of Property* (Philadelphia, 1951); idem, *Weströmisches Vulgarrecht. Das Obligationsrecht* (Weimar, 1956); and F. Wieacker, 'Vulgarismus und Klassizismus im Recht der Spätantike', *Sitzungsberichte der Heidelberger Akademie der Wissenschaften, phil. hist. Klasse* (1955), 3 Abhandlung (Heidelberg, 1955). An example of the older classic surveys is H. Brunner, *Deutsche Rechtsgeschichte* (Leipzig, 2 vols., 1887–92), 3rd edn. with C. F. von Schweim (Berlin, 1961). Scholars have differed in the weight they accord Roman influence, as well as in the spheres in which they detect it, whether in the style of the law, its specific legal content, rules for procedure or in verbal echoes. See also G. Kobler, *Das Recht im frühen Mittelalter* (Cologne and Vienna, 1971).

barbarian *leges*[2] and in the continuing knowledge of Roman law.[3] It is also apparent from the many types of official and private records, based on Roman precedents, which continued in use, and the new forms which evolved.[4] Given the long period of proximity and exchange in the frontier regions and within the Empire itself, it is only to be expected that there was much influence, knowledge and, possibly, cross-fertilization in terms of ideas and procedures.[5] The Carolingians, therefore, inherited and continued to promote the process of the accommodation of the written word within Frankish society, an accommodation not only encouraged by religious imperatives but also by the needs of secular government and law. The consequences and implications can be observed in four main areas. First, the use of writing in Carolingian government; secondly, the function and status of the *leges* or barbarian laws; thirdly, the stress on the written

[2] J. Gaudemet, *La Formation du droit seculier aux IV⁰ et V⁰ siècles* (Paris, 1957); *idem*, 'Survivances romaines dans le droit de la monarchie franque du V⁰ au X⁰ siècle', *Revue d'Histoire du Droit* 23 (1955) 149–206; and M. Kaser, *Das römische Privatrecht* II *Die nach-Klassischen Entwicklungen* (Munich, 1975). There are useful comments in Ian Wood, 'Disputes in late fifth- and sixth-century Gaul: some problems', in W. Davies and P. Fouracre, eds., *The Settlement of Disputes in Early Mediaeval Europe* (Cambridge, 1986), pp. 7 – 22. Many aspects of the survival and knowledge of Roman law in the middle ages are covered in the series *IRMA*. See also the discussion by Schott, '*Leges* Forschung', 43–6.

[3] P. Riché, 'Enseignement du droit en Gaule du VI⁰ au XI⁰ siècle', *IRMA* I.5.b.bb (Milan, 1965); G. Chevrier and G. Pieri, 'La Loi romain des Burgondes', *IRMA* I.2.b.aa (Milan, 1969).

[4] H. Steinacker, *Die antiken Grundlagen der frühmittelalterlichen Privaturkunde* (Leipzig, 1927); H. Fichtenau, *Arenga. Spätantike und Mittelalter im Spiegel von Urkundenformeln*, supplementary volume 18 of *MIÖG* (Vienna, 1957); P. Classen, *Kaiserreskript und Königsurkunde. Diplomatische Studien zum Problem der Kontinuität zwischen Altertum und Mittelalter* (Thessalonika, 1977).

[5] It is becoming increasingly clear how much day-to-day provincial Roman administration and record keeping, as distinct from the elaborate machinery of the central imperial government, survived the demise of the central western authority at the end of the fifth century. E. Posner, *Archives in the Ancient World* (Cambridge, Mass., 1972), pp. 86–223, discusses the record keeping of the late Empire. On the survival of the *gesta municipalia* into the early middle ages see Bruno Hirschfeld, *Die Gesta Municipalia in römischer und frühgermanischer Zeit* (Hamburg, 1904). See also Harold Steinacker, 'Zum Zusammenhang zwischen Antiken und frühmittelalterlichen Registerwesen', *Wiener Studien* 24 (1902) 301–6; and above all Eugen Ewig, 'Das Fortleben Römischer Institutionen in Gallien und Germanien', in E. Ewig, *Spätantikes und frühmittelalterliches Gallien* I (Munich, 1976), pp. 409–34; P. Classen, 'Fortleben und Wandel spätrömischen Urkundenwesens im frühen Mittelalter', in Peter Classen, ed., *Recht und Schrift im Mittelalter*, Vorträge und Forschungen 23 (Sigmaringen, 1977); and W. Bergmann, 'Fortleben des antiken Notariats im Frühmittelalter', in P.-J. Schuler, ed., *Tradition und Gegenwart. Festschrift zum 175-jährigen Bestehen eines badischen Notarstandes* (Karlsruhe, 1981), pp. 23–35. Extant remains of documents are being published in *ChLA* and work is well in train for the full description and identification of early mediaeval legal records, for example, by J. O. Tjader, *Die nichtliterarischen Papyri Italiens aus der Zeit 445–700* (Lund, 1955); U. Nonn, 'Merowingische Testament: Studien zum Fortleben einer römischen Urkundenform im Frankreich', *Archiv für Diplomatik* 18 (1972) 1–129; Werner Bergmann, 'Untersuchung zu den Gerichtsurkunden der Merowingerzeit', *Archiv für Diplomatik* 22 (1976) 151–86.

record in the *leges*; and fourthly, the production of such records. It is with the first three of these that this chapter will be concerned.

I THE USE OF WRITING IN CAROLINGIAN GOVERNMENT

In the increased use of writing in Carolingian government we are not simply observing the stages by which continuity becomes transformation. There is a deliberate impetus behind the new developments of the second half of the eighth century, and it is provided by the Carolingian rulers, exploiting levels of literacy and attitudes towards the written word already present.

Any discussion of the use of writing in administration, and the significance of the capitularies under the Carolingians, must take Ganshof's classic article as its starting point.[6] His contention that the use of the written word for administrative purposes survived as a debased legacy has been refined and strengthened by subsequent research. Studies of the Merovingian period and the legal processes involved in dispute settlement in particular have argued the case for the late Roman rather than the Germanic antecedents for the procedures and assumptions of Frankish judicial cases.[7] The impression created by Marculf's Formulary and others of the late Merovingian period, of resort to written means in a wide variety of cases, is reinforced by the surviving examples of Merovingian *placita*. Ganshof, moreover, pointed out that the *Lex Ribuaria*'s provision for a *cancellarius* was a possible reference to a scribe attached to a local count's court and responsible for the redaction of charters.[8] Yet he was cautious in expanding this reference to suggest that documents were part of an administrative routine conducted in writing in Austrasia as early as the seventh century. He identified an increase in the use of the written word for administrative purposes under Pippin III, while asserting that under Charlemagne the 'abundance of documentation [was] novel and revealing'.[9] He substantiated his opinion with a succinct summary of the types of document to be identified in the material extant, and therefore the

---

[6] F. L. Ganshof, 'Charlemagne et l'usage de l'écrit en matière administrative', *MA* 57 (1951), 1–25, Eng. trans. J. Sondheimer, in F. L. Ganshof, *The Carolingians and the Frankish Monarchy* (London, 1971), pp. 125–42. See also A. Dumas, 'La Parole et l'écriture dans les capitulaires carolingiens', in *Mélanges d'histoire du moyen âge dédiés à la mémoire de Louis Halphen* (Paris, 1951), pp. 209–17.

[7] See in particular Ian Wood, 'Disputes', and Paul Fouracre, 'Placita and the settlement of disputes in later Merovingian Francia', in Davies and Fouracre, eds., *Settlement of Disputes*, pp. 7–22, 23–43.

[8] The reference is to *Lex Ribuaria* 88, a list of those connected with a judicial court who must not receive bribes: nobles, the mayor of the palace, the *domesticus*, the count, the *grafio*, the *cancellarius*.

[9] Ganshof, 'L'Usage de l'écrit, trans. Sondheimer, in *Carolingians*, p. 126.

different business for which a written record or statement of some kind was required. There were political *acta*, such as the renunciation of all claims to Bavaria by Tassilo or the written arrangements for the succession issued in 806 (possibly the first such settlement to appear in written form). There is the possibility that written agendas for meetings, examples of which survive from 808 and 811, were sent out to the relevant persons in advance of the meeting. Ganshof suggested, moreover, that minutes of such meetings were apparently used as the basis for drafting instructions to *missi* or for framing capitularies, though some of these are so summary in form that they can presumably be understood as written reminders of orally delivered detailed instructions. Full written instructions to the *missi* also survive. An important testimony to the power of the written word in the king's name is the use of the *tractoria*, or requisition notes, by which transport, lodgings and provision could be obtained. Letters addressed to ambassadors, mobilization orders addressed to counts, bishops and abbots, requests for reports on royal and ecclesiastical estates and letters issued by such royal agents as the *missi dominici* to their subordinates are preserved, as are announcements to be made at the *placitum* or assembly of the people.[10]

There is a wealth of information in Ganshof's notes, all of them attesting to the use made by counts of the written word in the administration of the counties, but Ganshof introduces a note of unexplained scepticism when he stated that this use 'can only have been on a very restricted scale'. In Italy on the other hand, he continued, 'certain texts suggest that...the counts made a more extensive and systematic use of written documents which should not surprise us'. Two assumptions are made here by Ganshof without any justification whatsoever. The first is that we know the Franks were a barbarian kingdom and that any signs of using literate methods in government may safely be treated as aberrations from the normal, oral methods of doing things, which were ineffective anyway. The second is that Italy, the fount of civilization, obviously preserved and was able to preserve and carry on literate methods of government. It is not my intention to dispute or refute the assumptions concerning Lombard Italy, albeit I retain grave doubts concerning their validity. It is time, indeed, that the question of literacy and levels of Latin learning in Lombard Italy were tackled head on.

As far as Carolingian Francia is concerned, on the other hand, Ganshof was perplexingly dismissive of the mass of evidence he himself had gathered together. He seemed to wish to encourage in his readers a cosy

---

[10] These are Ganshof's classifications, not all of which are adhered to here, but they serve to illustrate the variety of text, and he provided examples of all these types.

superciliousness concerning the effectiveness of these ambitious but foolhardy Franks when he comments that 'It will be appreciated that the actual execution of such an order may well have fallen far short of what was intended' and 'we are dealing with instructions; how far they were carried out may have been another matter'.[11] He was right, of course, to be cautious and wary. There is not often proof that written instructions were carried out. Yet Mordek notes the Christianization of Saxony, and the reforms of coinage, for example, which are quite clearly implementations of capitulary decrees.[12] But such is the weight of Ganshof's authority, that his scepticism and caution have become the orthodox point of view and it is his qualifying phrases that have been registered rather than the outstanding quantity of information he actually presented. More crucially, his arguments, and those of many of the scholars who have since joined the debate, really relate to the effectiveness of the government itself rather than to the written means by which the requirements for it were communicated. That a count chose to ignore instructions tells us more about his attitude to central authority than it does about his ability to read or write and whether he had his own notary. A recalcitrant count, in other words, was not necessarily an illiterate one. Ganshof's generous acknowledgement that some places had a *cancellarius* or *notarius* appointed for the county, that it was intended that every bishop, count and abbot should have a notary, that the use of the written word for administrative purposes was an act of policy and that some returns of, for example, those swearing the oath were compiled, were outweighed by his conviction that many records were never compiled, and that effective use of written documents demanded a minimum of intellectual training which, he asserted, was a very weak point, particularly among the laity.[13] Such an assertion seems perverse in the light of the clear implications of the capitulary evidence that a practical level of intellectual training among the lay officials is assumed. It makes no sense to envisage a barrage of written communication directed at royal officials unable to make either head or tail of it.

The most obvious point to stress is that the aims and intentions of the king and his advisers were sent out in writing to those required to act on them. From many clauses in the capitularies, that is, the texts prescribing rules of law and ordering their implementation and/or prescribing

---

[11] *Ibid.*, p. 129.
[12] Hubert Mordek, 'Karolingische Kapitularien', in Hubert Mordek, ed., *Überlieferung und Geltung normativer Texte des frühen und hohen Mittelalters*, Quellen und Forschungen zum Recht im Mittelalter (ed. R. Kottje and H. Mordek) (Sigmaringen, 1986), pp. 25–50 at p. 46.
[13] Ganshof, 'L'Usage de l'écrit', trans. Sondheimer, in *Carolingians*, p. 135.

measures in particular cases, texts containing manifestos on policies, admonitions on behaviour or actions, pastoral advice or administrative changes, it is clear that, while counts also received oral instructions from the ruler and his agents, the *missi dominici*, written means were used as a matter of course. Diplomas and capitularies were generally addressed to counts and other agents. According to Louis the Pious' capitulary of 825, c. 26, repeated by Charles the Bald in 864, each count was supposed to receive a copy of a decree from the king, make known its contents to the people in his region by reading it aloud and see to its implementation.[14] This procedure assumes that the count could read or that he had someone in his entourage whose duty it was to do so. It does not assume that all the people could read. They were dependent on the oral communication made by the count. Nevertheless, that oral pronouncement was dependent on the written word.

Evidence of such communication being received by a count and the status it was accorded are extant. Among the texts in one of the manuscripts containing the episcopal statutes of Bishop Gerbald of Liège, is included the so-called *Capitula a missis dominicis ad comites directa*, that is, notes sent by *missi dominici* to counts, usually dated 806.[15] The *missi* admonish the count to 'reread' his capitularies, to 'recall the duties with which you have been charged orally and to strive to be so zealous with regard to those that you may receive both reward from God and fitting recompense from that great lord of ours' (that is, Charlemagne). The count is to 'show such solicitude for the rights of the lord emperor, in accordance with what [he has been told] in writing or orally'; he is to 'list the names' of the rebellious and send the list to the *missi* or else inform them when he next meets them. If he has doubts about his instructions 'with which our lord has charged you in writing or orally' he is to send someone to the *missus* for clarification. Further, the count is abjured to 'read this letter many times and keep it very safe, that you and we may use it as evidence to see whether you have or have not acted in accordance with what is written in it'.[16]

[14] *MGH Cap.* I. No. 150, c.26, p. 307, and *MGH Cap.* II, No. 273, c.36, p. 327. See also the comments by P. D. King in his introduction to *Charlemagne: Translated Sources* (Lambrigg, Kendal, 1987), pp. 33 and 35–6, and Karl-Ferdinand Werner, 'Missus, Marchio, Comes. Entre l'administration centrale et l'administration locale de l'empire carolingien', in W. Paravicini and K.-F. Werner, eds., *Histoire comparée de l'administration (IVᵉ – XVIIIᵉ siècles)*, Beiheft der Francia 9 (Munich, 1980), pp. 191–239, at p. 199.
[15] *MGH Cap.* I, No. 85, pp. 183–4. On Gerbald of Liège see Peter Brommer, ed., *MGH Capitula Episcoporum* I (1984), pp. 3–42, the initial identification in W. A. Eckhardt, *Die Kapitulariensammlung Bischof Ghaerbalds von Lüttich* (Berlin, 1956), and McKitterick, *Frankish Church*, pp. 50–2.
[16] The translation is King's, *Charlemagne*, pp. 258–60.

The brusque reply from Charlemagne to written questions for a *missus* in connection with the use of law books for guidance is relevant here too. The king had been asked whether a count and the *scabini* should receive a *solidus* for a written record of a judgement, or the scribe: 'Read the Roman law' he advised 'and act in accordance with what you find there. If it is a matter for Salian law, on the other hand, and you cannot find there what you must do, you are to raise the question at our general assembly.' Not only does it provide evidence of written communication between the king and one of his agents, it also clearly indicates the use of written records in court proceedings and the assumption that the *missus* possesses copies of the relevant laws. A list of the names of men who refuse to come to the *missus'* court is required by the king, and in a last impatient clause he sets down the answer to a query in writing in the hope that now the *missus*, who has heard it in the past, will register the answer:

And you wrote in the sixth article about bridges established in ancient times and about unlawful tolls. As regards this matter, it is our command that wherever it was the custom of old to take the toll, a lawful toll may be taken. This order too we have given you before, by our own mouth, and you have not understood it at all.[17]

Charlemagne's request for written information about the landed property of his vassals is an important preliminary to the host of estate inventories of the ninth century. Some, indeed, may have been in response to a request like that incorporated in the *Capitulare de iustitiis faciendis* from Boulogne in 811, which required each *missus* to have described in writing

what each person holds in benefice in his area of jurisdiction, how many enfeoffed *homines* there are on that benefice, how [they] have been cultivated, and who has bought or built up an allod from his benefice. Not only the benefices of bishops, abbots, abbesses, counts and our vassals are to be described but also our crown estates, that we may also be able to know how much of our own we have in the area of jurisdiction of each *missus*.[18]

This can be compared to an earlier requirement that *missi* produce written records concerning the general upkeep of buildings and estates,[19] and the more specific instruction to the stewards of a royal estate that 'they should record, in one document, any records, goods or services they have provided, or anything they have appropriated for our use, and, in another document, what payments they have made, and they shall notify us by letter of anything that is left over'.[20]

---

[17] *MGH Cap.* I, No. 58, cc.2 and 6, p. 145, trans. King, *ibid.*, pp. 267–8.
[18] *MGH Cap.* I, No. 80, c.7, p. 177, trans. King, *ibid.*, p. 267.
[19] *MGH Cap.* I, No. 49, c.4, p. 136; trans. King, *ibid.*, p. 258.
[20] *Capitulare de Villis* c.55, *MGH Cap.* I, No. 32, pp. 83–91 at p. 88, trans. Henry Loyn and John Percival, *The Reign of Charlemagne* (London, 1975), p. 71.

The capitulary for the mobilization of the army in 808 stipulates the need for copies of orders to be made:

it is our wish that four copies of this capitulary be made out: one copy is to be held by our *missi*, a second by the count in whose district these things are to be done (so that both our *missus* and our count will act precisely in accordance with what is set out in our enactment), the third by those of our *missi* who are to be set over our army, and the fourth by our chancellor.[21]

Mustering of the host was normally done by letter, or so the capitulary for the *missi* of 793 suggests when it says the king intends to notify the counts and *missi* by letter of his will as regards when and where they ought to assemble.[22] Appeals on ecclesiastical matters are to be accompanied by the metropolitan's letter explaining the issue.[23] The *missi* are to refer matters on which they cannot reach a just judgement by themselves to the king, with their written reports.[24] The *missi* receive a summary of what they should know as far as mobilizing the army is concerned.[25]

Many Carolingian capitularies mention that they are the record of the deliberations and decisions on the part of an assembly. The capitulary of Herstal of 779, for example, states that its contents were agreed by the bishops, abbots and counts gathered together with the king in one special council.[26] The illustration accompanying the *Quicunque vult* in the Utrecht Psalter, produced *c.* 820 at Hautvillers near Rheims, provides a striking impression of the proceedings of such a council. Four scribes making notes sit within the circle of delegates; a group of three more notaries consult a *rotulus*, while on two lecterns repose volumes, presumably law books of some kind, for consultation.[27] It is unfashionable to link manuscript images with anything the artist has seen in real life, but it is nevertheless highly probable that the Utrecht Psalter artist had a Frankish synod or assembly in mind when composing his drawing. Decisions about secular and ecclesiastical organization recorded in the capitulary were subsequently made known to the people in the regions administered by the delegates. In 803, for example, Count Stephen read out a new law to the people in his charge. For this purpose translations of the texts may well

---

[21] *MGH Cap.* I, No. 50, c.8, p. 138, trans. King, *Charlemagne*, p. 263.
[22] *MGH Cap.* I, No. 25, pp. 66–7, trans. King, *ibid.*, p. 223, and compare *MGH Cap.* I, No. 50, pp. 137–8, on what the *missi* should have for the mobilization of the army, trans. King, *ibid.*, pp. 261–3; compare also *MGH Cap.* I, No. 75, p. 168, trans. King, *ibid.*, p. 260, for an example of such a letter of mobilization sent to Fulrad of St Denis.
[23] *MGH Cap.* I, No. 28, c.6, pp. 74–5, trans. King, *ibid.*, p. 225.
[24] *MGH Cap.* I, No. 33, c.1, p. 92, trans. King, *ibid.*, p. 234.
[25] Cited above n. 16.
[26] *MGH Cap.* I, No. 20, prologue, p. 47, trans. King, *ibid.*, p. 203.
[27] Utrecht, script. eccl. 484, fo. 90v.

have been made where necessary.[28] How these texts were actually produced and transmitted is a separate issue which is addressed below.

If the written word can clearly be recognized as playing a fundamental role in communications and record making in the reign of Charlemagne, does it continue to play such a role? There are important indications that it does. Hincmar of Rheims in his *De Ordine Palatii*, for example, a tract on government written in 882 but purportedly based on an earlier description by Adalhard of Corbie written in the 820s, describes the use of writing in the process of consultation between the king and his advisers:

The matter for discussion was set before the counsellors in written form; the documents consisted of chapters, each with a separate heading. When the counsellors had received these chapters, they considered them for a day or more. Messengers chosen from the palace servants went back and forth between them and the king, supplying them with answers to their queries. Each matter was then explained orally to the king in his presence.[29]

As far as the assemblies are concerned, therefore, written communication plays an essential role. This could be dismissed as an idealized description were it not for the extant capitulary material from the reigns of Charlemagne, Louis the Pious and Charles the Bald, some of which has the character of agendas and notes for discussion. There have been attempts to categorize the procedure described as particularly pertinent for the reigns of either Louis the Pious or Charles the Bald. I see no reason why it cannot be understood as a generalized description, still appropriate when Hincmar was writing.[30] That the written mode was still taken for granted in the reign of Charles the Bald is apparent from his own capitulary legislation. In the edict of Pîtres of 864, for example, Charles the Bald stated:

we wish to make known to you in writing what we, with the consent and counsel (*consensus et consilium*) of our faithful men (*fideles*), have also decreed here and now...so that you can note it more thoroughly, and, by having recourse to the written copy which we have ordered to be distributed to each county where it will be read out and retained...we also wish it to be conveyed by the bishops or their officers to every county in their dioceses in straightforward language so that it can be understood by everyone... [c. 36]: Each man [archbishop and count] shall have

---

[28] According to a note in BN lat. 4995, the manuscript containing the capitulary for 803. See Karl-Ferdinand Werner, 'Das Geburtsjahr Karls des Grossen', *Francia* 1 (1973) 145 n. 114, and *idem*, 'Missus, marchio, Comes', p. 199 and n.27.

[29] T. Gross and R. Schieffer, eds., *Hinkmar von Reims De ordine Palatii* (Hanover, 1980), pp. 92–5, with German trans. Eng. trans. in D. Herlihy, *The History of Feudalism* (London, 1970), p. 225, but I here use, with grateful thanks to Dr Nelson, the translation she provided in her discussion, 'Legislation and consensus in the reign of Charles the Bald', in P. Wormald, ed., *Ideal and Reality in Frankish and Anglo-Saxon Society* (Oxford, 1983), pp. 202–27, at p. 216.

[30] See the important discussion by Nelson, 'Legislation and consensus'.

[the capitularies] transcribed throughout his diocese for the other bishops, abbots and counts, and all our other vassals, and shall read them out in their counties with everyone present so that our will and our decree can be made known to all.[31]

Further pronouncements of Louis the Pious in 825 for making capitulary texts available at the palace, from the moment they were issued, for copying by the archbishop and their counts were repeated in the capitulary of Servais in 853 as well as at Pîtres in 864.[32] Charles the Bald was apparently reliant on the written word to make his will known to his subjects, and in particular to those in authority on whom he depended for the maintenance of good government in his kingdom. In his requirement for copies of his legislation to be widely disseminated and copied, as well as being read to the people, he was reiterating wishes expressed in the decrees of his father and grandfather.

The royal agents and administrators were themselves required to deliver written reports. In 864, in the same edict as that from which the extract above was taken, Charles requested each count to compile a list of all the markets in his county with a statement about each to the effect of whether it had been in existence in the time of Charlemagne or Louis or himself or whether the count had established one on his own authority. These lists were to be brought to the king at the next assembly so that he could decide which markets were useful and necessary.[33] Further, the means for distributing the king's wishes are stipulated:

It is our wish that the archbishops together with the counts from their own cities should receive from our chancellor, either in person or through their representatives, those capitularies which we have laid down now and at other times in consultation with our faithful men. And each man shall have them transcribed throughout his diocese for the other bishops, abbots and counts, and all our other vassals, and shall read them out in their counties with everyone present, so that our will and our decree can be made known to all. But our chancellor shall note down the names of the bishops and counts who made it their business to collect them, and shall bring these names to our attention so that no one presumes to disregard this.[34]

The royal writing office was thus counting on the cooperation of regional writing offices under the auspices of the bishops to produce copies of the capitularies for further distribution.

Was all this emphasis on copies, written commands, consultation in written form and written reports mere wishful thinking? Would it not be

[31] MGH Cap. II, No. 273, Preface c.3 and c.36, pp. 311 and 327, trans. Simon Coupland, from a forthcoming volume. *The Vikings in Francia, Translated Sources.*
[32] MGH Cap. I,No. 150, c.26, p. 307, and MGH Cap. II, No. 260, c.11, p. 274.
[33] MGH Cap. II, No. 273, Preface c.3 and c.36, pp. 311 and 327.
[34] MGH Cap. II, No. 273, c.19, p. 318, trans. Coupland, *Viking Sources.*

carrying scepticism too far to interpret the consistent issuing of requirements in writing and expectation of response in writing as an ingenuous lack of realism on the part of Carolingian rulers and their advisers? They must have had some knowledge and conviction that something could be done to meet their requests, and that their subjects were sufficiently educated so to exert themselves because they could read what was required of them. The one or two surviving examples that can be cited for almost every kind of required record or report could be dismissed by the extreme sceptic as too few to be conclusive. They could, on the other hand, be accepted as fortunate instances, if pitifully meagre, of once common phenomena. Seen in the context of all the surviving evidence, with the Carolingians' clear statements of their reliance on written records for their administration and their assumptions that written decrees would be put into effect, the mass of extant written material assumes a new significance. The marked stress on the provision of written documents for central and local administration and legal record is reflected in the mass of material which survives. Even if we acknowledge the greater likelihood of survival of documents from the Carolingian period as compared to that of the Merovingian, especially as many of the Merovingian documents were probably written on papyrus, it can be recognized that in written instruments, as in book production generally, the difference between the Merovingian and Carolingian period was above all one of scale. When later politicians, ecclesiastical entrepreneurs or those simply anxious to defend the rights or jurisdictions of their own monastery or cathedral preserved vital Carolingian material in their cartularies and dossiers, it was partly because these documents were there to be preserved. There is every indication, as I have endeavoured to demonstrate so far in this chapter, that there was a prodigious output of documentation from the mid-eighth century onwards. There can be no doubt that the reliance the Carolingians placed on written records for their administration is a reflection and a function of their levels of literacy and assumptions concerning the effectiveness of the written word.

The implications of the capitulary evidence, in short, are that levels of at least pragmatic literacy were high enough for there to be some relation between the ideal of the capitularies and the realities of Frankish society as far as communications are concerned.

So far, the focus has been on the degree to which literate modes were employed in the process of communication, consultation and imparting information within the context of Carolingian government and administration. Stress has been placed on the implications of the capitulary evidence for the levels of pragmatic literacy among the lay, quite apart from the clerical, officials of the Frankish kingdoms. Nothing has been said, however, either of the process of transmission for its successful production or, more particularly, the status of the written text of the capitularies themselves. The question of the status of the written text requires a full-scale study which will tackle both the capitulary and royal diploma evidence, and cannot be addressed here;[35] the questions of transmission and production, on the other hand, have received concentrated attention in the last few years. Some comments on the purport of the most recent contributions to the discussion are therefore necessary, even though, for the most part, they raise more problems than they solve.

The most cogent contribution is that of Mordek.[36] He has insisted on the need to distinguish between the historical as opposed to the contemporary significance of the capitularies and legal texts. Our job is to try and determine the latter, and in so doing we encounter many of the same difficulties of interpreting the evidence as will be apparent in relation to the *leges*. It is no accident, moreover, that capitularies and *leges* are often part of the same collection.[37] The problem of the degree of authority conveyed by the actual written text of the capitularies may never decisively be settled, for we are hamstrung by the form in which this material has been preserved.[38] There are one or two precious survivors of notes and minutes taken at meetings, such as the famous Murbach statutes in the Colmar *rotulus* (Arch. Dep. du Haut-Rhin, Grand document No. 139 (*olim* 10G), Actes Généraux Lad. 12 No. 4) which a participant at the Aachen reform councils of 816 took home with him in his luggage, a version of the proceedings apparently actually written during the meeting and based on a draft of the conciliar *capitula*,[39] or the recently identified Munich *rotulus*, Clm 29555/2, containing matter relating to the reform councils of 813,[40] or what look like drafts for full capitulary texts in BN lat. 9008.[41] For the most part, however, we are dependent for our knowledge of the

---

[35] The ground work for such a study is R. H. Bautier, 'La Chancellerie et les actes royaux dans le royaumes carolingiens', *BEC* 142 (1984) 5–80.

[36] Mordek, 'Karolingische Kapitularien'. See also the discussions by Reinhard Schneider, 'Zur rechtliche Bedeutung der Kapitularientexte', *DA* 23 (1967) 273–94, and D. Hagermann, 'Zur Entstehung der Kapitularien', in *Festschrift P. Acht* (Kallmutz, 1976), pp. 12–27.

[37] For example, Montpellier 136, BN lat. 4417, 4626, 4628A, BL Add. 22398, Wolfenbüttel 50.2.Aug.4° (3530) and Blankenburg 130, Bamberg can. 12 (P.I.1).

[38] See, for example, the comments in McKitterick, *Frankish Church*, pp. 18–25, and *idem*, *Frankish Kingdoms*, pp. 331–2.

[39] A facsimile is provided with the volume by Mordek, *Überlieferung und Geltung*, and see Josef Semmler, 'Zur Überlieferung der monastischen Gestzgebung Ludwigs des Frommen', *DA* 16 (1960) 309–88, especially 322–4.

[40] See Mordek, 'Karolingische Kapitularien', p. 33.

[41] *Ibid.*, p. 32 n. 38, published in facsimile in Hartmut Atsma and Jean Vezin, eds., *ChLA* XVII, No. 655.

text of the capitularies on later and, supposedly, private compilations. The relatively large capitulary collection put together by Ansegis is held to be the most obvious instance of private initiative. I suggest, however, that there may be grounds for proposing a more formal initiative for his collection than is usually accepted.[42] It is worth considering, indeed, whether Ansegis' collection represents the contemporary evaluation of what was important in the bulk of capitulary material issued by Charlemagne and Louis the Pious. He has received much criticism for the fact that he included only twenty-six out of a possible one hundred or more capitularies, and scathing comments have been added about the inadequacies of the archive or archives to which Ansegis had recourse. But it is possible that his capitulary collection represents a systematic, deliberate and carefully structured selection. Is there any justification in condemning his efforts as futile because they do not match modern historians' estimates of his material? That the Carolingian rulers themselves referred to the Ansegis collection may have been for more weighty reasons than because there was no better one available. They regarded it as the useful digest that it was. But there are also other, smaller, compilations which demand attention.

The edict of Pîtres cited above made it clear that the regional, and especially episcopal, writing offices were assumed to be equipped to make copies of capitularies for further distribution. They would also, presumably, keep a record of pertinent capitularies for themselves. Much depended, therefore, on the efficiency, resources and reliability of the bishops concerned in their capacity as royal agents. It is worth noting here the possibility that bishops in the ninth century were also playing a much greater role in the judicial process than they had hitherto. That comital writing offices may have existed and played a similar role in the preservation of capitularies to that of episcopal ones should also not be dismissed out of hand. Any assumptions about inadequate capacity in this respect are totally unwarranted, even if it be acknowledged that firm evidence to prove that they were active is lacking at present. Nevertheless, there is no reason why some of the many capitulary and legal collections should not have been formed by and for counts.[43] Much rests, too, on the survival of particular ecclesiastical archives which may reflect this cooperative activity in the preservation of the capitularies. It is, no doubt, these two factors, that is, efficiency of the royal officers and of the archives, which can be observed in the overwhelming evidence for Hincmar of

[42] As suggested also in McKitterick, *Frankish Kingdoms*, p. 126.
[43] See the discussion of legal collections below, pp. 46–60.

Rheims' maintenance of the capitularies of Charles the Bald.[44] Some of the capitularies, as recorded by Hincmar and his secretaries, have the character of responses to particular problems subsequently generalized.[45] They can thus possibly be understood as texts which represent and expand the oral agreements of an assembly, transformed into texts of a more lasting character by the process of transcription. Other 'private' compilations of great diversity have also been signalled.[46] These include many different types of text – historical, canonical, philosophical, patristic and hagiographical; they form a great mass of material in dire need of investigation and assessment if we are to have a hope of understanding the meaning and status of the collections as collections, the texts they contain and the individuals and the society which produced them.

Despite the difficulties of interpreting the evidence, the literate modes employed for the dissemination and preservation of the capitularies are an unequivocal affirmation of the symbolic and practical value of the written word. One should remember that as early as the all-important *Admonitio Generalis* of 789, and in subsequent legislation, norms and uniformity are recommended and to be imposed through the medium of particular written texts – the *Dionysio-Hadriana* canon law collection, the Rule of Benedict, the Rome-approved sacramentary, a homiliary, Gregory the Great's *Cura Pastoralis* and the written law.[47]

Memory was not sufficient. A written tradition and written norms are drawn on at every juncture and in every sphere of activity, and their relevance and importance are insisted on by written means. The Carolingians reveal themselves as deeply committed to the written word for communication, administration and record.[48] The capitularies, in particular, by which the Carolingian rulers and magnates made known measures of legislation, and administration, exhortation, statements of policy and moral fervour, were part of a process of standardization, a striving towards unity within a disparate realm, and an attempt to consolidate authority.[49] As such, they constitute an eloquent witness to the exploitation of the written word by Carolingians. The implications for the

---

[44] Nelson, 'Legislation and consensus', p. 208.

[45] *Ibid.*, pp. 210–11.

[46] For example, BN lat. 4404 and others. Compare Mordek, 'Karolingische Kapitularien', pp. 37–40, and the collections discussed in Nelson, 'Legislation and consensus', pp. 205–7 (The Hague 10.d.2, Yale, Beinecke 213 and Vat. reg. lat. 291 with Vat. lat. 4982).

[47] *MGH Cap.* I, No. 22, cc.1–69 pp. 53–9, and see cc.72, 78, p. 60; *MGH Conc.* II. 1, council of Mainz (813), No. 36, Preface, pp. 259–60; *MGH Cap.* I, No. 33 (capitulary for the *missi* 802), c.26, p. 96.

[48] Werner, 'Missus, Marchio, Comes', adds much useful material on this.

[49] See McKitterick, *Frankish Church*, and Walter Ullmann, *The Carolingian Renaissance and the Idea of Kingship* (London, 1969).

degree and scale to which the Franks, both laymen and clerics, possessed literate skills are enormous. They point to an educated administrative class and to a deep penetration of literacy in Carolingian society.

II THE 'LEGES'

To the evidence of the use of writing in Carolingian government and the capitulary legislation must be added that of the *leges*, or collections of the 'national' laws of the peoples in the regions under Carolingian rule. These comprise the *Lex Salica, Lex Ribuaria, Lex Alamannorum* and *Lex Burgundionum*.[50] Their status as law is ambivalent. Do they reflect reality and represent attempts at describing social and legal practice already in evidence? Do they trail the introduction of particular practices, or do they make enactments and recommendations which are subsequently followed? Of what use were the laws in the courts? Were they resorted to for aid in reaching judicial decisions? What were the circumstances of their production, and how was knowledge of these laws disseminated and transmitted? Is their function primarily symbolic or is it practical? In considering these questions are we doing so in terms of the written texts that have come down to us, on the understanding that they represent oral law that is now unknown, or are we to distinguish by function the written law, *lex scripta*, from oral, legal pronouncements, and thus understand the written *leges* not so much as law but as minutes of oral pronouncements? Because the written form of the *leges* has given rise to so much argument, the form in which they have survived and considerations of the function and ownership of the manuscripts which contain these texts are of crucial importance. Yet to refer to the written form of the *leges* implies the existence of an oral form. In fact, the *leges* cannot be understood necessarily, or just simply, as a written version of custom. Both custom, an established usage which by long continuance has acquired the force of law or right, and law, a body of rules proceeding from formal enactment, may be sources of judicial decisions. Only a portion of the *lex*, in other words, is *lex scripta*. References, for example, to *Lex Salica* in sources from Merovingian Gaul are not necessarily to the written law (there is in any case no extant copy of *Lex Salica* datable to the Merovingian period) and *consuetudo* or custom is invoked as well. References to the Alemannic laws in charters reflect a similar situation; citations of *Lex Alamannorum* find no

---

[50] The *Lex Baiuuariorum* is also of importance but is not considered in detail here; on its transmission and application see Raymund Kottje, 'Die *Lex Baiuuariorum* – das Recht der Baiern', in Mordek, *Überlieferung und Geltung*, pp. 9–24. The *Lex Saxonum, Lex Frisonum* and *Lex Thuringorum* similarly cannot be disregarded, but for the purposes of this chapter I have concentrated on the main lines of law transmission.

parallel in any extant written version of the Alemannic laws. They must therefore be invoking unwritten law. As Nehlsen has pointed out, however, *lex* and *consuetudo*, law and custom, do not appear to have been juxtaposed as opposites in the sense of written and unwritten law so much as invoked as together constituting everyday practice.[51]

This is not, of course, a peculiarly early mediaeval feature. The late Roman period was one in which there was an increasing divergence between law in action and the law in the books. Early mediaeval *leges* seem to continue the Roman tradition of adaptation and change. Legal prescriptions and practice are increasingly at odds, new prescriptions are made to account for this, and new versions of the *leges* compiled, with, in Carolingian Francia at least, supplementary legislation to clarify or define certain matters such as Charlemagne's capitulary of additions to *Lex Ribuaria*. It appears, therefore, that the essential context for the understanding of the status of the written laws is one of continuous discussion and change, framed in terms of the authority that the written word could provide, and that our written texts represent more than mere minutes of decisions taken. I suggest, indeed, that the proliferation of texts of the laws in the Carolingian period reflects the growing understanding of the authority of the written word and an attempt to establish that authority in relation to legal procedure and judicial decisions.

This raises the question of the symbolic, as opposed to the practical, authority of the *leges*, if, indeed, they can be effectively distinguished. Wormald's arguments in favour of the predominantly symbolic function and primarily ideological character of the written laws,[52] or Nehlsen's independent observations concerning the obstacles in the path of any insistence on the *wholly* practical role of the written laws, must be given due weight.[53] In particular, Wormald has observed that the issuing of the *leges* of the Germanic kingdoms reflects the wish on the part of the Germanic kings to emulate the literary legal culture of the Roman and Judaeo-Christian civilization to which they were heirs, and to reinforce the links that bound a king or dynasty to his people. This does much to make sense of the wider context in which these written laws must be read. Nevertheless, the specific context of the written laws must also be

[51] H. Nehlsen, 'Zur Aktualität und Effektivität germanischer Rechtsaufzeichnungen', in Classen, ed., *Recht und Schrift*, pp. 449–502, at 454–71 and Schott, '*Leges* Forschung', 49. On written and unwritten law see, for example, W. W. Buckland, *A Text Book of Roman Law*, 3rd edn. revised by Peter Stein (Cambridge, 1966).

[52] Patrick Wormald, 'Lex scripta et verbum regis: legislation and Germanic kingship from Euric to Cnut', in P. Sawyer and Ian Wood, eds., *Early Mediaeval Kingship* (Leeds, 1977), pp. 105–38.

[53] Nehlsen, 'Aktualität und Effektivität', pp. 475–80.

understood. While ideology may have been an important incentive for the production of written laws, it could only have been effective if the value of written law and the symbol it represented were understood. Use of a symbol implies an audience that will appreciate its purport. It is in this context that the number of extant manuscripts of these laws dating from the ninth century is highly suggestive with respect to their practical relevance. The recommendations of the Carolingian rulers to judge wisely according to the written law must refer to books of law such as are represented by these manuscripts. For example, the Lorsch Annals of 802 record:

The emperor also assembled the dukes, the counts, and the rest of the Christian people, together with men skilled in the laws, and had all the laws in his realm read out, each man's law expounded to him and emended wherever necessary, and the emended law written down. And he declared that the judges (*iudices*) should judge in accordance with what was written and should not accept gifts, and that all men, poor or rich, should enjoy justice in his realm.[54]

Given the invocation of the personality principle that each man should have his own law, the passage would appear to be discussing the *leges*. It would have been possible to perform all the Carolingian counts' duties without recourse to written means. Judgement and record could have been, and often were, by oral pronouncement and memory, testified to by oaths from witnesses to the proceedings. One can compare the equilibrium maintained between written and oral evidence and records in the laws' statements themselves discussed later in this chapter. But a number of factors, including this law book evidence, suggest that in two stages of the judicial procedure written means were of growing importance both legally and socially. In the first place, there are indications in the Carolingian evidence that written law was, even if not actually used, then required to be used, by the counts. Royal legislation, such as the general capitulary for the *missi* in 802, required the judges diligently to learn the law composed for the people by wise men and to give judgements according to the written law, thus echoing the account provided in the Lorsch Annals. Other decrees of the first decade of the ninth century required counts, *missi dominici* and judges to possess copies of the law. Charlemagne's reply to his *missus* cited above assumed that the official had such a law book in his possession.[55] We have, in addition, telling instances of counts known to have possessed law books. Count Eberhard of Friuli bequeathed a copy of all the barbarian law codes to his eldest son Unruoch, possibly the very

---

[54] Lorsch Annals, *MGH SS* I, pp. 37–9, trans. King, *Charlemagne*, p. 145.
[55] *Responsa misso cuidam data* c.2, *MGH Cap.* I, No. 58, p. 145, trans. King, *ibid.*, p. 267, and see above p. 29.

codex prepared for him by Lupus of Ferrières, and his copy of the Lombard law to his daughter Judith![56] Eccard of Mâcon left copies of the Salic law to one of his friends, and volumes of the Burgundian law and Roman law to others.[57] It is likely that the great production of law books, especially after 802 and possibly in comital, episcopal and royal writing offices as well as monastic scriptoria, was specifically with the needs of judges and administrators in mind, and that this is what we are witnessing in the extant manuscripts of *leges* of which we have a remarkable abundance of ninth-century date. It is to these law books and their implications that I now turn.

III THE PRODUCTION AND TRANSMISSION OF WRITTEN LAW: THE CASE OF 'LEX SALICA'

Of vital importance in interpreting the significance of the written laws and their practical relevance is the form of the surviving evidence and the nature of its transmission. The testimony of the manuscripts has not hitherto been considered fully in the discussion of the function of the laws and thus a beginning will be made here in terms of one of the most problematic texts, the *Lex Salica*.

The *Lex Salica* exists in five versions (A, B, C, D and E) dating from before 800. The first three (A, the hypothetical B, and C) are supposed to represent the early Merovingian redactions, divided into sixty-five sections or Titles. A is the oldest and is dated *c.* 511, though the earliest manuscript of it extant is dated *c.* 770. D and E represent early Carolingian versions, presumed to have been compiled under Pippin (between 751 and 768) and Charlemagne (*c.* 798) respectively. E constitutes an amended version of D (in its turn based on A) and was divided into ninety-nine Titles. The sixth redaction of the *Lex Salica* is the *Karolina* (K), dependent on the Merovingian C text, produced *c.* 802, and divided into seventy Titles.[58] For simplicity's sake the *Lex Salica* redactions may be schematized thus:

Lex Salica A, B, C	65 Title text	Merovingian
Lex Salica D, E	100 and 99 Title text	Early Carolingian (before 800)
Lex Salica K	70 Title text	Carolingian (after 800)

[56] I. de Coussemaker, ed., *Cartulaire de l'abbaye de Cysoing et de ses dépendances* (Lille, 1885), pp. 3–4. For a fuller discussion of the significance of Eberhard's library and the bequest to his children see below, pp. 245–8, and the references there cited.

[57] M. Prou and A. Vidier, eds., *Recueil des chartes de l'abbaye de Saint-Benoît-sur-Loire*, Documents publiés par la Société historique et archéologique du Gâtinais V (Paris, 2 vols., 1900–7), I, No. XXV, pp. 61–7, and see below, pp. 248–50.

[58] K. A. Eckhardt, ed., *Lex Salica*, MGH Leges Germ. IV.1 (*Pactus legis Salicae*) and IV.2 (*Lex Salica* D,E) (1962 and 1969).

Additions were made to these texts both by the Merovingian and by the Carolingian kings, in the form of edicts and capitularies. These are found appended to the main texts in many of the manuscripts. There are also two further variants of interest: a systematized rearrangement of the *Karolina* redactions was made in north Italy in the second or third decade of the ninth century and is extant in two manuscripts; an Old High German version of the ninth century was compiled in the east Frankish region, but survives only in fragments.[59] As has been recognized, the vernacular version may be of the greatest importance in any assessment of the dissemination of knowledge of the law.[60]

The *Karolina* text had, as will be seen, wide currency. Was it an official set of laws or a code compiled with the knowledge of or under the aegis of the king? It is in relation to the production of the revised *Karolina* text that the statement in the Lorsch Annals cited above should be seen; it makes little sense in terms of the general emphases and methods of Charlemagne's government, discussed earlier in this chapter, to envisage any effort to produce law books on the scale the extant manuscripts indicate as unofficial. If there were evidence to support the notion of unofficial private compilation it would be easier to accept the notion of a proliferation of unofficial law books. The evidence, on the contrary, supports the notion of officially sanctioned production, and, in one crucial group of manuscripts (discussed below), actual official production in association with the royal court. I therefore accept the *Lex Salica Karolina* as the redaction sanctioned by the Carolingian king and his advisers. It is in this sense that it is an official collection. How it was issued and circulated, on the other hand, can only be learned from the manuscripts. Their message is not always unambiguous.

Extant manuscripts of the six versions of the *Lex Salica* are in abundance. Those dating from the ninth century, moreover, form the greater proportion. But there are significant peculiarities in the distribution of the redactions among these manuscripts which have been interpreted in many different ways. No fewer than sixty-nine of Eckhardt's eighty-four manuscripts of *Lex Salica* contain the *Lex Salica Karolina* redaction, and fifty-four of these date from the ninth and tenth centuries. This is the sort of proportion one might expect in the distribution of one edition of a text in relation to superseded versions of it. But it is also, by any reckoning, a prodigious number, for one text, of surviving manuscripts of similar date,

---

[59] Trier Ahd und Mhd Fragmente 4.

[60] The work of Ruth Schmidt-Wiegand is the most important in this context. See in particular her 'Die Malbergischen Glossen der Lex Salica als Denkmal des Westfränkischen', *Rheinische Vierteljahrsblätter* 33 (1969) 396–422, and the references cited by Schott, '*Leges* Forschung', 37nn. 40 and 41.

and must be acknowledged in assessments of the text's importance and dissemination. Scholars, however, have allowed themselves to be misled by the fact that the manuscripts of the earlier superseded versions A–E are at first sight produced at exactly the same time as the *Karolina* versions. This, they aver, is a sure sign of incompetence on the part of any judge, for how could he use an outdated legal text or permit one to be produced (if indeed he can be held responsible in relation to the production of the *leges*)? It is also held to undermine the status of the whole law code if different versions are in circulation at the same time. Murray, for example, is of the opinion that the existence of so many divergent forms at the same time and the apparent lack of any official attempt to abolish older versions or pronounce them invalid (as older issues of coinage might be called in and declared no longer current) constitutes too mighty an obstacle to acceptance of the *Lex Salica* as a developed or developing body of official law.[61]

The first practical rejoinder to this is that not only is the dating of the earliest redactions' codices for the most part too imprecise to be certain that they are indeed being copied appreciably later than the *Karolina*, but that it is begging the question to think in terms of rival texts being circulated. The coincidental existence of copying of two different versions of the same text, the one a more recent edition than the other, does not necessarily mean that both were equally valid in the same place at the same time, for the copies may be of very different origins and there may be other reasons why an older text was recopied. It should be stressed how few manuscripts there are of the pre-*Karolina* redactions – four A manuscripts, two of C, three of D and six of E. These may well represent survivors that escaped the cull, copies of earlier editions remade due to the unavailability of the modern up-to-date version, ignorance that such an up-to-date version existed in an area where communications were slow or for some reason had been interrupted, cussedness on the part of the commissioner of the codex concerned in preferring to have the text with which he was familiar recopied rather than the new one, simple failure to respond to the introduction of the *Karolina* quickly enough, slowness in the speed or efficiency at which the *Karolina* was disseminated and copies made available, or preference for an older version in a particular area. Some of these law books may have survived in a library in the same way

[61] Alexander C. Murray, *Germanic Kingship Structure. Studies in Law and Society in Antiquity and the Early Middle Ages* (Toronto, 1983), p. 128. See also, however, P. C. Boeren, 'Quelques remarques sur les manuscrits de la loi Salique', *Tijdschrift voor Rechtsgeschiedenis* 22 (1954) 33–67, who makes valuable comments on the practical use of the laws. It was he who stressed the significance of the copying of BN lat. 4632 by *Autramnus indignus advocatus laicus* mentioned below, p. 47.

that older out-of-date text books are retained by historically minded librarians nowadays who eschew the ridiculous 'steady-state library' principle. The *Lex Salica* codices in the library of St Gall are a case in point. St Gall possessed a copy of the D redaction made in 793 (St Gall 731), a copy of the E text dating to the beginning of the ninth century (St Gall 729), that is, probably copied before the issuing of the *Karolina*, and a volume containing the *Karolina* version copied later in the ninth century (St Gall 728). Thus scholarly or antiquarian motives could also account for the preservation or even recopying of particular redactions of the law. We should be careful not to draw conclusions too readily from a distribution and survival pattern which is at best arbitrary and where ecclesiastical institutions are the most likely places of ultimate preservation. Books that were once in constant use are also less likely to have survived intact. Too little is known in any case about the origins of each of the manuscripts concerned to draw conclusions with any confidence.

Another cause for suspicion of the *Lex Salica*'s effectiveness is the quality of the texts that are copied. The text often varies wildly from redaction to redaction, and even within manuscripts of the same 'family'. Sometimes such variations can be attributed to unintelligent copying, but the results on occasion are so hair-raisingly misleading, as in Wandalgarius' confusion of *hereburgii* and *rachinburgii* in St Gall 731, or the scribe who transcribed the heading *Pactum pro tenore pacis* as *Pactum pro timore pacis*,[62] as to jeopardize the utility of the texts. When these appalling mistakes are left uncorrected it decreases one's confidence in the user's knowledge of the law, whether written or unwritten. A cautionary note may perhaps be sounded in relation to this lack of expertise. It certainly reflects badly on the capabilities of the scribe, or else the quality of his exemplar if he knew what he was copying was wrong, but can a scribe be expected to possess an expert knowledge of the subject whose representative text he was transcribing? A particular defective or decadent copy does not necessarily negate the usefulness of the original text of the law or the capabilities of the person attempting to use it. That is, the defectiveness of a copy does not tell us anything of the person trying to use it. Carolingian judges may well have been as exasperated at the muddle and mistakes they found in their precious law books as the modern scholars who endeavour to make sense of them. We are not justified, moreover, in generalizing from particular inanities in copying to condemn not only the volume which contains them and its users, but also all copies of the law concerned.

---

[62] In the manuscript BN lat. 18237, discussed by Nehlsen, 'Aktualität und Effektivität', p. 474.

Discussion of the *Lex Salica* to date has involved a far from exhaustive survey of the texts, and has, in any case, been preoccupied with textual readings. It is striking, for example, how many ninth-century copies Eckhardt categorized but did not use for his editions. Although he consulted many of the A, D and E versions in the original, and all of them from photographs, he found little to interest him in the *Karolina* version. Of the sixty-nine *Karolina* copies, the majority of which date to the ninth century, he consulted only eight in the original and six more from photographs of the *Lex Salica* portion of each manuscript only. He compared the readings of a further twenty-one copies as they were recorded in such printed editions as those by Hessels[63] and Pardessus.[64] The remaining thirty-four he did not use at all. For the purposes of providing a text this was perhaps reasonable, though unwarrantable assumptions about the superiority of the A, D and E texts as against the *Karolina* version are implicit and open to criticism. But as far as assessing the historical significance or legal function of these laws is concerned, such selectivity is reprehensibly shortsighted. Four-fifths of these codices are Carolingian. How can conclusions about the quality of the *Lex Salica* texts or the effectiveness of the law they contained possibly be drawn in any credible way from a small sample of the available evidence? All the codices must be considered.

The whole question needs a wholesale re-examination on a scale impossible within the scope of this book but it is of some value to investigate the degree to which the form in which these laws were transmitted bears any relation to their function, or contemporary attitudes towards them.

First of all, can the circumstances of production of any of the early versions be established? This might help to soothe anxieties about the simultaneous copying of different editions of the same text. Unfortunately, such attempts at appeasement are stymied by the inadequacies of our knowledge. Of the A text manuscripts, the earliest, Wolfenbüttel Weissenburg 97, has been dated *c.* 770 and is thus consistent with production before the D version of Pippin became widely circulated. It was compiled in the north or east of the Frankish kingdom and also contains a summary version of the Breviary of Alaric (a digest of Roman law first compiled in the sixth century and still widely circulated in the ninth).[65]

---

[63] J. H. Hessels, *Lex Salica. The Ten Texts with Glosses and the Lex Emendata* (London, 1880).

[64] J. M. Pardessus, *La Loi Salique ou receuil contenant les anciennes rédactions de cette loi et le texte connu sous le nom de les emendata* (Paris, 1843).

[65] See the description by Hans Butzmann, *Die Weissenburger Handschriften* (Frankfurt, 1964), pp. 278–82.

Clm 4115 is another legal collection of late eighth- or early ninth-century date and contains, in addition to *Lex Salica*, the *Lex Ribuaria* and the *Lex Alamannorum*. It is from southern Germany and contains a number of German names entered in the ninth and tenth centuries.[66] BN lat. 4404, written between 800 and 814, is a book from the Tours region, possibly belonging to a magnate or court official, and also containing the *Lex Alamannorum*, *Lex Ribuaria* and the Breviary of Alaric, only the last of which has accompanying annotations.[67] Most of the sixteen pre-*Karolina* versions are 'law books', containing systematic selections of other Germanic laws and some Roman law. An exception is BN lat. 18237, which, owing to its inclusion of Isidore of Seville's *De legibus*, is better categorized as a school book.[68] Most, moreover, date at latest from early in the ninth century, except for Montpellier 136, copied after 819 and BN lat. 4627 (D text) and Berlin Phillipps 161 (E text) both of which were copied at the end of the ninth century, by which time it may be that distinctions between the three different Carolingian versions were not as important as they had been hitherto, or that intellectual rather than practical motives were uppermost.

The lesson to be learnt from the surviving manuscripts of the pre-*Karolina* redaction is that clear conclusions about its function in relation to the administration of justice cannot be drawn. The codices are, however, for the most part sufficiently early in date to suggest that the D and E manuscripts were copied, for whatever reason, before the later *Karolina* redaction could replace them, and that there may well have been personal or political reasons why some copyists continued to write out the 'Merovingian' A and C redactions of the laws rather than the early Carolingian ones.

The question of the judicial function of the *Lex Salica* cannot therefore be settled by a resort to the manuscript transmission of redactions A to E. The focus of attention should be on the fifty-four extant Carolingian manuscripts of the *Karolina* text, and the impression gained from them is very different.

The most crucial consideration in the transmission of the text of *Lex Salica* and its implications as far as its use in the administration of justice is concerned is that it is impossible to consider the *Lex Salica* in isolation

---

[66] Bischoff, *Schreibschulen* I, pp. 15–17.
[67] Eckhardt, ed., *Pactus legis Salicae*, MGH *Leges Germ.* IV.1, p. xiii and n. 1, and R. McKitterick, 'Some Carolingian lawbooks and their function', in Peter Linehan and Brian Tierney, eds., *Authority and Power. Studies on Medieval Law and Government Presented to Walter Ullmann on his Seventieth Birthday* (Cambridge, 1980), pp. 13–27 at p. 19 where I misleadingly suggested that this manuscript was from south of the Loire, without indicating how far south I meant.
[68] See below, pp. 46 and 47.

from the other *leges* or Carolingian capitulary legislation. The codicological context of *Lex Salica*, that is, what is in the codices in addition to the *Lex Salica*, precludes this, for it is quite clear that the surviving manuscripts represent different types of legal collection. From the information supplied in editions of *Lex Salica*, notably that of Eckhardt, this has not been apparent, but it is of the utmost importance to observe with what texts *Lex Salica* and the other *leges* were associated by compilers and scribes of books in the ninth century.[69] I provide, in tabular form for ease of consultation (Table A), therefore, a list of extant *Lex Salica* manuscripts, according to the labels provided by Eckhardt, with notes on their date, origin and content, and I classify them according to content first into law books, that is books containing a selection of, if not all, the *leges*, often including the capitulary collection of Ansegis or else a more personal selection of Carolingian capitularies, and in many cases also including the Breviary of Alaric, the form in which Roman law was most usually circulated in the Carolingian period. A second category is school texts about the law, identified by the inclusion of Isidore of Seville's section *De legibus* from his *Etymologiae*. The third category is that of ecclesiastical legal collections, comprising both canon law and secular law to which are often added Carolingian capitularies on ecclesiastical affairs.[70]

Examples of law books to be noted in Table A are St Paul in Carinthia XXV/4, 8, Wolfenbüttel 50.2.Aug.4° and Blankenburg 130, Lyons 375(303), BN lat. 4628, BL Add. 22398 and Egerton 2832, Leningrad O.v.II.11, and Vat. reg. lat. 338, all of which are collections of laws – Germanic or imperial Roman – and/or Carolingian capitularies containing material about royal and comital administration of law and order. Another of these 'law books' is the famous Wandalgarius codex, St Gall 731 (D9) which, for all its notorious mistakes, may well have been prepared by the notary Wandalgarius in a count's writing office for use by an official serving a region whose mixed population lived under Roman, Alemannic and Salic law.[71] Munich 8°132 is, on Bischoff's suggestion, probably a count's copy of the *Lex Baiuuariorum* from Ingolstadt for use in the Regensburg area.[72] Another notarial production may be recognized in the

---

[69] It should be noted, however, that R. Buchner's *MGH* edition of the *Lex Ribuaria* is exemplary in this respect, for he provides full details of all the codices containing the text of *Lex Ribuaria*, many of which also contain, of course, the *Lex Salica*: *MGH Leges Germ.* III.2.

[70] The Table is intended to serve as a preliminary guide and classification rather than as a dogmatic statement, as full details concerning the manuscripts listed thereon have not always been available. I am particularly grateful to Bernhard Bischoff for his help in verifying the dates and origins of these manuscripts.

[71] Compare McKitterick, 'Carolingian lawbooks', pp. 15–16.

[72] Bischoff, *Schreibschulen* I, pp. 249–50.

Lex Romana Raetica Curiensis, a personal compilation of late Roman law based on the Breviary of Alaric, made in the early ninth century, a copy of which was transcribed by Orsicinus, one of the 'local scribes' functioning in Rhaetia.[73] There are also the codices, such as Berlin Phillipps 1761, BN lat. 4626, 4417, 4418 and others, which, as I have suggested elsewhere, were apparently consulted by officials on various legal points and probably used in court. To the school books, BN lat. 4403A, 4629 and 18237 I have also discussed elsewhere, can be added Leiden Voss lat. Q. 119 and O. 86, BN lat. 4760, and Autun 36.[74] Of the utmost significance, furthermore, is the collection of *leges* and capitularies copied by Autramnus, who signs his name on folio 59r of BN lat. 4632. He was a lay advocate (*Autramnus indignus advocatus laicus*) working in the north of France, probably in the St Amand region, during the reign of Charles the Bald. This can only have been made for his own use.

Among the ecclesiastical legal collections, Berne 442, for example, is a collection of canon and secular law; Cambrai 625 contains canon law, papal decretals, fragments of penitentials, extracts from the Bible and the episcopal statutes of Theodulf of Orleans as well as the *Lex Salica*; Bamberg can. 12 (P.I.1) is an episcopal law collection and includes the capitularies of Aachen 801–13, the decrees of the Synod of Worms 829 and Hincmar's episcopal statutes; BN lat. 10758 is an historical and legal collection honouring the Carolingian house and is associated with Hincmar of Rheims; BN lat. 9654 accompanies the *Lex Salica Karolina* with much of the Carolingian ecclesiastical legislation; BN lat. 4628A, like BN lat. 10758, is a codex in which historical and theological, as well as legal, interests are represented, for it adds to the *Lex Salica* and its Carolingian augmentation, the Ansegis collection of Carolingian capitularies, a copy of Einhard's Life of Charlemagne, and the confutation of Elipandus of Toledo and Felix of Urgel's views on Adoptionism by Paulinus of Aquileia.

Each surviving Carolingian manuscript of the *Lex Salica* needs to be categorized in this way in order to give some sense of the intentions of the compilers. It should be stressed again, moreover, that although the main focus of this discussion has been on the *Lex Salica*, the fact that it almost invariably forms part of a legal collection of some sort, and that its most constant companion is the *Lex Ribuaria*, with *Lex Alamannorum* close behind, means that our attitude to the use and transmission of all the *leges* generally must be affected. In view of the prescriptions for the use of written records in the *Lex Ribuaria* and *Lex Alamannorum* discussed below, it is especially pertinent. As far as the *Lex Ribuaria* in particular is

---

[73] See below, p. 110.
[74] See McKitterick, 'Carolingian lawbooks', pp. 17–19, 25–6.

Table A *Carolingian legal compilations: the 'Lex Salica' manuscripts*

MS		Date	Origin	Category and content
A1	BN lat. 4404	s.ix^{in} (800–14)	Tours region	Law book (comital collection). *Leges Al., Bai., Rib., Sal.*
A2	Wolfenbüttel Weissenburg 97	c. 770	N. or N.E. France; scribe: Agambert	Law book. *Lex Sal., Brev. Alar.*
A3	Clm 4115	s.viii/ix	S. Germany	Law book. *Leges Sal., Rib., Al.*
A4	BN lat. 9653	s.ix^1	?Burgundy; provenance Lyons cathedral	Law book. *Leges Burg., Sal.* and add. capits. *Brev. Alar.*
C5	BN lat. 4403A	s.viii	Luxeuil	School book, includes Isidore, *De legibus, Lex Sal., Brev. Alar.* Annotated.
C6	BN lat. 18237	s.ix^2	W. France	School book, includes Isidore, *De legibus, florilegium* on kingship. *De iudicibus,* ecclesiastical capitularies. Or an ecclesiastical compilation.
C6a	Leiden BPL 2005	s.xvi	Low Countries	*Lex Sal.* (collation of a lost ninth-century copy).
D7	Montpellier 136	s.ix^1 (after 819)	France	Law book. *Lex Sal., Brev. Alar.* and Carolingian capitularies.
D8	BN lat. 4627	s.ix/x	France, a chancery	Law book with Marculf's Formulary; possibly a notary's collection.
D9	St Gall 731	793	W. Switzerland	Law book. The Wandalgarius codex (possibly a notary's collection): *Leges Sal., Al., Brev. Alar.*
B10	Fulda 507	s.xvi	Fulda	Law book. *Leges Sal., Rib., Al.*
C10	Fulda 508	s.xvi	Fulda	*Lex Sal.*
E11	Vat. reg. lat. 846	s.ix^1	*Leges* scriptorium	Law book. Many *probationes pennae* and annotations in tironian notes. *Lex. Sal., Brev. Alar., Pauli Sententiae,* Isidore, *De legibus.*

E12	BN lat. 4409	$s.ix^{ex}$	France	Roman law collection plus *Lex Sal.* and a formulary.
E13	Warsaw Quart. 480	$s.ix^{\frac{1}{4}}$	*Leges* scriptorium	School book or legal miscellany with Isidore, *De legibus, Formulae,* canon law, Brev. Alar., *Lex Sal.,* etc.
E14	St Gall 729	$s.ix^{\frac{1}{4}}$	*Leges* scriptorium	Law book. *Leges Sal., Al.,* Brev. Alar.
E15	BN lat. 4629	$s.ix^{\frac{1}{4}}$	Bourges	Possibly a law book subsequently used as a school book. *Leges Sal., Rib.,* with add. capits., *De Orthographia* and other didactic texts.
E16	Berlin Phillipps 1736	$s.x.^{med/2}$	France	Law book. *Lex Sal.* and add. capits., and capitulary for the *missi.*
			Karolina	
K17	Leiden Voss lat. Q. 119	$s.ix^{\frac{4}{4}}$	France. Used in Chartres	Law book. Isidore, *De Legibus,* Brev. Alar., *Leges Sal., Rib., Al., Bai.* Capitularies, but also includes Isidore *De legibus.*
K18	Leiden Voss lat. O. 86	$s.ix^{1}$	Paris region	A personal layman's collection? It includes the *Liber Historiae Francorum,* a formulary, prayers on the Trinity and *Lex Sal.*
K19	St Paul in Carinthia XXV.4.8	817–23	N. Italy or Aquilaeia	Law book. *Leges Sal., Rib., Bai., Al., Burg., Epit. Aegid.* and capitulary for count.
K20	St Gall 728	$s.ix^{\frac{3}{4}}$	E. France	A library copy of law? *Leges Sal., Rib. Ansegisus,* III and IV, add. capits. to *Leges Sal.* and *Rib.. Quaestiones* on the law. The codex also contains the St Gall library catalogue, compiled at St Gall.
K21	St Gall Stadtbibliothek 338	$s.ix^{\frac{1}{3}}$	Mainz, with $s.ix^{\frac{3}{3}}$ additions made at St Gall	Law book. *Leges Sal., Rib., Al.,* and prologue of *Lex Bai.*

Table A (*cont.*)

MS		Date	Origin	Category and content
K22	Berne 442	s.x$^{\frac{1}{4}}$	?E. France	Episcopal handbook of canon law and *Lex Sal.*
K23	Geneva 50	s.ix$^{\frac{2}{4}}$	?E. France	Miscellany of texts on *computus* by Bede and others, with *Annales Petaviani* and *Annales Masciacenses*. Contains no law text.
K24	BN lat. 4418	s.ix$^{\frac{1}{3}}$	Aachen region in association with the palace of Louis the Pious	Law book. *Epit. Aegid.* and *Epitome Iuliani*, *Leges Sal.*, *Rib.*, *Burg.*, *Visigothorum.*
K25	BN lat. 4417	s.ix^{ex}	?Burgundy	Law book. *Epit. Aegid.*, *Leges Sal.*, *Rib.*, *Al.*, *Bai.*, *Ansegisus.* Synod of Worms 829.
K26	BN lat. 4759	s.ix$^{\frac{2}{4}}$	Left bank of Rhine, E. France?	Law book. *Leges Sal.*, *Rib.*, *Al.*, *Bai.* Written in same place as BN lat. 4759A.
K27	BN n.a.lat. 204	s.ix^{1}	Tours style of script – *Leges* scriptorium	Law book. *Leges Sal.*, *Al.*, *Bai.*, *Burg.*, Tours Formulary, *Epit. Aegid.*, capitularies of Louis the Pious.
K28	BN lat. 4628	s.ix$^{\frac{2}{3}}$	N. France	Law book. *Leges Sal.*, *Rib.*, *Al.*, and add. capits., capitulary of 818/819 and capitulary to the *missi* on justice.
K29	BN lat. 8801	s.ix$^{\frac{1}{4}}$	N. France	Law book. *Lex Sal.* only. A pocketbook for a count or *missus*?
K30	BN lat. 10753	s.ix^{med}	France	Law book. *Leges Sal.*, *Rib.*, *Burg.*, Brev. Alar. add. capits., and some capitularies to 805.
K31	BN lat. 4626	s.xi	France	Private legal collection, including Isidore, *De legibus*, *Lex Sal.*, Brev. Alar.. Novels of Theodosius, capitularies of Louis the Pious and Charles the Bald.

	Shelfmark	Place	Date	Description
K32	BN lat. 9654	Metz	s.x	Law book. *Leges Sal., Rib., Al., Bai., Francorum Chamavorum*, capitularies from 814 to 884 (from 840 onwards for W. Francia) and Ansegis.
K33	BN lat. 10758	Rheims area	s.ix^{ex}	Historical and legal texts to honour the Carolingian house, *Lex Sal.*, Isidore, *De legibus*.
K34	BN lat. 4760	Lyons	s.x	Miscellany. *Lex Sal.*, add. capit., *Sent. de septem sentenis, Interrogationes Pippini et Resp. Alcuini, Comm. in Rom.*, etc.
K35	BN lat. 4628A	France	s.x/xi	Episcopal collection, including Ansegis, Einhard, *Vita Karoli* and texts on Adoptionism.
K36	BN lat. 4631	France	s.xv	Copy of BN lat 4628A? but includes Worms 829 and Louis the Pious, capitulary for 819.
K37	BN lat. 4630	France	s.xv/xvi	*Lex Sal.* only. Possibly a copy of the text in BN lat. 18238.
K38	BN lat. 4758	Burgundy	s.ix$^{\frac{1}{3}}$	Law book. *Leges Sal., Rib., Al., Bai.*
K39	BN lat. 4632	St Amand script. Written in St Stephen's church at Templève	s.ix^{4}	Law book. *Leges Sal., Rib., Al.*, add. capits., other capitularies. Belonged apparently to a lay advocate for it was written by *Autramnus indignus advocatus laicus.*
K40	BN lat. 3182	Brittany	s.x^{2}	Breton episcopal law collection with Breton glosses and insular canon law.
K41	BN lat. 4995	?France	S.ix	Capitulary collection (802–19), annals 708–800, extracts from *Lex Sal., interrogatio de legibus divinis et humanis.*
K42	BN lat. 4787	?France	s.ix$^{\frac{2}{3}}$	Law book. *Leges Sal., Rib., Al.*
K43	BN lat. 4788	?France	s.ix$^{\frac{2}{3}}$	Comital collection? Pocket copy. *Lex Sal.* capitulary of 816/817 and the capitulary *De Moneta* (sole extant copy).

Table A (cont.)

MS	Date	Origin	Category and content
K44 BN lat. 9656	s.x or xi	Probably N. Italy	Law book. *Lex Langobardorum*, capitularies for Italy, prologue to *Lex Bai.*, *Lex Sal.*
K45 BN lat. 10754	$s.ix^{\frac{3}{3}}$	?France	Law book. *Lex Sal.*, capitularies of 805 and 806. Tract on vices and virtues. Possibly a count's copy.
K46 BN lat. 18238	$s.ix^{\frac{1}{3}}$	?France	Law book. Fine copy, possibly episcopal. *Lex Sal.* and Ansegis III.
K47 Autun 36	$s.ix^{\frac{2}{3}}$	France	Miscellany. *Lex Sal.*, possibly originally a separate law book.
K48 Besançon 1348	$s.ix^{med}$	Probably E. France	Law book. *Leges Burg.*, *Sal.*
K49 Cambrai 625(526)	$s.ix^{ex}$	Brittany	Episcopal collection, including *Statuta* of Theodulf of Orleans.
K50 Lyons 375(303)	$s.ix^{1}$	Lyons area	Law book. *Brev. Alar.* and *Lex Sal.*
K51 BN lat. 4789	$s.x^{\frac{1}{4}}$	Provenance Rheims	*Lex Sal.*
K52 BL Egerton 2832 + Egerton 269 + BN lat. 4633	$s.x^{\frac{1}{4}}$	N.E. France	Law book. *Leges Sal.*, *Rib.*, *Saxonum*, *Al.*, *Bai.*, *Burg.*, add. capits., *Epit. Aegid.*
K53 BL Add. 22398	s.ix/x	Probably France	Law book. *Leges Sal.*, *Rib.*, Ansegis, add. capits. Pîtres 864. *Interrogationes Pippini et Resp. Alcuini.*
K54 Phillipps 3899	s.xv	Continent	*Lex Sal.*
K55 Copenhagen Gottorp 1943	$s.ix^{ex}$	E. France	Law book. *Leges Sal.*, *Rib.*, *Al.*, letter *formulae*, *Formulae salicae Lindenbrogii*, capitulary for 818/819.
K56 Hamburg in scrinio 141a	$s.ix^{\frac{3}{4}}$	Probably Corvey	Law book. *Leges Sal.*, *Rib.*, *Al.*, Ansegis capitulary of 829.

K57	Wolfenbüttel 50.2.Aug.4°	s.ix[1]	N.E. France	*Lex Sal.* and capitularies.
K58	Wolfenbüttel Blankenburg 130	s.ix[3/4]	N. Italy or Augsburg	Law book. *Leges Lombard., Sal., Rib., Burg., Al., Bai.,* and capitularies.
K59	Wolfenbüttel Gudianus 299	s.ix[3/4]	N.E. France	Law book. *Leges Sal., Rib.,* capitularies to 816.
K60	Wolfenbüttel Gudianus 327	s.ix[1]	N. France	Law book. *Leges Sal., A.*
K61	Nürnberg Cent. V. Anhang (App. 96, 1)	s.ix[1]	Germany	Law book. *Lex Sal.* and capitularies.
K62	Klitschdorf MS Quart, now Cologny Coll. Bodmer Cod. 107	s.ix[ex]	N.W. Germany	Law book. *Leges Sal., Rib., Al., Bai.,* capitularies, and Theodosian code.
K63	Bamberg can. 12 (P.I.1)	s.x[1]	Possibly Germany	Law book. Childebert edict add. to *Lex Sal.* and Ansegis.
K64	Bamberg iur. 35	s.ix[1]	N.E. France	Law book. *Leges Sal., Rib., Al.,* and *summula de bannis.*
K65	Bonn S.402	s.xi/xii	Probably Germany	Legal and historical compilation. Ansegis, Anon., *Vita Hludowici,* and *Einhard, Vita Karoli. Lex Sal.* with *Pactus* and prologues, and the text *Origo francorum.*
K66	Vat. reg. lat. 1036	s.xvi	Probably France	Law book. *Lex Sal.* add. capits of 803 and 805, Ansegis and the text *Origo francorum.*
K67	Vat. reg. lat. 1728	s.xvi	Probably France	Miscellany on music, grammar, Ansegis, lives of saints. *Lex Sal.* and add. capits.
K68	Vat. reg. lat. 520	s.ix[4]	Germany	Law book. *Lex Sal.*
K68a	Vat. reg. lat. 291	s.xvi[2]	Possibly France	Collection of texts on asceticism, with Decretio Childeberti on fo. 104.

Table A (cont.)

MS		Date	Origin	Category and content
K69	Vat. reg. lat. 338	s.ix^{med}	N. France	Law book (pocket copy). *Leges Sal.*, *Rib.*
K70	Vat. reg. lat. 857	s.ix$^{\frac{1}{4}}$	*Leges scriptorium*	Law book. *Leges Sal.*, *Al.* and abridged version of *Brev. Alar.*
K71	Vat. reg. lat. 991	s.ix$^{\frac{2}{4}}$	Lotharingia or possibly *leges scriptorium*	Law book. *Leges Sal.*, *Rib.*, *Al.*, *Bai.*, *Epit. Aegid.*, capitularies.
K72	Vat. reg. lat. 1050	s.ix^{med}	France (four scribes)	Law book. *Leges Sal.*, *Rib.*, *Burg.*, *Al.*, Isidore, *De septem gradibus*, tract on Frankish officials, *Formulae Turonensis*, prologue to *Lex Bai.*, capitulary of 803.
K73	Vat. reg. lat. 1128	s.ix$^{\frac{1}{3}}$	France, probably W. Frankish	Law book. *Leges Burg.*, *Rib.*, *Sal.*, *Al.*, *Visigothorum*, *Brev. Alar.*, *Notae iuris.*
K74	Rome Ottoboniana 3081	s.xv	Continent	Fragment of *Lex Sal.*
K75	Rome Vallicelliana C 20	s.xvi	Continent	Law book. *Leges Sal.*, *Bai.*, *Rib.*, *Al.*
K76	Florence Laurenziana 77.1	s.xii/xiii and s.xiv	Continent	Miscellany. *Lex Sal.* extracts and *Lex Bai.* prologue.
K77	Ivrea 4 (XXXIII)	s.ix^{med}	N. Italy	Law book. *Leges Sal.*, *Rib.*, *Burg.*, *Al.*, *Bai.*, capitularies to 818/819.
K78	Milan A 46 inf.	s.ix$^{\frac{1}{4}}$ & s.ix^{ex}	Rheims area	Law book. *Lex Sal.*, *Brev. Alar.*, *Epit. Aegid.*
K79	Modena Bib. Estense	s.xv (1490)	Not known, probably Continent	*Lex Sal.*
K80	Clm 29086	s.ix^{in}	Bavaria	*Lex Sal.* fragments.
K80a	Würzburg Fragmenta codd. mss. deperd. philol.	s.ix^{in}	France	*Lex Sal.* fragments.

K81	Leningrad O.v.II.11	$s.ix^{in}$	France	*Lex Sal.*, capitularies of 803, 806.
S82	Modena O.I.2.	c. 990/1 N.	Italy	Law book. *Leges Sal.*, *Rib.*, *Langobardorum*, *Al.*, *Bai.*, capitularies. Copied from the law book made for Eberhard of Friuli.
S83	Gotha Mbr.I.84	$s.x/xi$	?Mainz	Law book. *Leges Sal.*, *Rib.*, *Brev. Alar.*, *Ansegis.* Capitularies for Italy (including Pavia 855).

Dating conventions:

$s.ix$	ninth century
$s.ix^{in}$	beginning of ninth century
$s.ix^{\frac{1}{3}}$	first third of ninth century
$s.ix^{\frac{1}{4}}$	first quarter of ninth century
$s.ix^{\frac{2}{4}}$	second quarter of ninth century
$s.ix^{1}$	first half of ninth century
$s.ix^{med}$	middle of ninth century
$s.ix^{\frac{2}{3}}$	second third of ninth century
$s.ix^{\frac{3}{4}}$	third quarter of ninth century
$s.ix^{\frac{4}{4}}$	fourth quarter of ninth century
$s.ix^{2}$	second half of ninth century
$s.ix^{ex}$	end of ninth century
$s.ix/x$	turn of ninth century

Abbreviations:

add. capits.	additional capitularies to *Lex Sal.* and *Lex Rib.* made by Charlemagne and Louis the Pious
Brev. Alar.	Breviary of Alaric
Epit. Aegid.	Epitome Aegidiana
Lex Al.	*Lex Alamannorum*
Lex Bai.	*Lex Baiuuariorum*
Lex Burg.	*Lex Burgundionum*
Lex Rib.	*Lex Ribuaria*
Lex Sal.	*Lex Salica*

Note: On the Breviary of Alaric. the *Epitome Aegidius* and other epitomes of the Breviary of Alaric such as the so-called *Scintilla* in BN lat. 10753, see Jean Gaudemet, 'Le Breviaire d'Alaric et les Epitomes', *IRMA* I.2.b.aa (Milan, 1967), especially pp. 42–4.

concerned it is notable how rarely it is transmitted separately from the *Lex Salica*; only six out of the thirty-three available manuscripts are independent witnesses. Thus comments on the function of the *Lex Salica* in terms of its transmission are just as applicable to the *Lex Ribuaria*.[75] The great number among the ninth- and early tenth-century codices – about forty-five – which can in a tentative way be described as law books is highly suggestive. Even the later mediaeval copies of the Salic law may well be based on earlier collections, though their chief importance now is perhaps as a witness to a different, possibly more academic, interest in the barbarian laws in contrast to the Roman. It is difficult to believe that so many volumes of Germanic law were compiled in the Carolingian period for display purposes only. Undoubtedly they possessed a symbolic value, both as books *per se*,[76] and as written law, but until all of them have been examined they cannot categorically be denied a practical value as well. Lacking evidence to the contrary, and until and unless proved otherwise, indeed, I regard these books as having been of practical use. Many are well worn, with pages missing, and show signs of wear and tear to a degree remarkable in comparison with many of the more scholarly patristic and theological manuscripts which survive in such abundance from the ninth century. Those which can be categorized as school books, moreover, may indicate teaching of the law, even if only in terms of jurisprudence, within the monastic schools.[77] Such was possibly the purpose for which the famous Reichenau collection was intended:

Lex Theodosiana de diversis Romanorum legibus, lex Ribuaria lex Salica et lex Alemannica et capitula domni Karoli et domni Hludowici imperatorum addenda legibus necnon et alia capitula eius de nutriendis animalibus et laborandi cura in domestica agricultura in codice I
Item lex Ribuaria et lex Alemannica et capitula domni Karoli imperatoris addenda legibus et inventio sanctae crucis in codice I

[75] K. A. Eckhardt, *Lex Ribuaria. Westgermanisches Recht* (Göttingen, Berlin and Frankfurt, 1959), lists these, pp. 7–13, but fuller, and more accurate, details are provided by Buchner in *MGH Leges Germ*. III.2, pp. 32–40.

[76] See below, pp. 147–64. No doubt administration of the law remained oral in many instances and at many levels, but what the prodigious quantity of legal codices extant suggests is that the issuing of written law created what Stock termed 'textual communities'. That is, it is arguable that the law of a particular region, represented in physical and tangible terms by a written text, provided the most fundamental text on which a community in that region based its collective action. See Brian Stock, *The Implications of Literacy. Written Language and Models of Interpretation in the Eleventh and Twelfth Centuries* (Princeton, 1983), pp. 89–92. On the collective action of communities and its various manifestations see Susan Reynolds, *Kingdoms and Communities in Western Europe 900–1300* (Oxford, 1984). Her important observations and questions could be applied to the earlier middle ages with profit.

[77] There is no agreement on the teaching of law in schools, for neither the teaching itself, nor the schools, have been sufficiently defined. See Kottje, 'Die Lex Baiuuariorum', pp. 17–19, and his references, and Riché, 'Enseignement du droit'.

Item lex Salica et Alemannica et computatio annorum per sex mundi aetates in codice I
Item lex Salica in codice I
Item lex Alemannica et capitula domni Karoli in codice I
Item lex Alemannica in codice I
Item lex Langobardorum in codice I.[78]

Even here, however, some practical knowledge on the part of the abbot and the estate administrators can be envisaged. In a world in which resort to written texts for knowledge and wisdom, in the context of a religious faith and law of God received in written form, this is hardly to be wondered at.

If the classification of manuscripts according to content indicates a massive production of law books generally in the Frankish kingdoms throughout the ninth century, the palaeography of these codices has the potential to yield more specific information concerning the process and location of production. An important group of legal manuscripts which suggests the official production of legal material, for example, has been identified by Bernhard Bischoff and attributed to a '*leges* scriptorium'.[79] This '*leges* scriptorium' appears to have been a writing centre active in the 820s and 830s and specializing in the production of law books and legal material. Within this group some contain the *Lex Salica*, such as Vat. reg. lat. 846, Warsaw Quart. 480 and St Gall 729. That these codices all contain the E text of the *Lex Salica* and date from the first quarter of the ninth century perhaps reflects a stage at which the *Karolina* version was still gaining ground; this same scriptorium, however, also produced law books containing the *Karolina* version – Vat. reg. lat. 857 and BN n.a.lat. 204, and possibly also Vat. reg. lat. 991 – at about the same time or a little later. Other volumes of legal material produced by the same set of scribes are BN lat. 10756, fos. 46–61, containing charter formulae, Berlin lat.qu.150, Vat. reg. lat. 852, 857 and 1431 (fo. 74) and BN lat. 4408, a Roman law book containing the Theodosian code, excerpts from Isidore's *Etymologiae*, the Novels of Theodosius, an Epitome of the Institutes of Gaius, Paul's Sentences and excerpts from the *Gregorianum*, that is texts of the laws of the fifth-century Roman emperors and the interpretations and summaries compiled by various Roman jurists. It is a collection of fifth-century legal texts to be found in a number of Frankish manuscripts of both the Merovingian and Carolingian periods. Another Roman law book

---

[78] Lehmann, *Mittelalterliche Bibliothekskataloge* pp. 247–8.
[79] Bernhard Bischoff, 'Die Hofbibliothek unter Ludwig dem Frommen', in *MS* III, pp. 170–86, at p. 180, and compare Bernhard Bischoff, *Paläographie des römischen Altertums und des abendländischen Mittelalters* (Berlin, 1979), p. 257 n. 30. I am grateful to Bernhard Bischoff for providing me with information about additional members of this group.

whose contents are closely related to those of BN lat. 4408, for example, is BN lat. 4416, also a possible member of the '*leges* scriptorium' group. It contains, in addition to the Theodosian code and other late Roman legal texts, the *Leges Salica, Ribuaria* and *Burgundionum,* a *Chronica regis Visigothorum* and the Visigothic laws. The legal miscellany BN lat. 2718 is also to be attributed to the same scriptorium and provides useful clues concerning the type of scribe responsible for the collection as a whole. It contains a corpus of charters of Louis the Pious, which constitutes the so-called *Formulae imperiales e curia Ludovici Pii,* an official collection of fifty-five charter formulae thought to have been compiled under the direction of Fridugis, chancellor to Louis the Pious from 819 to 832, written almost entirely in tironian notes, the notarial shorthand. This legal shorthand was used by many Carolingian royal notaries and is also to be found in other members of the '*leges* scriptorium' group, such as Vat. reg. lat. 846. In BN lat. 2718 are also some of the most important of the capitularies of Louis the Pious (including the *Ordinatio Imperii* of 817, the capitularies of Aachen of 818 and 819, and the capitulary with additions to *Lex Salica*) and a small collection of Christian texts inserted here and there in the manuscript such as prayers and sermons by Cyprian and Caesarius of Arles, the *De anima* of Augustine and Charlemagne's letter to Alcuin and the congregation of Tours.[80] The Tours connection is reinforced by the script of the portions in normal Latin letter forms, for it is perhaps in the hand of Hirminmarus, one of the brethren at Tours and principal notary of Fridugis and Theoto, archchancellors to Louis the Pious. The script of all the manuscripts in the group, indeed, is in the Tours tradition and has been associated with Fridugis of Tours. That is, these legal codices reflect the activity of a small group of scribes presided over by the royal *cancellarius* and associated with the royal court, possibly actually located at the court itself.

To the palaeographical indications of the group can be added the observation by Buchner on the textual importance of one at least of the codices in it. He drew attention to the fact that the texts of the *Lex Ribuaria* and *Lex Baiuuariorum* in Vat. reg. lat. 991 represent the purest texts of the revised versions of these laws and suggested that the codex merited careful investigation to determine whether the other texts it contains, namely the *Leges Salica* and *Burgundionum,* the *Epitome Aegidiana* and various Carolingian capitularies, are of as high a quality. If it were the case, Buchner thought it would be possible to posit an edition of the laws emanating from

---

[80] See the description in the BN *Catalogue Générale des Manuscrits Latins* III (Paris, 1952), pp. 22–5. The sections in tironian notes have been published in facsimile by W. Schmitz, *Monumenta Tachygraphica Codicis Parisiensis 2718* (Hanover, 1882).

the royal chancery.[81] The combination of palaeographical and textual indications, therefore, suggests a most enticing possibility concerning the standing of the '*leges* scriptorium' and its products. Not only is there a concentration of the production of legal manuscripts in the reign of Louis the Pious and a writing centre specializing in copying laws, but there is clear evidence of royal notaries involved in the copying of these books. In other words, their production of written law is the work of a small group of scribes presided over by the royal *cancellarius* and associated with the royal court. The existence of such a '*leges* scriptorium' enhances the importance of extant copies of the written law; royal officials were closely associated with its production and dissemination.

Among the other law books listed in the Table, those compiled within an ecclesiastical or episcopal context may be distinguishable from those produced in connection with a count or lay official. Much work on each codex would be needed to establish this, but it may be noted here that the secular emphasis of the contents, the nature of the annotations, the fact that counts are mentioned by name in the texts and the provenance of a number of these law books strongly suggest comital initiative in their production, and use in connection with the administration of justice in the secular sphere. BN lat. 4404, Leiden Voss lat. O. 86, BN lat. 4628 and 8801, Vat. reg. lat. 338, Ivrea 4 or St Paul in Carinthia XXV.4.8, for example, have comital connections of this kind.[82] It may be that BN lat. 4632, a law book containing capitularies of Charlemagne and Louis the Pious as well as the *Leges Salica, Ribuaria* and *Alamannorum*, and written

---

[81] Buchner, *MGH Leges Germ.* III. 2, pp. 37–8, discussing Vat. reg. lat. 991.

[82] For details concerning BN lat. 4404 and 4628 see McKitterick, 'Carolingian lawbooks', pp. 19–20 and 24–5. For the addition of names of counts and other officials, and the incorporation of material relating to secular business, sometimes with annotations, in the other manuscripts see the full descriptions provided in the relevant manuscript catalogues and the suggestions with regard to Leiden Voss lat. O.86 in A. Holder, *Lex Salica emendata nach dem Codex von Trier Leyden (Vossianus O.86)* (Leipzig, 1880), p. 38; to Vat. reg. lat. 338 in Rudolf Buchner, *Textkritische Untersuchungen zur Lex Ribuaria* (Stuttgart, 1940), p. 90; to Ivrea 4 in Buchner, *ibid.*, p. 71, and Eckhardt, ed., *Lex Salica, MGH Leges Germ.* IV. 1, and on St Paul in Carinthia XXV.4.8 see Buchner, *Lex Ribuaria*, pp. 74–8, and Robert Eisler, *Die illuminierten Handschriften Kärnten. Beschreibendes Verzeichnis der Illuminierten Handschriften in Österreich* III, ed. Franz Wickhoff (Leipzig, 1907), pp. 100–2. This manuscript has a fine initial and two full-page illustrations, one of which depicts a man in full Frankish dress and a richly dressed woman (fos. 1v and 2r) which may have been intended as representations of the lay owners for whom the manuscript was written (just as a copy of the laws was made for Count Eberhard of Friuli), though Eisler interpreted this picture as one of the Annunciation! As well as the laws and capitularies (listed in Table A) it includes *Memoria quae domnus imperator suis comitibus precepit* and a list of names beginning: *Ostgrimo gastaldo iuravit, petrus scavinus similiter*, etc. Note also the copy of the *Lex Baiuuariorum*, now Munich 8°132, which Bischoff, *Schreibschulen* I, pp. 249–50, surmised was probably a count's copy from the Ingolstadt or Regensburg region.

by Autramnus in the third quarter of the ninth century, represents a law book copied by a man trained at St Amand but serving a local count; that monastery's extensive production of books for export is well documented.[83] Louis the Pious himself probably possessed BN lat. 4418, a law book produced in the Aachen region and associated with the court of Louis the Pious.[84] Where notarial interest is apparent, on the other hand, as in BN lat. 4627, St Gall 731 or BN lat. 4409, one may surmise that a notary could have put the collection together with the intention of its serving some useful purpose in connection with his judicial activities.

The compilation of these legal manuscripts is overwhelmingly consistent in its structure and content. These are not random collections but books with a purpose. It is difficult to imagine that this purpose could have been anything other than practical, whether for reference or for guidance in the day-to-day administration of the law. The codices represent what Carolingian counts and royal agents were supposed to use. That they survive in such remarkable abundance indicates a considerable degree of efficiency and organization in their production and dissemination. They constitute a vital body of evidence that deserves to be investigated in detail. That in some of the legal compilations charter formulae are included, moreover, most notably in those of the '*leges* scriptorium', suggests a close association of the written laws and written records. The laws themselves, indeed, prescribe the use of written records in legal transactions, and it is the implications of these prescriptions that we should now consider.

IV THE USE OF WRITING IN THE LEGAL PROCESS: THE EVIDENCE OF THE LAWS

The Carolingian period represents a crucial phase in the historical development of the use of writing in the legal process, and the assumptions implicit in using written documents to record or confirm legal decisions and rights. Most of this is manifest in the surviving documents themselves, but there is also much to be learnt from the statements about the use of the written word in legal transactions, and specific recommendations for the use of written documents in the *Leges Ribuaria, Alamannorum* and *Burgundionum.*

It is important to remember that there is in no sense a contrast between a Roman legal system dependent on written forms and an early mediaeval

---

[83] R. McKitterick, 'Manuscripts and scriptoria in the reign of Charles the Bald, 840–877', in E. Menesto and C. Leonardi, eds., *Giovanni Scoto nel suo tempo. L'organizzazione del sapere in eta' Carolingia* (Todi and Perugia, 1989). Compare above, p. 47.
[84] Bischoff, 'Hofbibliothek unter Ludwig dem Frommen', p. 180.

legal practice dependent on oral forms: classical Roman law had itself never regarded writing as more than the best kind of proof. Transactions such as the classical 'stipulations contract', indeed, were, at least in theory, oral. But the trend encouraged by the notaries was all towards writing as proof *par excellence*. The extensive use of documents in legal transactions was particularly evident in late Roman society, and so, judging from the recommendations in the early mediaeval *leges*, it continued to be. Let us therefore consider the instructions these laws contain for the use of written documents and in what contexts written documents were required. What was the legal status of written documents? How clearly are the written means envisaged as complementing other forms of legal proof – witnesses, oaths and ordeals? How early are written means perceived to be different from, and an acceptable substitute for, or, even, better than, oral forms? Do the prescriptions in the laws precede charter production or do they, as seems more likely, describe reality and recommend that which is already practised?

The earliest of the Germanic codes, the laws of Euric, dating to the fifth century, probably represents a blend of sub-Roman and Gothic elements.[85] For our purposes, however, it is the laws' tacit assumption of an extensive use of documents in legal transactions that is important.[86] *Lex Salica* in its earliest redaction, generally dated *c.* 511, on the other hand, makes no explicit reference to recourse to written documents for private transactions.[87] There is, however, a clear statement of the use of a royal charter as proof of a claim, and the punishment to be meted out to anyone challenging the king's order; the charter was to be produced in a public court. Reference is also made to the *ingenuus francus*, that is, the man freed by charter, in *Lex Salica* LXIX.1.[88] It reveals, however, far less evidence of written records than the Burgundian law, which appears to have taken

[85] For a stimulating discussion, with references, see Roger Collins, *Early Medieval Spain, Unity and Diversity 400–1000* (London, 1983), pp. 25–9, who draws on the interpretation of A. D'Ors, *El Código de Eurico. Estudios Visigóticos* II, Cuadernos del Instituto Jurídico Español 12 (Madrid, 1960), that the *Codex Eurici* is 'un monumento de derecho romano vulgaro'. But if the edict of Theodoric is invoked to support this, a text now thought to be not Ostrogothic of c. 500 but Visigothic of c. 450, containing Roman laws for Romans, it could be countered with the suggestion that in the mid-fifth century Roman law applied to Visigoths because they then had no independent status, whereas the code of Euric, before 484, constitutes an early reaction to newly acquired independent status and is more likely therefore to be a personal and Visigothic code. On the edict of Theodoric see G. Vismara, 'Edictum Theodorici', *IRMA* I.2.b.11 (Milan, 1967). On the code of Euric see also Schott, 'Leges' Forschung', 32–5.

[86] See for example, *Codex Eurici*, 281, 285, 286, 307, ed. D'Ors.

[87] See above, pp. 40–60, for discussion of the *Lex Salica* redaction.

[88] *Lex Salica* A (*Pactus legis Salicae* XIV. 4; *Lex Salica* D, XVI. 4; *Lex Salica* E, XVI.4, and compare LVIII.1, LVIII.5, LXI and LIX.1.7. See also J. F. Niermeyer, *Mediae Latinitatis Lexikon Minus* (Leiden, 1954), under *ingenuus francus*.

note of the laws of Euric in its assumptions, and some of its formulations. Indeed, either each successive set of barbarian laws appears to have been influenced by its predecessors, or else, more probably, each is independently showing similar survivals or adaptations of late Roman practice in the keeping of records simply because this was the common stock all of them received and used in areas of mixed population.

Not only charters in transactions such as exchanges, sales and gifts, but also written wills and the notarial records made of court proceedings were required by the *Lex Burgundionum*, laws sometimes attributed to Gundobad, king of the Burgundians from *c.* 480 to 516, with additional clauses made by his son Sigismund, king from 517 to 523. But the laws themselves were first issued in 517 by Sigismund.[89] In addition, from the Burgundian kingdom of the sixth century there is the *Lex Romana Burgundionum*, a digest of late Roman law compiled possibly under the auspices of the Burgundian rulers for the Roman people subject to them. It may be, however, a private, rather than an official, compilation. These Romans were exhorted to follow the written law when judging cases.[90]

The preface to the *Lex Burgundionum* records the acceptance by the Burgundians of a written form for the law. The constitution was to be signed by the counts 'so that the statement of the law which has been written as a result of our effort and with the common consent of all may maintain the validity of a lasting agreement'.[91] The counts, therefore, had to sign the constitution to indicate their acceptance of it as a correct statement of what had previously been an orally transmitted law, and this is likened to an agreement (reminiscent of the *Pactus legis Salicae*). But it does not necessarily imply that every agreement had to be confirmed by writing, only that writing was an important kind of proof of the agreement. It suggests too that the document, written and signed, had a legal status of its own.

The clear message of the Burgundian laws, moreover, is that the use of writing was a normal part of the legal process. In the preface, c. 7, for example, reference is made to the payments of 10 *solidi* to be given to the scribes (*notarii*) recording the decisions of the judges. Decisions in court, therefore, were recorded in writing. In the additional enactments at

---

89 The best edition of the *Lex Burgundionum* is that of L. R. de Salis, *MGH Leges Germ.* II, pp. 3–122, with an English translation by K. Fischer-Drew, *The Burgundian Code* (Philadelphia, 1949), quoted from in the following comments. On the *Lex* see Buchner, *Rechtsquellen*, pp. 10–12, and Schott, '*Leges* Forschung', 35–6.

90 On the *Lex Romana Burgundionum* see Chevrier and Pieri, 'La Loi romain des Burgondes'.

91 *Lex Burg.* first constitution c.7, trans. Fischer-Drew, p. 19.

Ambérieux by Gundobad (XXI.14) there is a further indication of the recourse to written communication in administration:

If anyone wishes to seek something by way of gift, let him come with letters from his count and let the counsellors (*consiliarii*) or mayors of the palace who are present receive those letters of the count and prepare letters of their own at our command for the guidance of the judge in whose territory [under whose jurisdiction] is found that property which is sought.[92]

The use of documentary evidence is required, or, at least, thought desirable, for a legal transaction to be valid. Wills, for example, are clearly assumed to have been made, for procedures are laid down for the course of action to be taken in cases where a will or instructions have not been left in writing. Similarly for sales: if anyone has bought a slave, field, land or house, the payment shall be forfeit if the transaction has not been recorded in writing and been subscribed by five or seven witnesses dwelling in that place. At least three witnesses are required for a document to be valid, preferably five.[93] This variable requirement for witnesses is one instance of the active adaptation of older Roman provisions. The recommendation recurs in the clause concerning wills, where it is stated that gifts and wills will be valid if the witnesses, five or seven in number, have appended their marks and signatures, while for lesser transactions three appropriate witnesses will suffice. In classical Roman law there were two alternative methods, civil and praetorian. Both required the presence of seven people, but in the civil form only five of the seven were technically witnesses. The *Interpretatio* to *Codex Theodosianus* 4.4.1 misunderstood the position and no doubt led to the confusion of later compilers. The different number of technical witnesses is adopted as a simple variable, for example, by the Burgundian (and other early mediaeval) compilers of the law and sometimes a spurious justification is invented.[94] The provisions for three witnesses for lesser transactions, on the other hand, appears to be a Burgundian innovation, and no clear guidance is provided concerning the definition of 'lesser'.

The recommendations concerning witnesses also enable us to observe some of the thinking concerning the relative value of documents and the oral testimony of witnesses. In manumitting slaves or serfs, for example, either a legally competent document or an enactment with the agency of five or seven native freemen acting as witnesses is required. In terms of

---

[92] *Lex Burg.* Add. XXI.14, trans. Fischer-Drew, p. 95.

[93] *Lex Burg.* XCIX.1 and 2, trans. Fischer-Drew, p. 85.

[94] *Lex Burg.* XLIII, trans. Fischer-Drew, p. 51, and *Codex Theodosianus* 4.4.1 respectively, ed. C. Pharr, *The Theodosian Code* (Princeton, 1952); and compare *Lex Burg.* LXXXVIII, trans. Fischer-Drew, p. 80.

later proof of the manumission having been effected, one document here
is being valued as the equivalent of the oral testimony of five or seven
freemen. On the other hand, the documents already mentioned in the
Burgundian code require five or seven witnesses to be valid. Further light
is cast on the matter by the acknowledgement in clause LX that some
barbarians, with two or three witnesses present, were willing to take
possession of property in the name of gift or inheritance contrary to
present custom which required a greater number of witnesses. Differences
are made explicit in LX.2: 'If any barbarian wishes to make a will or gift
either the Roman or the barbarian custom must be observed if he wishes
his actions to have any validity'. That is, he must either confirm the gift
by means of a legal written document in the Roman way, or he must have
five native freemen to act as witnesses to the transaction. This will make
it valid. The next clause goes on to define and suggest suitable and eligible
witnesses. Clause LXXXVIII, moreover, presents a further comment on the
relative status of oral testimony and written documents: with reference to
manumission without a written document (the implication is that this is
the inferior method), the manumission must be confirmed by five or seven
native freemen for it is 'not fitting to present a smaller number of witnesses
than is required when the manumission is in written form'.[95]

There is a clear indication in the Burgundian code, in other words, of a
consciousness concerning the different validation of legal actions according
to oral or literate methods, and, apparently, a sense of their opposition. The
tendency of the provisions concerning the use of oral testimony or written
documents is to favour the latter. Some ambivalence on specific matters is
retained, and there are problems acknowledged in the way in which a
written legal act had the potential to overthrow unwritten custom, or
manifested in the abuse of a written document to try and effect something
illegal. The case of Athala is pertinent here. While there is a clear
assumption in the Burgundian law that transactions and bequests
involving property are recorded in writing, Athala's case raised serious
problems: he had not given his son his legal, rightful and expected portion
but had transferred his property to other people by means of an 'illegal'
written title. Athala was attempting to use charters as a means of
disinheriting his son. The judgement nicely points the conflict: it was
decided that any man who would not hand over property legally belonging
to his son might do nothing adverse or prejudicial to them in writing, and
if he did do so, it would be invalid.[96] The fact that the legal requirement in

[95] *Lex Burg.* LX, LX.2, trans. Fischer-Drew, pp. 65–6, and LXXXVIII, trans. Fischer-Drew, p. 80.
[96] *Lex Burg.* LI.2, LI.4, LIII, trans. Fischer-Drew, pp. 58–9 and 61, and compare the case cited by Jack Goody, *The Logic of Writing and the Organization of Society* (Cambridge, 1986),

both classical and sub-Roman law is that most of a man's property had to go to his offspring highlights the difficulty of Athala's position and the ambivalent role of a charter in support of his case. In the sixth-century Burgundian kingdom, therefore, a written document's effectiveness was not unequivocally acknowledged, it would not necessarily be used, and, if used, it would not necessarily be honoured. While in the attempt of Athala we may have more a case of an individual against kin using any means at his disposal to get his own way, it is nevertheless of significance that the crucial issue is the status of a written document. We have in these laws generally an impression that written forms as a 'better' kind of proof were making headway slowly.

The *Pactus legis Alamannorum* was drawn up in the early seventh century, and the *Lex Alamannorum* about a century later. Whether the *Lex* in particular represents a code expressive of the independent duke's power or of the suzerainty of the Franks over the duke, an official, is disputed, though the scales seem weighted in favour of those who argue the case for the code's redaction in a short period of the relative independence of Alemannia under Lantfrid I before 724.[97] As far as procedure and the use of writing in the legal process are concerned, so late a date in comparison to the *Lex Burgundionum* or *Lex Salica* leaves open the possibility of external influences, as well as independent continuity with Roman practice.

Early indications of the Alemans' familiarity with and use of Roman literary forms are the references in Ammianus Marcellinus to the sending of letters to and from the Alemannic leaders of the fourth century. Constantius II wrote to the Alemannic king Vademanus in 361 asking him to attack Julian when hc usurped the imperial title. When a notary of Vademanus was captured by Julian's men some phrases of the letter were quoted and allusion was made to frequent letters between Julian and Vademanus. Further, in 372, Hortarius, an Alemannic noble in the Roman army, is accused of having written (*scripsisse*) treasonable things to the Alemannic king Macrienus. To these can be added Libanius' oration, recounting how the Alemannic envoy was sent to display the letter from

---

p. 148, about the will drawn up excluding a rightful heir in modern Ghana and the assurance of the villagers that after the death of the testator the son would be given his portion despite the provisions of the written will.

[97] Buchner, *Rechtsquellen*, p. 31, clearly outlines the issues, with full references to contributions to the debate to 1954. Schott, '*Leges* Forschung', 39–40, brings the discussion up to date, and see also his 'Recht und Gesetzgebung bei den Alamannen, Burgunden und Langobarden', *Ur- und frühgeschichtliche Archäologie der Schweiz* VI *Das Frühmittelalter* (Basle, 1979), and 'Lex Alamannorum', in A. Erles, E. Kaufman and R. Schmidt-Wiegand, *Handwörterbuch des deutschen Rechtsgeschichte* (Berlin, 1978), II, cols. 1879–86.

Constantius that made the land their own.[98] Whatever the means employed by the Alemans, the point is that they recognized and exploited the potential of the written word, particularly when dealing with the Romans. This recognition is evident in explicit form in their laws. The earlier *Pactus legis Alamannorum* preserves no indication whatsoever of the use of writing in the legal process apart from the fact that it survives in written form. It is another matter entirely with the *Lex Alamannorum*, where the influence of the church is now strongly in evidence. The Alemannic laws, indeed, bear witness to the enormous upheaval the church could cause in a newly Christian society's disposition of its property.[99] The role of the written word in this upheaval was crucial.

According to the Alemannic laws, a gift to the church had to be confirmed by means of a charter and attested by at least six witnesses whose names were to be recorded. The second clause of the law is even more explicit about the status of the written word. In the case of a son disputing the validity of a gift his now deceased father made to the church, the law is absolutely clear that an oath will not settle the issue. It is not only inadequate, it is inappropriate:

> Let him not swear, but let the charter that his father made be presented and let those witnesses who placed their hands on the charter together with the priest of the church as the law requires testify that they were present and saw with their eyes and heard with their ears that his father gave that property to the church and made a charter and called them as witnesses.[100]

This clause highlights the problems raised by the physical accommodation of the church in society and the nature of its landownership. Given the different categories of land – hereditary or ancestral and acquired land – how could the church be fitted into the normal patterns of inheritance? There are hints in the Bavarian and Burgundian laws, for example, that, as in the case of Athala cited above, hereditary land could not be granted

---

[98] Ammianus Marcellinus, ed. and trans. C. Rolfe (Loeb edn, London and Cambridge, Mass., 1971), 21.2.4–5 and 29.4.7. Compare 27.5.1 for the Goths doing the same. Libanius, *Orations*, ed. and trans. A. F. Norman (Loeb. edn, London and Cambridge, Mass., 1969), 18.52, and see 18.33 for the original sending of the letter. A. D. Lee, to whom I am indebted for these references, has suggested that one explanation for the ability of the Alemans to conduct correspondence of this sort may be the use of Roman prisoners, like Attila's secretary Rusticius, a prisoner from Upper Moesia, mentioned in Priscus' *Fragments*: John Martindale, ed., *Prosopography of the Later Roman Empire* (Cambridge, 1980), pp. 961–2.

[99] Compare the comments with respect to Anglo-Saxon England by Patrick Wormald, *Bede and the Conversion of England. The Charter Evidence* (Jarrow, 1984), p. 23.

[100] *Lex Alamannorum*, ed. K. A. Eckhardt, *MGH Leges Germ.* I, and compare II, which stipulates that precarial grants also have the gift by charter recorded and the precarial tenure confirmed in a letter, Eng. trans. Theodore John Rivers, *Laws of the Alamans and Bavarians* (Philadelphia, 1977), p. 66.

away from sons either by witness or by charter, but it is possible that acquired land or property could be, thus safeguarding the interests of the heir. The Alemannian clause above, however, may be an instance of a man choosing, or attempting, to give to the church hereditary ancestral land which the son had thought his by right. It is the charter which appears to make the transfer incontestable and to change the nature of the property. The power of the written word is such, in this case, that it can transform the status and future category of the land and constitute the legal proof that the new owner, whether church or monastery, is the legitimate one. The definition of criteria for determining the validity of a document should be seen in this context, as should the full description of the process of charter redaction.[101] The written word, in other words, was potentially more powerful than tradition: it could create a new category of inheritance, for the beneficiary had the right to choose recipients in any future bestowal of his wealth; it made it possible to divert and alter customary rights of succession. That there was resistance to this on the part of the families of benefactors is clear from the preliminary clauses of the *Lex Alamannorum*. While a charter can be produced the new owner is in a position at least to counter any challenge to his legal ownership. The witnesses to the charter can be called to acknowledge it as genuine and valid. In the case of a lost or destroyed charter, however, the man who regards the land as rightfully his and disputes his father's gift of it to the church can resort in church to the oaths of five witnesses in addition to his own, testifying that a charter never existed.[102] By oral denial of the existence of a written document, the normal inheritance pattern could be preserved.

There are many other assertions of the legal supremacy of the written charter in the code, usually, but not always, in relation to the endowment of the church. A layman, for example, could not gain possession of a church property without a charter. If he did not produce a charter, which he could obtain from a priest in a church, possession was to remain with the church.[103] Manumission of slaves was clearly to be carried out by means either of a charter or in a church, and sales were also to be confirmed in written form, so that there could be no dispute.[104] Regular

---

[101] *Lex Alam*. XLII.2 (XLIII). The year and the day are to be clearly indicated in the document. The procedure of charter redaction is outlined in I, trans. Rivers, pp. 81 and 66 respectively.

[102] *Lex Alam*. II.1,2; trans. Rivers, pp. 66–7.

[103] *Lex Alam*. XVIII, trans. Rivers, p. 72. There is a suggestion in this clause, moreover, that the church acted as a record keeper for deeds relating to property; for further consideration of this function see pp. 87–9 below.

[104] *Lex Alam*. XVI, XVII, XIX, trans. Rivers, pp. 72–3.

courts were to be held; but, unlike the Burgundian code, there is no hint that records of proceedings were to be made in writing.[105]

Owing to the exertion and example of the church, the charter in Alemannia in the early eighth century is apparently beginning to occupy a meaningful place in the legal process, in so far as it makes a written charter obligatory for a certain type of transaction to a certain type of beneficiary. But at this stage the charter did not constitute the only form of evidence. Quite apart from the procedure in the case of lost or destroyed documents, clause LXXXI, for example, speaks of a dispute between kindred being settled by duel and oath in the presence of a count, with symbolic use being made of a clod of earth rather than a piece of written parchment. Similarly the orders of duke, judge, count and *centenarius* (hundredman) are only to be valid if accompanied by an order, sign or seal. Such objects must also have been an additional means of identifying the person from whom the message came.[106] The use of symbolic objects in transactions was adapted for proceedings using charters. With the formal swearing in church to the validity of the written document and its deposition on the altar, it has clearly acquired the potency of the clod of earth recorded elsewhere in the code.[107] In transactions between laymen, the symbolic object, not the charter, is still required. In the next chapter it will be seen how successful the church was in its insistence on written evidence, and the extent to which its example was followed in secular legal proceedings.

The compilers of the Bavarian laws[108] intended the written law to be used in court, so that judgement could always be made correctly.[109] Much stress, moreover, is laid on the necessity for regular courts to be held, on the first day of each month, or after every fifteen days, or more often in troubled times. There are a number of references to the seal of the duke or count which was used to transmit his orders. This was presumably a symbol or token accompanying an oral message, though it is not impossible that it was attached to a letter.[110] It suggests that in Bavaria in

---

[105] *Lex Alam.* XXXVI and XLI, trans. Rivers, pp. 77–8 and 80.
[106] *Lex Alam.* LXXXI, XXII.2, XXVII. The penalty for killing the duke's messenger is severe, XXIX, trans. Rivers, pp. 96, 74, 75 and 76.
[107] Compare *Lex Alam.* XX.1 and LXXXI, trans. Rivers, pp. 66–7 and 96.
[108] Buchner, *Rechtsquellen*, pp. 26–9, with references to the discussions, especially those of Brunner and Beyerle. But compare the more recent assessment in Schott, 'Leges Forschung', 40–1. The best text is that of K. Beyerle, *MGH Leges Germ.* V.2 (1926). See too the lucid exposition offered by Kottje, 'Die *Lex Baiuuariorum*'. Strong but indirect evidence from the Alemannic laws is to be discerned in that of the Bavarians, usually dated 741–3, or at least 748, and produced under the auspices of Duke Odilo, though the kernel of the laws may well be much older than this. Both the Alemannic and the Bavarian laws may owe something to a common, Frankish, source, but despite the learning expended on these laws, their exact origin remains obscure.
[109] *Lex Bai.* II.14, trans. Rivers, p. 28.
[110] *Lex Bai.* II.13 and compare *Lex Alam.* XXVII.1, trans. Rivers, pp. 128 and 75.

the late eighth and early ninth centuries there were, as elsewhere, oral and written methods existing side by side. In the sale of property to individuals, for example (XVI.2), the transaction was to be considered legally valid either through a charter or through witnesses and 'the witnesses should be heard orally, since our law requires it'.[111] Again, buying or selling property (whether land, slaves, houses or forests) is to be confirmed through a charter or through witnesses so that afterwards there is no dispute; contracts or agreements are made either through writing of some sort or through three or more designated witnesses. These contracts are not to be altered for any reason provided the day and year are clearly indicated on them.[112] Yet there is also a clause concerning oral agreements for the selling of freehold land.[113]

As in the Alemannic laws, the link with the church in the promotion of the use of written documents is made quite clear in the context of bequests of freehold land or any property to the church.[114] In this case, the written means is the only legally valid way of establishing the change in possession. In terms very similar to those of the Alemannic laws, the law decrees that the donor must confirm in his own hand whatsoever he gives to the church by means of a charter, and he is to call six or more witnesses if he wishes; they are to place their hands on the letter and mark their names on the documents which is then placed on the altar. The property is then handed over in the presence of the priest who serves the church. The legal status of the written document as symbol and record is thus affirmed.

Although the *Lex Salica* does not refer to a recourse to written documents, there is no appropriate heading among the topics included in these laws under which such references might have been included. There are, for instance, no sections on ecclesiastical property in the *Lex Salica*. There is, however, ample evidence in the form of surviving charters and the Formularies of Marculf, Angers and Tours that the Franks in Neustria and elsewhere who regarded the *Lex Salica* as their 'national' law continued to use the written word to record agreements and trans-actions.[115] It is likely, furthermore, given the correspondence between the dissemination of the *Lex Salica* and the *Lex Ribuaria* stressed above, that the recommendations concerning recourse to written records in the Ripuarian laws would have been followed, especially in the wake of Carolingian expansion, and that its clauses, in some way that we cannot now

---

[111] *Lex Bai.* XVI.2, trans. Rivers, p. 160.
[112] *Lex Bai.* XVI.15, 16 and 17, trans. Rivers, pp. 163–4.
[113] *Lex Bai.* XVI.17, trans. Rivers, pp. 163–4.
[114] *Lex Bai.* I.1, trans. Rivers, p. 118.
[115] Ed. Karl Zeumer, *Formulae Merovingici et Karolini aevi*, MGH Formulae V (1886).

determine, were regarded by the Franks as complementing those of the Salic laws.

The provisions made by the *Lex Ribuaria*, a mid-seventh century set of laws, concerning the written word are the crucial context for the subsequent assumptions and procedures of the Carolingian mayors and Austrasian nobles in the conduct of legal business. The Carolingian mayor issued his own recension of it in the mid-eighth century.[116]

The status of the charter in the Ripuarian laws is certainly that of a document which facilitates the adjudication of a case. The charter is not a self-sufficient entity, or even by itself a sufficient legal instrument, but it is an essential part of the judicial and legal process. The laws in both the seventh- and eighth-century redactions make provision for the use of written documents in a number of important instances. A charter is drawn up to record the dowry and is thus an essential element in the marriage contract.[117] The provision a man makes for inheritance when he has no heirs of his own body is recorded in writing and is used in settling his estate.[118] A manumitted serf's freedom is recorded by charter and the code supplies a long list of instructions about the different cases in which, and according to which, circumstances such a charter of manumission is to be used. The word *tabularius* in this clause in fact was one coined to refer to a serf manumitted by charter. Originally the *tabulas* were what were produced to establish the new freed status. The procedure also seems to have many affinities with imperial Roman law. Freeing a serf according to Roman law had to take place in the presence of the priest, deacon or the whole clergy and people; the charter was received by the bishop. He, it

---

[116] On the *Lex Ribuaria* see Buchner, *Rechtsquellen*, pp. 21–6, and *idem*, *Textkritische Untersuchung zur Lex Ribuaria* (Stuttgart, 1940 and 1952); and Schott, 'Leges Forschung', 38. See also F. Beyerle, 'Zum Kleinreich Sigiberts II und zur Datierung der *Lex Ribuaria*', *Rheinische Vierteljahrsblätter* 21 (1956) 357–62, and R. Schmidt-Wiegand, 'Lex Ribuaria', in Erles, Kaufman and Schmidt-Wiegand, *Handwörterbuch des deutschen Rechtsgeschichte* II, cols. 1923–7. The *Lex Ribuaria* was Austrasian in origin. Beyerle suggested it represents Dagobert I's enterprise for his son Sigibert III (635–9) when the latter was made sub-king in Austrasia, though some parts no doubt go back to the first quarter of the seventh century. The best text is that provided by Rudolf Buchner, *MGH Leges Germ*. IV. But compare K. A. Eckhardt, *Lex Ribuaria. Austrasisches Recht in 7. Jahrhundert, Germanenrechte Neue Folge. West germanisches Recht* I (Göttingen, 1959), and *Lex Ribuaria* II (Hanover, 1966). That Austrasia was also the Carolingian heartland is crucial. There has even been a hypothesis that the Ripuarian laws are to be linked with the brief reign of Sigibert III's adopted Pippinid son Childebert III (?656–?662), son of the Pippinid mayor of the palace Grimoald.

[117] *Lex Rib*. XXXVII, trans. Theodore John Rivers, *Laws of the Salian and Ripuarian Franks* (New York, 1986), p. 186, though here and in the other translated extracts from the *Lex Rib*. I have not followed Rivers faithfully.

[118] *Lex Rib*. XLVIII, trans. Rivers, p. 190.

should be remembered, followed Roman law. It is worth considering the process in the Ripuarian laws in detail:

De tabulariis [concerning slaves freed by charter]
This we also command that every free Ripuarian, or man who has been manumitted by charter, who wishes to free his slave for the salvation of his soul or for a price (*precio*) according to Roman law, shall take this slave into the church in the presence of the priests, deacons or before the whole clergy and people, and hand him over to the bishop with the charters (*in manu episcopi servo cum tabulas tradat*) and the bishop will order the archdeacon to draw up a charter according to Roman law, which is what the church observes, and then the man himself and all his heirs shall be free and under the protection (*sub tuitione*) [of the church] and he shall give the church all the income from his position.[119]

In cases where the freedman's charter is challenged, the archdeacon and witnesses who subscribed the charter were required to come before the bishop, king or count and swear an oath that the *tabularius* (man freed by charter) was freed according to Roman law.[120] According to these and related provisions, the church determined to act as guarantor, and it is clear that the church played an active role in continuing what it understood to be Roman legal practice. Because the church followed laws classified as Roman, transactions involving the church had to accord with methods and procedures laid down in their collections of Roman law. Hence property transfer had to be recorded by charter. Church practice involved laymen. Gradually laymen began to use charters for their own transactions as well. This is clearly indicated by clause LVIII of the Ripuarian laws for the manumission for slaves, where 'Roman' law is urged as the method and rule to follow.

No comment is made in the charter about getting it proved valid without the scribe and witnesses saying it was, and the charter's validity in this case is only established after it has been challenged. Provision of the recommended course of action in case of such a challenge suggests that a charter was as yet not a completely accepted mode of transaction. Similarly in the case of sales, the Ripuarian laws state:

When someone buys something from someone else and the buyer wants the sale recorded in a charter, this should be done in court (*in mallo*). The buyer should pay the price and receive the object in the presence [of all] and the charter should be drawn up in public. If it is a small property it can be confirmed with seven witnesses, but if large it will need twelve witnesses. And if anyone later wishes to

---

[119] *Lex Rib.* LVIII, trans. Rivers, pp. 195–8, and compare *Conc. Aurelianense* 538, c.29, ed. C. de Clercq, *Concilia Galliae A.511–A.695* Corpus Christianorum Series Latina CXLVIIIA (Turnhout, 1963), p. 125.
[120] *Lex Rib.* LVIII.5, trans. Rivers, p. 196.

challenge the deed or declare it to be false, let it be proven valid by the witnesses or the *cancellarius* [court notary] with oathtakers [of the same number as the witnesses] to swear that it is genuine. If the charter be proved valid in court then he who challenges it shall pay to the *cancellarius* 45 *solidi* and to each of the witnesses 15 *solidi* and the charter will remain inviolable. But if the charter is forged then the man who challenged it shall receive what he demanded together with a 60 *solidi* fine and the *cancellarius* loses his right thumb or pays 50 *solidi* compensation and each of the witnesses must pay 15 *solidi*. When however the claimant pulls away the scribe's hand from the altar, or draws his sword before the church door, then let them both be confined so that within fourteen nights or within forty, they may present themselves before the king for combat.[121]

Clause LIX, therefore, is attesting to the validity of a deed of sale. Scribe and witnesses are to swear to it and to be compensated for the imputations against their integrity if the charter is proved valid. But in the fifth section of clause LIX an important addition is made concerning what should be done if the scribe were dead. The disputed charter is to be compared with three others he is known to have written, and if they look alike the charter on the altar is to be judged as genuine without further dispute. This is the first hint that some criterion of judgement other than oral testimony is being invoked. It is notable that it is a palaeographical one, based on comparison of the handwriting. If the seller and/or his heirs are still alive then they should affirm the validity of the charter.

There follows the important provision that all the procedures about sale should also apply to gifts and that proof will be accepted whether in the form of witnesses' dispositions or the written decision.[122] The clause then continues: 'He who comes to judgement and has a charter can say when challenged, " I do not hold this unlawfully but have it because of this charter."' If someone cannot obtain a charter, on the other hand, a particular number of witnesses is specified according to the value of the thing sold or given.[123]

Further clauses follow on the legal strength of a royal charter. Anyone contesting a royal charter, for example, without producing a contradictory charter, must pay with his life.[124] The additions made to the Ripuarian laws under Charlemagne are also of significance, namely that a man who has no son and wishes to make someone else his heir must make a written conveyance before the king or count and the *scabini* of the *missus dominicus* in the relevant district.[125]

[121] *Lex Rib.* LIX, trans. Rivers, p. 199.   [122] *Lex Rib.* LIX.7, trans. Rivers, p. 199.
[123] *Lex Rib.* LIX.8, trans. Rivers, p. 199.
[124] *Lex Rib.* LX.6, trans. Rivers, p. 193.
[125] *Capitulare legi Ribuariae additum* 803, c.8, *MGH Cap.* I, No. 41, p. 118, trans. Loyn and Percival, *Charlemagne*, pp. 85–6. The implication may be that a written conveyance is intended here, the word used being *traditio*.

According to the Ripuarian laws, therefore, a charter was required for the sale or gift of goods, large or small, and for the manumission of slaves. If the gift or sale concerned the church, a charter was essential. The written word thus had an established place in both secular and ecclesiastical transactions. Instructions for the procedure to be followed in the case of challenges to a written charter suggest that disputes were anticipated. Such disputes may reflect some unease or lack of acceptance, in every case, of written proof on the part of the population. On the other hand, challenging the validity of a particular document is not unknown even in societies where the legal status of a written deed is undisputed. Oral methods, moreover, were still employed; there are provisions in the *Lex Ribuaria* for oathswearing in a church or on relics and before presented numbers of witnesses.[126] Nevertheless, the status of writing as proof is considerably enhanced in these legal provisions.

We have seen some of the ways in which written records, at least in so far as they are discussed in the law codes, achieved recognition and independent legal status, and were recommended by the compilers as the preferred mode of record. These early laws, most of which are to be dated to the vital period of the mid-seventh to late eighth centuries when the Carolingian mayors were consolidating their authority over the whole of northern Francia, reveal a gradual accommodation of written methods in the legal process in so far as this is represented by the laws. But did anyone take any notice of what was recommended in the law codes? Does the ideal practice described bear any relation to reality? There are any number of specific manifestations of charter forms, the use of these charters in the legal process and the resort to written evidence in judicial proceedings, for which there is much evidence not only in Alemannia, but also elsewhere in the Frankish kingdoms, from the mid-eighth century onwards. In 748, for example, Pippin III, while still mayor of the palace, settled a dispute between Christiana, Hrodgar, advocate of the abbey of St Denis, and Abbot Amalbert of St Denis over the villa of Marneil and its dependants. Hrodgar produced a charter proving the villa to have been given to St Denis, and Christiana submitted to the judgement made by Pippin and his *fideles*. Three years later, shortly before he assumed the royal title, Pippin settled a dispute between Fulrad, abbot of St Denis, and Hormung, abbot of Maroilles, over the oratorium of St Martin *in pago Hainovio* and its possessions and dependants. Again a charter was produced to prove possession, and it was recognized as genuine. Unfortunately, the document

---

[126] *Lex Rib.* X, XI, LXVII and LXVIII, and compare the *Capitulare legi Ribuariae additum* (803) which refers to men freed by penny throw as well as by charter in cc.9 and 10, and the importance of swearing on relics in the presence of witnesses is reaffirmed.

does not specify the methods by which the charter's validity was determined. A third case is that between Fulrad of St Denis and Legitemus, advocate of abbess Ragana of Septemolas over Corberie *in pago Tellau*. Fulrad produced a *testamentum* to say the land concerned was left to St Denis and Legitemus produced a charter to say it had been given to Septemolas. Fulrad's *testamentum* was the one recognized as genuine.[127] In all three cases the written evidence is the deciding factor. The temptation to forge documents must have been great, and it is of the greatest significance that some of the boldest forgeries of the middle ages are Carolingian.[128] The power of the written word could be exploited to deceive as well as to prove. In these examples, and others available to us, it is also notable that all parties to a transaction appear to have access to the records made of it, either in their own possession or in some safe archive.

Hübner's list of *Gerichtsurkunden*, however inadequate it may be, nevertheless includes in its inventory of some 600 records of Frankish judicial proceedings no less than 134 for which charters and the witnesses were called in to testify to the process in dispute, and a further 130 which verify that neither charter nor witnesses could be brought forward.[129] Charters were clearly hardly negligible as evidence, but the resort on occasion to both the oaths of the witnesses and the judicial proof by ordeal is also not lacking. The use of such phrases as 'to alienate by charter' or 'to manumit by means of a charter' which recur in the Carolingian capitularies, however, surely suggests that the charter is not a mere record to be set on one side in favour of alternative methods of proof.[130] Although the charter may well have had a dispositive function in some contexts but not in others, its status as material witness in disputes is clearly high.[131] We find charters playing a central role in dispute settlements in the ninth century, though very few of these have been examined in any detail. A

[127] The charters of Pippin are discussed by Ingrid Heidrich, 'Titulatur und Urkunden der arnulfingischen Hausmeier', *Archiv für Diplomatik* 11/12 (1965/6) A16, A19, A20*, pp. 243–6, and G. Pertz, ed., *Diplomata maiorum domus e stirpe arnulforum*, MGH *Leges* (1872) nos. 18, 21 and 22, pp. 104–8.

[128] For example, the Le Mans forgeries exposed by Walter Goffart, *The Le Mans Forgeries* (Princeton, 1962), or the pseudo-Isidorean decretals: H. Fuhrmann, *Einfluss und Verbreitung der pseudoisidorischen Fälschungen, von ihren Auftauchen bis in die neuere Zeit*, Schriften der Monumenta Germaniae Historica 24 (Stuttgart, 1972–4).

[129] R. Hübner, 'Gerichtsurkunden der fränkischen Zeit I Die Gerichtsurkunden aus Deutschland und Frankreich bis zum Jahre 1000', ZSSR, GA 12 (1891), appendix, 1–118.

[130] See, for example, MGH *Cap.* I, No. 77, c.6 p. 171, and No. 104, c.7 p. 215 on manumission by written documents; see *ibid*, No. 68, c.5 p. 158, No. 98, c.1, p. 205, and No. 104, c.7, p. 215, lines 1 and 9, for *per cartam alienare* and *per cartam dimittere*.

[131] See, for example, the discussion by P. Gasnault, 'Les Actes privés de l'abbaye de Saint-Martin de Tours du VIIIᵉ au XIIᵉ siècle' *BEC* 112 (1954) 24–66.

splendid exception is the case heard in 857 in the kingdom of Charles the
Bald. The disputants were requested to produce their title deeds, and the
validity of these was discussed. They were judged to be false and perforated
in the manner described in the Ripuarian laws; oral testimony was also
invoked to reach the decision, for even the scribe of one of the charters
concerned was present.[132] More studies such as this of the *Gerichtsurkunden*
inventoried by Hübner in which charter evidence is invoked would deepen
our appreciation of the role of written records in the daily practice of the
law. It would be absurd, of course, to suppose that oral procedures were
not used and in many cases wholly relied upon. Yet one gets a clear sense
that even if these charters are not wholly dispositive in function, what we
are observing in these documents is first of all the practical manifestation
of prescriptions contained in the law codes concerning written records,
and secondly a transition from charters as documents establishing record
and proof of ownership to charters which in themselves constitute the
legal transaction. Even as records, the charters are vital for their
documentation of the move 'from memory to written record', for the part
the written charter played in ritual transaction, the symbolic role of
writing in legal business and, as we shall see in the following chapter, the
extensive network for their production.

[132] Discussed by Janet Nelson, 'Dispute settlement in Carolingian West Francia', in Davies
and Fouracre, eds., *Settlement of Disputes*, pp. 45–64, at pp. 56–7, with an English
translation of the text. The Latin text is printed, *ibid.*, pp. 248–50, after M. Thévénin,
Textes relatifs aux institutions privées et publiques aux époques mérovingienne et carolingienne
(Paris, 1887), pp. 120–3. A further instance of a charter playing a key part in judicial
proceedings is that referred to in the Polyptych of Irminon in relation to a claim to
property, IX.268, in the edition of B. Guérard, *Polyptyque de l'abbé Irminon* I (Paris, 1844),
p. 111. Other narrative sources, such as Flodoard's History of Rheims, are replete with
references to charters; see too the *Miracula sanctae Genovefae*, *AA SS* Jan. I, p. 149, c.17,
where the use of a charter is stipulated in the gift of a villa.

3 ✺ A literate community : the evidence of the charters

I THE IMPORTANCE OF CHARTER EVIDENCE

A crucial body of evidence for demonstrating the use of writing in legal transactions is the charter material, since legal transactions involving property, whether moveable or immoveable, were recorded in writing throughout the early middle ages. Charters are single-sheet documents recording gifts or sales of land or moveable property, the manumission of slaves, the grant of land in *precaria* (in which the donor would usually retain the use of the land in exchange for a rent or services during his lifetime) or exchanges of property.[1] Nearly all the surviving charters from the early middle ages on the Continent are either royal diplomas or charters relating to a particular institution, most usually a monastery or cathedral church.[2] There is thus a heavy ecclesiastical bias in the sources, but allowance should be made for the circumstances of the survival of documents: institutions are more likely to be successful in preserving their archives than private individuals, but we cannot assume that only the church was concerned in legal transactions involving writing. The number of private gifts to the church, and the occasional documents concerning wholly lay transactions of land which have survived, make it

---

[1] On mediaeval charters generally the essential handbooks remain H. Bresslau, *Handbuch der Urkundenlehre für Deutschland und Italien* (Berlin, 1889), with the 2nd edn in two vols: I (Leipzig, 1912), II, ed. H. W. Klewitz (Leipzig, 1931); A. de Bouard, *Manuel de diplomatique française et pontificale* I *Diplomatique générale* (Paris, 1925) and II *L'Acte privé* (Paris, 1948); and A. Giry, *Manuel de diplomatique* (Paris, 1894). A useful introduction is provided by Leonard E. Boyle, 'Diplomatics', in James M. Powell, ed., *Medieval Studies. An Introduction* (Syracuse, 1976). The precarial grant involving *cens* or dues appears to have been a Carolingian development: see J.-F. Lemarignier, 'Les Actes du droit privé de Saint-Bertin au haut moyen âge. Survivances et déclin du droit romain dans la pratique franque', *Revue Internationale des Droits de l'Antiquité* 5 (1950) (Mélanges F. de Visscher IV) 35–72, at 44.

[2] A case in point is the preponderance of St Denis charters in the Frankish documentary material from the Merovingian period. It has led to a suggestion of a special role enjoyed by St Denis for both the production and preservation of royal charters: see, for example, David Ganz, 'Bureaucratic shorthand and Merovingian learning', in P. Wormald, ed., *Ideal and Reality in Frankish and Anglo-Saxon Society* (Oxford, 1983), pp. 58–75, and his references.

possible to treat the charter evidence as pertaining to legal transactions generally.[3] Rather than shedding light only on the church's use of the written word for its legal business, therefore, the charter material provides vital information concerning the conduct and record of a society's methods of gift, endowment and exchange, and the status of the written word within a community.

It is not only for the information they yield concerning the uses of literacy, however, that charters deserve scrutiny. When a group of them concerning a particular ecclesiastical institution can be identified, they witness to the piety and devotion of the laity of a region. Charters were drawn up not only on behalf of kings, dukes, ecclesiastical magnates and counts, but also for their wives and sisters, cousins and kinsmen, and for the lesser 'gentry' and landed freemen. They record the subtle accommodation in a Christian context of the Germanic custom of gift exchange.[4] Under Germanic law, a gift was a form of nominal gift exchange, for some benefit was required in return. Alternatively, a gift could be made as a result of a relationship of dependence between the parties. In the cases of land grants to monasteries, the gift exchange blended the material and the spiritual, the Germanic and the Christian. For the material wealth it received, in exchange the monastery offered prayers for the soul of the donor. With its material welfare increased, its spiritual power was enhanced. Without the material base afforded by the gifts of pious laymen and laywomen, and, above all, the new recruits from the lay population for the religious community, the monastery could not survive. Even the monastery that aimed to be self-sufficient needed the first gift of land and permission to establish itself where it did, and the first group of men ardent for the religious life.[5] The ties of land, kinship and gratitude anchored the monastery within the community.

The monastery that was really withdrawn from the secular world was thus an impossibility in western Europe in this period: it administered to

---

[3] There are a number of examples reproduced and discussed in the volumes of *ChLA*. See, too, de Bouard, *Manuel de diplomatique* II *L'Acte privé*.

[4] E. Levy, *West Roman Vulgar Law. The Law of Property* (Philadelphia, 1951), p. 57.

[5] In St Gall's case, for example, we lack any foundation charter as such. In the case of such monasteries as Echternach, however, we have the full text of the grant made by the noblewoman Irmina to the Englishman Willibrord, in C. Wampach, ed., *Geschichte der Grundherrschaft Echternach im Frühmittelalter* I.2 *Quellenband* (Luxembourg, 1930), No. 1. The grant made by the wealthy landowner Adroald to Bertin, Mommelin and Ebertram in 649 was the beginning of the great abbey of Sithiu-St Bertin; see B. Guérard, ed., *Cartulaire de l'abbaye de Saint-Bertin*, Collection des Cartulaires de France III (Paris, 1840), pp. 18–19. We know of the disused Merovingian *palatium* or royal *villa* at Fulda granted to Boniface and his followers; see Boniface, *Ep.* 37, and Eigil, *Vita Sturmi*, *MGH SS* II, pp. 366–77. We know also of the land ceded to Reichenau by Charles Martel; see P. Classen, ed., *Die Grundungsurkunden der Reichenau*, Vorträge und Forschungen 24 (Sigmaringen, 1977). There are many other such cases, either recorded in charters or in the lives of the founders and patrons.

the religious needs of the surrounding population. As its essential link with the holy, the visible contact with God and his saints, as well as the focus of religious loyalties and devotion, and service to the cult of the local saint, the surrounding population, for its part, was dependent, before the provision of its own local churches, on the monastery. When a donor made a grant to a church *pro remedium animae meae*, for the salvation of my soul, he meant every word. His grant was an insurance against damnation and an assurance of the welfare of his immortal soul. Yet it was also a token of the lay Christian's participation in the religious life, and his own contribution to the promotion of the Christian faith. The charter evidence thus has much to tell us about the religious role of the monastery in an early mediaeval community, and how faith was expressed in gifts, usually of land.

Concentration on the charter evidence from a particular institution as evidence for the growth of its wealth, and the patronage and devotion from local families that it enjoyed, however, ignores the implications of this rich and fascinating material for the social relationship between the monastery and the population of the neighbouring districts. Sprandel, in an evocative phrase, saw the monastery (in his case, St Gall) as both lord and neighbour within the community (*Als Herr und als Nachbar also stand der Kloster dem Land gegenüber*).[6] He concentrated on the monastery's lordship and administration. I wish rather to focus on the monastery's neighbourliness and its participation in the life, and, above all, in the legal business, of the community, and to do so through the lens provided by the charter evidence. We may, by this means, be able to observe the extent to which a monastery acted not merely as a keeper of records concerning its own land, but fostered and contributed to the transmission and preservation of legal methods and literate forms of record. We can explore whether the charter evidence yields information concerning the levels and uses of literacy on the part of both monastery and community. We may determine whether the monastery and the church are in any sense the instigators, or merely the beneficiaries, of legal practice. We may thereby observe another effect that Christianity and the heritage of the late Roman world had on early mediaeval society and the role of the written word.

II THE CHARTERS OF ST GALL

A body of charter material that can assist us in answering these questions is that from the monastery of St Gall. To focus on one major collection has the obvious danger that it is unrepresentative. Sufficient material of

---

[6] R. Sprandel, 'Das Kloster Sankt Gallen in der Verfassung des karolingischen Reiches', *Forschungen zur Oberrheinischen Landesgeschichte* 7 (1958) 57.

comparable significance from regions throughout the Frankish kingdoms survives, however, to suggest that the examination in detail of one particular region and its population, on the basis of the information yielded by a major monastery's charters, can establish not just its specific differences but also its more general similarities.

Nevertheless, the charter material from St Gall is unique for the Carolingian period in a number of obvious ways. In the first place, it is easily the largest body of charters to have been preserved by any Carolingian ecclesiastical institution, and, indeed, the largest extant collection from early mediaeval Europe.[7] More crucially, the greater proportion of its 839 charters dating from before 920 has been preserved in the 'original', that is, the document written at the time of the transaction.[8] The charters which comprise this collection were first arranged in about 815. A further systematic ordering was made towards the end of the ninth century on geographical principles, which presumably corresponded to the divisions of the St Gall estates made for administrative purposes.[9] The charters were kept in drawers marked with Roman numerals, and on the verso of each charter a short summary of the contents (donor and land) was added by whoever was responsible for the archive. The position of the superscription, and the creases visible in most of the charters, indicate that they were folded up into thin, finger-shaped packages before being filed in the drawers. No cartulary was compiled; unlike most mediaeval ecclesiastical institutions, St Gall chose to keep the records of its property in the original documents rather than to copy the main details into a register. A cartulary of the royal and papal charters was compiled in the fifteenth century, but not until the beginning of the seventeenth century were the charters collected together and printed in the *Codex Traditionum Sancti Galli*. Some of the charters were lost through looting in 1531. Others were appropriated by the scholar Goldast (d. 1635) during his sojourn at St Gall. It was through Goldast's heirs that the

---

[7] H. Wartmann, *Urkundenbuch der Abtei St Gallen* I and II (700–920) (Zurich, 1863), hereafter cited as W. For convenience, in this and subsequent references, the Wartmann edition charter number will be cited rather than the archive shelf mark. The latter is easily retrievable from Wartmann's Table, II, pp. 418–28. It should be noted that for the dating of the charters and their places of redaction I have followed the new revisions of Michael Borgolte in his 'Chronologische Studien zu den alemannischen Urkunden des Stiftsarchivs St Gallen', *Archiv für Diplomatik* 24 (1978) 54–202, which are augmented and summarized in Michael Borgolte, Dieter Geuenich and Karl Schmid, *Subsidia Sangallensia I Materialen und Untersuchungen zu den Verbrüderungsbüchern und zu den ältern Urkunden des Stiftsarchivs St Gallen* (St Gall, 1986), pp. 323–475.

[8] For comments on the originality of the charters of St Gall see Bruckner in *ChLA* I, p. viii, and II, pp. xii–xiii.

[9] Albert Bruckner, 'Die Anfänge des St Gallen Stiftsarchivs', in *Festschrift Gustav Binz* (Basle, 1935), pp. 119–31.

charters in his possession reached the Stadtbibliothek Bremen and were restored to St Gall only in 1948.

Because we have most of the original charters, we have a full record not only of the total content, with the details of the land granted to the monastery (information which would also be preserved in a cartulary copy) but also the essential protocol and eschatocol, that is, the introductory and concluding phrases and formulae, with the information these contain concerning donors, scribes, the office of the scribe, the place where the charter was drawn up, the names of the witnesses and the local lord and the actual handwriting of the scribe himself. The palaeography of the charters indeed provides unique assistance in any attempt to map the existence of local scribes, as opposed to those provided by the monastery. It is thus essential for an assessment of the extent to which the Alemannian population of the St Gall region and the monastery could use literate modes and resort to the written word.[10]

Let us first consider, briefly, the historical background against which the St Gall charters, the monastery itself and the Alemannian region it served should be placed. In doing so, a question that should be uppermost is the degree to which written culture could have survived from the late Roman period.

III THE SURVIVAL OF WRITTEN CULTURE IN ALEMANNIA AND RHAETIA

The region between Lake Constance and Lake Geneva had been part of the Roman world, and there were Christians, certainly as far north as Zurich, by the fourth century. In the fifth century the Burgundians were settled round Lake Geneva, and in the sixth and seventh centuries the Alemans occupied the north-eastern part of Switzerland and divided Rhaetia from Burgundy. Although the Alemans were pagan and Germanic, many localities within the area they controlled remained Romanized and Christian. It is impossible to imagine that there would have been no interaction between the different groups. We cannot think in terms of hermetically sealed communities but of local farmers, elders, merchants and pedlars, labourers and servants, who would have had some degree of contact with one another, and who cannot have been totally ignorant of their respective habits and methods of day-to-day living. Any transactions

---

[10] The palaeography of the oldest St Gall charters was studied by Albert Bruckner, 'Paläeographische Studien zu den älteren St Gallen Urkunden', *Studi Medievali* 4 (1931) 119–30, 360–70, and his findings are incorporated into the descriptions in *ChLA* I and II. The palaeography of the ninth-century charters, however, has not been properly studied hitherto.

between different local communities concerning land, rights of way or use of common ground or water would necessarily have involved a familiarity with each other's legal customs, and any transaction would naturally have been decided according to a conscious choice of which legal tradition to follow. We should envisage this kind of mixed community and mixed legal tradition in every part of the Frankish realms and the areas gradually brought under Frankish rule. It is, moreover, to be expected that those accustomed to recording their legal transactions in writing would have been unhappy at a purely verbal procedure reliant on memory for its validity. It may therefore be due to the assertion of familiar written modes of record by one section of an early mediaeval community, drawing on its Roman past, that we owe the gradual adoption of written modes by other sections. The church, in its preservation of Roman methods of record, and anxiety to document its endowment, would have been a crucial catalyst in this development.

The Franks started to extend eastwards in the sixth century as part of the territorial aggrandizement of the sons of Clovis. They conquered Burgundy by 534 and Rhaetia shortly thereafter. The Alemans thus became the object of both the political expansion and the missionary zeal of the Franks, but it was not until early in the period of rule by the Carolingian mayor of the palace, Pippin III, who appropriated the Frankish throne in 751, that the Alemans were conquered by the Franks and the area came under Frankish overlordship, and, presumably, Frankish influence.[11]

Alemannia and Rhaetia were thus areas with a mixed Romano-Germanic population, Romanized to an undetermined extent, and Christian for some two centuries before the Frankish conquest. It should come as no surprise, therefore, that the earliest charters from the region in the aftermath of Frankish conquest should resemble both late Roman documents and the Merovingian charters extant from Frankish Gaul.

The St Gall region appears to have been one with a Roman and Christian population of some size. Watered by the Sitten and Thur rivers, it is in the old Roman region of Arbon, bounded by Lake Constance and the Seerücken in the north, and by the Alpstein, of which Säntis is the highest peak, in the south. It was a thinly populated and thickly forested region in the early middle ages. There is evidence of a late Roman *castellum*

---

[11] For discussions of the early history of the region see K. Schmid, 'Königtum, Adel und Kloster zwischen Bodensee und Schwarzwald', *Forschungen zur Oberrheinischen Landesgeschichte* 4 (1957) 225–51; K. Reindel, 'Bistumsorganization im Alpen-Donauraum in der Spätantike und im Frühmittelalter', *MIÖG* 72 (1964) 277–310; R. Moosbrugger, *Die Schweiz zur Merowingerzeit* (Berne, 1971); E. Meyer, *Handbuch der Schweizergeschichte* I (Zurich, 1972); B. Behr, *Das alemannische Herzogtum bis 750* (Berne, 1975); and H. Büttner, *Frühmittelalterliches Christentum und Fränkischer Staat zwischen Hochrhein und Alpen* (Darmstadt, 1961), especially pp. 7–54.

and *vicus* at Arbon itself, between Romanshorn and Steinach on the shores of Lake Constance. It was built *c*. 284–305, and appears to have acted as a regional centre, a function enhanced by its harbour. The last reference to Roman troops in the area is in the early fifth century; the garrison then was presumably withdrawn as part of Honorius' general retraction.[12] Some Romanized Christians seem to have remained in the region and at Arbon itself. Jonas of Bobbio in his Life of Columbanus, and the oldest *Vita sancti Galli*, for example, talk of *Arbona castrum* and of Willimar the *presbyter castri* whose house was beside the *castrum*.[13] The latter source also refers to *Romani* in the Arbon area. At the beginning of the seventh century the Alemans began to become more numerous in the Arbon region, and it is thought that they hastened the lapse, if lapse there were, of the population into paganism, or at least only nominal Christianity. Our sources here, however, the *Vita Columbani* and the *Vita sancti Galli*, may well be exaggerating the degree of paganism in order to make the achievement of the missionaries more notable. They specifically refer in fact to pagan practices only in the vicinity of Bregenz, a long-ruined city, where Gall, a Frankish or Alemannian follower of Columbanus, broke up the idols of the people of Bregenz and threw them into the lake.[14]

IV THE FOUNDATION OF ST GALL

The monastery of St Gall itself was founded on the site of this same Gall's hermitage. Rather than follow Columbanus to Italy, he had established himself beside a waterfall of the River Steinach in the great forest of Arbon. Whether a small community of religious remained at this hermitage until the eighth century and prompted the local dignatories, Waltram and Boden, to enlarge and regularize the community is not clear. Whatever the case, the life of Otmar, first abbot of St Gall, records that Waltram and Boden asked Bishop Victor of Chur to recommend someone to direct the cell of Gall.[15] Victor sent Otmar, possibly his kinsman, who had been a priest in the diocese of Chur. This connection with the Rhaetian diocese of Chur is important for the subsequent history of St Gall, but it is also an indication, if this link represented one of Arbon's many connections with the old Roman province of Rhaetia Prima and its episcopal seat at Chur,

[12] A useful summary of St Gall's history is provided by Sprandel, 'Kloster St Gallen', 9–27.
[13] Wetti, *Vita sancti Galli* c.30, *MGH SS rer. merov.* IV (1902), p. 274.
[14] *Ibid.*, and compare Jonas of Bobbio, *Vita Columbani* c.27, *MGH SS rer. merov.* IV (1902), p. 103.
[15] *Vita Otmari* c.1, *MGH SS* II, p. 42. Compare Walafrid Strabo, *Vita sancti Galli* II, c.10, *MGH SS rer. merov.* IV, p. 319.

that the dismal picture of the state of Christianity near Lake Constance painted in the early lives of Columbanus and Gall is not correct. Apart from Otmar, a number of Rhaetians were among the first members of the new monastery. Gall himself had also had links with Rhaetia; his disciple John was Rhaetian, and Gall preached at John's enthronement as bishop of Constance.[16]

From its foundation in *c.* 719 the monastery of St Gall went from strength to strength and attracted gifts from the Alemans among whom it had been established. Certainly most of the personal names recorded in the charters are Alemannian. The earliest gifts were from before the 740s and were made by Gotefrid, *dux* of the Alemans, Rodulfus, Erfoin and his sons Teotar and Rotar, Aloin, Rinulf and Petto (W.1–6). These were the beginnings of the provision of the essential material base for the work of the monastery.[17] By the beginning of the tenth century, the lands of St Gall extended between Lake Constance and Lake Zurich, with the bulk of its estates concentrated in the present-day cantons of Thurgau, St Gall and Zurich.[18] The monastery also came into possession of a number of estates in the Vorarlberg on the eastern side of the Alpstein. North of Lake Constance, in present-day Baden-Württemberg and Bavaria, St Gall's properties extended north as far as Donaueschingen, Rothweil and Ulm, with a concentration round Legau, and in the west to the Rhine and the areas near Basle and Freiburg. The monastery's properties, and presumably the population, at this stage appear to have been most dense in the long valley from Rorschach to Winterthur and Zurich and on its lower mountain slopes and meadows.

[16] *Vita sancti Galli* cc.23–5, *MGH SS rer. merov.* IV, pp. 269–70. The connection with Victor of Chur is a clear indication of Frankish and even the Carolingian interest in the background of the foundation of St Gall and its subsequent development. Like Abbo of Provence's family, combining the Frankish and Roman traditions, the Viktoriden of Chur owed their position to a long history of family control over a crucial border region in the Alps since the Frank Zacco had been placed there by the Merovingians; see O. P. Clavadetscher, 'Die Einführung der Grafschaftverfassung in Rätien und die Klageschriften Bischof Viktors III von Chur', *ZSSR KA* 39 (1953) 46–111, 'Zur verfassungsgeschichte des merowingischen Rätien', *Frühmittelalterliche Studien* 8 (1974) 60–70. The family of Viktor is known primarily from an eighth-century will; see E. Meyer-Marthaler and F. Perret, eds., *Bündner Urkundenbuch* I (Chur, 1955), No. 17, pp. 13–23. For comparison with Abbo of Provence, see P. J. Geary, *Aristocracy in Provence. The Rhône basin at the dawn of the Carolingian Age* (Stuttgart, 1985), pp. 119–25.

[17] How important a factor this was in the foundation of monasteries has been stressed by K.-F. Werner, 'Le Rôle de l'aristocratie dans la christianisation du nord-est de la Gaul', *RHEF* 62 (1976) 45–73.

[18] A useful guide, with maps, to the St Gall estates is still Meyer von Knonau, 'Der Besitz des Klosters St Gallen in seinen Wachsthum bis 920 nach Wartmann, Bd. I und II', *Mitteilungen zur vaterländischen Geschichte* 13 NF 3 (St Gall, 1872) 87–225, but is now superseded by Borgolte, Geuenich and Schmid, *Subsidia Sangallensia* I, with a new map of St Gall's early mediaeval estates.

V THE SCRIPT OF THE ST GALL REGION

The script of this region also reflects the divers elements that contributed to its development. Even with the acknowledgement that the bulk of our palaeographical evidence from the seventh, eighth and ninth centuries comes from St Gall itself, the history of the monastery's own minuscule and the evidence provided by the handwriting of both its charters and its books, especially in the eighth century, is a clear indication of the possible script types available.[19]

The script written in the old Roman province of Rhaetia Prima, that is, the Chur region, served by the bishop of Chur, had some kinship with such north Italian types as the scripts of Nonantola and Vercelli. The best examples extant are St Gall 348 (*CLA* VII, 936) and Monza a. 2 (4) (*CLA* III, 383), a Gelasian sacramentary and copy of the Dialogues of Gregory the Great respectively. It is characterized by what Lowe terms an 'adroit alternation of shaded and unshaded strokes' and is rather delicately drawn.[20] Its most distinctive letter forms are those of the 'a', formed as if with two contiguous 'c's, and the low looped 't', which in combination with other letters reminds one forcibly of Beneventan minuscule. These features reveal the script to be directly derived from late Roman cursive, and its letter forms as a whole are an important indication that one source of books and exemplars for the diocese of Chur was northern Italy. It is possible, moreover, that there was some continuity in the use of writing in the region from the late Roman period to the eighth century. One or two inscriptions, some palimpsests in St Gall manuscripts possibly from the Chur region, and some tantalizing legal, linguistic and artistic traces provide some stepping stones from the late Roman to the early mediaeval period. As far as one can tell from the surviving episcopal lists of Chur, moreover, the bishop, and, therefore, an administration of some kind, continued to function throughout the sixth and seventh centuries; until the early Carolingian period Chur was within the sphere of the metropolitan of Milan. Although no identified examples survive, it seems most likely that Roman provincial cursive was known in the area in the fourth and fifth centuries, and that in the early mediaeval private charters of the Lombard kingdom from such centres as Bergamo, Como and Milan, we have useful script-type analogues for Rhaetia.[21]

[19] Recorded in Bruckner, *Scriptoria* II and III.
[20] *CLA* VII, p. ix. Compare L. Schiaparelli, *Influenze straniere nella scrittura italiana dei secoli VIII and IX*, Studi e Testi 47 (Rome, 1927).
[21] See, for example, G. Bonelli, *Codice Paleografico Lombardo* (Milan, 1908); L. Schiaparelli, *Il codice 490 della Biblioteca Capitolare di Lucca e la scuola scrittoria lucchese (sec. viii–ix)*, Studi e testi 36 (Rome, 1924); and A. Petrucci, 'Il codice n.490 della Biblioteca Capitolare di Lucca: un problema di storia della cultura medievale ancora da risolvere', *Actum Luce* 2 (1973) 159–74.

Alemannian pre-caroline minuscule, on the other hand, is a solid, robust and fairly bold script. Lowe noted its fondness for the 'nt' ligature, even in the middle of a word, and the 'simpler, less intricate and more rustic ornament'.[22] The most typical examples are St Gall 44 of *c.* 760-81 (*CLA* VII, 899), St Gall 213 (*CLA* VII, 922) and the books written by Winithar, an active charter writer between 761 and 763, such as St Gall 70 (*CLA* VII, 903). The finest example of ninth-century Alemannian minuscule is the famous copy of the pure text of the Rule of Benedict, St Gall 914, written by the Reichenau monks Tatto and Grimalt.

Only gradually did a distinctive 'St Gall book hand' develop; the earliest known scribes of St Gall, for example, Petrus, *c.* 720, and Silvester, 731–64, write a Rhaetian type of script. Given the substantial contingent of men from Rhaetia in the early years of the monastery, Rhaetian minuscule was an important formative influence on St Gall book hand. Combined with Alemannian minuscule, and from the second half of the eighth century, the Frankish pre-caroline and caroline hands, it contributed to its development. A clear St Gall version of the caroline minuscule emerged by the third decade of the ninth century, and is associated with the scribe Wolfcoz (820–30).

Both Rhaetian and Alemannian minuscules were indigenous scripts and had evolved independently from late Roman cursive and half-uncial. That the scripts should survive in the eighth century (and in a few fragments from the seventh century) in association with St Gall should not deceive us into ignoring the implications of this phenomenon. For a script to survive and evolve in a recognizable way, that is, with the antecedents identifiable, in ways similar to the evolution of scripts in Gaul and northern Italy, must mean that written culture, even if only to a very limited degree, never actually died out in the region. We are emphatically not dealing with the introduction of script and written culture to this area with the foundation of St Gall and the conquest of the Franks. Rather, it was an area in which Christianity and a lingering association (in the case of Rhaetia at least) with northern Italy, if not Rome itself, ensured the survival of the civilization it represented. The charter evidence, indeed, can indicate far more precisely than has been understood hitherto where, for what reasons and in what ways a written culture was preserved. St Gall itself would only have been the success it became if the ground had already been prepared, with a receptive and sympathetic population and one, moreover, quite clearly accustomed to regulating its life according to laws and established custom and resorting to written records to do so.

---

[22] *CLA* VII, p. ix. Other early examples of Alemannian minuscule written in the St Gall and Lake Constance regions are St Gall 2, 6, 12, 40, 212, 225, 259 and 249 (*CLA* VII, 893b, 895, 897, 898, 921, 928, 935, 937 and 938.)

Both Alemannian and Rhaetian minuscule were used in the St Gall charters as well as in its books. The Alemannian minuscule of Bremen charter 2, for example, dated 744 and written by Hiringus *lector*, is in a hand closely related to the book hand of the earliest St Gall books.[23] Two charters written by Audo *clericus*, on the other hand, probably at Gebhardswil in the Gossau region, are in an early Rhaetian charter minuscule and barbarous Latin (or perhaps it would be fairer to call it good Rhaetian). Other early charters which can be attributed to St Gall monks are written in similar hands as are those of local, apparently non-monastic, scribes such as Weringis *cancellarius*.[24] In other words, scribes within and without the monastery in so far as we can determine their status are writing similar local scripts. It suggests that the first members of the St Gall community brought their writing skills with them. How then did monks learn to write? How was script uniformity or a recognizable 'house style' within a monastic community achieved? Receiving the tonsure and taking one's vows did not miraculously transform a man into a competent, or even an incompetent, scribe. Still less did simply joining a monastic community do so. One cannot assume that the scribes of the earliest St Gall charters, even in the cases where they were members of the St Gall community, were St Gall-trained. The founding members of St Gall must already have been able to write. They were recruited as adults from a population that already had adult scribes not yet, or at least, not necessarily, in clerical orders. The implications of this for the possible levels of literacy in Alemannia and Rhaetia are enormous. After all, the insistence on the observance of Roman law in matters relating to ecclesiastical property does not necessarily establish that only the church could provide scribes. Given the need for written records made clear in the Frankish Ripuarian and the Alemannian codes, the possibility is indicated of a local law court with scribes attached in some way to it and the

---

[23] Drawn up at Benken monastery for Beata (W.7) and compare W.10. He also calls himself *monachus*. On this scribe see Borgolte, who suggests that 'Hiring' was a member either of the Benken community or conceivably of Reichenau itself, for it is possible that Benken north of Lake Zurich was a dependent cell of Reichenau: Michael Borgolte, *Geschichte der Grafschaften Alemanniens in fränkischer Zeit*, Vorträge und Forschungen Sonderband 31 (Sigmaringen, 1985), pp. 34–5.

[24] See, for example, the St Gall scribes Silvester (*ChLA* II, 161, 160, 41; W.6, 11 and 12) and Marcus (*ChLA* I, 50; W.17). Marcus also wrote W.16, which survives only in a late ninth-century copy, is recorded as witness in 761 in W.27 and 29 and as *praepositus* in 766 in W.49; his minuscule shows some hints of insular influence as well as similarities with the hand of Winithar. The work of local scribes may be seen in the charters written by, for example, Lantherius (*ChLA* II, 70, 84; W.68, 78; W.14 is a ninth-century copy of Lantherius' earliest charter of 751), Audo (*ChLA* I, 40, 44; W.8, 9 of 744) and Bero, (*ChLA* I, 45; W.15 in 752). Lantherius writes a cursive charter hand, Audo a Rhaetian minuscule and Bero an 'Alemannian Alsatian charter cursive minuscule'. Both Bero and Lantherius operated in the area near Basle.

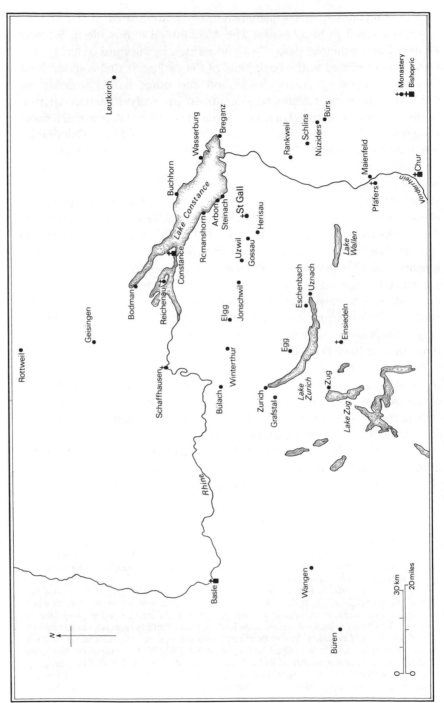

Map 2 The St Gall region and principal places referred to in the text

necessary means of training these scribes. It is possible, therefore, that the earliest scribes featuring in the St Gall charters, whether members of the monastic community or not, had been trained in the local courts or local count's writing office. Others among the earliest scribes were perhaps taught by the local priest. If this be so, the monastery was not the only promoter of the use of written records.

At the beginning of St Gall's history, therefore, there is a close relationship, reflected in the hands responsible for the charters and the manuscripts of St Gall, between the scripts used in Alemannia and Rhaetia and those employed by members of the community of St Gall. Among the charters of the late eighth and the ninth centuries in both the informal cursive script and the more formal book hand, many were written by scribes whose handwriting can also be seen in some of the books still extant from the monastery. Clearly we cannot envisage a writing office at St Gall staffed only by scribes responsible for charters. The monks wrote books as well as charters. But they did not write all the charters. Bruckner in his *Scriptoria Medii Aevi Helvetica* acknowledged some notable local, non-St Gall scribes, but he tended to exploit the charter scripts as evidence for the script of St Gall. Thus, any hands found in charters but not in any extant manuscripts would simply be evidence of more inmates of the monastery who conducted business for it. It is possible, however, that the charters can be understood as a repository of regional script types rather than as a reflection of the scripts of one centre. As such they constitute crucial evidence for the relationship between the monastery and its environs; they suggest that the monastery, contrary to what is usually assumed, did not exert a monopoly over record making generally, still less over the documents concerning transactions involving itself. Local scripts may signal local scribes. Even in the cases of the many St Gall duplicates in St Gall book hands where the script itself can tell us little about the scribe (most of which dated from the later ninth century when the monastery's charter production had become more streamlined), the indications of the earlier material are sufficient to ensure that we do not accept these later charters literally at their face value as evidence of the monastery's assumption of the role of chief record maker. It may well have acted as chief record keeper, and been similar in function to the earlier *gesta municipalia*, but that is another matter entirely.[25] There would appear to be, in other words, a far more complex relationship between monastery and local community as far as legal transactions were concerned than has been envisaged. It is this relationship and its implications for uses and levels of literacy within the community that need to be analysed. The key

[25] Compare above, p. 24 n. 5.

issues involved are the process of the redaction of the charters, the role of the witnesses, the place of the redaction and transaction, and the identity of the scribes.

VI CHARTER PRODUCTION AND THE PROCESS OF REDACTION

Charter structure

The context of charter production and the process of redaction are best tackled by means of a detailed consideration of charter structure. The size of the charters varies greatly. They tend to be trapezoid in shape rather than regularly rectangular. The parchment on which they were written was not ruled, and the text is written on the flesh rather than on the hair side. Opisthographs are rare; usually only the drafts, where these survive, are recorded on the verso.[26] Vertically arranged charters, that is, with the script parallel to the shortest side and the parchment tall and narrow rather than short and wide, or square shaped charters, occur comparatively rarely and seem to have been used only for precarial grants by those whom we can identify definitely as St Gall monks. In the eighth-century charters, the format is consistent, with the chrismon or symbolic invocation in the top left-hand margin and usually a discernible break between the date and subscription clauses. The chrismon takes two main forms. It is either a serpentine line snaking downwards round the vertical shaft, or it takes a form derived from the chrismon on royal charters, with a vertical line traversed by an arrangement of oblique strokes and some use of tironian notes of varying complexity. Each scribe had his own characteristic chrismon. It can therefore be of some assistance, sometimes, in determining which of a group of charters attributed to a particular scribe is actually written in his hand rather than being a copy. Scribes were, however, capable of using a variety of forms for their chrismons, and could adopt the royal diploma type of chrismon, sometimes associated with a legal notary, simply if they happened to fancy it. Too much faith should not perhaps be pinned on the form of the chrismon. It is nevertheless worth noting that the serpentine form of chrismon is by far the commonest, and used by both St Gall scribes and those I shall designate as local. Similarly, the less common notarial form is also used by both categories of scribe.

Few charters begin without a capital letter, carefully picked out, and it is rare to find a simple cross. After the chrismon there is usually a verbal invocation such as *in dei nomine* or *in christi nomine* followed by the name of the donor: *Ego Rinulfus* (W.5), *Ego Kisa* (W.379) or a combination of

---

[26] A. Bruckner, ed., *Die Vorakte der älteren St Galler Urkunden* (St Gall, 1931). See too the lucid description of the St Gall charters provided by Bruckner in *ChLA* II, pp. vii–xiii.

invocation and name: *Ego in dei nomine Meginbreht* (W.378). The donor adds then his motive in making the grant, usually an expression of piety, concern for his immortal soul or the spiritual rewards resultant on gifts to the church. Rinulfus states, for example (W.5): *Ego Rinulfus cogitavi dei intuitum vel divinam retributionem vel peccatorum meorum veniam promerere.* Rihbert (W.130) offers: *In dei nomine. Perpetrandum est unicuique quod evangelia vox admonet dicens: Date et dabitur vobis. Igitur ego Rihpertus et coniunx mea Kebasinda tractantes pro dei timore vel remedium anime nostre vel pro aeterne retributione.* There is considerable latitude exercized by the scribes concerning the order in which these three preliminary elements, invocation, name of donor, donor's motive, are set down.

After these preliminaries, the name of the recipient, usually given in terms both of the institution (St Gall) and the abbot, is recorded. The scribe on behalf of Rumolt (W.504), for example, writes: *trado ad monasterium sancti Galli, ubi modo Grimaldus abbas preesse dinoscitur.* The present tense is used. Immediately thereafter the names of the property or properties and all appurtenances, such as serfs, woods, water, meadows and vineyards, are listed and the terms on which the gift is made are stipulated, the nature of the ownership is defined, and prayers for the souls of the donor and his family may be requested. Often a penalty clause is included and the fine to be paid by anyone failing to uphold the validity of the charter is stated. W.394 and W.504, for example, add that anyone disputing what is set out in the charter should be dealt with according to the procedure given in the Alemannic law code.

The order in which the information concerning witnesses, scribes, date, place of redaction and commissioner or rogator of the charter is provided in the eschatocol or final protocol is also variable. The details of place of redaction, and of scribe, usually recorded in a past tense, need further comment. From this information it is clear that the charter was drawn up in the presence of witnesses gathered together in a particular place, often a local *placitum* or assembly, or a court; the implication of this for the degree of participation in the literate modes of the legal process is considerable.

A precarial grant drawn up at Winterthur on 2 February 856, for example (W.446), was in the presence of Count Odalric and the people (*Actum in Wintarduro coram Oadalrico comite et cetero populo*). A charter of 20 April 845 at Steinach (W.394) notes simply that it was drawn up in the presence of the eighteen witnesses, whose names are listed each preceded by a *signum*, usually in the form of a cross. Other charters use the phrase *publice* or *in villa publice*, or in the presence of those whose *signa* are appended to the document: *Acta Chirihaim villa publice* (W.241, 819);

Actum presentibus, quorum signacula continentur (W.5, 735). Very occasionally the fact that the charter was written at a local *mallus* or court is recorded, as on 10 September 745: *Actum in Craolfestale in mallo publici* (W.11, 744).

By convention, the witnesses' (*boni homines* or *seculares homines*) names, almost without exception, were written by the scribe of the body of the charter. No conclusions therefore can be drawn concerning the ability of the witnesses to write from their signatures. In one or two instances, however, the name of a witness written in a different hand from either that of the body of the charter or, at least, that which recorded the other witnesses' names, suggests an autograph signature. Bruckner drew attention, for example, to W.71, the note *Adalungus scripsi et subscripsi* in a different hand from the rest of the charter written by Waldo; W.100, where the name Agino may have been added by Bishop Agino himself in confirmation of his will; and W.83, where Waldo himself adds his own subscription in a charter written by Helfant.[27] Some of the *signa* in W.338, moreover, a charter written for Adalbert by the local scribe Atto *clericus* at Ottenbach in 831 in a nasty, cramped, inexpert, cursive script, are in different hands, possibly autograph: Albger, for example, wrote a clear caroline minuscule, Wipertus a hand showing Rhaetian influence and Pernwic a far more regular minuscule hand than Atto the scribe. The witnesses' presence, nevertheless, would appear to be crucial; it is arguable that it was essential for the legal validity of the document. Under Alemannian law, at least seven witnesses were required for a charter to be valid. Many of the charters exceed this number; the average is eight or nine, though sometimes as many as twenty-three names are listed. A few charters have less than seven witnesses. Well over 10,000 names are recorded in the extant charters from St Gall though the same person could, and does, appear in more than one charter. Aimo, for example, witnessed five charters between 818 and 825, four at Rankweil (W.235, 254, 255, 270) and one at Schlins (W.293). Brothers, sons, uncles and cousins, widows, mothers, wives, sisters and daughters appear often as witnesses to their kinsman or kinswoman's business, though the women are more usually mentioned as donors or relatives of the donor whose agreement to the grant has been deemed necessary. In many cases it is clear that a landowner would call on a group of relatives, friends and neighbours to validate a transaction, but the records of witnesses also suggest gatherings of local freemen specifically for the conduct of business. The legal status of the witnesses, despite these requirements in the law, is a little ambiguous. How necessary was their presence to the validity of the transaction?

[27] Noted by Bruckner, *ChLA* II, p. xi.

Research on the witnesses' names and the kin groups to which the witnesses belong has indicated their invariable presence at transactions and the necessity for it.[28] Bruckner and diplomatists before him have been certain that the witnesses were present during the transaction, but Bruckner at least thought the charter was executed afterwards, so that autograph participation on the part of the witnesses in the charter redaction process was not necessary.[29] The charter texts themselves stress that the transaction took place in the presence of witnesses. Bearing in mind the status of the charters as dispositive documents discussed in the preceding chapter, and the particular formulae used for what was done in the presence of the witnesses in the St Gall corpus of charters, it seems clear that the witnesses were indeed required to witness the actual redaction of the charter, simply because of the crucial role the written document played in the contract.[30]

After the list of witnesses, the name and, usually, the status of the scribe is added in a formula that can sometimes incorporate the date clause. Other scribes record the date in a separate clause. An example is the formula of Hratbert (W.241): *Ego in dei nomine Hratbertus conzlarius scripsi et subscripsi. Notavi viii idus April anno VI regnante domno Hludowico imperatore et sub Erchangario comite.* The *subscriptio* of the scribe is given in an elaborately decorated form rather than simply in writing. Some of these *subscriptiones* are quite ornamental and centre on the word *subscripsi*. As for the chrismons, however, so for the *subscriptiones*: the scribe could vary his individual one so that it is not necessarily a reliable guide to the identity of the scribe. In copies or duplicates the *subscriptio* was usually reduced to a simple dome formed by an enlarged tall 's' with *sub* written inside.

There would seem to be four main categories of scribe represented by the writers of the St Gall charters as far as this can be determined from the

[28] On the status of witnesses see the following: Giry, *Manuel de diplomatique*, pp. 613–16, Georges Tessier, *La Diplomatique royale française* (Paris, 1962), pp. 208–9; and O. Guillot, *Le Comte d'Anjou et son entourage au XIe siècle* (Paris, 1972), pp. 5–16, for some historical implications of witness lists. See also R. Allen Brown, 'Some observations on Norman and Anglo-Norman charters', in Diana Greenway, Christopher Holdsworth and J. Sayers, *Tradition and Change. Essays in Honour of Marjorie Chibnall* (Cambridge, 1985), pp. 145–64, at pp. 156–8.

[29] *ChLA* II, p. xi.

[30] Above, pp. 66–72. The assumption here is that the formula *Actum in* ... is equivalent to *Facta carta* ..., rather than signalling a difference in practice. The word *actum* itself could refer simply to the verbal agreement but its use in other contexts, such as Carolingian legislation, appears to signify a written document. For example, *MGH Cap.* I, No. 100, c.3, p. 208: *Et placuit nobis ut quiscumque de fidelibus nostris hoc actum a nobis iussum habuerit ad inquirendum per regnum nostrum ... quales seniores homines in ipsa loca fuerint manentes.* I suggest that the act of writing is intended also in the charter formula *Actum in.* Compare Sprandel, 'Kloster St Gallen', 84, who also recognizes writing taking place as part of the action, and the discussion below, pp. 104–15.

palaeography of the documents: local scribes trained locally, St Gall-trained scribes who acted as local village scribes, St Gall-trained scribes who belonged to the monastic community and wrote charters both at St Gall and elsewhere on its behalf and, finally, locally-trained scribes who subsequently became brethren at St Gall. In some respects this is too simple, for the production of charters is thereby divorced from its political and social context. It is to this, and the role of the monastery in it, that we should now turn.

The process of redaction

Let us consider the process of redaction. In the absence of a contemporary description of the process by which a charter was drawn up, we are dependent on the internal evidence of the charter and its format. It is difficult to determine, in this situation, at precisely what stage of a legal transaction the charter was drawn up. Factors which have to be borne in mind are the length of time it would take a scribe to write a charter and how many charters he would be expected to draw up in the space of one meeting. Do some donation charters represent the assembly for the purpose of that one grant, or would it be more likely for a scribe to function for a number of different donors or transactions at any one time, as Amalger and his deputies do at Uznach and Eschenbach in 829 (see below)? Solving this last named problem is made particularly difficult because we have only the charters from one recipient. Other records that may have been made for other persons and institutions at the same meeting are now lost. The corpus of charters from Rankweil, for example (see below), attest to the non-monastic transactions that could be made, as do the handful of grants to such places as Marchtal (referred to in W.81), the churches dedicated to St Martin at Jonschwil (W.227), St Martin at Löffingen (W.240), St Martin at Rohrbach (W.140), St George at Wasserburg (W.137) and St Peter at Rangendingen (W.139).

Both Sprandel and Borgolte have suggested the procedures for charter redaction.[31] Neither envisages a long interval between legal transaction and the written record made of it. Borgolte takes the more positive view that the legal transaction and the production of the charters were closely related events conceptually and that there was no significant time lag between them. He stressed also the importance of legal business for the

---

[31] Sprandel, 'Kloster St Gallen', 87–8; Borgolte, 'Chronologische Studien', 92–134. Yet it would be foolish to be too categorical about the process. Undoubtedly variations from this procedure occurred, with transactions being concluded in one place on a certain date and the document being drawn up elsewhere. The latter procedure, however, was not always followed.

Alemans generally. But neither Sprandel nor Borgolte pursued the possibility of local, non-monastic scribes being responsible for the charters. Sprandel, for example, could only envisage charter scribes being either attached to the monastery as monks or as agents in some way that we can no longer determine.[32] In other words, he could not detach charter production from a monastic context. Under Cozpert (817–42) even the use of agents in outlying areas changed. Cozpert, he argues, organized charter production and thereafter it was concentrated at St Gall.[33] This part of Sprandel's thesis is more persuasive, for it creates the picture of the monastery carving out a specific function for itself in the community in legal matters, and the chronological distribution of monastic scribes, as we shall see, shows them increasingly predominant after 820. The whole argument, however, does not allow for legal activity generally in which St Gall participated, nor for a social and legal procedure in which scribes could be accepted and used by both parties to a transaction. If one thinks instead in terms of legal activity with Alemannia, of which the charters from the St Gall collection constitute our sole remaining information, the evidence seems to me to suggest two different possibilities concerning the process of redaction.

In the first, we may envisage a group assembling in a villa, a local court or, as Alemannic law stipulates, a church. The group consists of the donor, a representative of the recipient, at least five, and preferably seven, witnesses provided by the donor and the *cancellarius* or scribe. The gift is explained orally; it is possible then that the parchment is laid on the altar, and the scribe jots down a quick draft on the hair side of the parchment, noting the name of the donor, the witnesses and the properties concerned. The scribe subsequently writes out a full version of the transaction on the parchment's flesh side, with all the conventional apparatus of chrismon, *subscriptio, formulae*, date clause and so on. The whole process would be carried out on the same day as the transaction and we may perhaps imagine that it was done while other cases were being heard in court, or even while a feast was being held to celebrate the gift. The drafts or *Vorakte* and the scribbled notes on the backs of charters extant are so brief that only a short interval between draft and full version is conceivable.[34]

---

[32] Sprandel, 'Kloster St Gallen', 64–5.   [33] *Ibid.*, 89–91.

[34] See Bruckner, *Vorakte*, and Paul Staerkle, *Die Rückvermerke der ältern St Galler Urkunden* (St Gall, 1966). Sprandel, 'Kloster St Gallen', 711, on the process of redaction, surmised that the place recorded in the charter was not necessarily where the actual document was drawn up but where the transaction or conveyance took place. This is of course possible, though does not preclude the scribe being based at the place chosen for the transaction (see below, pp. 104–15). For earlier views on the role of the charter in conveyance see Oswald Redlich, 'Geschäftsurkunde und Beweisurkunde', *MIÖG Ergänzungsband* 6 (1906) 1–16.

On the other hand, the surviving drafts may indicate the notes based on advance notice of the grant to be made. If, as seems to be the case, judging from the activities of such monastic scribes as Cozpert, Liuto, Albrih, Liuthart or Elolf,[35] the St Gall monks occasionally travelled long distances in order to be present at the signing of the charter, we have surely to entertain the possibility that a notice of intent, whether orally or in writing, had been sent to the monastery, and that an agreement had been reached about the place where the parties concerned were all to meet. There are, of course, large numbers of the St Gall charters which bear no record of witnesses from the abbey; most of those that do, appear to be precarial grants, and must surely mark the last stage in a series of negotiations. The suggestion, by Bruckner and others, that witnesses placed their hands on a blank piece of parchment, moreover, does not make much sense.[36] The witnesses' function was to verify that the charter had been written; any investigations concerning disputes include requests that the witnesses confirm that they have seen a charter written.[37] Their hands were therefore placed on the document after it had been covered with writing rather than before, if at all, and their presence, as argued above, was essential for the charter's redaction. A slight modification of this would be that the scribe could have prepared much of the document in

[35] Cozpert (or Gospert), scribe between 817 and 829, wrote ten charters at St Gall itself as well as such centres as Uzwil, Leutkirch, Henau and Stammheim. See W.222, 278, 279, 284, 285, 287, 288, (as subdeacon) 303, 309, 317, 326, 328, 330, 334, 348 and 385 (as deacon). He wrote a caroline minuscule of some character with a few cursive elements. Not all the surviving charters in Cozpert's name are his autograph. Wartmann took W.288 to be in Cozpert's hand and judged the rest accordingly. W.278, 279, 317 are in the same hand, not the same as 288 (278 and 317 have been corrected); W.314, 330 and 334 also look like contemporary copies, for example. Liuto, scribe between 845 and 876 wrote eleven charters in a variety of centres north of Lake Zurich. Except for W.599, a copy, all seem to be 'originals' and all are written in a neat St Gall book hand (W.396, 399, 537, 550, 554, 555, 560, 561, 568, 580, 599) but not all by the same hand. Albrih was responsible for twenty charters between 851 and 876, drawn up at St Gall, Gossau, Pfohren, Uznach, Uzwil, Kempraten, Wolfenweiler, Zell, Mönchaltorf and Birndorf. All the surviving charters: W.360, 392, 409–12, 416, 430–2, 438, 448, 491, 492, 500, 506, 508, 574, 575, 594, are in caroline book hands but not all by the same scribe. The following, for example, appear to be contemporary copies or duplicates: W.360, 392, 410, 416, 594, and possibly 448 and 506. Liuthart, scribe of twelve charters between 858 and 872, and *bibliothecarius* (from 867), drew up charters at Egg, St Gall, Romanshorn, Wasserburg, Pfäffikon and Buchhorn (Friedrichshafen) and wrote a small and regular caroline minuscule book hand, which, allowing for some enlargement over the fourteen years, appears in each of his charters (W.459, 464, 498, 499, 507, 523, 525, 526, 529, 530, 538 and 557). Elolf, active from 902 to 912 at Mönchaltorf, Bütschwil, Reichlingen, Büren, Niederhelfenschwil, Rickinbach, Amriswil, Hohenfirst, *Pacenhova* (?Betznau) and St Gall, also wrote a neat and regular caroline minuscule book hand if the charters extant in his name (W.722, 725, 729, 736, 737, 742, 744, 747, 757, 762 and 764) are indeed in his hand rather than that of the duplicator. The beehive is curiously diagrammatic and may be Elolf's own.
[36] Bruckner, *ChLA* II, p. xii.   [37] See above, pp. 71–2.

advance provided with information by the donor. At the meeting itself all that would then remain to be done would be to record the names of the place, the witnesses, his own name and the date. The layouts of some of the charters, with a clear space between the body of the charter and the final protocol, and the spilling over in a few instances of the names of the witnesses onto the back of the charter, indicating that more witnesses turned up than space had been allowed for, and, occasionally, a clearly different hand recording witnesses' names, make this procedure the more likely one.[38]

One further stage is suggested by the palaeography of the charters and goes some way to explaining why so many charters, purporting to be written by the same scribe, are not actually in the same hand. Deciding whether or not a particular charter is the 'original' or 'contemporary copy' seems to be a highly subjective process. It is quite common for a set of charters supposedly by one scribe, such as in the group of charters by Hadabert, or Bero, or Salomon, for more than one hand to be at work. Conversely, those by Edilleoz written between 845 and 854 are all arguably in the same hand.[39]

A possible explanation for this phenomenon is that two copies of a charter, the 'original' and a duplicate, were made at each transaction, one for the donor and one for the recipient and that each party provided a scribe, though only one was the official *scriptor*. We can recognize duplicates in those charters which record the name of a scribe who can be identified as a local scribe on other grounds, but which are written in a St Gall book hand and have unconvincing chrismons and *subscriptiones*. It is

[38] For example the charter of Sundramnus (W.646) in 885. In this case a space was left for the insertion of the witnesses' names, and not all of it was used. Similarly the charter of Fridahelm (W.657) in 887 was written in two stages by two different people, with the witnesses' names being recorded by a different hand from that of the body of the charter. It may be significant that both these examples date from the late ninth century. One can compare Anglo-Saxon England where there is one possible instance of a blank charter being used: see Susan Kelly, 'Anglo-Saxon lay society and the written word', in R. McKitterick, *The Uses of Literacy in Early Mediaeval Europe* (Cambridge, forthcoming).

[39] See the comments in n. 35 above. Hadabert (770–809) wrote W.58, 106, 152, 200, but only 106 appears to be his autograph, an Alemannian charter minuscule closely related to contemporary book hands (compare the facsimile in *ChLA* II, 111). The others are later copies. It may be possible to identify Hadabert with the scribe of St Gall 44 and 260. Bero (883–95) wrote W.631, 689 and 699 in a fairly regular caroline book hand with a few cursive elements. W.699 appears to be a contemporary copy. Salomon (778–822) wrote W.82, 108, 122 and 150 with facsimiles in *ChLA* I, 88, 107, II, 120, 133. He was a *cancellarius*, and wrote all of 82, 108 and 122 but none of 150 (*ChLA* I, 133). Edilleoz (845–54) wrote W.394, 402, 404, 427, 428, 436 and 437. His script is a rather rough caroline book hand with some ligatures and letter forms such as 'a' and 'g' from the old Alemannian minuscule, but W.427 and 428 could be contemporary duplicates, for the caroline hand is much neater than in the other documents. Compare the comments by Sprandel, 'Kloster St Gallen', 43, 62–3, 71, 90, 118–19.

possible that the procedure for the provision of duplicates became more strictly observed in the course of the ninth century. This could explain the greater number of apparent St Gall copies of charters among the later ones. A few instances of both the original and the duplicate being preserved add weight to my hypothesis about the regular production of copies. The second copy, in these cases, presumably came into the abbey's possession when the donor himself joined the community.[40]

Whatever the case, it is clear that the process of charter redaction was one that was subject to rules we now know little about. It was altogether more complex, and required a higher degree of social and legal organization and greater reliance on the validity of the written word than we have hitherto appreciated. The gathering together of the parties to the transaction, the commissioning of a scribe, the provision of the parchment, ink and writing equipment, the notification of intent and the making of the record in writing – a record perceived as the essential validation of the transaction – mark a stage beyond the dependence on memory.

VII THE CONTEXT OF LEGAL TRANSACTIONS

The witness lists

So far I have been concentrating on the indications provided by the charters concerning the procedure of record making. Can they also tell us something of the preceding negotiations and the physical context of the transactions? Examination of the witness lists on the one hand, and of the scribes and places of redaction on the other, sheds some light.

One example of witness groups, among many possible, must serve (see Table B). On 20 April 829 a public meeting was convened at Uznach at the eastern end of Lake Zurich. Four of the charters drawn up at this meeting survive, for they concerned St Gall. The landowners, Gerhart, Witolt and Hagastolt, Aldegund and her advocate Ratingis made grants to the abbey (W.318, 319, 320). Further, Thiotin and his sons Engilram and Thiotin were accorded use of their land by Abbot Cozpert in return for an annual payment (W.321); it is likely that this charter is the pair of the normal twin charters recording a gift to the abbey and its return *in precariam*.[41] With these landowners, and the representatives of the abbey, who on this

---

[40] For example, two charters written by Alphart (W.346 and 347) in 834 survive in two copies each apparently made by Alphart and a contemporary copyist. Two original copies of W.335, written by Thiothart of St Gall at Gossau in 830 can also be cited, among others.

[41] Note that Sprandel also discusses this case and others in a sensitive section on witness groups generally, 'Kloster St Gallen', 113–33.

Table B. *Witness lists at Uznach and Eschenbach, 20 April 829, in the administrative region of Count Gerold*

	Uznach W.318	Uznach W.319	Uznach W.320	Uznach W.321	Eschenbach W.322	Eschenbach W.323	Eschenbach W.324
Witnesses							
Perahger	✓	✓	✓	✓	✓	✓	✓
Thiotpert	✓	✓	✓	✓	✓	✓	✓
Reginpert	✓	✓	✓	✓	✓	✓	✓
Heribold	✓	✓	✓	✓	✓	✓	✓
Uuazo	✓	✓	✓	✓	✓	✓	✓
Erchanolf	✓	✓	✓	✓	✓	✓	✓
Lantolt	✓	✓	✓	✓	✓	✓	
Paldram	✓	✓	✓	✓	✓	✓	
Perolf	✓	✓	✓	✓	✓	✓	
Rather	✓	✓	✓	✓	✓	✓	
Egilpert	✓	✓	✓	✓	✓	✓	
Hunolf	✓	✓	✓	✓	✓		
Hehtolf	✓	✓	✓	✓	✓		
Peratolf	✓	✓	✓	✓	✓		
Hiltipold	✓				✓	✓	
Cunzo	✓				✓	✓	
Woldreg	✓				✓	✓	
Liupher	✓					✓	
Witolt	✓				✓	✓	
Hagastolt	✓					✓	✓
Amalger				✓			✓
Reginhart				✓			✓
Friduric				✓			✓
Ruadkar				✓			✓
Hunolt				✓			
Engilbert				✓			
Pernwic				✓			✓
Gerbald				✓			✓
Salvo				✓			
Isanpert							✓
Landowners and commissioners	Gerhart	Witolt and Hagastolt	Aldegund	Thiotin	Wolfher (Esgithorf)	Epurhart	Liupher
Scribes	Thiothart *ad vicem Amalgeri prepositi*	Amalger	Rihpert	Rihpert *ad vicem Amalgeri*	Rihpert *ad vicem Amalgeri*	Rihpert *ad vicem Amalgeri*	Rihpert *ad vicem Amalgeri*

occasion were Abbot Cozpert in person and his advocate Wolfhart, were the scribes Amalger (W.319), Thiothart (W.318), Rihpert (W.320, 321) and a large group of freemen who served as witnesses. Twenty men witnessed Gerhart's grant and the first fourteen listed on Gerhart's charter also attested the other three documents. In addition, the precarial grant was witnessed by an additional eight men not recorded in the three donation charters. This group, headed by Amalger *prepositus*, is probably to be recognized as the contingent from the monastery. At Uznach, therefore, on this spring day in 829, were gathered together at least forty-two people concerned with a set of transactions. What is of great interest is that most members of the assembly appear to have decamped to nearby Eschenbach (or else had arrived at Uznach from thence), a distance of some 7 kilometres, the same day, for three further charters drawn up at Eschenbach for St Gall were commissioned by Wolfher, Epurhart and Liupher (W.322, 323, 324). The last named freeman's precarial grant from Abbot Cozpert is preserved. Wolfher's witnesses (W.322) include all those for Gerhart (W.318), except for Hehtolf, Liupher and Witolt, but Liupher's presence is certain from the fact that the precarial grant was in his favour. Similarly, the list of witnesses for Epurhart's charter corresponds to that of Wolfher, with the exception of the omission of Hunolf and Hiltipold. The same eight additional witnesses attested the precarial grants in both Uznach and Eschenbach, with an extra one, Isanpert, at Eschenbach. Esgithorf, mentioned as the place of redaction of W.322 appears to have been part of Eschenbach.

Who wrote these charters? Rihpert, scribe of two of the Uznach charters, is recorded as scribe, again acting *ad vicem Amalgeri*, at Eschenbach. Apart from these five charters he is also recorded at St Gall and Bussnang, at first as *diaconus* and then as *presbyter*, and was active from 827 to 838. He wrote a small, neat and regular caroline minuscule book hand, if indeed the extant charter is in Rihpert's own hand rather than in the duplicate made for St Gall.[42] Rihpert could have been either the scribe provided by St Gall or the local scribe approved for the transactions by both St Gall and the lay landowners involved. Amalger of St Gall, *prepositus* and *presbyter* on whose behalf Rihpert writes, was, judging from his handwriting, a locally-trained scribe. His function as *prepositus*, extending Sprandel's hypothesis concerning *prepositi*, could have been that of local, monastery-appointed agent or bailiff.[43] On the other hand, he could be an example of a man who joined the community as an adult.

---

[42] Rihpert (827–38), scribe of W.304, 320, 321, 322, 323, 324, 339 and 375 at St Gall and Bussnang as well as Uznach, Esgithorf and Eschenbach. Compare Sprandel, 'Kloster St Gallen', 68.   [43] *Ibid.*, 61–72.

There is no knowing why the move from Uznach to Eschenbach was necessary. It may have been a matter of the hospitality available for the party from St Gall, other transactions that needed to be made, or, possibly, the incapacity of one of the principals concerned to travel to the other centre. That witnesses travelled about attending courts or legal business meetings on a regular basis is suggested by the number of those recorded who turn up elsewhere. If we consider only one or two of those present at Uznach and Eschenbach this is clear. Rather, for example, is also included among the nine witnesses at Uzwil on 2 June 824 (W.278) and four months later at St Gall itself (W.284). He may be identified with the Rather who with twenty-six others attested a charter at Gossau on 7 July 830 (W.335) and conceivably as late as 845 at Steinach (W.394), as well as again at St Gall in 832 (W.341, 342, 348). The distances involved, as can be seen from Map 2, make such movements plausible; business may well have taken Rather away from his normal stamping ground east of Lake Zurich. Uuazo, another Uznach and Eschenbach witness, may be the same Uuazo who attended the public *mallus* at Egg, 30 kilometres or so from Eschenbach, sometime after 841 (W.565, 566, 567). The fact that this is twenty years later, however, may indicate a son or other relative rather than the man himself.

The Uznach and Eschenbach incident is unusual in that two places are involved on the same day. But the incidence of the same witnesses acting at a particular place on one or more occasions can be observed many times in the extant charters. At Leutkirch in the Allgäu, for example, seventeen witnesses are recorded in 797 (W.144), of whom four, Altman, Ebracher, Gisalbold and a certain Cuntbold, possibly the son of Cunthart, occur again fifteen years later, together with eleven new names. Altman, Ebracher and Ruadpold (son of Hruadhar?) witnessed a succession of charters issued on 6 June 824; Diodolt, Cuntbold, Siutolf, Raffolt and Nandger survive from the 812 charters and there are six new names (W.279–82). By 860, the last in the series from Leutkirch (W.470), an Altman (presumably the son of the Altman who witnessed charters in 797, 812 and 824) and Scrutolf are the only survivors from earlier transactions, but a host of new names, some sixteen, represent the men who have now attained their majority. Many have name elements in common with earlier witnesses – Heriprand (797), Gisalher (824), Thiother (860), Hiltiprand (797), Hildipold (860) – which may indicate kinship. Some of these witnesses, moreover, also were present at the church of Nibelgau (Leutkirch) for a number of other transactions (W.117, 168, 183, 311 and 470).

Sprandel has suggested an important indication of the degree to which witnesses were organized in his notion of the witness leader. He cited, for example, the landowner Othere of Jonschwil. Like a later Othere he acted as witness at Glatt, Rickinbach and Algetshausen. The later Othere appears to have been an *Eigenkircheherr* in Jonschwil and is called in one of the charters (W.227) *venerabilis laicus*. The little Eigenkloster at Jonschwil in his possession was closely related to St Gall and Othere gave many estates to the great abbey, as is testified by a number of charters (W.648, 727 and 738). In W.738 Othere is named as *advocatus* of the donor. Othere's brother was Notker Balbulus. Othere acted as witness in a number of different local centres, and in a large judicial gathering in 890 he was described as the first of the *principes* of the Thurgau (W.680). Other witness leaders, such as Amalung, Heitar, Amalrich or Wolfhart, can be identified from the witness lists of a region. They provide evidence of those landowners who had sufficient standing within the local community to act as leaders, and could muster together the brave men and true to attest to the legality of a transaction. Sprandel concludes that witness leaders, often with such titles as *centenarius*, are connected to witness groups, and have a wider sphere of activity than any one witness group. In the Thurgau and Zurichgau the witness leaders were more active in the whole area in which St Gall possessed estates. In other words, it is possible to identify an administrative region in which the witness leader is active. Within this region smaller witness communities are active, and among these are the smaller and middling landowners, all freemen. The witness leader was also, then, the head man of a local community and in some sense was the representative of authority, royal authority, in the localities.[44]

The witness lists as a whole suggest, first, that the local men, often members of a wide kin group, attended regular meetings and legal courts, and witnessed transactions, and, second, that the personnel from St Gall joined these meetings when the transactions concerned them. Many of the donors' names, moreover, appear in the witness lists, so that research, such as that conducted by May[45] and by Borgolte,[46] above all, on both witnesses and donors has provided information concerning the families involved.

May, for example, has documented the prominent role played in the establishment of St Gall by the family of Waltram, *tribunus Arbonensis*, in the early eighth century.[47] Possible relatives of this Waltram among the St

---

[44] *Ibid.*, 113–33.

[45] Ulrich May, *Untersuchungen zur frühmittelalterlichen Siedlungs-, Personen- und Besitz-geschichte anhand der St Galler Urkunden* (Berne, 1976).

[46] Borgolte, *Grafschaften Alemanniens*, and see his comprehensive bibliography for smaller studies of the Alemannian population. Borgolte has effectively exploited, in particular, the information in the date clauses of the charters referring to counts.

[47] Waltram has been linked with the Waltramshuntare region near Romanshorn on the shore of Lake Constance. According to the *Casus sancti Galli* of Ratpert, Waltram was a

Gall charter corpus are Waldrata, the widow of the dead *tribunus* Waltram, and her son Waldbert (W.35, dated 779), who gave their properties at Romanshorn, including a church, to the monastery. Waltram must therefore have been an *Eigenkircheherr*. The family appear to have owned a sizeable portion of land in this region south of Lake Constance, as well as in the Uzwil, Glatt, Gossau and Appenzell areas. Other members make gifts to St Gall from it or witness the gifts of others in the region between 779 and 909.[48] They also joined the community of St Gall. One of Iso's students, for example, was a Waltram, and between 886 and 909 an active monastic charter scribe, Waltram, is recorded successively as monk, subdeacon, deacon and *bibliothecarius* of St Gall.[49]

Adalgoz, benefactor of St Gall, was another *Eigenkircheherr*. The name Adalgoz appears thirty-two times in thirty-one charters, and most of the references are to the same or related Adalgozes.[50] The first Adalgoz received, in his role as custodian of the church at Rohrbach, land from Heribald. The charter, drawn up at Rohrbach on 28 December 795 by Starcho *indignus presbyter*, unfortunately only survives in a later, ninth-century copy, but Starcho appears to have been a local scribe, and only at a subsequent stage does Adalgoz's land come into St Gall's possession. Besides the charter references to Adalgoz and his family, some of the Adalgoz kindred are included in the confraternity book lists of Pfäfers, St Gall and Reichenau, as are many other lay benefactors of these monasteries.[51] May's work has indicated how many of these, and those recorded as witnesses, were landowners, on however small a scale, in eastern Alemannia. Borgolte has considerably augmented and consolidated this preliminary study.[52]

founder and benefactor of St Gall. Walafrid Strabo, *Vita sancti Galli* II, c.10, *MGH SS rer. merov.* IV, p. 319, adds that Otmar, the first abbot, was Waltram's choice, and that it was he who approached the bishop of Chur for someone to establish a monastery on his estates on the Steinach. Waltram is also supposed to have asked for the protection for his monastery from the Carolingian mayors Carloman and Pippin, but there is no charter evidence to support this. Compare Sprandel, 'Kloster St Gallen', 12.

[48] See, for example, W.44, 120, 185, 208, 325, 419, 444 and 478, and the discussion in May, *Untersuchungen*, pp. 46–55, 64–82.

[49] W.651, 672, 697, 709, 723, 749 (and in W.761: here the scribe was Notker, *ad vicem Uualtrammi bibliothecarii*). Waltram wrote a neat caroline minuscule book hand of the St Gall type, but 723 and 749 are not in the same hand as the other four.

[50] May, *Untersuchungen*, pp. 111–19, and his references.

[51] See, for example, P. Piper, ed., *Libri confraternitatum Sancti Galli, Augiensis, Fabariensis, MGH Necrologia Germaniae* I (Berlin, 1884, and Munich, 1983), 60, 9; 113, 36; 115, 24; 314, 17; 396, 8; or J. Autenrieth, D. Geuenich and K. Schmid, eds., *Das Verbrüderungsbuch der Abtei Reichenau, MGH Libri Memoriales et Necrologia, Nova Series* I (Hanover, 1979), Altcoz 102, D1.

[52] Borgolte, *Grafschaften Alemanniens*.

Centres of charter production

Under Alemannian law, the *mallus* or local court was required to be held at least once a fortnight, or more frequently in times of trouble. If we look at the records of the places where charters were drawn up, it may be possible to determine where these meetings were held on a regular basis and whether or not particular scribes can be associated with regular meeting places. Apart from St Gall and the royal residences, there are 255 places where charters were drawn up, though not all are located or named in the charters (see Map 3). Almost half of the identifiable places among these, 120, are recorded only once as a place for charter redaction. Many of these are houses of individuals, or a local church, and may probably be understood as the only time at which the donor made a grant to St Gall. About thirty charters, for example, have the place-name suffix *-wilare*, that is, in someone's villa, as in *Adaldrudowilare* (Adriatsweiler) or *Chuniperteswilari*. It may be that places with the *-hova* (Hof) suffix can also be so categorized. A further forty-six places were used only twice for the drawing up of charters for St Gall. One of these, however, was the royal judicial court at Zurich, and other instances of a place known for only one or two charters, such as Gurtweil, Geisingen or Grafstal, being referred to as the gathering place for the local *mallus* are warnings not to dismiss too readily these places as of only short-term or local importance. Further, even those places with only one or two charters recorded there are known to us because one transaction concerned St Gall. It may be that many more non-monastic or, at least, non-St Gall agreements took place at these. The single charter places may therefore provide crucial indications of centres for secular judicial proceedings, especially in areas far from St Gall itself. For the twenty-five places where three or four charters were drawn up, and still more for those from which five to ten documents are extant, it is possible to be much more confident that one may be dealing with a local judicial centre. Some of these, such as Winterthur, Elgg, Wängi, Uster, Schlins, Romanshorn, Stammheim, Buchhorn and Eschenbach, arguably served as regional centres for the purposes of charter redaction, the hearing of judicial disputes and the assembly of the local notables for legal business as required under Alemannian law. There can be no doubt at all that Leutkirch, Rankweil (Vinomna), Gossau, Uznach and Wasserburg, for all of which there are more than ten charters, served this function. Some of the local royal residences, such as Rottweil or Bodman, could also have been judicial meeting places. To the instances of centres where a *mallus* or *placitum* was held, such as Egg under Count Kerold, Eschenbach, Rankweil,

Munzach, Stammheim, Gurtweil, Grafstal and Geisingen,[53] can be added the centres where assemblies were held under the presidency of a tribune, count, royal *missus* or judge (see Map 4). Count Rocharius, for example, presided over an assembly at an unnamed centre, possibly Geisingen or somewhere in the Argengau, *c.* 824 (W.277). The court at Gams (*curte Campesias*) and its scribe Priectus *cancellarius* are named in a charter of 835 (W.353); Priectus added in a subsequent charter that he wrote *de iusso Teudones iudices* (W.354). At Winterthur between 843 and 876 a meeting was held in the presence of the count (W.388), and again in 856 in the presence of Count Odalric and the rest of the people (W.446). At Rindal in 842/849 an assembly was convened in the court of Luitwin (W.407), the presence of the royal *missi dominici* is recorded at *Hostrahun* in 834/851 (W.417), and of judges at Tänikon in 789 (W.120). The meeting at Kirchen in Breisgau in 868 was described as taking place *in cubiculo regis publice* (W.534 and compare W.661: *Actum Chiriheim curtam regiam*). In another Kirchen, north-west of Lake Constance, an assembly a century earlier was presided over by the tribune Albuin (W.42). To these may be added the meetings held in specified churches, such as that of St Laurence at Bülach, St Benignus at Pfäffikon, St Laurence at Binzen or St Michael at Eschenbach.[54] In the cases of one or two of these centres, such as Egg or Winterthur, there would seem to be a sufficient spread of the charters chronologically to posit the centre as one selected for the local *mallus* or court with some regularity, possibly because it was the residence of the local official, judge, court or tribune. The vast majority of charters, moreover, refer to the gathering being held in a public place or in a villa 'publicly' in the presence of those who sign, of 'good men' (*boni homines*) or of 'many people'. These too may be small local courts or judicial meetings. Undoubtedly some of these charters are the outcome of one-off meetings to make a particular grant to an institution, but overall there is ample indication in the body of the charters that many have to be seen in

---

[53] Egg: of the charters W.459, 460, 565, 566 and 567 at Egg, only 565 and 566 mention the public *mallus*; Eschenbach: only W.297 mentions a *placitum*; Rankweil: only W.187; Munzach: W.II Anh. 16; Stammheim: W.II Anh. 18; Gurtweil: W.643; Grafstal: W.11; Geisingen: *Gisinga coram misso Roacharii Comitis in publico placito* (W.325 – 27th April, 829).

[54] W.206, 205, 195, 490 and 641 respectively. To these can be added the following churches: St Martin at Ewattingen (W.145); St Martin at Rohrbach (W.140); St Martin at Leutkirch (W.144); Ringwil (W.365); St Gall at Uznach (W.448); St Gall at Wurmlingen (W.581); St Geor at Wängi (W.658); St Leodegar at Bussen (W.684 – note that the first stage of this transaction took place in the villa *Diethereskiriha*, for it was, unusually, business conducted in two stages 1: *Acta et levata*; 2: *firmata et perpetrata*); St Alexander at Aadorf (W.691); Henau (W.738); before the altar of St Saviour at Herisau (W.750, 758 and 759).

Map 3 The charters of St Gall: places of redaction

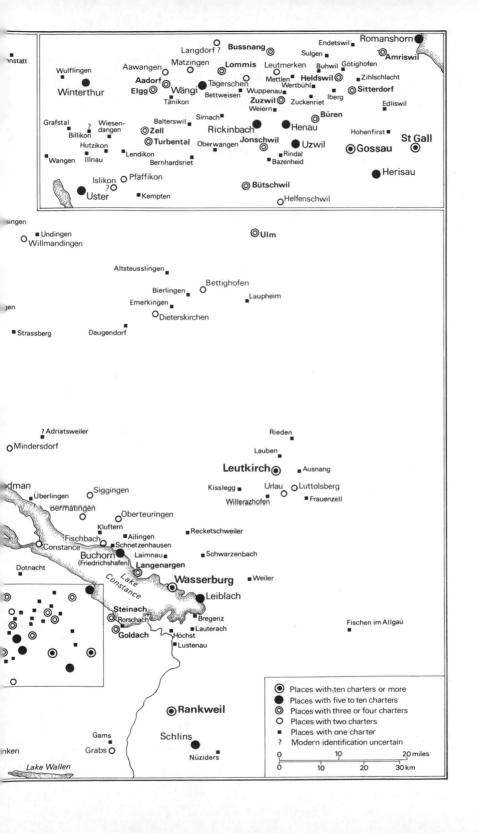

nstatt

Wulflingen ■

Aawangen ○

Winterthur

Aadorf ◉

Elgg ◉   **Wängi** ◉

Tänikon ■

Grafstal ■   ? Wiesen-
              dangen
Billikon ■

Hutzikon ■

Wangen ■   Illnau ■

Langdorf ? ○

Matzingen ○

Bussnang ◉

Endetswil ■   **Romanshorn** ●

Sulgen ■

◉ **Amriswil**

Lommis ◉   Leutmerken ■   Buhwil ■   Götighofen ■

Mettlen ■   **Heldswil** ◉   Zihlschlacht ■

Tägerschen ◉   Wertbühl ■   ◉ **Sitterdorf**

Bettweisen ■   Wuppenau ■

Zuzwil ◉   Zuckenriet ■   Iberg ■   Edliswil ■

Weiern ■

Sirnach ■

Balterswil ■

◉ **Zell**

◉ **Turbental**

Lendikon ■

Bernhardsriet ■

Islikon ○   Pfäffikon ○

? ○

Uster ●

■ Kempten

Rickinbach ●   **Henau** ●

Jonschwil   Oberwangen ■   ◉ **Büren**

◉ ◉   **Uzwil** ●

Rindal ■
Bazenheid ■

◉ **Bütschwil**

Hohenfirst ■

○ **Gossau**   **St Gall** ◉

● **Herisau**

○ Helfenschwil

singen

○ ■ Undingen
Willmandingen

◉ Ulm

Altsteusslingen ■

Bierlingen ■

Emerkingen ■

gen

Bettighofen ○

Laupheim ■

○ Dieterskirchen

■ Strassberg   Daugendorf ■

? Adriatsweiler ■

○ Mindersdorf

dman

Überlingen ■   ○ Siggingen

Bermatingen ■

Kluftern ■

Fischbach ■   ○ Ailingen

Constance ○   ■ Schnetzenhausen

Buchorn ●   Laimnau ■
(Friedrichshafen)

Langenargen ●

Dotnacht ■

Rieden ■

Lauben ■

Leutkirch ◉   ■ Ausnang

Kisslegg ■   Urlau ◉ Luttolsberg

Willerazhofen ■   ○   ■ Frauenzell

○ Oberteuringen

■ Recketschweiler

■ Schwarzenbach

Lake Constance

Wasserburg ●   ■ Weiler

● Leiblach

Steinach ●

◎ Rorschach

Goldach ●

Bregenz ■

■ Lauterach
Höchst ■
■ Lustenau

Fischen im Allgäu ■

◉ **Rankweil**

Gams ■

Grabs ○

nken

Lake Wallen

Schlins ●

Nüziders ■

◉	Places with ten charters or more
●	Places with five to ten charters
◎	Places with three or four charters
○	Places with two charters
■	Places with one charter
?	Modern identification uncertain

0   10   20 miles
0   10   20   30 km

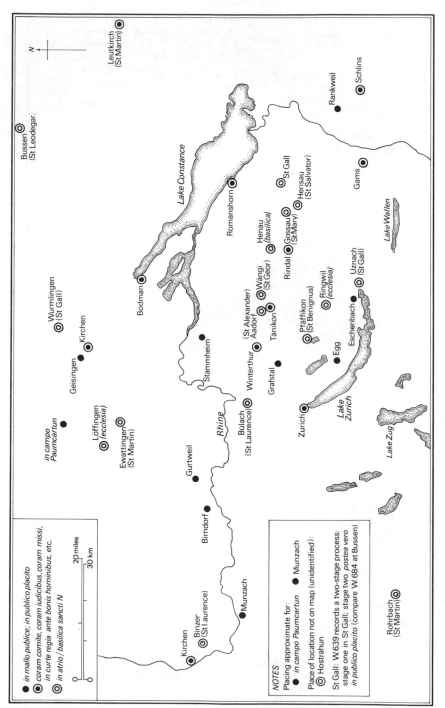

Map 4 Locations of a *mallus* or local court referred to in the St Gall charters

a more public setting than this. The implications for the recourse on a habitual scale to literate methods of concluding transactions, with the provision of scribes and recording of decisions, and thus to the levels of literacy in local concentrations of populations throughout eastern Alemannia, are considerable.

It is worth looking at a small selection of these centres in some detail, in order to identify the scribes and their functions and the possible status, and 'catchment area' of the meeting place itself.

The centre which produced the largest number of charters outside St Gall itself was Rankweil or Vinomna in the Rhaetian Vorarlberg, consistently described in the charters as a *vicus*. It is separated from the St Gall, Thurgau and Zurich regions by the Alpstein. The land referred to in the charters probably came into St Gall's possession at a later stage, for few of the documents are actually donations to the monastery.

The indications are that written culture, even if to a very limited degree, survived in early mediaeval Rhaetia. It is possible that there were local scribes, perhaps associated with other places than Chur itself. The Vinomna evidence is crucial in this respect, for in the thirty charters drawn up there we appear to have a group of local scribes. Dominant is the priest Andreas (fl., 817–51) and his pupils Valerius (825–44) and Vigilius (825). Willimannus *clericus* (864) and Eberulfus (881 and 896) *diaconus et cancellarius* (who drew up a charter for Valerius undoubtedly in the latter's old age), Orsicinus *presbyter* (852/859) (also the scribe of St Gall 722, the *Lex Romana Raetica Curiensis*), Edalicus *clericus* (826) and Bauco (806) can also be closely associated with them. The priest Drusio is also recorded as scribe of nearby Schlins (*c.* 826).[55] That Andreas may have been the official scribe as well as the parish priest of the *vicus* of Vinomna in the Vorarlberg is suggested by the fact that he also drew up charters at Schlins, Bürs and Nüziders. Andreas and the other Vorarlberg scribes, moreover, can be associated palaeographically. There is nothing to connect them with St Gall. Their script is Rhaetian cursive minuscule, or else Alemannian minuscule clearly influenced by Rhaetian. In Bauco's Latin, Rhaetian dialect is detectable. Andreas himself writes a clear Rhaetian type with few ligatures and many caroline elements. Some of his charters are written in a more cursive style, with elevated loops on the ascenders and a tall looped 'c' and 's', which suggest some notarial training. He does not use a chrismon or a *subscriptio*, but these omissions, together with his

---

[55] Andreas: W.224, 235, 243, 250, 253–6, 262, 264, 415 (at Rankweil); W.258, 260, 261, 265, 266, 270 and Zurich C.35 (*ChLA* II, 178) (at Schlins); W.247 (at Nüziders); W.248 (at Bürs). Valerius: W.259, 289, 293, 391. Vigilius: W.290. Eberulfus: W.72, 165, 173, 174, 180, 705. Willimannus: W.501. Orsicinus: W.421. Edalicus: W.296. Bauco: W.187. Drusio: W. Anhang 4, 5 and 6.

distinctive opening formula: *in christi nomine, dulcissime mihi atque amantissime et unica afeccione colende*, and closing formula: *Facta carta...* or *Facta donatio...* are characteristic of the Vinomna corpus and can be counted as consistent regional variants.

Valerius and Vigilius refer to Andreas as their *magister*. They appear to have succeeded him in office and their script is very similar to that of their master. Caroline elements become increasingly predominant in the scripts of the other scribes. There are so many similarities in this group of charters – in script, layout and formulae – quite apart from their being drawn up in the same place, as to indicate a local centre and a scribe, Andreas, who was required to cope with a substantial enough volume of business for him to think it necessary to initiate two of his subordinates into the techniques of charter preparation and writing. Thereafter there were three, four or more scribes active in the area at the same time who could write charters. We have no idea how dense the population was, but it is likely that these men were only part-time scribes as required, and had other occupations and responsibilities. Even Eberulfus, who refers to himself as *cancellarius*, the term the Alemannian law code used for the charter writer, was also a deacon (later a priest) and presumably therefore assisted the priest at the *vicus* of Vinomna. Orsicinus, like Drusio, may have been a priest elsewhere, though the chronology would permit us to count him as one of the successors of Andreas. He may have acted in a public notarial capacity in the region, for his copy of the *Lex Romana Raetica Curiensis* (St Gall 722) suggests that he was conversant with the law at least to the extent of being required to copy it in an official capacity. But the text, usually dated to the late eighth century, has the character of a private selection of extracts from the *Lex Romana Visigothorum*, designed for practical use, such as a public notary might make, or a public official might consult.[56] It bears signs of Frankish influence and is thought to give a good sense of the survival of late Roman 'vulgar law'. It is known to have been used in Rhaetia in the ninth century, at least from 852 or 859.[57]

Some of these Rankweil charters were for the *scultaizus* or local official Folquin. A charter drawn up at Schlins by Andreas (Zurich C 35) on behalf of Estradarius and Solvanus, granting a property to Folquin, appears to

---

[56] On the *Lex Romana Raetica Curiensis*, see R. Buchner, *Die Rechtsquellen*, Beiheft to W. Wattenbach and W. Levison, *Deutschlands Geschichtsquellen im Mittelalter* (Weimar, 1953), pp. 37–9, and his references.

[57] W.421, for example, cites it. On Rhaetian law and charter practice, see E. Meyer-Marthaler, *Rätien im frühen Mittelalter. Eine verfassungsgeschichtliche Studie*, Beiheft der *Zeitschrift für schweizerische Geschichte* 7 (Zurich, 1948), and *idem*, 'Die ältesten rätischen Urkunden des Klosters St Gallen', *Zeitschrift für schweizerische Kirchengeschichte* 49 (1955) 125–32.

represent the donation of a portion of land belonging to this wealthy landowner which did not come into the possession of St Gall. The only hint that there may actually have been a local law court held at Rankweil is Bauco's charter of 806 (Bremen 18, W.187) which notes that it was drawn up *in campos mallo publico*, identified by Bergmann and Borgolte as Vinomna, that is, Rankweil. If this identification be correct, and bearing in mind that Eberulfus gives his status as *cancellarius*, then Andreas the local priest and his assistants and successors may have been more than the local men who could write out documents when required. They may have served as official judicial notaries, that is, as *Gerichtsschreiber*, when the court was convened. It would thus be an important indication that the local priest could serve the community in more than the spiritual way and, further, that it was not only the personnel of the monastery who could do so.

There were other scribes writing in the Vorarlberg area, or in the Rhaetian script, who can be identified as local scribes, though it is not clear whether they too were based, or functioned, at Rankweil or in its environs. Other eighth- and ninth-century Rhaetian local scribes are Werdo, Weringis, Silvester, Perincher and Johannes. Another Orsicinus appears in a charter on behalf of *cancellarius* Erchanbertus for Duke Bernhard of Suabia and Waldo of Chur (W.779) and in 933 he wrote for Lubricio *cancellarius* (W.790). In the tenth century, moreover, there are also charters written by Umbertus *cancellarius* (931, W.789) and Paulinus *cancellarius* (974, W.814); the latter comes from the Vorarlberg near Pfäfers. These scribes attest to the continuing activity of local notaries.

Uznach at the eastern end of Lake Zurich was also a regional centre of some importance. Its position gave it a catchment area, just as that of Gossau in the north-east ensured its ability to serve a substantial area. But it does not appear to have had a resident scribe serving it as Andreas served Rankweil. No less than ten scribes can be associated with Uznach; three of these have links, by their note that they were writing *ad vicem*, with others, so that a further four who may have served this region can be added.[58] Their activities were not confined to Uznach itself, for all drew up

[58] The scribes operating at Uznach did so over a period of about fifty years, between 829 and 874. See W.251, 300, 301, 306, 318, 319, 320, 321, 350, 427, 436, 448, 522, 582. For Rihpert, see above, n. 42. Christianus: W.283 (at Gossau), 300, 301 (both at Uznach), wrote a very simple minuscule of the Rhaetian type, which is distinctive and consistent. Heribald: W.286, 292, 294, 295, 298, 306, 329 (only 306 was written at Uznach), probably a St Gall scribe, who travelled as far afield as Pfohren, Gossau and Wängi. Possibly only W.298 survives in Heribald's own hand. Amalger: W.219, 297, 315, 319 (only 319 at Uznach), wrote an early caroline minuscule with many cursive elements in the manner of a trained notary in W.219, but the other three charters are St Gall copies. One, W.319, is reproduced in Bruckner, *Scriptoria* III, Plate XLVI. Thiotart:

charters at other places. Rihpert for example wrote between 827 and 838 at St Gall, Lauterach, Eschenbach and Bussnang as well as at Uznach. Christianus and his deputy Heribald can be identified, as well as on occasion Amalger, who drew up charters *ad vicem Christiani* at Eschenbach. Thiothart and Rihpert in their turn acted for Amalger and also as independent scribes. Another scribe is Edilleoz, for whom Albrih acted as deputy. Two others to be associated with this group are Uozo (a colleague of Thiothart) and Engilbert *monachus* of St Gall. St Gall's contribution to the charter scribes of the Uznach region were Engilbert, Thiothart, Rihpert, Heribald, Albrih and Edilleoz, all of them monks. Amalger is referred to in one of Thiothart's charters as *prepositus*. If he is to be identified with the Amalger *presbyter* who writes a bunch of charters in the same region, then this is a prominent member of the St Gall community. Christianus, Walthere and Berngar on the other hand appear to have been local scribes. Berngar and Walthere were priests, Heribald a subdeacon, and Christianus simply calls himself unworthy (*indignus*) so could be a lay notary or a cleric.

At Gossau in the north-east another regional centre can be posited. Some of the scribes active at Uznach – Heribald, Albrih, Thiothart and Christianus – were also active here. But Iltibrant, whose one surviving charter is full of silly mistakes, which, if not a poor copy, points to inadequate training and a shaky grasp both of Latin and how to write (W.603, 877–80), may be the local priest acting as scribe, as may Suzzo *diaconus* (W.659 and 660). St Gall itself appears to have supplied other scribes to this place; its proximity to St Gall makes this readily explicable.

Although at Leutkirch in the Allgäu there are a number of local scribes similar to the group at Rankweil, the long arm of St Gall could extend this far. Of Ratbot, who wrote one charter in 810 (W.210), nothing is known, for even his charter survives only in two late ninth-century copies made at St Gall. Cunzo, on the other hand, presents us with a fascinating set of

W.318, 335, 345, 349, 350, 355, 356, 358, 362, 363, 364, 365, 367, 369, 374, 377, 378, 382, 403, 405, 446, 490, 534, 541, 553, was an immensely active St Gall scribe in a number of centres besides Uznach who wrote a practised caroline minuscule book hand, though again not all the charters attributed to him are written by his hand. It is possible that W.356 is a copy, and W.378 describes itself as a copy. Thiothart's script in W.362 is illustrated in Bruckner, *Scriptoria* III, Plate XLVII, and see also Wartmann's comments appended to W.318. For Edilleoz, see above n. 39. Vozo *prepositus*: W.350, Thiothart acts for him at Uznach. Engilbert: W.413, 502, 509, 510, 515, 540, who was active in a number of centres, wrote in a spiky sloping caroline minuscule with one or two lingering cursive features such as loops on the the ascenders. W.509 and 510 may be St Gall copies. Walthere: W.522, 528 (at Ringwil), who wrote rather an old-fashioned Alemannian minuscule for the date (867), which supports the hypothesis that he is to be recognized as a local scribe. Berngar (Perincher/Perahtger/Bertgar/Peringer): W.176, 201, 206, 207 and 251.

possibilities. Cunzo *presbyter* was responsible for three charters (W.280, 281, 282) dated 6 June 824 and drawn up at Leutkirch, far to the north-west of Lake Constance in the Allgäu, for three local landowners: Werinpold, Lantpert and Wolvold. He wrote a pre-caroline hand with some transitional forms and a very distinctive 'g'. But his script is also to be found in several St Gall manuscripts (115, pp. 196ff; 128, pp. 1–122; 129, pp. 3–22, 198–9; 130; 287; 626, pp. 97–219) and he was the main scribe of St Gall 168.[59] Was Cunzo then a St Gall monk? There is no extant reference to him as such and he gives himself only the title *presbyter*. Are we certain that books written in the St Gall book hand and now in the St Gall library were actually written in the St Gall scriptorium? This is perhaps going too far; it may be simpler to think in terms of St Gall sending Cunzo, as one of the brethren in charge of estate management, out to Leutkirch to record the three gifts. A further, more interesting, possibility, however, is that Cunzo the priest was trained at St Gall, established his reputation as a scribe while a student there by writing essential texts for the abbey library, and subsequently went to serve Leutkirch as its local or parish priest, in which capacity he also served as local scribe.[60] On this interpretation Cunzo would become an instance of the role of monastery as seminary and promoter of literate skills, contributing to the community in a substantial way.

This would not preclude St Gall commissioning its own scribes to record many of the gifts made to it, especially in centres close to home. Cozbert's membership of the St Gall community, for example, is not in doubt. He is listed in the St Gall confraternity book as Cozpertus *monachus* and was responsible for no less than eighteen charters drawn up in the St Gall and Thurgau areas between 817 and 829.[61] It is also to his initiative that the growing activity of St Gall charter scribes is attributed.[62] His rather uncertain caroline hand, with its distinctive 'a' and 'g' forms can also be seen in three manuscripts from St Gall: St Gall 121 (p. 1 lines 6ff) and 123, and Zurich C 41 (fos. 103–121v, 130v lines 40–1, 143v, 144v–145, 247).[63] He also wrote one charter *ad vicem Cunzonis presbyter*, commissioned

---

[59] See Bruckner, *Scriptoria* II, Plate XL, and his discussion, pp. 26–8. Compare Bénédictins du Bouveret, *Colophons des manuscrits occidentaux des origines au XVIe siècle* (Freiburg, 1965), No. 3229, and Meyer-Marthaler, 'Die ältesten rätischen Urkunden', 127.

[60] On the scriptorium and growth of the abbey library at St Gall see Bruckner, *Scriptoria* III pp. 11–43; Franz Weidmann, *Geschichte der Bibliothek von St Gallen seit ihrer Gründung um das Jahr 830 bis auf 1841* (St Gall, 1841 and 1845); Johannes Duft, *Die Stiftsbibliothek St Gallen, der Barocksaal und seine Putten* (St Gall and Sigmaringen, 1982); and J. M. Clark, *The Abbey of St Gall as a Centre of Literature and Art* (Cambridge, 1926).

[61] Cozpert: see above, n. 35.

[62] Sprandel, 'Kloster St Gallen', 24–6, 46–50.

[63] Bruckner, *Scriptoria* II, pp. 26–8 and Plate XLII, and III, pp. 22–3.

by a certain Gerold, at Leutkirch in 824 (W.279). Other scribes sent out by St Gall to Leutkirch were Marcellus *diaconus*, active in other places on behalf of the St Gall *prepositus*, and Mauvo, another active St Gall charter scribe, who is recorded also at St Gall itself, Constance and Bütschwil between 788 and 800.[64]

A predecessor of Cunzo as the local scribe and priest at Leutkirch and serving Nibelgau as well, on the other hand, is the priest Cacanwardus (fl. 797–805). Cacanwardus wrote a rather crude Alemannian minuscule, full of ligatures. Only one of his three surviving charters does so in an original.[65] A number of other scribes, for example, Alphart and Oto appear in charters at both Leutkirch or Legau and also in other villages nearby. Oto can be categorized as a local scribe serving the local population; Alphart is a St Gall scribe.[66]

At Romanshorn, we find the monastic scribes who were serving also as scribes at Uzwil, Uznach and Egg respectively, namely Wolfcoz, Thiothart and Liuthart.[67] We are bound to conclude that in this more densely populated region of the Thurgau, Canton St Gall and Canton Zurich, the St Gall monks could be assigned to serve whole regions. It is thus all the more important to determine whether or not we are dealing with a monastic or local scribe. Romanshorn appears to have acted as the

[64] Marcellus: W.424, 429, 441, 470 (854–60), wrote charters also at Hinwil, St Gall and Gündlingen. Mauvo: W.117, 131, 132, 133, 135, 141, 143, 146, 153, 155, 160, wrote an Alemannian charter minuscule and was a very active scribe. The original charters surviving are reproduced in *ChLA* II, 126, 127, 128, 132, 135, 141, 149, 152. His hand develops from a rapid cursive to a clear book hand. He used the chancery form of chrismon, if indeed it is by him. W.131, 132, 133 and 160 could be by a different scribe.

[65] Cacanwardus: W.144, 168, 183. W.168 is in his hand. W.144 is one of those transactions conducted in two stages, for it states that the charter was drawn up in the church of St Martin at Leutkirch and afterwards before Hiranhart the judge.

[66] Alphart: W.305, 307, 311, 336, 346, 347, 351, 361 (827–37), active in a number of centres, wrote a clear and regular caroline minuscule book hand. In W.307 he appears to ape the royal diplomas with his flourishes on the 'o' and his elaborate beehive. The plate in Bruckner, *Scriptoria* III, Plate XLVII, only reproduces his sober text script and could, indeed, be the hand of one of Alphart's colleagues rather than Alphart himself. Oto: W.199 (809), wrote a pre-caroline Alemannian minuscule with cursive elements. His charter is unusually long in format and the membrane, with a suede-like surface on both sides, appears to have been prepared in a different way from the others. His chrismon was one of the chancery type.

[67] See above, nn. 58 and 35, for Thiothart and Liuthart. Wolfcoz (817–22): W.228, 236, 242, 244, 245, 246, 249, 252, 269, 271, 273, 274, wrote a caroline minuscule of the Alemannian type. He also is the scribe of St Gall 20. Compare Bruckner, *Scriptoria* II, Plate XXIX (W.238), and Plate XXX (St Gall 20, p. 111). But he is not to be confused with Wolfcoz 2, one of the scribes at Romanshorn (840–67): W.383, 395, 398, 426, 445, 493, 494, 524, who wrote a neat St Gall book hand and who gives his title as *monachus*. The Romanshorn charters are W.364, 494, 507, 577, 600, 621 and 671. That is, the earliest is 837 and it may not have been much before this date that St Gall established itself as the provider of scribes for this centre.

episcopal residence for Saloman of Constance, and at a very early stage it became part of the St Gall estates. There seems to be no doubt that all the scribes serving Romanshorn were provided by St Gall: Hartmann (876–93), for example, who also wrote charters at Stammheim, Eccho *monachus* (868–82), who writes also at Wittlingen and St Gall itself, and Lantpret *monachus* (873–89) who is present at Hutzikon and St Gall.[68] The same seems to be the case for Buchhorn on the opposite side of the lake and easily accessible by boat. There the scribes are monks whose activities are also recorded at other places in the vicinity, such as Rorschach, Steinach and Bussnang, in the late ninth century.

These examples of regional centres, as can be seen from Map 3, could be multiplied. Apart from the many places at which only one or two charters are recorded, it is only at Rankweil or Vinomna that we appear to have a judicial meeting place totally independent of St Gall's charter writing services. This, however, can be attributed to the fact that most of these charters did not concern St Gall. To the ranks of regional centres, however, must be added St Gall itself. From 765 it shows a steady increase in the number of times transactions were enacted there. Between 765 and 800 there were eleven, in the next twenty-five years there were sixteen meetings recorded. From 825 to 850 the number increased to twenty-five, and reached a peak of thirty-nine in the next quarter century, falling off to a total of nineteen in the period 875 to 920.

VIII THE STATUS AND OFFICE OF SCRIBES

The 'cancellarii'

We need to consider the status and office of local scribes in more detail. In the foregoing discussion, it has been clear that many of those serving their villages, hamlets or local landowners and *Eigenkirchenherren* as notaries were the local priests. In the final versions of the charters, moreover, the office or status of the scribe is given so consistently that one is justified in considering the possibility that some of the engrossers of charters among the local clerics were not in orders at all, or else were members of only the lowest ecclesiastical grades. Apart from the 23 royal notaries whose names are recorded in the St Gall corpus, most of the 244 remaining scribes are in clerical orders of some kind: *subdiaconus* (8), *diaconus* (27), *presbyter*

---

[68] Hartmann: W.600, 634, 635, 636, 639, 710. Wartmann suggested that the Hartmann who wrote W.710 was a different Hartmann. But it is simply that this charter survives in a contemporary duplicate made by another scribe. Eccho: W.542, 579, 621. W.621 is a contemporary copy. Lantpret/Lantbert: W.571, 595, 671, wrote a rather uneven book hand. W.595 is a copy.

(78), *monachus* (54) and *prepositus* (3). A small group use the term *clericus* (14), a word perhaps sufficiently elastic in the ninth century to refer simply to his writing function when used in this context. Some scribes belong to the low ecclesiastical grade of *lector* (7).

There remains a substantial number (53) who simply sign their names and give no extra indication of status. Only Rodo, the scribe of a charter of 779/780/782 actually records that he is *laicus*, though he also states that he has attained the grade of *lector* (W.93). Only a fifth of the total number of scribes (that is, 54 out of 267) known, therefore, are definitely monks and members of the community of St Gall or one of its dependent cells.

But there is also a significant group who give their function as *cancellarius* or *notarius* (13), and whose lay or clerical status is ambiguous. The status of *Theotpertus presbyter et cancellarius sub Warino comite*, is clear. He engrossed a charter at Fischbach on Theotram's behalf between 763 and 767. Theotpert was perhaps the head of Count Warin's writing office and his chaplain. Unfortunately, there is some doubt as to whether his surviving charter is his autograph. Others among the *cancellarii* and the *notarii* who drew up the charters in the St Gall corpus, however, appear to have the character of the public notaries associated with local judicial courts discussed below.[69] Certainly, while their use of standard legal formulae is not conclusive proof of notarial training,[70] their handwriting may be a more reliable indication of a non-monastic background. Hadarichus, *cancellarius*, for example, who wrote a charter for Reginhard at Buchheim in 804, may have been the notary to Count Odalric (W.179). He had a good command of the legal formulae, and wrote a fine, somewhat elaborate, chancery cursive hand with Alemannian traits, full of character and flourishes. The chrismon is an ornate form of the chancery type and he used a distinctive signum-sign before the names of the witnesses. Madalfridus at Ausnang (W.447, dated ?856), another local scribe who might have been trained at St Gall, also appears to have had some 'chancery' training, for his caroline minuscule has many cursive elements and flourishes. The high-backed curly 'c' in particular suggests familiarity with the royal charter hands. Hratbert *cancellarius* similarly wrote a script with cursive traits (St Gall 1394 XIII p. 138). A *notarius* who served

[69] See below, pp. 118–20.
[70] On the formulae see the study of the use of Marculf's Formulary by H. Zatschek, 'Die Benutzung der *Formulae Marculfi* und anderer Formularsammlungen in den Privaturkunden des 8. bis 10. Jahrhunderts', *MIÖG* 42 (1937) 165–267, and the comments by Borgolte, *Grafschaften Alemanniens*, pp. 36–40; W. John, 'Formale Beziehungen der privaten Schenkungsurkunden Italiens und das Frankenreichs und die Wirksamkeit der Formulare', *Archiv für Urkundenforschung* 14 (1936) 1–104.

Bermatingen and Kluftern, and who visited St Gall, was Maio, a priest active as a scribe between 779 and 813.[71] He wrote an accomplished Alemannian charter minuscule with a very individual chrismon. Priectus, who wrote a caroline minuscule script with some cursive elements of the Rhaetian type, can also be identified as a local public notary.[72] He gives himself only the title *cancellarius* and was possibly the comital notary at Gams, and a layman. Salomon *cancellarius* on the other hand was a deacon. Active from 778 to 797, he served north of Lake Constance and wrote a distinctive Alemannian charter minuscule.[73] Zezzo *presbyter* at Mengen in 861 may well be another local *cancellarius*, but we hear of him only indirectly as such, and no original specimen of his handwriting survives. The script of the *cancellarius* Weringis on the other hand, a neat Alemannian charter minuscule, with many features reminiscent of Merovingian cursive, points to his scribal training having been that of a notary.[74] Christianus is identified as a *cancellarius* by other scribes acting for him. The three charters in his own hand which survive, dated 824 and 826, are a simple minuscule with rather stumpy, round letters, and very consistent ductus.[75] Vunolf's single surviving charter, from 795, is in a crude and ugly Alemannian charter minuscule, and the Latin is very bad. It has every sign of being an inexpert local product.[76] Salerat and Bernegarius, a priest, moreover, appear to have been responsible for keeping records at the local counts' court at Zurich, and Hunolt at Bodman in 849 may have been the local notary rather than a royal chancery official.[77]

[71] Maio: W.87, 119, 198, 211, and compare the facsimiles in *ChLA* I, 92, 93 and II, 119. He wrote an Alemannian charter minuscule, rather crude and rapidly written. W.211 is a later caroline minuscule copy.

[72] Priectus: W.353, 354 (835), though probably only W.354, written in a hand full of cursive elements and reminiscent of Rhaetian minuscule, is Priectus' autograph.

[73] Salomon: see n. 39.

[74] Zezzo: W.487 (W. Anhang 7) Weringis: W.64, 120, 129, 178. W.64 was engrossed by Waldo (see *ChLA* I, 77), W.120 by Weringis himself (see *ChLA* II, 122), W.129 by Adam (see *ChLA* II, 124 and compare 117) and W.178 appears also to be a copy. Weringis was one of the Thurgau *cancellarii* discussed by H. Bresslau, 'Urkundenbeweis und Urkunden schreiber im älteren Deutschen Recht', *Forschungen zur Deutschen Geschichte* 26 (1886) 46, 55, 57–8.   [75] Christianus, see above n. 58.

[76] Vunolf: W.138 (and see *ChLA* II, 134). A copy of this charter was made at the monastery of St Gall in the second half of the ninth century, no doubt because of the crudeness of the original.

[77] Salerat: W.193 (807), wrote a clear caroline minuscule apart from his use of pointed 'a', a curious reversed 'g' and a flamboyant 'z'. Bernegarius: W.148, 163 (dated 796/797/799/800 and 801), appears to have had notarial training, for his accomplished Alemannian minuscule contains many cursive elements. One of his charters (W.148) was also copied soon afterwards with additional witnesses recorded in *Urkundenbuch St Gallen* I, 140. Note that Bernegarius the priest is described as the son of the donor Wolfbold in W.148. Hunolt: W.408 (849/850) is a monastic copy. His own script does not survive. On the back of the charter is written *Exemplar traditionis Salamonis de Linzgone*. In the Breisgau in 800/801/803/804 Plidolf *cancellarius* is recorded at Hartkirch (W.II Anh. 2).

The problem of 'Gerichtsschreiber'

There are comparable instances of comital notaries further to the west in the Frankish kingdoms. Apart from the cases discussed at the end of this chapter, it is possible that the scribes of two of the Arnulfing mayoral charters were officials with a function towards the mayor similar to that enjoyed by the referendaries in relation to the Merovingian kings.[78] Deotinus, too, was temporarily in charge of the writing office of John, the count of the palace of Pippin I of Aquitaine, and had a scribe Nectarius working under him.[79]

Did these notaries have a more public function? The terms *cancellarius*, *notarius* and *emanuensis* occur in a great many charters from all over the Frankish regions and not just in this sample from St Gall.[80] In a classic article published a century ago, Harry Bresslau formulated his hypothesis concerning the existence and activity of *Gerichtsschreiber* or public notaries on the basis of the *cancellarii* recorded in the charters.[81] Bresslau drew attention to the importance of the scribe or *cancellarius* in the *Lex Ribuaria* (LIX. c.5), the role of the *scabini* or law court assessors in the Carolingian period in the verification of charters and the emphasis in the capitulary of 805 on the need for every bishop, abbot and count to have a notary.[82] Wishing to establish the relationship between ideal and reality in the everyday working of the law, he wondered whether the existence of any of these required scribes could be discerned in the charters and suggested the identification, as public scribes or notaries, of a number of scribes in the charters of the Arnulfing mayors, Werden, Prüm, Lorsch, Metz, Trier, Weissenburg, some west Frankish centres and St Gall. That is, he found scribes he felt able to propose as *Gerichtsschreiber* in areas under Salic, Ripuarian and Alemannic law. Only in Saxony and Bavaria could he find no *cancellarii* before *c.* 800. In these regions, on the contrary, the transactions were validated by the witnesses, and the charter itself, like Anglo-Saxon charters, appears to have had a primarily symbolic and evidentiary function. Bresslau's theories have since found both supporters

---

[78] Ingrid Heidrich, 'Titulatur und Urkunden der arnulfingischen Hausmeier', *Archiv für Diplomatik* 11/12 (1965/6) 71–279 at 205–7 and A10, A11, A13 and A14; see also Chrodegang, referendary to Charles Martel at No. A.12 and also her criticisms of the concept of *ämtliche Gerichtsschreiber*, ibid., pp. 207–12.

[79] Léon Levillain, ed., *Recueil des Actes de Pépin I et Pépin II rois d'Aquitaine (814–848)*, Chartes et Diplômes relatifs à l'histoire de France publiés par les soins de l'Académie des Inscriptions et Belles Lettres (Paris, 1926), p. xxx and No. XII, pp. 44–7.

[80] See below on Fulda, pp. 127–9.

[81] Bresslau, 'Urkundenbeweis und Urkundenschreiber', 1–66.

[82] *MGH Cap.* I, No. 43, c.4, p. 121; the reading is that in Wolfenbüttel Blankenburg 130.52, fo. 78. On the *rachimburgii* and *scabini*, see F. N. Estey, 'The *scabini* and the local courts', *Speculum* 26 (1951) 119–29.

and sceptics and it is worth considering briefly the main contributions to the debate. On the basis of his work at Werden, for example, Blok has mounted the strongest objections to Bresslau, maintaining that many of these so-called *cancellarii* were monks of the beneficiary abbey and therefore to be understood as referring to the function the scribe had just fulfilled. That is, a *cancellarius* is to be understood as a man, monk or otherwise, who writes a charter, rather than as an official with the specific function of charter writing.[83] Staab, on the other hand, drawing strength from his reading of the Prüm material, stoutly supported and extended Bresslau's views. He posited the existence of regional law court notaries, town scribes and monastic scribes in the Middle-Rhine region from the mid-eighth century onwards and suggested that extending one's findings from any centre ran the risk of groundless extrapolation.[84] Blok's concentration on Werden, for example, had not allowed sufficiently for Werden's particular history and geographical position. Sandmann's work on Fulda, on the other hand, does take Fulda's particular circumstances into account. She nevertheless argues the case for monastic monopoly, but adds the notion of monastic *cancellarii* drawing up charters for the monastery.[85] Johanek is more sympathetic to Staab's views.[86] Classen, however, despite his convincing documentation of Late Roman precedent for much of the legal process in the Germanic kingdoms, and in particular for the use of the written word, states baldly that he finds the notion of a court in any region equipped with a notary improbable.[87]

There is a danger in the consideration of the problem of the *Gerichtsschreiber* of letting the separate case studies determine the issue in terms of existence or non-existence of public notaries. The reality was

---

[83] Dirk Blok, *Een diplomatisch onderzoek van de oudste particuliere oorkunden van Werden* (Amsterdam, 1966), especially pp. 122–49.

[84] F. Staab, *Untersuchungen zur Gesellschaft am Mittelrhein in der Karolingerzeit*, Geschichtliche Landeskunde 11 (Wiesbaden, 1975).

[85] Mechthild Sandmann, 'Wirkungsbereiche Fuldischer Mönche', in Karl Schmid, ed., *Die Klostergemeinschaft von Fulda im früheren Mittelalter*, Münstersche Mittelalterschriften 8 (Munich, 1978), pp. 692–791, at pp. 704–14.

[86] Peter Johanek, 'Zur rechtliche Functionen von Traditionsnotiz, Traditionsbuch und früher Siegelurkunde', in Peter Classen, ed., *Recht und Schrift im Mittelalter*, Vorträge und Forschungen 23 (Sigmaringen 1977), pp. 131–72, especially p. 140 and n. 35.

[87] Peter Classen, 'Fortleben und Wandel spätrömischen Urkundenwesens im frühen Mittelalter', in Classen, ed., *Recht und Schrift*, pp. 13–44. The use of formularies may make identification of public notaries easier. Zatschek's investigation of the use of the Formulary of Marculf, for example, demonstrates the rapidity with which this collection gained currency among charter writers in western Europe. He accepts the existence of local scribes and thinks it most likely that the formulae for charters were first used by them and handed on from one notary to another and to, for example, the monks of St Gall, who, in their turn, adopted the formulae: Zatschek, 'Benutzung der *Formulae Marculfi*'.

clearly much more complex. While some charter material indicates a limited role for monastic *cancellarii*, other collections suggest most forcefully the existence of public local scribes. These findings are not mutually exclusive. The evidence requires us to be more flexible in our definition of the function and social position of the *cancellarii* and *notarii* to be found in the charters. The different role of monastery and church within the diversity of the Frankish kingdoms as far as charter redaction is concerned, and the possible historical and social reasons for these differences, should be acknowledged and investigated further, rather than fruitless efforts being made to reconcile conflicting conclusions one way or another. Some may indeed have been monastic *cancellarii* serving the local community. Others fulfilled the function of notary at a law court as part of their duties as members of a count's household, as freemen whose responsibility it was when occasion demanded to perform this task, as the local priests possessed of literate skills and basic knowledge of how to write a charter, or as the priests attached to an *Eigenkirche*. All these can be recognized in the St Gall charters and, once the possibilities are clear, in the charters preserved from other centres as well. In the latter case, we rarely have the assistance of the palaeographical evidence but the handwriting of the St Gall charters at least is of crucial assistance in this respect.

The handwriting of the St Gall charters

An examination of the script of all the original St Gall charters, indeed, reveals a clear distinction between the book hands – Alemannian and Rhaetian minuscule and caroline minuscule – used by the St Gall monks, and the more cursive scripts of the local scribes. As the St Gall influence becomes more widespread, the script becomes more uniform.

It is the palaeographical evidence above all which demonstrates the contribution the monastery of St Gall made to scribal provision in Alemannia. It indicates a growing preponderance of St Gall scribes responsible for the redaction of documents concerning gifts and sales to, or exchanges with, the monastery. As the distribution maps show, the work of the scribes when charted shows a clear differentiation between the wide-ranging activities of St Gall scribes, sent out far and wide to represent the monastery and record gifts, and the localized activity of the local scribes, including the *cancellarii*, who operated within a small area. There is no doubt that particular groups of scribes can be associated with particular areas. It is not impossible to imagine, for example, that a scribe based at Leutkirch or Nibelgau could be available to draw up charters for donors at nearby Willerathof, Litoldberg, Otsrumloh or Lauben. In many instances, indeed, particularly in the eighth century, scribes are recorded in one centre only. Some exceptions to this are Weringis *cancellarius* (761–89) who drew up charters in a number of places in the Thurgau, all within about 20 miles of each other.[88] On one occasion, in 761, Weringis went to St Gall itself to write a precarial charter for the abbot and the brothers Erinpert and Amalpert, for whom he had already, presumably, drawn up the first charter of this precarial agreement (W.29).[89] Weringis, moreover, had local deputies and successors: Adam, who acted at Elgg and Jonschwil in 788 and 796 respectively, and Vunolf at Tägerschen in 795.[90]

Wasserburg, on the north shore of Lake Constance, was served by Hadabert (770–809), who also wrote charters for the inhabitants of nearby Langenargen and Oberteuringen,[91] and in this area there are other local scribes such as Kerram (784), Deodultus (799), Moathelmus at Laimnau,[92] Adalhard at Langenargen (794)[93] and Hartker *clericus* (770/771/773/774) at Ailingen.[94] At Fischbach, on the other hand, two scribes, Waldo and Theotbald, are also to be found writing charters at Heidenhofen, Schwarzenbach, Oberndorf, Überlingen, Uster and St Gall itself. They are early examples of monks going out into the community,[95]

---

[88] See above, n. 74.

[89] See *ChLA* II, 165.

[90] Adam: W.118, 142, wrote Alemannian charter minuscule with many Rhaetian elements. See *ChLA* II, 117 and 124. Vunolf: see above, n. 76.

[91] Hadabert: W.58, 106, 152, 200. Only one original survives, the rest are later copies, see *ChLA* II, 111. Bruckner considered his even Alemannian charter minuscule to be closely related to contemporary book hands, and thought he was probably a St Gall monk. He could, on the other hand, have been the local scribe at Langenargen at the end of the eighth century.

[92] Kerram: W.101 (784), at Wasserburg; see *ChLA* I, 106, and compare *ChLA* I, 105, to which it is very similar. See too Sprandel, 'Kloster St Gallen', 125. Deodultus: W.156 (799), also at Wasserburg; see *ChLA* II, 145, who wrote a small Alemannian minuscule with some cursive elements; see Sprandel, 'Kloster St Gallen', 163. Moathelmus: W.52 (769), which unfortunately only survives in a copy of the second half of the ninth century.

[93] Adalhard: W.137 (794), which survives in two copies.

[94] Hartker: W.32, 59, written in Alemannian book minuscule (W.59) and 'St Gall minuscule' (W.32) according to Bruckner in *ChLA* I, 54 and 72. They are clearly not written by the same person.

[95] Waldo: W.25 (W. Anhang 1), 57, 61, 62, 63, 71, 74, 75, 76, 77, 79, 80, 83, 84, 86, 88, 89, 95, 96 (759–82), an accomplished charter redactor, who wrote a distinctive Alemannian charter minuscule. Compare *ChLA* I, 71, 74, 75, 76, 77 (for Weringis), 78, 85, 86, 89, 94, 95, 96. See also, E. Munding, *Abt-Bischof Waldo* (Beuron, 1924), and Sprandel, 'Kloster St Gallen', 37–42. Theotbald: W.23 (758). Other instances of monks who wrote charters at one or more places outside the monastery could be cited, such as Winithar (W.30, 39), who wrote a charter at Weigheim as well as St Gall itself, quite apart from the St Gall manuscripts extant in his engagingly sprawling, thick, 'rather gauche' Alemannian minuscule – see *CLA* VII, 893a, 894, 896, and *ChLA* I, 57, 60.

122   *The Carolingians and the written word*

complemented later in the eighth century by such industrious monks as Mauvo, who turns up at Bütschwil, Constance, Leutkirch and St Gall.[96]

For the rest, the evidence of scribes during the eighth century is highly suggestive. Those who can definitely be associated with the monastery of St Gall or one of its dependent cells are in the minority. There are, on the other hand, many scribes who are active in places as far away as Lörrach, Rottweil, Stammheim, Leutkirch, Kembs and Rankweil, that is, in present-day Breisgau, Baden-Württemberg, Bavaria and Graubünden as well as St Gall, Zurichgau and Thurgau.

In the first half of the ninth century there are fewer instances of local scribes in the distant districts, and increasing scribal activity on the part of St Gall, especially in the Thurgau. In this latter region, indeed, very few local scribes (Walthere is one) are operating by the middle of the ninth century.[97] St Gall scribes are now operating on the north shore of Lake Constance and the upper reaches of the Rhine.[98] But Hilteratus, Oto, Wanilo and Hadarichus in Baden-Württemberg,[99] Salerat in the Zurichgau,[100] the Andreas group at Rankweil (see above), Ysanbertus in the Breisgau,[101] Beratker and Lantherius at Egringen[102] and Erchanmarus at Lörrach[103] still function as local scribes.

The next quarter century, from 850 to 875, reflects the peak of charter production at St Gall itself, for it is in this period that St Gall scribes are clearly predominant. A few local scribes at Egg, Leiblach, Goldach, Grabs, Wetzikon (Ratpoldeskiricha) and other small centres, especially northwest of Lake Zurich, remain independent.[104] It is noticeable how much the

---

[96] Mauvo: see above, n. 64. The bishop of Constance may also have been able to supply scribes, see Pertigarius (Bertgar) *diaconus* (W.151 and *ChLA* II, 144) and Bobosinnus *clericus* (W.111, *ChLA* II, 115).

[97] Walthere: see above, n. 58.

[98] See Map 3.

[99] Hilteratus: W.237 (818), wrote a neat cursive pre-caroline Alemannian hand. Oto: W.199 (809), see n. 66. Wanilo: W.170 (802). His charter, drawn up at Deislingen, is particularly interesting for it survives in two copies, original and duplicate, both in the same hand, a rapid pre-caroline Alemannian minuscule. Hadarichus *cancellarius* at Buchheim: W.179 (804), may have been a notary of count Odalric and was well in command of the legal formulae. His hand is a very nice example of chancery cursive and gives every indication of being that of a trained notary.

[100] Salerat: W.193 (807), see above, n. 77.

[101] Ysanbertus: W.167 (802), who wrote an extraordinarily curly hand with many cursive elements showing no sign of a connection with St Gall.

[102] Beratker: W.162 (800), whose Alemannian cursive minuscule hand was clear but lacking finesse. Compare Sprandel, 'Kloster St Gallen', 124–6. Lantherius: W.439 (855?).

[103] Erchanmarus: W.196 (808), who wrote in a slightly backhand script with a 'chancery-style' cramped and elongated *subscriptio*.

[104] Egg: W.459, 460, 565, 566 and 567. The St Gall scribes Otine and Liuthart were responsible for the first two. Otine's charters (855–65) indicate a newly emerging St Gall charter form. It is more regular, the first word is slightly enlarged, the date clause is

St Gall scribes' activity is concentrated in the region east of Lake Zurich and south of Lake Constance. Gossau is prominent as a writing centre. In places such as Uznach and Goldach, monastic and local scribes appear to coexist. But generally the net of St Gall has spread even wider in the Thurgau, and its predominance in this region at least is maintained to the end of the ninth century and into the early tenth.

A hint of the process of change is provided by the career of Salacho. He appears to have been the local scribe at Büren until 898, but by 902 he had been replaced by the St Gall monk Elolf, who thereafter seems to have borne responsibility for drawing up charters in the area.[105] This suggests that St Gall seized the opportunity when it could to extend its scribal provision in nearby districts. It could, on the other hand, reflect the disintegration of training procedures for local scribes. Of the other places where once a local scribe was available, Gossau maintained its local scribes, such as Suzzo and Iltibrant, at least until 887, but centres, such as Herisau, Buchhorn (Friedrichshafen) and Winterthur, were regularly served by St Gall scribes.[106] One interesting development is the emergence of Mönchaltorf, a cell of St Gall, as a writing centre in the district north of Lake Zurich, served by the monks Elolf, Sigibert, Engilbert and Waltram.[107]

written in rustic capitals and set out at the bottom of the sheet and *scripsi et subscripsi* is written out in full rather than expressed with the 'beehive'. Paldene, operating between 841 and 872, appears to have been the local priest. He wrote an irregular and somewhat inexpert caroline minuscule, and the formulae used are very simple. They look like the work of someone who did not draw up charters often. Compare Wartmann's comments on W.565. Leiblach: W.452, 457, 462, 609 and 645. The St Gall monks Herimot, Reginbert and Purgolf wrote W.457, 609 and 645 respectively; Irminfrid, scribe of W.452, however, appears to have been a local subdeacon. (He also wrote W.425 and 461 at St Gall). Goldach: W.402, 444, 451 and 466. As well as the St Gall scribes Otine and Edilleoz (W.402, 466) was the local priest Lel (855–7), who wrote a rough caroline minuscule with cursive elements. Grabs: W.401 and 458, the scribes of which, Laveso *presbyter* and Cianus, were local. Cianus's hand (W.458, 858) was a very cursive minuscule with Rhaetian elements, and with no pretensions. Wetzikon: W.456, 531 and 596. Ratpert *monachus*: W.596 (876), was complemented by the local scribes Dancho, W.456 (850–8), who wrote *ad vicem* Adalbert scribe of W.531 (860). The surviving Dancho charter is unfortunately the St Gall copy, and the Adalbert one appears to be so as well.

[105] Salacho: W.669, 715, who wrote a large, rounded irregular hand, basically a caroline minuscule but with some cursive features, such as the shape of the 's' and the 'd'. Compare Sprandel, 'Kloster St Gallen; 122, and for Elolf, see below, n. 109.

[106] For Suzzo and Iltibrant, see above, p. 112. Herisau: W.589, 598, 750, 758, 759, (875–909), by the monks Purgolf, Benedict, Thioto, Notker and Udalrich. Buchhorn (Friedrichshafen): W.369, 557, 629, 649 and 652 (838–86), by the monks Thiothart, Liuthart, Trudpret, Emicho and Waltram. Winterthur: W.446, 513, 514, 631, 656 (856–86), by the monks Thiothart, Folchard, Pero and Ratbert. A local scribe, Wiartus, appears to have been active before then, judging from one charter, dated between 843 and 876 (W.388), written in a ragged Zurich type of caroline book hand with occasional cursive treatment of 'g'.

[107] See above, p. 103 and below p. 124, and compare, for example, W.655, 691, 770 and the charter of Luitfritus *presbyter*, a monastic scribe in 775 (W.73).

Some St Gall monks were particularly productive in this later period. B/Purgolf (874–82), for example, was present north of Lake Constance at Leiblach and Wasserburg, as well as in a number of key centres in the Thurgau. In 879 he travelled east to Urlau in the Vorarlberg. Ratbert's activity spread over a longer period, from 876 to 902, and his special area appears to have been the western Zurichgau, dealing with monastic business as far afield as Gurtweil, Singen, Winterthur, Wiesendangen and Wetzikon (Ratpoldeskiricha). Cozolt (885–90), perhaps, affords an instance of the extent to which a monk could act as substitute for a local scribe. Besides his charters at Kirchen and Theuringen, he also wrote a charter at the public *mallus* at Gurtweil.[108] Waltram (886–908) later *bibliothecarius* of St Gall, Sigibert (899–914) and Elolf (902–14) are further examples of the itinerant notarial service offered by St Gall.[109]

The significance of the distribution of scribes

The distribution of scribes over the period 700 to 920 thus shows the increasing preponderance of monastic scribes and a decreasing number of local scribes. The difficulty here is the fortunes of the monastery itself. The general picture is one of contraction and consolidation, rather than continuing expansion, and with an increasing web of local ties and connections in the immediate vicinity of the monastery. There was undoubtedly a decrease in gifts as the first ardour of generosity cooled. Families connected with the abbey may well have continued to act as patrons but it may be it was in the form of gifts in kind, and in personnel, rather than in landed endowment, now that the material base of the foundation was secure. Political changes must have had their effect.[110] It is possible too that the apparent dearth of local scribes in the later charters of St Gall is a function of the pattern of survival of charters from the region, as well as the decrease in land gifts made to St Gall. Scrutiny of the later mediaeval charters of St Gall and all their palaeographical indications would be needed to determine whether the pattern of local and monastic scribes observed in the eighth and ninth centuries is one that continues into the late tenth, eleventh and twelfth centuries. The extant early

---

[108] Cozolt: W.643, 654 and 677, wrote an unexceptional caroline book hand with standard ligatures. Compare Sprandel, 'Kloster St Gallen', 75.

[109] Waltram, see above, nn. 47, 48 and especially 49. Sigibert/Sigipret: W.717, 718, 719, 731, 732, 743, 746, 770, 775. All seem to be in his own neat caroline hand. Elolf: W.722, 725, 729, 736, 737, 742, 744, 747, 757, 762, 764. He appears to have written all these, but there is some variation in the format, especially the placing of the *Ego* clause and the appearance of the beehive. If not written by Elolf one would have to argue for the same scribe producing all the copies, which would be most unusual.

[110] Some indication of these is provided by Borgolte, 'Chronologische Studien', 190–200.

mediaeval evidence is an eloquent indication of the local communities who had scribes among them and who employed them to record their legal transactions. The subsequent histories of these local communities, and their levels of literacy, need to be pursued, for, as the influence of the monastery waned, so the older patterns and habits of life may have reasserted themselves, particularly in the areas other than the Thurgau and St Gall itself.

But it is also clear from the St Gall material that the provision of *cancellarii*, or, at least, scribes who could act as the recorders at legal assemblies and transactions, was one vital service the monastery could perform, and that St Gall did so increasingly in the course of the ninth century as its own administrative arrangements became more organized. Thus, the increasing occurrence of monastic or monastic-trained scribes points to a growing role on the part of the monastery as the promoter of the use of the written word, and maker and keeper of records. The monastery was able to draw at first on the expertise that existed already in the community in which it established itself, and then contribute to the formal procedures of the community on an increasingly pervasive scale. But it never exerted a monopoly. The monastery had a role in the conduct of public legal business. We now have the surviving remnant of that business in the documents concerning the monastery. But it would be contrary to the evidence to conclude that only in transactions concerning the monastery were written means employed. The church did not introduce methods; it adopted and extended existing methods. The relationship of monastery and community was complex and carefully nuanced. It made a decisive contribution to the uses of literacy within the community.

If the prominence of St Gall itself as a meeting place for legal business be seen within the context of a community running its affairs, some of which concern the monastery itself, then the charter material has revealed important information concerning the administration and functioning of the law in the early middle ages, the role of the monastery in this, and the extent of the resort to literate modes for it. What we have is the outward and visible manifestation of the collective activity of the village and rural communities concerned, to ensure the observance of the law, and the validity and legal standing of their decisions. This activity on the part of the local community included the religious house at its heart. The charters thus give some sense of the local organization and intimate social interaction between the secular and monastic groups in which these meetings and transactions took place. They bear witness, indeed, to a high degree of organization and cooperation between layman and cleric, and a crucial social service offered by the monastery in Frankish society. The implications for the levels of literacy within the community, moreover, are considerable.

The great variety of hands apparent in these charters, not to mention the different script types, provide an overwhelming indication of the number of people who could write in this region. The evidence for local *Gerichtsschreiber* or public judicial scribes and notaries also indicates a certain level of organization and training within the community, quite apart from the implications for the social status of the scribe. If one regards the scribes represented in the charters as the most competent and reliable products of small groups taught to write by the local priest, as Andreas taught his two pupils Vigilius and Valerius, or of the boys sent for basic instruction to the external school of the great monastery in their midst, then one has to recognize the degree to which these scribes are the top level of several in the use and practice of literacy. We have to add to this the widespread participation in literacy on the part of the donors and witnesses, many of whom in their turn act as witnesses and donors. The conclusion appears unavoidable that the population of Alemannia resorted as a matter of course to the written word as much for the conduct of their legal business as for their religion. Undoubtedly their habits were fostered and promoted by the monastery. It may even be the case that the monastery played an increasingly preponderant role. Nevertheless, the old view of the literate clergy and monks superior to an illiterate population cannot be sustained. We are, rather, dealing with a literate community, in which many degrees of literacy and its use are represented, and of which the monastery, and the local priests, formed a part.

IX CHARTER PRODUCTION ELSEWHERE IN THE FRANKISH KINGDOMS AND ITS IMPLICATIONS

The problem remains, of course, of how far the specific conclusions from the St Gall evidence concerning Alemannia and Rhaetia may be generalized for the rest of the Frankish kingdoms. While the particular role played by the monastery in the context of the legal business of the community may well be unique to St Gall, there are sufficient indications in private charters from elsewhere in the Frankish kingdoms that, first, the resort to literate modes for the conduct of business on the part of the lay population and, secondly, the contribution of both secular clergy and monks to this can be paralleled in a number of different regions. Only in rare instances, however, is information concerning the scribe of the charter afforded in the cartulary copies in which most early mediaeval charters survive. Charter evidence from elsewhere, reflecting the resort of members of small communities to the written word to record their generosity and devotion to God and his local representative saints, is an eloquent witness to the widespread participation in literacy on the part of those who acknowledged the Carolingians as their rulers. Only a brief survey of its potential can be attempted here.

Among the collections of charters from elsewhere in the Frankish kingdoms, that from Fulda has been the most exhaustively studied.[111] Many features of this evidence are analogous to those of St Gall. Indeed, the St Gall evidence helps to explain the more ambiguous information concerning scribes and their functions in the Maingau and Grapfeld area around Fulda from the mid-eighth century onwards, for in Fulda's case we lack not only the original documents and their precious palaeographical information, so crucial in the case of St Gall, but we also lack the names of the scribes. Only rarely were these retained by the later copyist. As far as the acceptance of, and recourse to, documentary methods to contract and record agreements are concerned, the Fulda evidence shows many local landowners and freemen involved as donors and witnesses. Here in Hesse as in Alemannia, there is widespread participation in literacy on the part of the Frankish population, spurred on to pious donations by the establishment of Fulda and other monasteries by the zealous English missionaries.[112] It is nevertheless clear that it was not the monasteries which introduced written methods to the population. These existed already. How else could the charters produced be Frankish in form and content from the beginning, despite the Anglo-Saxon character of the original foundation?[113] The way in which the monastery made its contribution to the process of charter redaction in the area, on the other hand, is indicated by the small selection of documents which provide details of the scribe. A number, for example, were drawn up by an *emanuensis* or *cancellarius*. Wolfram for example, was active from 752 to 774, and twenty-three of his charters survive.[114] Uuinibaldus, Abraham,

---

[111] Schmid, ed., *Klostergemeinschaft von Fulda*.

[112] E. E. Stengel, ed., *Urkundenbuch des Klosters Fulda* I.1 (Marburg, 1913) and I.2 (Marburg, 1956), up to 802. For the charters from 802 to 1342, see E. F. J. Dronke, *Codex Diplomaticus Fuldensis* (Aalen, 1962, reprint of 1850 edition). Hereafter cited as Stengel and Dronke.

[113] A clear comparison of Frankish and Anglo-Saxon charter practice can be found in Bruckner's introduction to *ChLA* IV.

[114] Wolfram (752–74), for example, Stengel 59: *Ego Uuolframnus [e]ma[nu]ensis rogatus scripsi et notavi diem et tempus quo supra.* His other charters are Stengel 18, 22–33, 37, 40, 41, 44, 55, 59, 61, 66 (Dronke 8–10, 11B, 12–14, 17–20, 23, 26, 27, 30, 31, 33, 35, 36, 39, 40, 42, 45). Those for which the place of redaction is recorded were written at Mainz. For a critique of Stengel's comments on the *cancellarii* and *emanuenses*, especially on public scribes at Mainz, see Staab, *Gesellschaft am Mittelrhein*, and compare the discussion of the *Gerichtsschreiber* problem above, pp. 118–20.

Widolaicus, Wigolt, Erhart, Einhart, Asaph, Hiltibald, Engilger and
Uuelimanus do not specify that they are members of any of the
ecclesiastical grades.[115] Reccheo on the other hand is *cancellarius* and
presbyter.[116] They may well be local scribes or even public notaries. Some
of these, such as Hiltibald, Asaph and Uuelimanus, are responsible for a
series of charters. This suggests that their function was a more or less
permanent one and that they were recognized as the scribes for the district
they were serving. In some cases, as with the scribes in the St Gall charters,
a career may be traced through the charters. Theotricus, for example,
wrote charters between 27 January 800 and 15 August 812. In 800 he
described himself as *notarius* and *emanuensis in dei nomine*. By 809 he had
taken orders and signed himself *presbyter* for the first time. Whether he had
entered the service of the archbishop of Mainz by then is not clear, but
three years later he wrote a charter on the orders of Richolf, archbishop
of Mainz.[117] Similarly, Theotmar was a *cancellarius* in 821, subdeacon two
years later and a deacon by 830.[118] Occasionally there appears to be a local
priest drawing up charters. Vodalrichus, for example, acted for Ratulf and
Machelm who were selling land in the Grapfeld to Fulda.[119] Notaries and
secretaries could be in orders, but not necessarily from the beginning of
their careers. That they subsequently attained ecclesiastical rank, however,
suggests some common training for both notaries and priests, and it may
be that in this respect either the monastery of Fulda or the cathedral *familia*
of Mainz itself provided this service, just as St Gall may have done.[120]

[115] Uuinibaldus (754–68): Stengel 48, 49, and Dronke 15, 16, both at Urmitz. Abraham
(785): Stengel 157, 158, and Dronke 71, 78, at Fulda. Widolaicus (781): Dronke 72, 73.
Wigolt (782): Dronke 76. Erhart (785): Stengel 163 and Dronke 82, at Paderborn; he
also appears to have acted as witness between 789 and 802 for a number of charters
drawn up in the Worms and Mainz regions. Einhart (788–91), probably to be identified
with Einhard, author of the *Vita Karoli*: Stengel 175, 189, 191, 234, 240, and Dronke
87, 102, 183, 184, 185 (at Fulda); Stengel 240 is a charter of donation by a couple called
Einhart and Engilfrit, possibly the scribe's parents. Asaph (778–801): Stengel 84, 187
(Strasburg) 254, 281 (Strasburg), and compare Dronke 98, 148, 171, 178, 179, 208,
225. Hiltibald (790–9): Stengel 185, 195, 196, 231, 245, 248–53, 255–7, 260, and
Dronke 143–7, 149–51, 154. Engilger (798): Stengel 258 and Dronke 152. Uuelimanus
(775–88): Stengel 71, 72, 76, 80–2, 87, 88, 160–2, 177, 179, and Dronke 52, 53, 55,
58, 59, 63, 64, 79–81, 90, 92. Abraham and Einhart at least were members of the Fulda
community, even if not as professed monks but as pupils in the school.

[116] Reccheo at Milz in 799 or 800; compare Stengel 264 and Dronke 213. See also Racholfus
(801): Stengel 275 and Dronke 165. Inguis (812–15): Dronke 264, 290, 309. Oltfrid
(804): Dronke 209. Reginprahtus (813): Dronke 279, 284.

[117] Theotricus (800–12): Stengel 263, 266, 267, 270, 283, 284, 285, and Dronke 156,
160, 161, 164, 174, 175, 176, 218, 222, 224, 244, 245 (*presbyter*), 270 (*Ego Theotricus
ex iussione domni Richolfi archiepiscopi scripsi*).

[118] Theotmar (821): Dronke 395, 407, 408, and compare Dronke 444, 445, 451, 453.

[119] 25 June, 793, Stengel 197 and Dronke 106.

[120] See the comments of Sandmann in her section on monks as charter writers in
'Wirkungsbereiche Fuldischer Mönche', pp. 704–14.

Yet the apparent ability of the Fulda monks themselves to act as *cancellarii* makes any clear understanding of the respective social context of the scribes, without the assistance of their handwriting, difficult to obtain. Ramvoltus, for example, wrote a charter *ex iussu Baugulfi* (abbot of Fulda)[121] and Hradulf, simply *cancellarius* in some of his charters, is *cancellarius Fuldensis* in others, though he does not describe himself as *clericus* until 814, added *scolasticus* in the same year and in 822 recorded himself as subdeacon. Not till 834 did he sign himself as *presbyter*.[122] But could he have been a 'public' notary who acted for Fulda? There seems little doubt, however, that Fulda monks served the secular world. While Ascrichus *ostiarius* and Liubharius and Asger wrote many charters for their monastery and remained within the community, Theotmar, scribe for many Fulda charters in the 850s, subsequently rose to become *archicapellanus* to the Frankish king.[123] Sandmann's invaluable study of the activities of Fulda monks, moreover, documents their work as charter writers, witnesses, messengers for the abbot and the monastery, on the king's service, as estate administrators and as priests. Most of the twelve priests in the famous Hatto charter of 845, for example, were already members of the Fulda community in 825/826 and had been monks for about twenty years. The distribution of places in the Fulda charters also suggests that, like the St Gall monks, the Fulda brethren travelled out to different centres themselves. Not until the 770s, however, do they appear as the scribes of charters. Further, the chronological distribution of the Fulda charter scribes suggests that one individual at a time was designated main scribe, with one or two assistants, and that this main scribe was accorded the title of *cancellarius*. This interpretation is arguable, yet the lesson from the St Gall evidence suggests that we are observing not merely an aspect of the internal organization of the monastery of Fulda, but also a clue to the recognition its services gained in the outside world.[124]

Other cartularies are more enlightening for their documentation, in the private, as distinct from royal, diplomas they contain of the ordinary lay

[121] Ramvoltus (800, 801): Stengel 268, 278, and Dronke 168.
[122] Hradulf (812–34): Dronke 273, 277, 291, 297, 298, 302–4, 377, 396, 400, 404, 411, 413, 414, 416, 418–20, 423–6, 430, 434, 454, 475, 487.
[123] Ascrichus (824): Dronke 433, 435–7, 439, 440–4, 452. Liubharius (835–7): Dronke 488, 490, 508, wrote *iussu domini* Hraban Maur, who was archbishop of Mainz (from 847 to 856) as well as abbot of Fulda. Liubharius could have been an episcopal rather than a monastic scribe. Asger (776–855): Dronke 54, 66, 70, 85, 88, 93, 94, 101, 103, 116, 117–19, 122–4, 126–30, 132–42, 219, 334, 360, 422, 428, 535, 563. Theotmar, see above, n. 118.
[124] Sandmann, 'Wirkungsbereiche Fuldischer Mönche', pp. 716–18. Sandmann's work is of fundamental importance. Further investigation must proceed from the basis she has provided to determine the roles of Fulda and Mainz as charter producers throughout the ninth century.

population's participation in literacy than for the knowledge they afford concerning scribes. Wendy Davies' work on the cartulary of Redon, however, has suggested that there were people scattered in the villages of ninth-century Brittany who could draw up a document when necessary, and that these skilled people might most commonly have been local priests. She notes that of the twenty-three individuals named as scribes in the Redon corpus of ninth-century charters, 'three seem to have been working for Redon, since they were either termed monks or produced records for a wide range of location in which Redon had interests'. The other scribes on the other hand are 'notable for their limited range', with some at major centres such as Angers and Nantes but others only in one of the *plebes*. As in eastern Alemannia, so in eastern Brittany, records were sometimes made at the local chief landowner's residence, and there appears to have been provision of secretarial services in the villages for the transfer of property rights.[125]

Further to the east, at Tours, only about ten originals survive among the hundred or so private charters recording transactions with the abbey of St Martin. It is thus rare to find a scribe's name recorded, but Gasnault has been able to distinguish a group of scribes active outside the abbey of St Martin.[126] A donation charter of 813 for Count Helingar, for example, was written by Hagroardus *emanuensis*, who may have been the count's own notary,[127] and Rainardus, scribe of a charter of 846 for Count Odo, may have been writing at a public court at Châteaudun.[128] A canon of St Martin's on the other hand stood in for Isarnus *cancellarius* at a public *mallus* presided over by the *vicecomes* Adraldus. Isarnus himself took notes at a *placitum* in 878, and we hear of another *cancellarius*, the *presbyter* Aurelian, at Blois.[129] For other transactions, it is St Martin's which provides the scribes, such as Audebert in 791, Wichardus in 841, Odalric in 887, Archanaldus who wrote seventeen charters for Tours between 892 and 920, Leodramnus in 937 and Walter in 940.[130] The descriptions provided by the St Martin scribes suggest that from the end of the ninth

---

[125] A. de Courson, ed., *Cartulaire de l'abbaye de Redon en Bretagne* (Paris, 1863); and W. Davies, 'People and places in dispute in ninth-century Brittany', in W. Davies and P. Fouracre, eds., *The Settlement of Disputes in Early Mediaeval Europe* (Cambridge, 1986), pp. 65–84, at pp. 68–70; see also W. Davies, *Small Worlds* (London, 1988), pp. 146–60.

[126] Pierre Gasnault, 'Les Actes privés de l'abbaye de Saint-Martin de Tours du VIIIᵉ au XIIᵉ siècle', *BEC* 112 (1954) 24–66.

[127] *Gallia Christiana* XIV, *Instrumenta*, col. 15.

[128] BN, Collection de Touraine-Anjou, I, fos. 67 and 68.

[129] Jacques Joseph Champollion-Figeac, *Documents historiques inédits* I (Paris, 1841), p. 457; E. Mabille, 'Les Invasions normandes dans le Loire et les pérégrinations du corps du Saint-Martin', *BEC* 30 (1869) 427; and E. Favre, *Eudes, comte de Paris et roi de France* (Paris, 1893), p. 243: *ad vicem Aureliani presbiteri ex pago Blesinse dominici cancellarii*.

[130] Gasnault, 'Actes privés', 27–9.

century the head scholar of St Martin's was also the *cancellarius*. Was he, like the Fulda *cancellarius*, an abbatial notary who could also serve the lay population in that capacity? Our information here is unfortunately too meagre to be sure.

Again, in the surviving records from Fleury, there is evidence of local and monastic scribes working in the area.[131] Among the private charters are a number of *notitiae* or reports of the local court. At Autun in 815, for example, Ermembert *clericus* wrote up the proceedings of the public *mallus* presided over by Count Theodoric of Autun. He acted again two years later at a *mallus* before the *vicecomes* Blitgar, and again in 818 for Blitgar, who this time is named as a *missus*, and Count Theodoric. All these records concerned the status of *servi*.[132] Godelarius was another scribe at Autun in 818.[133] He and Ermembert were probably public notaries to the extent that they were required to serve at the court in Autun when the *mallus* was convened. It is possible that Gautbertus *notarius*, who wrote the donation charter for Count Eccard of Mâcon in 876, was that famous individual's personal secretary.[134] He might, however, be better recognized as the successor to Ermembert and Godelarius, for he acted also for the sons of Count Theodoric of Autun in 885.[135] To these men may be added the scribes Laurentius *clericus* and Matebert.[136] A Laurentius *monachus*, however, is recorded as witness in a charter of 907. If it be the same man, he can either be seen as one who became a monk later in his career, or as an instance of a local secretarial service provided by the monastery of Fleury, especially in transactions concerning itself.[137] For the precarial grants drawn up at Autun in 908, the scribe was Bernard, but his status is not clear. Gunfred, who wrote the precarial charter in 924 at Perrecy-les-Forges called himself *notarius* in 932 and also acted at Cisa Villa in 936. He appears to have been the local scribe.[138] Amalbert *monachus*, on the other hand, wrote for his abbot in 940, Andreas *monachus* in 941 and Vulfadus in 942.[139] There seems every reason to suppose, in other words, that some scribal facilities at Autun and at Perrecy-les-Forges for the *mallus* and for legal transactions involving property, as well as the

[131] M. Prou and A. Vidier, eds., *Recueil des chartes de l'abbaye de Saint-Benoît-sur-Loire*, Documents publiés par la Société historique et archéologique du Gâtinais V (Paris, 2 vols, 1900–7).
[132] *Ibid.*, Nos. X, XI, XII, pp. 24–9.
[133] *Ibid.*, No. XIII, pp. 29–30.
[134] *Ibid.*, No. XXVII, pp. 74–8.
[135] *Ibid.*, No. XXX, pp. 83–5.
[136] *Ibid.*, Nos. XXXI (889), XXXIII (898), XXXII (895), pp. 85–92.
[137] *Ibid.*, No. XXXV, pp. 95–7.
[138] *Ibid.*, Nos. XXXVI (Bernard), XL, XLII, XLIII (Gunfred), pp. 97–9, 104–5, 107–10.
[139] *Ibid.*, Nos., XLVI, XLVII, XLIX, pp. 119–25.

provision of scribes by the monastery, were maintained throughout the ninth and tenth centuries.[140]

The evidence of private charters surviving from St Symphorien of Autun is too meagre to yield more than the name of Boso canon of St Symphorien acting as scribe in the tenth century.[141]

In the large corpus of charters from Echternach, there is, among the few indications of scribe provided, a similar hint of local, episcopal and monastic scribal provision. Huncio *presbyter*, scribe of the foundation charter, for example, was probably the scribe provided by Basinus bishop of Trier. Laurentius and Virgilius, scribes of others among the early charters were brethren at Echternach. Laurentius drew up charters for Echternach at Würzburg and Chelles. Ansbald, *monachus*, wrote his own donation charter at Walre in 712. Docta *presbyter*, scribe of a charter for Engelbert at Diessen in 712, is possibly a local priest. For the most part, the twelfth-century compiler of the *Liber aureus Epternacensis* omitted the details of scribe and witnesses from the charters he copied into his cartulary. While we have an abundance of records documenting the piety of the laity who gave of their wealth to the monastery, it is rare that we have information concerning the exact means and personnel they employed. The earlier charters, of the first three decades of the monastery's existence, do often include a scribe's name. Occasionally an original charter is extant, such as the gift made by Godoin and his son Helmerich, on 20 July 762 at Echternach, now Weimar, Urkunde No. 47. The script of the body of the charter is a rough, pre-caroline minuscule with many cursive features. The *subscriptio* of Helmerich, scribe as well as donor, suggests that he had had notarial training.[142]

The occasional references to scribes in the tiny group of Carolingian private charters from St Bertin/Sithui also testify to the lack of monopoly on the part of the monastery, though also to the contribution made by the monks to local charter writing activities.[143] Charters from the dioceses of

---

[140] On Fleury see the material assembled in A. Vidier, *L'Historiographie à Saint-Benoît-sur-Loire et les miracles de Saint Benoît* (Paris, 1965).

[141] A. Déléage, *Recueil des actes du prieuré de Saint-Symphorien d'Autun de 696 à 1300* (Autun, 1936). Compare this meagre material with the charters discussed by Jean Richard, 'La Mention du chancelier dans les actes privés du XIe siècle en Bourgogne', *BEC* 112 (1954) 67–80.

[142] Wampach, ed., *Geschichte*, Nos. 3 (and compare 10), 8, 17 (Laurence at Chelles), 16 (Vigilius), 20 (Docta), 21 (Ansbald), 47 (Helmerich: and see the facsimile in Wampach, ed., *Geschichte*, II).

[143] See Lemarignier, 'Les Actes du droit privé de Saint-Bertin', 35–72, and Guérard, ed., *Cartulaire de Saint-Bertin*, I. XVIII (704): Erchembodus *lector* is the scribe; he probably succeeded Erlefrid as abbot. Of Chrodberthus (I. XX (708)), on the other hand, we know nothing. Winidmar, scribe of I. XXIX (723), could have been an episcopal scribe. Other scribes such as Henricus *diaconus* (I. XLI (776)) could well have been called on by

Sens, Marseilles, Weissenburg, Freising, Salzburg, Passau, Regensburg and Lorsch, to select examples at random, are of comparable significance.[144]

It will be apparent from the sketchiness of the examples provided that there is nothing as substantial as the St Gall evidence from elsewhere in the Frankish kingdoms to convey anything like the richness of that prodigious body of charters. Compared with the hundreds of scribes, the rich variety of scripts and the host of private donors evidenced from eastern Alemannia, the handful of scribes and patrons, and only an occasional original private charter, from the rest of the Carolingian world is tantalizingly inconclusive. Yet, given the small scraps which correspond to patches in the rich St Gall fabric, the incidence of *cancellarii* and *notarii*, the existence of local scribes, whether priests or associated with particular counts, and the scribal services provided for the community by the monastery itself, it appears that there is a significant number of instances of the uses of literacy beyond

the vendors of the land in question. Guntbertus *sacerdos* (I. LII (807), and LIV (811)) was praised by Folcuin for his services as scribe and the books he provided for his monastery's library, so he is one scribe at least about whose monastic status there is no doubt, and there are many other monastic scribes recorded in Book II of Folcuin's compilation of St Bertin charters which witness to St Bertin's charter production in the ninth century.

[144] The charters of Weissenburg in particular are ripe for investigation within this context. See the edition by Anton Doll (from the *Nachlass* of Karl Glöckner), *Traditiones Wizenburgenses: die Urkunden des Klosters Weissenburg 661–864*, Arbeiten der Hessischen Historischen Kommission Darmstadt (Darmstadt, 1979), and see in particular the section on scribes, pp. 115–51, a model provision of the precise sort of information that is needed. Limits of space preclude discussion in detail of these collections of charters, but I hope others will undertake their analysis. The nature of the religious community, its connections with the surrounding population and its activities revealed in this type of evidence are separate questions which I shall address in the book I am preparing on the tenth-century church for Oxford University Press. See also the charters of Sens in Maximilien Quantin, *Cartulaire générale de l'Yonne. Recueil de documents authentiques pour servir à l'histoire de pays qui forment ce département* (Auxerre, 2 vols., 1854–60); Marseilles: Benjamin Guérard, ed., *Cartulaire de l'abbaye de Saint-Victor de Marseilles*, Collection des Cartulaires de France VIII (Paris, 1857); and for other French cartularies see Henri Stein, *Bibliographie générale des cartulaires français ou relatifs à l'histoire de France*, Manuels de bibliographie historique 4 (Paris, 1907). Freising: of the many donation charters of Freising about thirty refer to privately built or endowed churches, that is, they provide evidence of the Christian piety of the local population in the same way as the charters of Echternach, Fulda and St Gall. See Theodor Bitterauf, *Die Traditionen des Hochstifts Freising* I (744–926), Quellen und Erörterungen zur bayerischen Geschichte, NF 4 (Munich, 1905); and also Max Heuwieser, *Die Traditionen des Hochstifts Passau*, Quellen und Erörterungen zur bayerischen Geschichte, NF 6 (Munich, 1930); and Josef Widemann, *Die Traditionen des Hochstifts Regensburg und das Kloster St Emmeram*, Quellen und Erörterungen zur bayerischen Geschichte, NF 8 (Munich, 1942). On Salzburg, see Bernhard Bischoff, 'Salzburger Formelbücher und Briefe aus tassilonischer und karolingischer Zeit', in *Sitzungsberichte der Bayerischen Akademie der Wissenschaften, phil. hist. Klasse* (Munich, 1973). For the charters of Cluny (for comparative purposes), see Auguste Bernard, *Recueil des chartes de l'abbaye de Cluny*, Documents inédit sur l'histoire de France (Paris, 1876); and for those of Lorsch, see Karl Glöckner, *Codex Laureshamensis* (Darmstadt, 3 vols., 1929–36); and F. Knopp, ed., *Die Reichsabtei Lorsch. Festschrift zum Gedenken an ihre Stiftung 764* (Darmstadt, 2 vols., 1973–7).

the walls of a monastery, the bounds of the cathedral close or the royal chancery, from widely separate and scattered parts of the Carolingian world. The indications of the practical use of literacy and the advantages to be had from the deployment of the written word gained from the assumptions made and convictions voiced in the legal material discussed in the preceding chapter are enhanced and reinforced by the crucial charter material examined here. Despite widely diverse backgrounds and historical developments, the written word was woven into the structure and conduct of many local communities. The status and value of writing was taken for granted, on however small a scale or amateur a level. The Franks had indeed passed from memory to written record.

Yet the use of documents in legal transactions and judgements is only one, pragmatic, aspect of a society's reception and utilization of the written word. Further aspects are the role of the book, the impact of the written word of Christian revelation and the degree to which anything more than a basic level of pragmatic literacy was attained by the Franks. Let us start with the role of the book in its economic and social context, and consider the book first of all as a symbol of wealth.

4 ❧ *The production and possession of books: an economic dimension*

I VALUES AND PRICES FOR BOOKS

I have been afraid to send you Bede's *Collectanea* on the apostle taken from the works of Augustine, chiefly because the book is so large that it cannot be concealed on one's person nor very easily contained in a bag. And even if one or the other were possible, one would have to fear an attack of robbers who would certainly be attracted by the beauty of the book, and it would therefore probably be lost to both you and me.[1]

Lupus of Ferrières' opinion, expressed to Archbishop Hincmar of Rheims in 858, that one of his books would be attractive to thieves as an object of material value, as an object to be stolen and resold, is borne out by the number of books to which this did happen. The chronicle of the monastery of St Hubert in the Ardennes, for example, records that St Hubert lost a number of books, among them a psalter, written in letters of gold and decorated with pearls, that had been given to the monastery by the Emperor Louis the Pious. The thieves sold the psalter in Toul, where it was bought in good faith by a woman described as the 'mother of Bruno'.[2]

In one case at least the Vikings were book-thieves. Valenciennes 293, a ninth-century copy of Plato's *Timaeus* in the translation by Calcidius, has a note on the verso of the first folio recording that it had been bought from a pirate. As Hucbald of St Amand owned this book, according to the twelfth-century catalogue of the library of St Amand, he may well have made the purchase.[3] The Stockholm *Codex Aureus* (A 135) is another famous article of stolen goods ransomed from Vikings. On folio 11 of this manuscript, a note in Anglo-Saxon minuscule explains that the book was obtained from a heathen army by the ealdorman Aelfred for gold and given by him and his wife Werberg to Christ Church Canterbury. Emile Lesne has

---

[1] Léon Levillain ed., *Loup de Ferrières. Correspondance* (Paris, 1964), Ep. 108.
[2] *Chronicon Sancti Huberti*, MGH SS VIII, p. 579.
[3] BN lat. 1863, fo. 201, printed by L. Delisle, *Le Cabinet des manuscrits de la Bibliothèque Impériale* I (Paris, 1868), pp. 448–58, at p. 454.

135

suggested that books in which runes have been found, such as Douai 12 and the St Vaast Gospel Lectionary (Arras 1045) may have suffered a similar fate.[4] Whether one can extrapolate from these few instances, as Lesne does, and say that the Vikings made a practice of stealing books in order to sell them back to their owners for silver and gold, must remain in question; the evidence seems insufficient to generalize in this way.

Even outside the 'black market', books certainly could be bought and sold for substantial sums. According to Einhard, Charlemagne directed in his will that his books should be sold and the money, obviously expected to be a substantial amount, distributed to the poor.[5] In the tenth century, Gerbert of Rheims, later Pope Sylvester II, used large sums of money to pay copyists and acquire copies of authors in Germany, Rome and Lotharingia. He wrote, for example, to Ebrard, abbot of Tours, asking for books and promising money for the scribes.[6] In a letter to Abbot Romulf he mentions that he has sent the sum of 2 *solidi* for copying a text, possibly a work by Cicero, because Romulf had written to tell Gerbert that the cost 'would be a considerable amount, but the size of the volume we cannot guess. We will send more if you request until you shall say "it is enough" because the work has been completed.'[7] Centres lacking the resources to produce their own books, such as those to which the monastery of St Amand exported fine sacramentaries and gospel books,[8] presumably paid for the books they needed and acquired in kind or in coin.

The prices these books fetched is rarely known. The earliest Carolingian book price known to me is the sum of 8 *denarii* given between 835 and 842 by Regimbert, monk and scribe of Reichenau, for a volume containing the Lombard laws and an account of the passion of Servulus.[9] It is not known

---

[4] E. Lesne, *Histoire de la propriété ecclésiastique en France* IV *Les Livres, 'scriptoria' et bibliothèques* (Lille, 1938), pp. 480–1. On the Stockholm *Codex Aureus*, see J. J. G. Alexander, *A Survey of Manuscripts Illuminated in the British Isles* I *Insular Manuscripts 6th to 9th Century* (London, 1978), pp. 56–7 and Plate 152.

[5] O. Holder-Egger, ed., *Einhardi Vita Karoli, MGH SS i.u.s.* (Hanover, 1911), pp. 37–41.

[6] Gerbert, ed. F. Weigle, *Die Briefsammlung Gerberts von Reims, MGH Der Briefe der deutschen Kaiserzeit* II (Berlin, Zurich and Dublin, 1966), Ep. 44.

[7] *Ibid.*, Ep. 116.

[8] See A. Boutemy, 'Le Scriptorium et la bibliothèque de Saint-Amand d'après les manuscrits et les anciens catalogues', *Scriptorium* 1 (1946) 6–16; but the manuscript evidence does not accord with Boutemy's theory, namely, that St Amand's book production is only evident after their return from St Germain-des-Prés in 884, as it was then they had to rebuild the library after Viking depredations. A. d'Haenens, *Les Invasions normandes en Belgique au IXe siècle* (Louvain, 1967), pp. 134–6, notes some of the manuscripts and charters taken with them by the brethren when they fled from the Vikings, and subsequently restored to the monastery: see McKitterick, *Frankish Kingdoms*, pp. 207–9, and Jean Deshusses, 'Chronologie des grands sacramentaires de Saint-Amand', *RB* 87 (1977) 230–7.

[9] Lehmann, *Mittelalterliche Bibliothekskataloge*, p. 260, lines 19–20: *In XIX libello habetur lex Longobardorum et passio servuli, quem emi VIII denariis.* Compare the price of the *Leges Visigothorum* under Recceswinth and Erwig (649–72 and 687–702), *Leges Visigothorum*

to whom this book belonged before it came into Reichenau's possession. Its curious pairing of texts suggests it was someone who had Italian connections. Some idea of what the price of this book meant in relation to the cost of living can be gained by comparing it with the price of bread recorded at the Synod of Frankfurt in 794.[19] There, 1 *denarius* could purchase a dozen two-pound wheaten loaves. The cost of the Reichenau law book, therefore, would have been the equivalent of ninety-six two-pound loaves of bread.

A law book with a saint's life included would undoubtedly have cost less than the Golden Psalter bought at Toul by the mother of Bruno, but we have unfortunately only an inductive notion of the relative cost of books rather than secure knowledge. Some help may be sought from late antique sources. There is no reason to suppose that the *relative* cost of books and the services of scribes mentioned in Diocletian's price edict, for example, had become substantially less by the ninth century. In 302, a parchment maker would be paid 40 *denarii* for a quaternion, measuring a foot, of white or yellow parchment; for 100 lines of the 'best writing' a scribe could earn 25 *denarii*, the price being reduced for 'writing of the second quality', and a notary would be paid 10 *denarii* for writing 100 lines of a petition or legal document.[11] Other hints at the costliness of books are in the prices for pens and ink: one pound of ink was priced at 12 *denarii*, ten Paphian or Alexandrian reeds made from a single joint (that is, reed pens) at four *denarii* and twenty reed pens of second quality also at 4 *denarii*.[12] A leather container for five reed pens cost 40 *denarii*.[13] It is difficult to translate such prices into estimates of the price of books in the early fourth century, but Marichal has suggested that the *Aeneid* in writing of the 'first quality' (that is, capitals) would have cost 3,400 *denarii* and a copy in writing of the 'second quality' (that is, a cursive script?) would have cost 2,600 *denarii*). This is a calculation based on the number of lines and estimated number of quaternions. To buy a copy of the *Aeneid* according to the Diocletianic scale of prices, a teacher would have to have taken fifty-two students for a month, or a farmer would have had to sell 184 pounds of pork or 160 litres of wine.[14]

V.4, 22., ed. K. Zeumer, *MGH Leges Germ.* I *Leges Visigothorum* (Hanover, 1902), p. 226. The price was doubled, from 6 *solidi* to 12, under Erwig. The Reichenau catalogue, Lehmann, *Mittelalterliche Bibliothekskataloge*, p. 256, also refers to the sale of books by Kernentit and Ericho, but no prices are given.   [10] *MGH Cap.* I, No. 28, c. 4, p. 74.

[11] E. R. Graser, ed. and trans., 'The Edict of Diocletian on maximum prices', in Tenney Frank, ed., *An Economic Survey of Ancient Rome* V (Baltimore, 1940), pp. 305–421, at pp. 342–3 (section VII, 38, 39, 40, 41).

[12] *Ibid.*, section XVIII, 11a, 12 and 13, p. 369.   [13] *Ibid.*, section X, 17, p. 354.

[14] R. Marichal, 'L'Ecriture latine et la civilisation occidentale du Ier au XVIe siècle', in M. Cohen and J. Sainte Fare Garnot, *L'Ecriture et la psychologie des peuples*, XXIIe–*Semaine de Synthèse – Centre internationale de Synthèse* (Paris, 1963), pp. 199–247, at p. 215.

One may perhaps infer, especially with the little known about the more strictly comparable ninth-century Byzantine and the Jewish Cairo Genizah community's book prices in relation to annual income, where a book could cost as much as two-thirds of the annual income of an official of middling status, that a book in the Carolingian period could cost the purchaser a very high proportion of an income. The grander and more richly decorated the book the higher the cost.[15]

In the absence of markets in the modern economic sense, it must be acknowledged that the prices of books when recorded, or guessed at from the likely cost or relative scarcity of the materials that made them, are not market prices but contained major social and symbolic elements which we can only begin to understand in the total perspective of the role of the book and of writing in Carolingian culture. Did the combining of a saint's life with a law code in the Reichenau volume enhance or detract from its value? This volume could be held to express, on the other hand, the essential tension and interdependence of the secular and the spiritual in the Carolingian world, and the many levels on which such concepts as value need to be understood. In the role of the written word in gift giving and exchange, legal transactions, formulation of the law, enhancement and expression of social status and material wealth, it may be possible to surmise the ways in which the Franks determined social value. Some of these concerns will be examined in this chapter.

II THE COST OF PRODUCTION

Membranes

The high price of books was, of course, directly related to the cost of their production. The necessary quantities of parchment, quill or reed pens and ink were relatively easily obtainable, in that the sheep, cow, goat, rabbit or squirrel skins for the parchment, the common reed (*phragmites communis*) and goose quills for the pens, and gall nuts, organic salts of iron and lampblack for the ink were in abundant supply in western Europe. Unfortunately there is very little precise information concerning the techniques of book production in the Carolingian period, other than that which can be derived from the books themselves. Only rarely, for instance,

---

[15] On Byzantium, see L. D. Reynolds and N. G. Wilson, *Scribes and Scholars. A Guide to the Transmission of Greek and Latin Literature* (Oxford, 1974), p. 56; N. G. Wilson, 'Books and readers in Byzantium', in *Byzantine Books and Bookmen*, A Dumbarton Oaks Colloquium (Washington DC, 1975), pp. 1–15, at p. 3; and C. Mango, 'The availability of books in the Byzantine Empire 750–850', in *ibid.*, pp. 29–45, at p. 39. For the Cairo Genizah community see the references cited below, n. 93.

as in the statutes of Abbot Adalhard of Corbie (822), is there a reference to a parchment maker.[16] Corbie apparently only had one parchment maker at this time, and he was a layman. Skins, if they are to be any use for parchment making, must be fresh and put to soak soon after the animals have been killed; it may be that one man in a monastery the size of Corbie was in fact sufficient to supervise the treatment of the skins of newly killed animals. Corbie's own livestock included cattle, sheep, goats and pigs, so that there was the potential for a regular supply of skins. Whether skins for parchment making would only have been available at particular killing seasons is not known, but it seems most likely. The season of the year in which the animals are slaughtered determines the fat content, and thus the quality, of the skins. The possibility cannot be excluded, moreover, that some centres imported their parchment from a supplier who was able to work in close proximity to an abattoir, rather than preparing their own skins. The parchment supply at even the major writing centres may not necessarily have been constant or sufficient to cope with the demands of commissions from elsewhere. When Humbert, bishop of Würzburg (833–42), for example, commissioned copies of Hraban Maur's commentaries from Fulda, he sent a large supply of parchment for the work.[17]

The quantity of parchment required for one volume varied greatly according to the format and length of the book. A small law book or collection of saints' lives, a collection of treatises by Augustine or a grand, complete Bible would require very different numbers of skins. Calculating the numbers of skins necessary for a book is fraught with uncertainties. There is no secure knowledge of the size of cow or sheep skins in the period before the selective breeding of livestock. Reed has calculated that a two-month-old lamb skin in modern times would measure 300 mm. × 600 mm., that of a goat – in his opinion the most common source of parchment before the tenth century – would provide pieces approximately 900 mm. × 900 mm., and that of a sheep – best slaughtered when the animal was eight to twelve months old – would have been 'somewhat' smaller.[18] As far as smaller books are concerned, it is impossible to estimate how many leaves or bifolia could be made from offcuts of the sheets for larger books. In estimating the number of calf skins (presumably used because larger than sheep skins) which supplied the vellum for the *Codex Amiatinus*, Bruce-Mitford calculated that an entire calf skin was used for

---

[16] J. Semmler, ed., *Consuetudines Corbeienses*, in *Corpus Consuetudinum Monasticarum* I (Siegburg, 1963), pp. 364–418, at p. 367.

[17] *MGH Epp.* V, Ep. 26, p. 440, lines 15–20, and compare the answers he received, *ibid.*, Ep. 27, pp. 441–2.

[18] R. Reed, *Ancient Skins, Parchments and Leathers* (London and New York, 1972).

each bifolium of 505 mm. × 780 mm. and thus that 515 skins were used for the entire volume.[19] The *Codex Amiatinus* is a pandect of a very large format, similar to that of the great Tours Bibles. Some idea of the number of skins required for smaller books can be gained if we take the *Codex Amiatinus* measurements for one skin of approximately 500 mm. × 750 mm. and calculate how many smaller bifolia could be cut from a skin of this size. The result can only be very approximate and to some degree speculative, but will provide, nevertheless, some indication of the relationship between the number of folios in a book and the number of calf or sheep or goat skins used to make them.

A random selection of library books written in the St Amand scriptorium in the ninth century yields the following estimates (these estimates can be altered according to the size of skin thought to be available; they thus give only a very approximate notion of the quantity of pelts used).[20]

Valenciennes 72, Jerome's commentary on St Matthew, 119 fos., 141 mm. × 116 mm. – 5 skins

Valenciennes 76, commentary *De musica* attributed to Bede, 139 fos., 286 mm. × 195 mm. – 35 skins

Valenciennes 162, Augustine, *De anima*, 88 fos., 182 mm. × 130 mm. – 6 skins

Valenciennes 173, Isidore of Seville, *Synonyma*, 154 fos., 223 mm. × 165 mm. – 20 skins

Valenciennes 293, Plato, *Timaeus*, 154 fos., 258 mm. × 218 mm. – 16 skins

Valenciennes 404, Virgil, *Opera*, 232 fos., 315 mm. × 257 mm. – 58 skins

Valenciennes 406, treatises on logic and rhetoric, 149 fos., 218 mm. × 148 mm. – 19 skins (with a lot of waste)

Valenciennes 415, poetry of Milo and Hucbald of St Amand, 66 fos., 186 mm. × 149 mm. – 4 skins

The requirements of the three great Tours Bibles on the other hand – the Moutier-Grandval Bible (BL Add. 10546, 449 fos., 510 mm. × 375 mm.), the Bamberg Bible (Bamberg A.I.5, 423 fos., 477 mm. × 362 mm.) and the Vivian Bible (BN lat. 1, 423 fos., 500 mm. × 380 mm.) – at one skin per bifolium would have been a total of 648 skins. These measurements do not, naturally, take possible binders' trimming into account. Nevertheless,

[19] R. L. S. Bruce-Mitford, *The Art of the Codex Amiatinus* (Jarrow, 1967), p. 2.

[20] It should be noted that the measurements given are the conventional ones for the page area of the codex. The width of the bifolium would be twice the second measurement given in each case, or more if the edges were trimmed by a binder.

when one recalls that the extant ninth-century manuscripts from Tours alone number, according to Rand's survey, some 170 codices, and that this in all probability represents but a small proportion of that monastery's output during the Carolingian period, some inkling of the sheer volume of material used in book production can be gained, and thus a rather different perspective on the economy of an ecclesiastical estate which could boast a scriptorium.[21] The books, moreover, are an eloquent witness to the degree of organization, skill, speed of working and concentrated physical effort deployed in the preparation, stretching and drying of the wet, unhaired and limed animal pelts. They argue for the manufacture of parchment and writing materials on a large scale, possibly in particular centres. It can be surmised that the greatest centres of learning, the most productive scriptoria and the possessors of large libraries also had extensive landed estates and much livestock.[22]

What we know of the extent and richness of the estates, endowments, privileges and degree of royal or noble patronage of some of the main scriptoria in the Carolingian period fully corroborates the suggestion that there is a relationship between the material wealth of a centre and its book production. In other words, the size of a centre's library and the number of books it produced in its own scriptorium may be a reflection not only of its learning but also of its wealth and the degree of patronage it enjoyed. Some of the wealthiest abbeys, such as St Amand and Tours, also produced books for export to or on commission from other centres as well as for their own use; book production was an integral part of their economy. It was also a fundamental part of the Carolingian economy. This economic dimension to literacy should never be ignored.

Pigments

If parchment, pen and ink were more readily available, in relative terms, the same may not be said of the different pigments and gold and silver (or tin) dust for illuminating books. The Merovingians had made many important contributions to the conventions of book decoration,

---

[21] E. K. Rand, *A Survey of the Manuscripts of Tours* (Cambridge, Mass., 1929).

[22] As J. L. Nelson has expressed it: 'No scriptoria without sheep and cows!', in 'Charles the Bald and the church in town and countryside', *Studies in Church History* 16 (1979) 103–118, at 105. Parchment in western Europe would not seem to have been in such short supply as in Byzantium: see Wilson, in *Byzantine Books and Bookmen*, pp. 1–2. On the estates of St Amand, for example, see H. Platelle, *Le Temporel de l'abbaye de Saint-Amand* (Paris, 1962), and 'Le Premier cartulaire de l'abbaye de Saint-Amand', *MA*, 4th series, 11 (1956) 301–29. On Corbie, see L. Levillain, 'Les Statuts d'Adalhard', *MA*, 2nd series, 4 (1900) 333–86; and A. Verhulst and J. Semmler, 'Les Statuts d'Adalhard de Corbie', *MA*, 4th series, 17 (1962) 90–123 and 233–69.

particularly in the emphasis on ornament and in the distinctions between types of script.[23] Yet they were but a necessary preliminary to the glories of Carolingian book art. Carolingian scribes and artists drew not only on the three centuries of book production under the Merovingians, but also on the newly arrived insular ideas and conventions, and on revived techniques and iconography from the fourth, fifth and sixth centuries. The result is a rich corpus of books, many of them sumptuously decorated with narrative or allegorical pictures, ranging in date from the late eighth to the late ninth centuries. Among the producers of these, a number of leading schools of book painting have been identified. There are, for example, the groups of gospel books associated with the court of Charlemagne – the Ada school and the Coronation Gospels or Palace school – which produced such manuscripts as the Ada, Soissons, Godescalc, Lorsch, Harley, Aachen, Coronation and Xanten Gospels, or the books from the great schools of book painting of the reigns of Louis the Pious and Charles the Bald, such as Rheims, Tours, Metz, the Palace school of Charles the Bald and the Franco-Saxon school.[24] Many of these books were written on purple-dyed parchment and lavishly embellished with gold ornament as well as being written in gold and richly painted.

While most of the raw materials for these pigments were likely to have been procurable in western Europe itself, so that it is unnecessary to posit long-distance trade, the laboriousness of extracting the colour and the expense involved meant that use of colour in books is a vital indicator of the wealth of a donor or producer. Purple dye, for example, was phenomenally expensive. Diocletian's price edict gives some indication of how the addition of purple dye could raise the price of silk: 1 pound of white silk was priced at 12,000 *denarii*, but raw silk dyed purple was 150,000 *denarii* per pound.[25] It was procured drop by precious drop from shellfish, most commonly the shellfish *murex*, though many other molluscs yield porphyry dye. Bede described the 'great abundance of whelks, from which a scarlet-coloured dye is made, a most beautiful red which fades neither through the heat of the sun nor exposure to rain; indeed the older

---

[23] H. Zimmermann, *Vorkarolingische Miniaturen* (Berlin, 4 vols., 1916–18); C. Nordenfalk, 'The beginning of book decoration', in *Essays in Honor of George Swarzenski* (Berlin and Chicago, 1951), pp. 9–20; and *idem, Die Spätantiken Zierbuchstaben* (Stockholm, 1970).

[24] These manuscripts and Charles the Bald's role as patron are discussed in R. McKitterick, 'Charles the Bald (823–877) and his library: the patronage of learning', *EHR* 95 (1980) 28–47. The best survey of Carolingian book painting is by W. Koehler, *Die karolingischen Miniaturen* I-IV (Berlin, 1930–), a series being continued by F. Mütherich. A selection of illustrations of Carolingian manuscript paintings is to be found in F. Mütherich and J. Gaehde, *Carolingian Painting* (London, 1977), and J. Hubert, J. Porcher and W. Volbach, *Carolingian Art* (London, 1970).

[25] Diocletian, edict on maximum prices XXIII.1, in Frank, ed., *Economic Survey*, p. 382.

it is the more beautiful it becomes'.[26] These whelks were to be found in the seas round Britain to which the Carolingians also had access. Bede's implication, however, is that the colour was used for dyeing cloth, rather than that the pigment was used for paint. Roosen-Runge, in his study of the pigments of the Lindisfarne Gospels, indeed, has demonstrated that the source of the purple dye and pigment used in early mediaeval manuscripts, such as the Royal Bible (BL Royal I.E.VI) and the Ada school manuscripts associated with Charlemagne, was the kermes beetle or *Kermococcus vermilio*, found on the kermes oak in southern Europe, whose dried eggs yield an extract. Mixed with alum, this produces the colour carmine, in shades from reddish violet to purple. With the reagent acetic acid *kermes* also provides various shades of orange and brown *vermiculum*. Alternatively, a range of purple hues, from reddish purple through deep plum to mauve can be derived from *folium*, a pigment prepared from the juice of the fruits and flowers of the *tournesol* or *morella* plant. It is a reddish liquid whose colour alters according to the pH, that is the acidity or alkalinity of the reagents added, whether wood ash, stale urine or quick-lime. According to Theophilus, a twelfth-century writer on artists' materials, these would yield red, purple and blue respectively, that is, *folium rubeum*, *folium purpureum* and *folium saphireum*. Pink could be made from *folium purpureum* added to white lead. The opaque flesh colour was made with *kermes* plus white lead.[27]

Use of purple, whether from *kermes* or *folium*, especially for the colouring of whole pages in a book, was symbolic of great wealth, high social status and prestige. Investigation of the provenance of manuscripts using purple-dyed or painted parchment might well uncover royal associations for many of them, for it is possible that ownership of purple books was a royal prerogative. Christopher de Hamel has reminded us recently of the use of purple parchment, written in gold, in books in antiquity, and that it was a practice that may have survived to the Carolingian period through its continued use in Constantinople. He suggested, moreover, that manuscripts written in gold on purple had a promotional value in symbolizing imperial culture.[28] The sumptuously ornate copies of the Christian gospels

---

[26] Bede, *Historia Ecclesiastica*, I.1: *Sunt et cocleae satis abundates quibus tinctura coccinei coloris conficitur, cuius rubor pulcherrimus nullo umquam solis ardore, nulla valet pluuiarum iniuria pallescere sed quo vetustior eo solet esse venustior.* B. Colgrave and R. A. B. Mynors, eds., *Bede's Ecclesiastical History of the English People* (Oxford, 1969), p. 14. H. Roosen-Runge, in T. D. Kendrick, T. Julian Brown, R. L. S. Bruce-Mitford *et al.*, *Evangeliorum quattuor codex Lindisfarnensis* (Olten and Lausanne, 1956 and 1960).

[27] Kurt Wehlte, *The Materials and Techniques of Painting*, trans. Ursula Dix (New York, 1975), p. 111, notes that this carmine is not to be confused with the red derived from the female cochineal insects, *Coccus cacti*, which replaced *kermes* in the course of the sixteenth century.   [28] C. de Hamel, *A History of Manuscript Illumination* (Oxford, 1986), p. 46.

in royal possession written in gold on purple parchment can be seen as further expressions of the relationship between the ruler and the faith he protected and promoted, a reflection of his majesty and, in a sense, part of his regalia. The written word thus becomes a symbol of royal authority and responsibility.

Apart from purple, some of the colours used in book painting in the middle ages were rarer than others; not all the sources from which colours were extracted in the later middle ages, such as lapis-lazuli or ultramarine, were necessarily available in the early middle ages. The mineral lazurite, from which lapis-lazuli is refined, for example, is found mainly near Lake Baikal, in the USSR, and in Tibet, but also in Spain. Yet the pigment imported to western Europe in the thirteenth century via Persia and the Mediterranean may have been a purified blue already prepared from lapis-lazuli. Ultramarine, also made from lapis-lazuli, is first recorded in a recipe in 1271. Most colours, whatever the source, were laboriously extracted from the raw materials. It suggests that an artist, while mixing his own binding media – glair or size – with the pigments himself, must have been dependent on some source of supply.[29] In a well-organized workshop or one producing a large number of illuminated manuscripts, such as that of Tours, some part of the estate economy may have been geared to the provision of artists' pigments. The sources are unanimously silent on this; it is only from the richness and variety of the colours in the extant books that the essential economic foundation and organization necessary for the production of books may be deduced.

Elements such as carbon, gold, silver, tin, mercury and sulphur, minerals such as the natural deposits of mineral salts or oxides in iron and carbonates of copper and the coloured earths, and vegetable extracts such as saffron from the dried stigmas of *Crocus sativus*, are all natural sources of colours. In addition, there are the artificial manufactured salts which include all the organic lake pigments (that is, pigments produced by the double decomposition of salts in solution and which owe their colour to vegetable or insect dye-stuffs).[30] White lead, for example, was procured by

[29] Glair: egg white beaten until it is stiff and then left to settle into a watery liquid which can be mixed with any proportion of water and pigment and which flows smoothly from brush or pen. Size: the gelatine obtained from boiling scraps of parchment or cartilage tendons in water. Size or fish glue were particularly important as binding media for the grounds on which gold dust was laid.

[30] For all of what follows concerning binding media and pigments I am dependent on Daniel V. Thompson. *The Materials and Techniques of Medieval Painting* (London, 1936); Wehlte, *The Materials and Techniques of Painting*; Ernst Berger, *Quellen und Technik der Fresko-, Oel- und Tempera- Malerei des Mittelalters von der Byzantischen Zeit bis einschliesslich der Erfindung der Ölmalerei* (Munich, 1912), and Herman Kühn, Heinz Roosen-Runge, Rolf E. Straub and Manfred Koller, *Reclams Handbuch der Künstlerischen Techniken, Farbmittel*

an elaborate and dangerous process from the deposit formed on lead when it was exposed for some weeks to vinegar vapours combined with those of fermenting tan bark or dung. This white could be mixed with most colours apart from verdigris (green) and orpiment (yellow, a sulphide of arsenic) with which it was incompatible. Bone white made from calcined bones was used with these two substances. Reds are abundant in nature in red stone or clay. The best was haematite, a form of pure iron oxide. Minium (red or orange lead) was produced by roasting white lead in the open air. Alternative sources of red, such as cinnabar (a red sulphate of mercury for which the chief sources in the classical period were Spain and Mount Amiata in Italy) and vermilion (made by mixing and heating mercury and sulphur together and grinding the result), were much more expensive. Vermilion in particular is said to have been as expensive as gilding before the twelfth century. A further and cheaper supply of red was madder, a field plant which grew wild in Italy and was cultivated in the Frankish kingdom. The *Capitulare de Villis*, for example, notes that the stewards are to supply the women's workshops with woad, vermilion and madder.[31] Woad, a native European weed, was the commonest source of blue, though because it exhausts the ground it grows on it was a difficult and expensive procedure to supply it. Fine blues were rare and costly. The pure ultramarine blue from lapis-lazuli, the Persian blue mineral, and indigo, however, are not thought to have been much used in western Europe before the thirteenth century. More likely sources before that and, indeed, still cheaper thereafter, were azurite (there are deposits near Lyons and in Hungary) and 'turnsole' (that is, *Crozophora tinctoria*), a plant in abundance in the south of France. Greens were obtained from various vegetable substances (sap and iris), malachite, green earth such as celadonite (found near Verona) and glauconite (found in Czechoslovakia), and verdigris (an acetate of copper and vinegar). Sources of yellow included bile of tortoise, *massicot* or *giallorino* (a yellow oxide of lead produced from the roasting of orange lead which was often used to make lighter greens), orpiment (a sulphide of arsenic found in Asia Minor),[32] saffron yellow (from the *Crocus sativus*; other types of crocus could be used but they were not so good), some yellow ochres (from the Siena region),

Buchmalerei, Tafel- und Leinwandmalerei (Stuttgart, 1984). Detailed study of early mediaeval pigments and their sources and methods of preparation is to be undertaken by the newly established Forschungstelle für Technik mittelalterlicher Buchmalerei in Göttingen under the direction of Solange Michon and Robert Fuchs, and initiated by Heinz Roosen-Runge himself.

[31] *MGH Cap.* I, No. 32 c. 43, p. 87.
[32] Diocletian's edict on maximum prices (Greek text) XXXII.55 mentions orpiment (Frank, ed., *Economic Survey*, p. 419) but no price has survived.

buckthorn and weld berries, and, of course, gold. Gold writing used a prodigious quantity of gold because of the technique of making an ink with gold dust. A great many ounces of gold could be used for a book written in gold letters. It was also an immensely laborious process, and one requiring great skill, to grind the gold properly and then produce a usable liquid with which to write or paint.

A late eighth-century manuscript, Lucca 490, fos. 217r–231r, contains a number of recipes for artists' pigments including many of those mentioned above.[33] So too does the rather later treatise, *De diversis artibus* of Theophilus, dated variously between the tenth and twelfth centuries.[34] While some of the pigments used in Theophilus' time and later, about which we are relatively well informed, may not have been used in the book paintings of the ninth century, the costliness, laboriousness and the great skill and precision required in handling those colours that were available is quite clear. The technical mastery necessary before one was ready to draw or paint should not be underestimated. Nor should the implications of the occurrence of certain pigments for trading and commercial links far and wide between western and eastern Europe and even India and Africa, in which the Arabic countries must have played a key role, be ignored. The pigments and their raw materials used in the most richly decorated books were emphatically not just from local sources. There can be no doubt that the owner of a mediaeval manuscript would have some inkling at least of the costliness of the paints and the technical perfectionism expended upon the preparation of parchment, ink and pigments. While it may not have added in any obvious way to the aesthetic value of the object it did represent an important element in its intrinsic value. A reckoning of the quality of the pigments, parchment and workmanship would undoubtedly be included in the estimate of a book's material value. Books were treasures in a very real sense.

[33] Dated by E. A. Lowe, see *CLA* IV, 303c, and for a full description and references, see L. Schiaparelli, *Il codice 490 della Biblioteca Capitolare di Lucca e la scuola scrittoria lucchese* (*sec. viii–ix*), Studi e Testi 36 (Rome, 1924). The text has been edited by H. Hedfors, *Compositiones ad tingenda musiva* (Uppsala, 1932), and E. Berger, *Beiträge zur Ent- wicklungsgeschichte der Maltechnik* III (Munich, 1912). Compare M. Berthelot, *La Chimie au Moyen Age* I (Paris, 1893). Red lead, moreover, is called *siricum ex plumbu* in the Lucca manuscript, and Bishop Frothar of Toul asked for some red lead from Abbot Aglemar, along with some other pigments: *Unde peto ut nobis mittas ad decorandas parietes colores diversos qui ad manum habentur videlicet auri pigmentum, folium indicum, minium, lazur, atque prusinum et de vivo argento iuxta facultatem.* Cited by J. von Schlosser, *Schriftquellen zur Geschichte der Karolingischen Kunst* (Vienna, 1892), p. 310.

[34] C. R. Dodwell, ed. and trans., *Theophilus, De diversis artibus* (London, 1961), Book I.

Binding

A book's intrinsic value could be further augmented by its binding. As the protective but rich covering for a gospel book, for example, a binding of precious stones, metal or ivory was similar in function to a reliquary. Such rich embellishment of books was not, of course, an invention of the Carolingians. There are some shreds of evidence that the Merovingians bound some of their books in decorative rich covers: six of Knögel's compilation of 1078 references to works of art in pre-Carolingian sources refer to Frankish jewelled, gold or silver gospel book bindings.[35] But this is a meagre harvest compared with the abundance of Carolingian references to, and examples of, ornate book covers. In the Carolingian period, too, a binding could represent more than a material complement of the sacred text; personal wealth and status also found an outward symbol in the ornateness of the covers of books. Nor should the significance of bejewelled covers be forgotten; given the symbolic meaning attached to particular gems, the jewels on a book could act as a reflection of the splendour of heaven.[36] The life of a patron saint of a centre, doctrinal and theological works, personal prayer books or copies of secular law codes could be given rich bindings, though most of the surviving examples are attached to liturgical books.[37] Rich books could be provided with densely ornamented 'carpet' or decorated pages, simulating rare fabrics and enhancing the protection or 'cover' of the text just as relics could be wrapped in costly silks and placed in jewelled caskets.[38]

Flodoard tells us that Hincmar of Rheims commissioned a gospel book for the church of Rheims, written in gold and silver and with the binding decorated with gold and pearls. A sacramentary and lectionary executed for Hincmar were covered with silver and ivory and a book on the birth of the Virgin and the sermons of Jerome was bound, on Hincmar's orders, in gold and ivory.[39] One of the most famous of the surviving Carolingian ivory

---

[35] E. Knögel, 'Schriftquellen zur Kunstgeschichte der Merowingerzeit', *Bonner Jahrbücher* (1936) 1–258. Only 22 of her 1,078 items refer to manuscripts, and of these, 9 are from Frankish sources.

[36] On lapidaries see, for example, Peter Kitson, 'Lapidary traditions in Anglo-Saxon England: part I, the background; the Old English lapidary', *Anglo-Saxon England* 7 (1978) 9–60.

[37] Some of the 'treasure bindings' have been discussed by Paul Needham, *Twelve Centuries of Bookbinding 400–1600* (New York, 1979), especially pp. 21–9. See, too, A. Goldschmidt, *Die Elfenbeinskulpturen aus der Zeit der karolingischen und sächsischen Kaiserzeit VIII-XI Jahrhundert* (Berlin, 1914–20).

[38] A point made by Robert G. Calkins, *Illuminated Books of the Middle Ages* (London, 1983), p. 31, in a sensitive and stimulating study of the structure and rationale of 'programmes' of mediaeval book decoration.

[39] Flodoard, *Historia Remensis ecclesiae*, MGH SS XIII, p. 479.

book covers belonged to the Lorsch Gospels, produced at the court school of Charlemagne, one panel of which is in the Victoria and Albert Museum.[40] It is carved in the style of the late antique five-part imperial diptychs, with modelling of the draped clothes and of the faces in the late antique manner. In the top section of the panel is Christ in a roundel, and in the bottom section are scenes associated with the Nativity, the Nativity itself and the Annunciation to the Shepherds. The middle section depicts Mary with Jesus, flanked by John the Baptist and Zacharias. The Lorsch Gospel covers resemble other Carolingian gospel book covers in that they depict scenes described in the gospel story or else those which are symbolic of the message of the gospels. A late ninth-century ivory panel from Lotharingia, now in the Victoria and Albert Museum, for example, illustrates the adoration of the Magi and the presentation of Jesus in the temple. The Lindau Gospel covers, on the other hand, sculptured in gold and ornamented in precious stones, depict simply a large cross. These bindings are now separated from the books to which they once belonged, but in some cases, such as St Gall 53 or the Psalter of Charles the Bald (BN lat. 1152) or the Munich *Codex Aureus* (Clm 14000), the original covers in all their glory remain. Of other covers we know only from descriptions in contemporary sources, such as the *evangelium auro et gemmis optime paratum, et intus auro scriptum*, one of the books received by Odo, king of the Franks, from St Denis in 888 (possibly Clm 14000)[41], or the *evangelium argento paratum* received by Adalhard, son of Eberhard, count of Friuli, by his father's will.[42] Carolingian references to gospel books covered in gold or silver and written in letters of gold or silver are in fact relatively common.[43] Sometimes covers were provided to bind older books. Ermentrude, a noblewoman, re-covered in gold and pearls a gospel book used at St Père de Chartres.[44]

III BOOKS AS WEALTH

The value of books as loot and a source of rich ransoms and the great cost of their manufacture are obvious justifications for regarding books as luxury items of importance for their intrinsic value. Can it be argued from

[40] The iconography of the covers is discussed by W. Braunfels, *The Lorsch Gospels* (New York, 1967), and by M. Longhurst and C. R. Morey, 'The covers of the Lorsch Gospels', *Speculum* 3 (1928) 64–73.

[41] BN lat. 7230, fo. 117v, printed in P. E. Schramm and F. Mütherich, *Denkmale der deutschen Könige und Kaiser* (Munich, 1962), p. 95.

[42] I. de Coussemaker, ed., *Cartulaire de l'abbaye de Cysoing et de ses dépendances* (Lille, 1885), p. 3.

[43] See, for example, the library catalogues printed by G. Becker, *Catalogi bibliothecarum antiqui* (Bonn, 1885), and the treasure inventories in B. Bischoff, ed., *Mittelalterliche Schatzverzeichnisse* (Munich, 1967).

[44] F. de Mely and E. Bishop, *Bibliographie générale des inventaires imprimés* (Paris, 1892), p. 314.

this that the acquisition of wealth was uppermost in the mind of anyone acquiring a book; that the possession of books could be a reflection of status; that books had a function in gift giving as material objects; that books represented wealth in the same way as land, precious metals, coins, animals or slaves? Was the costliness of a book one reason why libraries came to be regarded as the proper appurtenance of kings? When did this begin to be so?

We have long been accustomed to the possession of books being one manifestation of wealth and status in the later middle ages. One need only recall the beauties of the libraries of Margaret of York and the dukes of Burgundy, with their commissioned masterpieces of Flemish illumination; the same circle provided the context for Caxton's early work as a printer.[45] Nor were the great libraries confined to the nobility; the library of Louis de Gruthuyse, burgher of Bruges, rivalled, in its magnificence, that of the Burgundian duke himself.[46] In late mediaeval France, the king, his brother and his nobles collected books.[47] Above all, there was the library of Charles V of France (1364–80), described for us by Christine de Pisan, which was designed not only to satisfy the personal tastes of the royal family, but also to facilitate the studies of the *savants*.[48] Charles V's library in fact epitomizes the dual role of the great late mediaeval libraries, for they were symbols of wealth, status and rank as well as the repositories of the intellectual and spiritual wealth of Europe. That this abundance of intellectual wealth was later sought out in the libraries of Europe can be illustrated from the well-known delight and gratification of Poggio Bracciolini at his discoveries of classical texts in the monasteries of Langres, Cluny, Fulda and St Gall. Of St Gall, for example, he writes:

There amid a tremendous quantity of books which it would take too long to describe we found Quintilian still safe and sound though filthy with mould and dust...beside Quintilian we found the first three books and half the fourth of C. Valerius Flaccus' Argonauticon and commentaries on eight of Cicero's orations by Q. Asconius Pedianus.[49]

[45] These collections are amply documented in the exhibition catalogues: *Marguerite d'York et son temps* (Brussels, 1967); *Le Siècle d'or de la miniature flamande. Le Mécenat de Philippe le Bon* (Brussels, 1959); and *La Librairie de Philippe le Bon* (Brussels, 1967). See also Lotte Hellinga, 'Caxton and the Bibliophiles', *Communications of the Eleventh International Congress of Bibliophiles* (Brussels, 1981), pp. 11–38; N. F. Blake, *Caxton and his World* (London, 1969), pp. 46–83; and George D. Painter, *William Caxton* (London, 1976), pp. 59–71.

[46] The only full-scale study is still J. B. B. van Praet, *Recherches sur Louis de Bruges, seigneur de la Gruthuyse* (Paris, 1831).

[47] Delisle, *Cabinet des manuscrits* pp. 6–71, recounts the history of the royal libraries of France.

[48] *Ibid.*, pp. 18–19, and see François Baron, *Les Fastes de Gothique. Le siècle de Charles V* (Paris, 1981), pp. 276–362.

[49] Phyllis Walter Goodhart Gordan, trans., *Two Renaissance Book Hunters. The Letters of Poggius Bracciolini to Nicolaus de Niccolis* (New York and London, 1974), Appendix: Letter III, pp. 195–6.

Historians of the later middle ages, and indeed of the early middle ages, take it for granted that books were valuable, that they were considered as treasure and that people also wanted books for their intellectual and religious import. But when did this first become the case in barbarian Europe after the transformations of the fifth century? How did it come about that the possession of books was prized for such a complex of reasons? What were the consequences for the role and function of books in the middle ages? As far as the books belonging to kings, written and decorated in gold, are concerned, de Hamel has proposed, very convincingly, a clear association between the gold of the books, stressed in the dedicatory verses to such manuscripts as the Godescalc Gospels and the Dagulf Psalter, and the importance of gold in an early Germanic culture as a mark of wealth and status and the ability to be a generous gift giver. 'In the most primitive sense, a Frankish prince distributed gold, and books were gold.'[50]

The status of books as wealth in every sense in the early middle ages has, however, to be demonstrated on rather more substantial evidence than the sale or theft of manuscripts I have detailed above. The bulk of the evidence for the evaluation of books in the early mediaeval period comes in fact from the Frankish kingdoms in the late eighth and the ninth centuries. I suggest that this is no accidental survival of evidence, but that it was in the Carolingian period that some of the most important and influential developments took place in people's attitudes to books and their treatment of them. In the value placed on books we can observe the material dimension of literacy as well as of learning.

The importance of the written word to the Christian faith and the emphasis the Carolingian Renaissance placed on the provision of books to serve the Christian faith has already been stressed. Whereas in the Merovingian sources, admittedly too meagre to support firm conclusions, it is almost exclusively gospel books and psalters, that is, the books containing the word of God, which are revered, Carolingian scholars appear to have elevated all books into a special category. Such scholars as Theodulf of Orleans and Alcuin thought that the content of a book and its spiritual value far exceeded its material value. So, too, the labour of the pen and of the mind which produced a book was worth far more than any other kind of labour. Alcuin, for example, concludes his poem on scribes with the comment 'it is better to write books than to dig vines / One fills

---

[50] De Hamel, *Manuscript Illumination*, p. 46. A recent essay on the reasons for the value human beings placed and place on precious metals, gems, ivory or pearls is Grahame Clark's *Symbols of Excellence* (Cambridge, 1986).

the belly but the other serves the soul'. Hraban Maur expressed the holiness of the scribes' task rather more eloquently:

> As God's kingly law rules in absolute majesty over the wide world
> it is an exceedingly holy task to copy the law of God.
> This activity is a pious one (*pius labor*) unequalled in merit
> by any other which men's hands can perform.
> For the fingers rejoice in writing, the eyes in seeing,
> and the mind at examining the meaning of God's mystical words.
> No work sees the light which hoary old age
> does not destroy or wicked time overturn:
> only letters are immortal and ward off death
> only letters in books bring the past to life.
> Indeed God's hand carved letters on the rock
> that pleased him when he gave his laws to the people,
> and these letters reveal everything in the world that is
> has been, or may chance to come in the future.[51]

In the dedicatory verses to one of his Bibles, Theodulf extolled the beauty of its cover, resplendent in gold, ivory and pearls, but stressed the greater splendour of the contents. The heavenly wisdom contained in books, said Alcuin in his poem *Ubi libri custodiantur*, is more precious than any treasure.[52]

The content of a book is assumed by Alcuin and Theodulf to be either the Bible text itself or writings which led one to an understanding of them. A reverence for the wisdom couched in writing could be extended to embrace many different categories of text and book. One of the most interesting extensions is the Carolingians' appreciation of particular books for their antiquity, or of a particular history and provenance known for a volume. This appreciation was more than mere connoisseurship: it was, first, a recognition of the spiritual, and possibly even material, enhancement of value a special association could lend a text, and, secondly,

[51] *MGH Poet.* I, p. 320, trans. Peter Godman, *Poetry of the Carolingian Renaissance* (London, 1985), No. 11, lines 13–14, p. 139. I am grateful to Peter Godman for allowing me to quote from his translation. Hraban, *ibid.*, No. 36, p. 249, from the text in *MGH Poet.* II, p. 186. This idea is the reverse of that propounded by the Desert Fathers. See, for example, the reproof offered by St Anthony to one of his brethren who had preferred to study rather than help with the manual labour in the vegetable garden. The greater claims of intellectual study and spiritual growth over the exertion of manual labour appear to be made more frequently from the Carolingian period onwards. Compare the arrangements Boniface made for Fulda (751), where the monks 'keep no servants but are content with the labour of their hands' (R. Rau, ed., *Bonifatii Epistulae Willibaldi vita Bonifatii* (Darmstadt, 1968), Ep. 86, p. 290) with Adalhard's statutes for Corbie in 822 (Semmler, ed., *Consuetudines Corbeienses*), which give a clear picture of a large body of servants employed by the monastery to do the heavy work as well as many of the lighter tasks (trans. L. W. Jones, in Walter Horn and Ernest Born, *The Plan of St Gall* III (Berkeley, 1979), pp. 101–23). [52] *MGH Poet.* I, pp. 539 and 332.

it was an awareness of the need for particular works and the necessity to search for them. But it also involved a growing understanding of how the history of the transmission of a text, and the age and provenance of a volume containing a text, might affect the text itself. It is this growing understanding that appears to be reflected in, for example, the efforts of both Alcuin and Theodulf of Orleans to revise the text of the Bible,[53] in the move to provide a correct text of the liturgy, so that it would not mislead people into incorrect practice,[54] or the energy Lupus of Ferrières invested in procuring second or third copies of texts for the purposes of collation.[55] This new way of thinking about books and texts on the part of the Carolingians is behind the many observations they made concerning the antiquity or associations of codices they owned. At Fulda, for example, the venerable *Codex Bonifatianus* 1, containing a sixth-century uncial text of the Old Testament with annotations probably by Boniface of Mainz, was apparently a valued possession of the monastery. *Codex Bonifatianus* 2, an eighth-century copy of Isidore of Seville's *Synonyma* in Luxeuil minuscule, was enhanced in value by the belief that it was the book with which Boniface had tried to defend himself from his Frisian murderers.[56] The earliest Würzburg library catalogue, discussed in the following chapter, lists at the head of the first column the item *Actus apostolorum*. Lowe identified this manuscript with Oxford Bodleian Library Laud gr. 35, a venerable sixth-century uncial codex, and suggested that it was listed first because it was regarded as the most important book in the Würzburg collection.[57] Other Carolingian libraries possessed a number of fifth-, sixth-

[53] On Alcuin's and Theodulf's revision of the Bible, see Bonifatius Fischer, 'Bibeltext und Bibelreform unter Karl dem Grossen', in W. Braunfels, ed., *Karl der Grosse. Lebenswerk und Nachleben* II *Das Geistige Leben* (Düsseldorf, 1965), pp. 156–217; idem, *Die Alkuin Bibel* (Freiburg, 1957); F. L. Ganshof, 'Alcuin's revision of the Bible', in F. L. Ganshof, *The Carolingians and the Frankish Monarchy*, trans. J. Sondheimer (London, 1971) pp. 28–40; and E. Dahlhaus-Berg, *Nova Antiquitas et antiqua Novitas. Typologische Exegese und isidorianisches Geschichtsbild bei Theodulf von Orléans* (Cologne and Vienna, 1975), pp. 39–76.

[54] For comments on liturgical revision the following may be found useful: McKitterick. *Frankish Church*, pp. 115–53, and D. Bullough 'Alcuin and the kingdom of heaven: liturgy, theology and the Carolingian age', in Uta-Renate Blumenthal, ed., *Carolingian Essays*, Andrew W. Mellon Lectures in Early Christian Studies (Washington, 1983), pp. 1–69.

[55] Lupus, ed. Levillain, *Loup de Ferrières. Correspondance*, Ep. 1. See also the suggestive remarks made by Donald Bullough in his 'Roman books and Carolingian Renovatio', *Studies in Church History* 14 (1977) 23–50.

[56] *CLA* VIII, 1196, and see M. B. Parkes, 'The handwriting of St Boniface: a reassessment of the problems', *Beiträge zur Geschichte der deutschen Sprache und Literatur* 98 (1976) 161–79; *CLA* VIII, 1197. *Codex Bonifatianus* 3 (*CLA* VIII, 1198) is also thought to have been owned by Boniface. It is a gospel book, the 'Cadmug Gospels', written in Irish minuscule of the eighth century.

[57] E. A. Lowe, 'An eighth-century list of books in a Bodleian manuscript from Würzburg and its probable relation to the Laudian Acts', *Speculum* 3 (1928) 3–15, reprinted in L. Bieler, ed., *Palaeographical Papers 1907–1965* (Oxford, 2 vols., 1972), I, pp. 239–50.

and seventh-century codices. Two fifth-century volumes, the Palatinus Virgil (Vat. pal. lat. 1631) and a fragment of Livy (Vienna 15) were at Lorsch.[58] The seventh-century Ashburnham Pentateuch (BN n.a. lat. 2334) was at Tours by the end of the eighth century if not before,[59] and the fifth-century Virgilius Romanus (Vat. lat. 3867) was at St Denis until the fifteenth century.[60] St Amand possessed a late seventh-century copy of the chronicle of Eusebius written at Luxeuil (Valenciennes 495).[61] Lyons provides what appears to be an instance of wholesale and zealous gathering of legal and theological texts dating from the sixth to the eighth centuries by those responsible for the library in the ninth century.[62] Many of these codices were written, if not at Lyons, then certainly in scriptoria in the region round Lyons in the Merovingian period, and contain in addition to their texts (predominantly legal and patristic writings) annotations ranging in date from the sixth to the ninth centuries. Lyons 604, for example, a copy of Augustine's *De Civitate Dei*, is written in sixth-century half uncial and is glossed in a contemporary cursive, as well as by the Carolingian controversialist of Lyons, Florus the Deacon.[63] The *Codex Bezae* (Cambridge University Library Nn.2.41), a fifth-century Greek and Latin Gospels and Acts of unknown origin, is among the manuscripts annotated by Florus – indeed, it is the most famous of these – and was therefore in Lyons by the ninth century. The annotations in these and many others of the 300 or so surviving manuscripts and fragments from the Merovingian period attest not only the esteem with which the texts they contained were regarded, but also the fact that they continued to be read.[64] They provide further testimony to the important survival in the Merovingian period of certain habits and attitudes of mind concerning books on which the Carolingians were to draw, and build.

The library catalogues of the eighth and ninth centuries reveal the compilers' recognition, in particular cases, of the antiquity of a book. The reference in the list of Abbot Wando's books (742–7) in the *Gesta abbatum Fontanellensium* to *id est codicem unum Romana littera scriptum in quo continetur expositio brevis trium evangelistarum, id est Iohannis, Mathaei et Lucae*, that is, a gospel book written in 'Roman letters', is presumably an indication that the manuscript was written in either capitals or uncials

[58] *CLA* I, 99; X, 1472. See Bischoff, *Lorsch*, pp. 118–21.

[59] *CLA* V, 693a.   [60] *CLA* I, 19.   [61] *CLA* VI, 841.

[62] The corpus of early Lyons codices was discussed by E. A. Lowe, *Codices Lugdunenses Antiquiores* (Lyons, 1924), but see my remarks in 'The scriptoria of Merovingian Gaul: a survey of the evidence', in H. Clarke and M. Brennan, eds., *Columbanus and Merovingian Monasticism* (Oxford, 1981), pp. 173–207, at pp. 177–84.

[63] C. Charlier, 'Les Manuscrits personnels de Florus de Lyon et son activité littéraire', *Mélanges E. Podechard* (Lyons, 1945), pp. 71–84.

[64] On these manuscripts, see R. McKitterick, 'The scriptoria of Merovingian Gaul'.

and possibly therefore before the mid-eighth century.[65] It can also be understood as the compiler's identification of the letter forms in the book as of a particular type, with particular textual and historical associations. The annotator of the St Gall catalogue was rather more forthcoming. Against the entry: *Eiusdem de deo liber I differentiarum eucherii et de questiunculis sancti augustini et de floratibus* in vol. I he wrote *vetustissimo*; a collection of the passions of *omnium apostolorum nec non et quorundam martyrium* was described as *antiquissimo* and a further collection of passions of the saints was noted as *antiquo*. In additions to the catalogue made by the annotator a *vitae patrum in volumen vetustissimo* and a *sermo de epiph. et alius cypriani et alia quaedam in libellulo valde vetusto* are recorded. Antiquity was not necessarily a guarantee of quality as far as this annotator was concerned: witness his pungent remarks on a number of works – he described a *liber prosperi promissionum et predictorum dei vol. I* as *vetus et falsatus*.[66]

Many copies of older manuscripts were made in the ninth century; the number of classical and late antique works, especially, which have survived in ninth-century copies (often the earliest extant copies) is well documented.[67] Quite apart from the more famous illustrated codices such as the Berne *Physiologus* (Berne 318) and the Paris Terence (BN lat. 7899), copied at Hautvillers near Rheims in the first half of the ninth century, there are such manuscripts as Oxford Bodleian Library Laud lat. 104, a superb volume of the letters of Sidonius Apollinaris, probably written at the court of Louis the Pious and the earliest extant copy of Sidonius' works.[68] Oxford Bodleian Library Class. lat. 279, containing the letters of Seneca, was copied from an exemplar which, judging from the omissions and disorders in the text, could have been 'little more than a bundle of rags'.[69] The Cicero codex copied in the Tours region, now BL Add. 47678, was made from a late antique exemplar.

[65] F. Lohier and J. Laporte, eds., *Gesta sanctorum patrum Fontanellensis coenobii* (Paris and Rouen, 1936), p. 66, and compare the entry for Gervold's books (787–806) which also included a gospel book written in Roman letters: *volumen quatuor evangeliorum Romana littera scriptum*, ibid., p. 90, that is, surely, written in uncial script.

[66] Lehmann, *Mittelalterliche Bibliothekskataloge*, p. 74. This is probably to be translated as 'an old and corrupt [text]' of the fifth-century writer. Prosper of Aquitaine's *Liber de praedictionibus et promissionibus Dei*, printed in *PL* 51, cols. 733–854. That is, it was a poor and unreliable copy.

[67] See L. Traube, *Vorlesungen und Abhandlungen* II (Munich, 1911), pp. 121–37; Reynolds and Wilson, *Scribes and Scholars*, pp. 70–108; and the two exhibition catalogues: R. W. Hunt, *The Survival of Ancient Literature* (Oxford, 1975), and Rome, Biblioteca Apostolica Vaticana, *Survie des classiques latins. Exposition de manuscrits Vaticans du IVe au XVe siècle* (Vatican, 1973). L. D. Reynolds, *Texts and Transmission. A Survey of Latin Classics* (Oxford, 1983).

[68] Hunt, *Survival*, p. 49.

[69] L. D. Reynolds, *The Medieval Tradition of Seneca's Letters* (Oxford, 1965), p. 25.

Both Hincmar of Rheims and Lupus of Ferrières, moreover, provide a personal insight into the necessity felt for rescue operations. In a letter to Orsmar, bishop of Tours, Lupus requests the loan of the commentaries of Boethius on the *Topica* of Cicero in the library of St Martin. The book was written on papyrus (*in chartacio codice*) and Lupus promised that he would 'take very good care of it and... return it at an opportune time'.[70] Hincmar tells us of the fate of the book containing the life, miracles and death of Remigius of Rheims, 'written in an antique hand' (*manu antiquaria scriptum*). It was increasingly neglected. Hincmar relates how in Charles Martel's time the few priests at Rheims made ends meet by trading in a small way, frequently wrapping up the money they took in pages torn from books. Thus the book of St Remigius, already rotted by damp and gnawed by mice, lost the greater part of its remaining pages. It was hard work for Hincmar to find a few of the dispersed pages here and there, but find a few he did and he used them to construct his new Life of Remigius.[71] Many precious theological, biblical, grammatical, legal, scientific and philosophical texts from the pre-Carolingian period must also have been salvaged in this way.[72]

IV GIFT GIVING AND EXCHANGE

As a treasure, the book played an important role in gift giving and exchange.[73] The gift of a book, as much as the gift of gold or jewels, enhanced the donor's status and when donated to a church or saint ensured the saint's favour. Kings, queens, noblemen and women, bishops, abbots, monks, priests and pilgrims made gifts of books to churches, monasteries and saints for the benefit of their immortal souls and to honour the saint. Lothar, sacristan of St Amand, ordered two volumes, now Laon 298 and 299, to be written for the patron saint of his monastery. In 832,

[70] Lupus, ed. Levillain, *Loup de Ferrières. Correspondance*, Ep. 53.
[71] MGH SS rer. merov. III, pp. 251–2.
[72] On Carolingian copying of older manuscripts, see also Traube, *Vorlesungen und Abhandlungen*, p. 132; idem, *Die Textgeschichte der Regula Sancti Benedicti*, 2nd edn (Munich, 1910), pp. 7 and 91; and Alexander Souter, 'The sources of Sedulius Scottus' Collectaneum on the Epistles of St Paul', *JTS* 18 (1917) 184.
[73] On gift exchange, see P. Grierson, 'Commerce in the dark ages: a critique of the evidence', *TRHS*, 5th series, 9 (1959) 123–40. The classic anthropological studies are those of E. E. Evans Pritchard, *The Azande: History and Political Institutions* (Oxford, 1971); N. A. Chagnon, *Yanomanö: The Fierce People* (New York, 1968); and Max Gluckman, *Politics, Law and Ritual in Tribal Society* (Oxford, 1965), pp. 47–50. See also Bryony Orme, *Anthropology for Archaeologists* (London, 1981), pp. 180–90. Christopher de Hamel expressed the role of the book in gift giving admirably, in de Hamel, *Manuscript Illumination*, p. 46: just as Charlemagne rewarded his soldiers with land and booty so his 'Cohorts' of monks 'were rewarded for spiritual service in the same way'. That is, with wealth in the form of books.

a pilgrim to St Sauveur of Redon deposited on the altar a mass book decorated with gold and silver.[74]

Most of these gifts were of liturgical books, but there are also many records of personal collections of books for a centre's library, and for use in the school, being donated by zealous bishops, abbots, monks and masters. Wando, abbot of St Wandrille, gave his books to that abbey.[75] Erlebald of Reichenau,[76] Manno of St Claude (Jura),[77] Agobard of Lyons,[78] Hucbald of St Amand,[79] Gerward of Lorsch,[80] Iskar, abbot of Murbach,[81] Hincmar of Rheims,[82] Dido, bishop of Laon, Bernard and Adalelm of Laon[83] and Grimalt and Hartmut of St Gall[84] were all donors to the libraries of their communities. The Reichenau catalogue of 823–38 also records a series of gifts of one or two books made by individual priests and monks.[85]

Books could also be commissioned or given to mark political occasions. The Lothar Gospels, for example (BN lat. 266), is thought to have marked the reconciliation of Charles the Bald with his brother Lothar at Péronne in 849 and was commissioned by Lothar.[86] On the occasion of his

---

[74] A. de Courson, ed., *Cartulaire de l'abbaye de Redon en Bretagne* (Paris, 1863), p. 128.

[75] Lohier and Laporte, eds., *Gesta Fontanellensis coenobii*, IX.2, pp. 66–8.

[76] Lehmann, *Mittelalterliche Bibliothekskataloge*, pp. 252–4.

[77] His manuscripts are discussed by L. Delisle, 'Notes sur trois manuscrits à date certaine', *BEC* 29 (1868) 217–19, and *idem*, 'La Bibliothèque de l'abbaye de Sainte-Claude de Jura: esquisse de son histoire', *BEC* 50 (1889) 31–54.

[78] See E. Boshof, *Erzbischof Agobard von Lyon: Leben und Werk* (Cologne, 1969), pp. 159–69; Lesne, *Les Livres*, 'scriptoria' et bibliothèques, p. 109; and S. Tafel, 'The Lyons scriptorium', *Palaeographia Latina* 4 (1925) 60–73, especially 52.

[79] Delisle, *Cabinet des manuscrits*, pp. 312–13.

[80] Bischoff, *Lorsch*, pp. 54–7, and *idem*, 'Die Hofbibliothek unter Ludwig dem Frommen', in *MS* III, p. 172 n. 19.

[81] K. E. Geith and W. Berschin, 'Die Bibliothekskataloge des Klosters Murbach aus dem IX[te] Jht', *Zeitschrift für Kirchengeschichte* (1972) 61–87, at 66–8.

[82] F. L. Carey, 'The scriptorium of Rheims during the archbishopric of Hincmar', in L. W. Jones, ed., *Classical and Medieval Studies in Honor of Edward Kenneth Rand* (New York, 1938), pp. 41–60. See, too, J. Devisse, *Hincmar, archevêque de Reims* (Geneva, 1976).

[83] J. J. Contreni, *The Cathedral School of Laon from 850 to 930. Its manuscripts and masters*, Münchener Beiträge zur Mediävistik und Renaissance Forschung 29 (Munich, 1978), pp. 30–40.

[84] Lehmann, *Mittelalterliche Bibliothekskataloge*, pp. 82–9, and B. Bischoff, 'Bücher am Hofe Ludwigs des Deutschen und die Privatbibliothek des Kanzlers Grimalt', *MS* III, pp. 187–212.

[85] Lehmann, *Mittelalterliche Bibliothekskataloge*, p. 256.

[86] See H. Kessler, *The Illumination of the Books of Tours* (Princeton, 1977), pp. 127–8, and D. Bullough, '*Imagines regum* and their significance in the early medieval west', in G. Robertson and G. Henderson, eds., *Studies in Memory of David Talbot Rice* (Edinburgh, 1977), pp. 223–76. The manuscript is not to be identified with the one Lothar gave to Prüm; on its possible provenance, see Schramm and Mütherich, *Denkmale*, p. 123. Compare the list of presents reputedly given in 926 by Hugh the Great to King Aethelstan of England to mark the occasion of Hugh's betrothal to Aethelstan's sister, in Schramm and Mütherich, *Denkmale*, p. 96.

coronation as king of Lotharingia in the cathedral church of Metz in 869, Charles presented the canons of Metz with his First Bible (BN lat. 1) and his Psalter (BN lat. 1152). Presents in gratitude and acknowledgement of patronage, or even in the hope of stimulating further patronage, could also be made in the form of books. Charles the Bald's First Bible had been presented to him by the brethren and abbot of the monastery of St Martin of Tours and his Second Bible (BN lat. 2) was given him by the monastery of St Amand in about 870. Both Tours and St Amand were patronized by the king.[87] Patronage itself could take the form of a gift of a book. New York Pierpont Morgan Library G57 was written at St Amand and presented by Queen Ermintrude to the convent of Chelles. (Here some return, as true gift *exchange*, such as the nuns' prayers for Ermintrude and her family, was probably expected.) The Emperor Lothar presented a richly bound and decorated copy of the gospels to the monastery of Prüm. The recently discovered St Hubert Gospels were probably a diplomatic gift ordered by Abbot Gauzlin from his own scriptorium of St Amand, to encourage Louis the Younger to render Gauzlin and his party assistance in the political disputes of 879–82.[88] Many of these manuscripts are still extant. Most are fine examples of book production and possess richly decorated bindings as well as illuminated pages and gold and silver lettering.

At the simplest level, these gifts represent wealth deployed in the service of religion – an investment in the hereafter. The ability to make such gifts is, furthermore, indicative on a material level of the wealth of the donor.

V THE POSSESSION OF BOOKS

Not only the giving but also the possession of books was an indication of wealth and status. That this status involved a degree of intellectual attainment bears out the 'prophecy' made by Sidonius Apollinaris three centuries earlier: 'For now that the old degrees of official rank are swept away, those degrees by which the highest in the land used to be distinguished from the lowest, the only token of ability will henceforth be a knowledge of letters.'[89] Most of the private owners of books in the

[87] The development of the relationship with St Amand is discussed in McKitterick, 'Charles the Bald', 42–7.
[88] The Lothar Gospels are listed in the inventory of Prüm for 1003, cited by Lesne, *Les Livres, 'scriptoria' et bibliothèques*, p. 10. On the St Hubert Gospels see R. McKitterick, 'The Gospels of St Hubert', in *Art at Auction. The Year at Sotheby's 1985–86* (London, 1986), pp. 154–7.
[89] W. B. Anderson, ed. and trans., *The Poems and Letters of Sidonius* (Cambridge, Mass., 1936), Ep. VIII.2.

Carolingian period were clerics. Lupus of Ferrières' avid acquisition of the classics and theology,[90] the corpus of philosophical and theological works belonging to Wulfad of Bourges[91] and the predominantly legal collection of Hincmar, archbishop of Rheims, are among the best known.[92] Other Carolingian scholars, Manno, Martin of Laon, Hucbald of St Amand and Einhard, and the Carolingian kings, Charlemagne, Louis the Pious and Charles the Bald, all possessed small libraries.[93] There is evidence that lay aristocrats, too, were the owners of books.[94] The implications of this evidence for the level of lay literacy are considered in a later chapter. It is the context of some of the more specific pieces of this evidence about libraries, however, that is so important for an understanding of the evaluation of books in the early middle ages, quite apart from what it reveals about aristocratic wealth. The books belonging to Counts Eberhard of Friuli and Eccard of Mâcon are mentioned in their wills. The full implications of this are not always realized, owing to the separation of the book lists from the rest of the text in older editions and the continued use of these editions.[95] These documents show us not only how wealthy these magnates were in terms of their moveable and immoveable property, but also what they considered to be precious among their possessions. The

---

[90] See E. Pellegrin, 'Les Manuscrits de Loup de Ferrières', *BEC* 115 (1957) 5–31; C. H. Beeson, *Lupus of Ferrières as Scribe and Text Critic* (Cambridge, Mass., 1930); and R. J. Garièpy, 'Lupus of Ferrières: Carolingian scribe and text critic', *Medieval Studies* 30 (1968) 90–105.

[91] The manuscript list of these was edited by M. Cappuyns, 'Les *Bibli Wulfadi* et Jean Scot Erigène', *Recherches de Théologie Ancienne et Mediévale* 33 (1966) 137–9.

[92] See Carey, 'The scriptorium of Rheims'.

[93] On the royal libraries see, B. Bischoff, 'Die Hofbibliothek Karls des Grossen', 'Die Hofbibliothek unter Ludwig dem Frommen', and 'Bücher am Hofe Ludwigs des Deutschen und die Privatbibliothek des Kanzlers Grimalt', in *MS* III, pp. 149–69, 170–86 and 187–212; and McKitterick, 'Charles the Bald'. On private ownership of books in the Byzantine Empire see Wilson, in *Byzantine Books and Bookmen*, pp. 1–18. For book ownership among the Jewish communities in early mediaeval Egypt, as evidenced from the Cairo Genizah collection now in Cambridge University Library, see the articles by N. Allony, 'Three book-lists from the Cairo Genizah', *Kirjath Sepher* 36 (1960–1) 389–402 and 517–24; 'The book-list of R. Josef Rosh ha-Seder', *ibid.* 38 (1962–3) 531–7; 'Four book-lists', *ibid.* 43 (1967–8) 121–43; and (with A. Scheiber) 'An autograph book-list of R. Josef Rosh ha-Seder', *ibid.* 48 (1972–3) 152–72.

[94] Pierre Riché discusses the libraries and the treasure of some lay aristocrats in two separate articles: 'Les Bibliothèques de trois aristocrates laïcs carolingiens', *MA* 69 (1963) 87–104, and 'Trésors et collections d'aristocrates laïcs carolingiens', *Cahiers Archéologiques* 22 (1972) 39–46, without making the essential connection between books and treasure. K. Christ, however, recognized the importance of the status of liturgical books as treasure in his contribution to G. Leyh, ed., *Handbuch der Bibliothekswissenschaft* III.3 (Wiesbaden, 1953), pp. 243–426, trans. Theophil M. Otto, *The Handbook of Medieval Library History* (Metuchen, N.J., 1984), as did Emile Lesne in *Histoire de la propriété ecclesiastique en France* III *L'Inventaire de la propriété. Eglises et trésor des églises du commencement du VIIIe à la fin du XIe siècle* (Lille, 1936).

[95] For example, Becker, *Catalogi*, and those who use his flawed edition.

wills list all their possessions – lands, villae, tenants, mills, rents and treasure. It is in the section on treasure that the books are included.

Eberhard and his wife Gisela divided their belongings and the properties they possessed in Lombardy, the east Frankish kingdom, Hasbaye, Toxandria and Cysoing among their seven children.[96] The will lists the grants of land for each child first, then the gold and silver articles, among which are one or two liturgical books. Unruoch the eldest son, for example, was to receive an *Evangelium eum auro paratum... missale cum argento et auro paratum, lectionarium similiter tabulas eburneas auro paratas*. There was also a separate section in the will headed *De libris etiam capelle nostre divisionem inter eos facere sic volumus*, and these were also divided among the children.

Eccard of Mâcon's will also listed his lands, works of art, books, animals and weapons, all mixed up together.[97] Similarly, the grant Walgarius, Eberhard of Friuli's chaplain, made to the abbey of Cysoing in *c*. 865 listed all the land he possessed in the Tournaisis and his treasure, which included his books,[98] and Fulrad, abbot of St Denis, left to that monastery in 777 his lands, mills, herds, gold, silver, books and bronze *ornamenta*.[99]

In time of danger, moreover, books were the object of the same precautions as the vestments and church plate. For fear of the Slavs the monks of St Gall sent their books to the island monastery of Reichenau for safety; in the face of the threat from the Northmen, the monks of St Vaast transported their ecclesiastical *ornamenta* and books to Beauvais; the monks of St Amand are reputed to have taken their books with them when they fled to St Germain-des-Prés in 882 and the monks of St Philibert of Noirmoutier retrieved only the *bibliotheca* from their lost treasures, precious books and royal charters after a Viking raid.[100] They were not only saving their material wealth, they were also preserving virtually irreplaceable texts.

---

[96] De Coussemaker, *Cartulaire*, pp. 1–5, reprinted in Schramm and Mütherich, *Denkmale*, pp. 93–4.

[97] M. Prou and A. Vidier, eds., *Recueil des chartes de l'abbaye de Saint-Benoît-sur-Loire*, Documents publiés par la Société historique et archéologique du Gâtinais V (Paris, 2 vols., 1900–7), I, p. 59.

[98] De Coussemaker, *Cartulaire*, pp. 5–7.

[99] Edited with commentary and facsimile by M. Tangl, *Das Mittelalter in Quellenkunde und Diplomatik. Ausgewählte Schriften* I (Berlin, 1966), pp. 540–81. Merovingian charters of 653 and 723 refer to sacred books in the enumeration of church plate: *MGH Diplomatum Imperii Tomus* I (Hanover, 1872), pp. 20 and 83 (Nos. 19 and 93).

[100] Platelle, *Le Temporel de Saint Amand*, p. 60, discussed the evidence; see too d'Haenens, *Les Invasions normandes*, especially pp. 131–6, and P. Riché, 'Consequences des invasions normandes sur la culture monastique dans l'occident franc', *Settimane* 16 (1969) 705–21. See also *Chronicon Namnetense*, ed. R. Merlet, *Chronique de Nantes* (Paris, 1896), c. IV.

This way of thinking about books as treasure is even more clearly demonstrated in the inventories of property surviving from the Carolingian period. It is these inventories which represent the most important evidence for the quantification of wealth in the early middle ages.

Frankish polyptychs and ecclesiastical inventories owe something on the one hand to the late Roman censuses of population and descriptions of property made for purposes of tax and the allocation of civil obligations,[101] and on the other hand to the early Christian 'liturgical inventories', describing the *ornamenta ecclesiae*, such as the extracts from the *Acta Munati Felicis* incorporated into the record of the proceedings against Silvanus, bishop of Constantinople, accused by his deacon Nundinarius in 320 of being a *traditor*; church plate, vestments and liturgical codices were enumerated in the course of the search for books.[102] Later inventories of the fourth and fifth centuries such as that of the *Ecclesia Cornutiana*[103] also include books in the description of the church property.

Very little evidence of either kind of document, liturgical inventory or estate description, survives from the Gallo-Roman or Merovingian period in Frankish Gaul, but the registers for tax purposes appear to have been used by the Visigoths, Ostragoths, Lombards and Franks. Of great significance for our knowledge of Merovingian inventories, for instance, is the recently discovered fragment of a Merovingian polyptych from Tours (BN n.a. lat. 2654).[104] English evidence for inventories of monastic or ecclesiastical estates, or for royal wills which mention books, is almost non-existent before the late tenth century.[105] It seems to have been the

---

[101] The discussion by B. Guérard, *Polyptyque de l'abbé Irminon* I (Paris, 1844), is still useful. See too J. Susta, 'Zur Geschichte und Kritik der Urbarialaufzeichnungen', *Sitzungsberichte der phil.-hist. Klasse der Kaiserlichen Academie der Wissenschaften* 138 (Berlin, 1897), No. VIII, and Lesne, *L'Inventaire de la propriété*. It will be evident how much I am indebted to Lesne's masterly survey.

[102] These proceedings and other early inventories are edited in F. Cabrol and H. Leclercq, eds., *Dictionnaire d'archéologie chrétienne et de liturgie* (Paris, 15 volumes in 30, 1903–53), VIII.1, cols. 1396–418.

[103] *PL* 127, cols. 993–6.

[104] See the evidence cited by Guérard, *Polyptyque de l'abbé Irminon*, and Gregory of Tours, *Historiae* V.28 and IX.30. In some of the Merovingian royal charters, such as *MGH Diplomata Imperii* I, Nos. 84 and 86, are to be found what could perhaps be described as rudimentary inventories. On the Tours tax lists BN. n.a.lat. 2654, see P. Gasnault, *Documents comptables de Saint-Martin de Tours à l'époque mérovingienne* (Paris, 1975), and for a general survey, see Robert Fossier, *Polyptyques et censiers*, Typologie des Sources du Moyen Age Occidental fasc. 28 (Turnholt, 1978).

[105] The tenth-century English evidence is edited by A. J. Robertson, *Anglo-Saxon Charters* (Cambridge, 1939), Appendices I and II. See also F. Harmer, *Select English Historical Documents of the Ninth and Tenth Centuries* (Cambridge, 1914); D. Whitelock, *Anglo-Saxon Wills* (Cambridge, 1930); and *idem, English Historical Documents I ca. 500–1042* (London, 1979). On the books associated with Aethelstan, see T. Gottlieb, *Über Mittelalterliche Bibliotheken* (Leipzig, 1890), pp. 278–80; N. R. Ker, *Medieval Libraries of Great Britain*

from Rome

Carolingian kings who instituted (or revived) the practice of making detailed inventories of property. This is of some significance when assessing the Carolingian attitude towards wealth.

The intervention of the king or his *missi* made the execution of an inventory obligatory. As early as 751 a survey of church property was made for Pippin,[106] and in 787 Charlemagne ordered Landri, abbot of Jumièges and Count Richard to make an inventory of the property of St Wandrille.[107] In 807 the *missi* were enjoined to send the king information about the properties of the churches in their regions,[108] and again in 811–13 detailed descriptions of the benefices and estates in each *missaticum* were requested.[109] The Staffelsee inventory, the only portion of the *descriptio* of Augsburg diocese to have survived, was produced at this time.[110] Charlemagne wanted all his officers to send him an account of their administration and in his *Capitulare de Villis* proposed directives for introducing order into the administration of the royal estates.[111] Louis the Pious continued his father's policy.[112] One inventory made at his request survives in its entirety; it is the *descriptio* made in 831 of St Riquier and was incorporated by Hariulf into his *Gesta ecclesiae Centulensis*.[113] In 853, Charles the Bald charged his *missi dominici* with making inventories of the treasure, vestments, books and property of the ecclesiastical estates and to send these inventories to him.[114] No more reference is made to the royal orders in the preamble to the *descriptio* after the reign of Charles the Bald. An inventory seems to have ceased to be required by the secular authority from the end of the ninth century, but even before that time it is likely that many ecclesiastical establishments drew up polyptychs of their estates on their own initiative. Certainly the polyptychs of St Germain-des-Prés

(London, 1964), under Bath, Worcester, Winchester and Canterbury; and the masterly survey of the evidence by Simon Keynes, 'King Aethelstan's Books', in M. Lapidge and H. Gneuss, eds., *Learning and Literature in Anglo-Saxon England. Studies Presented to Peter Clemoes* (Cambridge, (1985), pp. 145–201.

[106] *Annales Alemannici, MGH SS* I, p. 26.
[107] Lohier and Laporte, eds., *Gesta Fontanellensis coenobii*, p. 82.
[108] *MGH Cap.* I, No. 49, c. 4, p. 136.
[109] *Ibid.*, No. 80,c. 5, p. 177.
[110] Bischoff, ed., *Schatzverzeichnisse*, pp. 90–1. The Staffelsee inventory is on fo. 9r–9v of Wolfenbüttel Helmst. 254 (the rest of the codex contains the *Brevium exempla ad describendas res ecclesiasticas et fiscale*, letters from Pope Leo III to Charlemagne and Charlemagne's *Capitulare de Villis*). It is dated 811.
[111] *MGH Cap.* I, No. 32, pp. 82–91, and see the discussion by R. Latouche, *The Birth of the Western Economy* (London, 1961), pp. 176–210.
[112] Compare Ermold the Black, ed. E. Faral, *Poéme sur Louis le Pieux* (Paris, 1964), lines 1171–5.
[113] Hariulf, ed. F. Lot, *Hariulf, Chronique de l'abbaye de Saint-Riquier Ve siècle–1104* (Paris, 1894), p. 86.
[114] *MGH Cap.* II, No. 259, c. 1, p. 267. *Ecclesiae quoque luminaria et ornatum debetum ordinent et thesaurum ac vestimenta seu libros diligenter inbrevient et breves nobis reportent.*

(drawn up by Abbot Irmino), St Amand, St Rémi of Rheims and St Bertin, and the statutes of Adalhard of Corbie fall into this category.[115]

The inventory, polyptych or *descriptio* usually took the form of an enquiry made on the spot either by the royal *missi* or by the prelate of the church to which the *missi* had been sent. The buildings, lands, treasure, library, houses, dependents, tenants, labourers, vineyards, rents, services and equipment were all described. The inventories of property and treasure are almost exclusively ecclesiastical. They were made primarily in the interests of the possessor, while the treasure listed is for the most part impersonal property in that it belonged to God's service. Often the treasury of the poorest of establishments, such as Bergkirchen near Jesenwang or the parish church of Bibereck near Dachau, both in the diocese of Freising, consisted of no more than the essential vestments, a missal and a lectionary. Others possessed some silver vessels, candlesticks or silver or jewelled crosses. A treasure list made at Thannkirchen in 858 includes a missal, a lectionary, a 'history in one volume', an exposition of the Psalms (possibly that of Cassiodorus), a penitential, the *Cura Pastoralis*, an exposition of St Matthew's Gospel and a *computus* as well as the customary service books. The books were kept in two different places.[116] In other words, it is not just the liturgical books that are considered to be the wealth of any centre. Similarly, BL Harley 2790, fo. 263, has a late tenth- or early eleventh-century list of books in the *armarium* of the cathedral of Nevers; it contains works for studying the liberal arts, liturgical books, a cross, caskets, phylacteries, chalices and censers. Most of the original treasury inventories are themselves entered in gospel books, though psalters, lectionaries and other *Pracht Codices* are also used. Eleventh-century and later inventories occur in early gospel books that were obviously the prized possession of a particular centre. BL Harley 2826, for example, an early ninth-century gospel book, contains a tenth-century inventory of the treasure at the church of Eller. A gospel book produced at Tours in about 840, now Wolfenbüttel Cod. 2186, contains an inventory of the canonesses' house at Erstein, founded in about 840 by Irmgard, wife of the Emperor Lothar. The inventory includes what is probably a reference to the gospel book in which it had been entered: *evangelium 1 aureis litteris scriptum exteriusque.*

A further impulse to the making of inventories was the invasion of the Northmen. Clm 6333 contains a palimpsested fragment of a list of property

---

[115] Guérard, *Polyptyque de l'abbé Irminon*, discussed St Amand, St Germain-des-Prés and St Bertin. On the latter, see G. W. Coopland, *The Abbey of Saint Bertin and its Neighbourhood* (Oxford, 1914).

[116] Bischoff, ed., *Schatzverzeichnisse*, pp. 23–5 and 94.

belonging to St Bavo's monastery in Ghent, made in 800; in the Ghent Livinus Gospels (s. ix), is a twelfth-century copy of another list made in 851 on the return of the monks to St Bavo's after their flight from the Northmen.[117]

An important function of the inventory, polyptych or *descriptio* was ratification in writing of the right to possession of the items listed. Royal and synodal diplomas confirming the properties would be assimilated into the document. In 858, for example, the *descriptio* of Notre Dame of Soissons was made in the presence of Charles the Bald's *optimates*, confirmed by them and countersigned by fifteen bishops and abbots.[118] Wenilo of Sens' *descriptio* was confirmed by Charles the Bald in 848.[119] Inventories thus served to define, maintain and defend rights to property and wealth. It is important to remember the functions of an inventory and how it could be given a new facet when considering the function of book inventories, or library catalogues, in the next chapter.

As we shall see in the next chapter, the lists of books originally forming part of the church's or abbey's inventory of its treasure gradually developed into independent book inventories or library catalogues, representing descriptions of the intellectual wealth of a centre and a quantification of the knowledge any one centre had at its disposal. While in the catalogues the material wealth these books represent is neither dominant nor even explicit, the original motive and context of these catalogues is a salutary reminder of the economic dimension to literacy and learning in the Carolingian period. The books the Carolingians produced and owned are self-conscious manifestations and displays of their wealth.[120] Over 7,000 books from the Carolingian ateliers of the ninth century survive. How many may once have existed can only be guessed at, but Bischoff once suggested 50,000. Such an investment of wealth cannot be ignored. Book ownership as much as land ownership was a mark of social status and means. As part of the trade in luxury items (which many would have regarded as necessities), the book trade deserves to be recognized as a crucial indication of what men and women were prepared to spend their money on. Furthermore, the books surviving from the Carolingian period are a clear and rarely fully appreciated index of Carolingian prosperity. No historian can afford to ignore the evidence of

---

[117] *Ibid.*, pp. 36–9, and see P. McGurk, 'The Ghent Livinus Gospels and the scriptorium of St Amand', *Sacris Erudiri* 14 (1963) 164–204.

[118] Cited by Lesne, *L'Inventaire de la propriété*, p. 10.

[119] G. Tessier, ed., *Recueil des Actes de Charles II le Chauve* (Paris, 1943), diploma of 24 February 848, I, pp. 275–9.

[120] Bischoff, 'Die Hofbibliothek Karls des Grossen' and 'Panorama der Handschriften-überlieferung aus der Zeit Karls des Grossen', *MS* III, pp. 149–69 and 5–38.

the books produced and owned when assessing the level and range of economic activity under the Carolingian rulers.[121] It was an economy in which the cultivation of literacy and learning played a fundamental part.

Books in the late eighth and the ninth centuries were thus assessed on a number of different and complementary levels: the material value related to the cost of production and added to the book by embellishing it with decoration and pictures and binding it in a precious binding; the intellectual or spiritual value attached to a book because of its content and importance for the Christian faith; the value attached to a book because of its associations and its antiquity; the importance of books in gift giving or gift exchange; the role of books as an index of status and wealth. Nevertheless, it is doubtful that the material value of a book in the early middle ages ever became separated from its religious, spiritual or intellectual importance as it could when treated simply as an object of rarity or work of art of a particular kind. All books, however grand and however high their intrinsic value, were to be used as well as treasured. In respect to the role and function of, and attitudes towards, books throughout the middle ages, as to so much else, the Carolingians made a vital contribution.

---

[121] Apart from the articles by Bischoff cited above see the articles cited in n. 93. Nor should the Ottonian rulers be forgotten, especially Otto III: see F. Mütherich, 'The library of Otto III', in Peter Ganz, ed. *The Role of the Book in Medieval Culture*, Bibliologia. Elementa ad librorum studia pertinentia 4 (Turnhout, 1986), pp. 11–25.

5 ❧ The organization of written knowledge

From the economic imperatives behind the production and possession of books, let us now turn to the intellectual and spiritual ones. It has long been accepted that in the Carolingian period the Franks did much to consolidate their intellectual and cultural heritage from classical antiquity and the early Christian church, and to lay the foundations for subsequent developments in education and scholarship in Europe.[1] Such, indeed, was their zeal, intelligence and sheer productiveness in so doing that the whole period is generally classified as a 'Renaissance', despite the inevitable ambiguities and assumptions of such a term.[2] That these Carolingian efforts to promote education and learning had among many results the establishment of an accepted canon of standard 'school texts' and the creation of large libraries has become clear in the works of such scholars as Bischoff, Glauche, Illmer, Lehmann and Traube.[3] They have exploited the rich evidence in the form of surviving books from the period, indications in the writing of contemporary scholars of books available to them, and the library catalogues and book inventories of a number of the most important of the Carolingian monastic and episcopal centres. There is in all this evidence a clear preoccupation with the Bible and the particular types of knowledge and scholarship this generated, for the effort to understand the Bible and Christ's teaching is one of the clear impulses

---

[1] For details, see McKitterick, *Frankish Kingdoms*, pp. 140–68 and 200–27. The best coverage of the period before the eighth century is Pierre Riché, *Education et culture dans l'occident barbare VIᵉ–VIIIᵉ siècles* (Paris, 1962), Eng. trans. J. J. Contreni (Columbia, South Carolina, 1976).

[2] For the classic discussions see *Settimane* 1 (Spoleto, 1954) and *Settimane* 27 (Spoleto, 1979).

[3] See in particular Bernhard Bischoff, 'Die Bibliothek im Dienste der Schule', MS III, pp. 213–33; Günter Glauche, *Schullektüre im Mittelalter. Entstehung und Wandlungen des Lektürekanons bis 1200 nach den Quellen dargestellt*, Münchener Beiträge zur Mediävistik und Renaissance Forschung 5 (Munich, 1970); Detlef Illmer, *Formen der Erziehung und Wissensvermittlung im frühen Mittelalter. Quellenstudien zur Frage der Kontinuität des abendländischen Erziehungswesen*, Münchener Beiträge zur Mediävistik und Renaissance Forschung 7 (Munich, 1971); Paul Lehmann, *Erforschung des Mittelalters* (Stuttgart, 5 vols., 1959–62); Ludwig Traube, *Vorlesungen und Abhandlungen* (Munich, 1911).

165

of Carolingian education and learning.[4] What has not yet been considered, however, is the role of the library catalogues and the inspirations behind their creation in forming a canon of wisdom and learning. This chapter will argue, on the contrary, that the book lists should be understood as a dynamic expression of literate and intellectual aspirations.

The general context of these crucial pieces of evidence, that of the Carolingian promotion of the written word, and the more specific context, that of the relationship between library catalogues and the inventories of wealth discussed in the previous chapter, have not been given sufficient weight. The catalogues may provide information concerning the libraries which produced them and the books listed in them. But their implications as far as the Carolingians and the written word are concerned are far more wide-reaching. They are expressive of yet another link between the secular use of literacy (for inventories and legal records) and the ecclesiastical dissemination of learning.

Let us consider, first of all, the contents and organization of the extant catalogues from the mid-eighth century to the end of the ninth, and the libraries they record, before considering the host of problems and questions they raise.[5]

I THE ESTABLISHMENT OF MONASTIC LIBRARIES

It is not possible to speak confidently of libraries in the Merovingian period, for the evidence extant is insufficient to establish the existence either of large scriptoria (in the sense of ateliers producing a homogeneous style of script) or of libraries between the sixth and mid-eighth centuries. Only exceptionally were a number of scribes trained to write a similar script which differed markedly from the current book hands and which, with its characteristic minuscule, uncial, display scripts or capitals, amounted to a house style which is instantly recognizable.[6] Such a case is Luxeuil.[7]

---

[4] A point stressed by John J. Contreni, 'Carolingian biblical studies', in Uta-Renate Blumenthal, ed., *Carolingian Essays*, Andrew W. Mellon Lectures in Early Christian Studies (Washington, 1983), pp. 71–98.

[5] The most recent introduction to mediaeval library catalogues is that by Albert Derolez, *Les Catalogues de bibliothèques*, Typologie des Sources du Moyen Age Occidental, fasc. 31 (Turnhout, 1979). It is admirably lucid but he does not address the problems of origin, organization or transmission, and focuses primarily on the period from the twelfth century onwards. A useful survey of libraries in the middle ages generally is provided by Karl Christ, 'Das Mittelalter', in G. Leyh, ed., *Handbuch der Bibliothekswissenschaft* (Wiesbaden, 1953), Parts III and IV, Eng. trans. T. M. Otto (Metuchen, NJ, 1984).

[6] See R. McKitterick, 'The scriptoria of Merovingian Gaul: a survey of the evidence', in H. Clarke and M. Brennan, eds., *Columbanus and Merovingian Monasticism* (Oxford, 1981), pp. 173–207.

[7] Identified by E. A. Lowe, 'The "script of Luxeuil": a title vindicated', in L. Bieler, ed.,

Sometimes a Merovingian library can be posited and some of its contents indicated, as in the foundation of Corbie.[8] How large the libraries at such important centres as Tours, St Denis, Rheims or Lyons were in the Merovingian period is impossible now to gauge, even if the fact that these centres had collections of books is not in doubt. The evidence for libraries in Gaul in the Merovingian period is thus very meagre. So is that for Merovingian book production, though it far exceeds for the seventh and early eighth centuries any of the efforts of the British Isles, Spain or Italy. That relative wealth should never be forgotten. There are obvious dangers in an argument from silence, but the problems of survival from the Carolingian period are likely to have been no less than for those from the Merovingian period. Yet from the Carolingian period there is a veritably astonishing amount of evidence concerning both book production and libraries, quite apart from a rapid expansion and foundation of new monasteries in the course of the eighth century.[9] It represents a real increase in the quantity, and the quality, of book production, and suggests an overall purpose withal. These books constitute the most eloquent witness to the Carolingians' conviction of the paramount importance of the written word, not least in the design, layout and treatment of letter forms in the books themselves.[10]

It is clear that the monasteries, as centres of book production, played a vital part in the promotion of the written word. But how did they come to contribute so much in this sphere, when in the early years of the Christian church monks were not famed for either learning or scribal activity? One obvious but highly significant aspect of early mediaeval monasticism in Gaul was that the monastic convert in the fourth century and later, as Clare Stancliffe has pointed out, tended to be a well-born aristocrat, an ambitious intellectual or an educated official. Inevitably such men could not undo their literary education when they rid themselves of their material possessions and became monks. In her words, these *conversi* 'refashioned the rigorous monasticism of Egypt in a manner appropriate to their own cultural background'.[11] Thus the newly recruited members of

---

Palaeographical Papers 1907–1965 (Oxford, 2 vols., 1972), II, pp. 389–98, and see my comments, 'The scriptoria of Merovingian Gaul', pp. 184–92.

[8] David Ganz, 'The Merovingian library of Corbie', in Clarke and Brennan, eds., *Merovingian Monasticism*, pp. 153–72.

[9] Bischoff, 'Bibliothek im Dienste der Schule'.

[10] I discuss this aspect of book production in 'Text and image in the Carolingian world', in R. McKitterick, ed., *The Uses of Literacy in Early Mediaeval Europe* (Cambridge, 1990).

[11] Clare Stancliffe, *St Martin and his Hagiographer. History and Miracle in Sulpicius Severus* (Oxford, 1983), pp. 27–9, at p. 29. See also Jacques Fontaine, 'Valeurs antiques et valeurs chrétiennes dans la spiritualité des grands propriétaires terriens à la fin du IVe siècle occidental', in J. Fontaine and C. Kannengiesser, eds., *Epektasis: mélanges patristiques*

the early monastic communities in Gaul carried over from their secular life their respect for their literary heritage, their assumption of its necessity and the place of reading and writing in its preservation, and accommodated it to the new monasticism. We can see this, for example, in the fitting occupations, with the stress on reading, recommended for the nuns addressed by Caesarius of Arles.[12] As part of the monastic tradition of early mediaeval Gaul, therefore, literacy and learning had their parts.[13] The Rule of St Benedict, though a later introduction to Frankish Gaul, and one not universally adopted (or at least not in an unadulterated form), nevertheless had in chapter 48 an essential latitude in the provisions for reading as part of the daily discipline which enabled it the more rapidly to be adapted to Frankish monastic practice.[14] Carolingian commentaries on the Rule, when extrapolating on Benedict's advice for reading, add details of their own monastery's custom. Hildermar's commentary, written *c.* 820, is particularly interesting in this respect, for it describes the record kept of borrowed books by the librarian and, by implication, the library provided by the monastery to serve the needs of the brethren.[15] The very diversity of monastic practice throughout the Merovingian and Carolingian periods and the different social assumptions of monastic founders and the members of their communities, so strongly a part of the aristocratic milieu in their enjoyment of patronage and endowment and in their personnel, had much to do with the preservation within the ecclesiastical context of the old aristocratic cultural traditions of late antiquity. Nevertheless, what that culture actually comprised, changed. In place of the former preponderance of classical and pagan authors in late antique education and literary culture there was now a Christian emphasis, and a growing body of new authors and new works to form a distinctive culture and intellectual tradition in its own right.[16] It is this which, for the Carolingian period, the library catalogues do so much to chart.

offerts au Cardinal Jean Daniélou (Paris, 1972), pp. 571–95; and Martin Heinzelmann, *Bischofsherrschaft in Gallien. Zur Kontinuität römischer Fuhrungschichten vom 4. bis zum 7. Jahrhundert. Soziale, prosopographische und bildungsgeschichtliche Aspekte* (Munich, 1976), pp. 185–211.

[12] Caesarius of Arles, *Regula*, ed. G. Morin, *S. Caesarii Arelatensis episcopi regula Sanctarum Virginum aliaque opuscula ad sanctimoniales directa ad normam codicum nunc primum edidit* G. Morin, Florilegium Patristicum 34 (Bonn, 1933).

[13] Of particular value is Franz Weissengruber, 'Monastische Profanbildung in der Zeit von Augustinus bis Benedikt', in Friedrich Prinz, ed., *Mönchtum und Gesellschaft im Frühmittelalter*, Wege der Forschung 312 (Darmstadt, 1976), pp. 387–429.

[14] A useful discussion is that by Karl Christ, '*In caput Quadragesimae*', *Zeitschrift für Bibliothekswesen* 60 (1943) 33–59.

[15] Hildemar, ed. Rupert Mittermüller, *Vita et regula SS.P.Benedicti una cum expositione regulae a Hildemaro tradita* (Regensburg, New York and Cincinnati, 1880).

[16] Some of the early development is surveyed by Riché, *Education et Culture*.

II THE DEVELOPMENT OF FRANKISH LIBRARIES: THE EVIDENCE OF THE EARLIEST CATALOGUES

Close examination of this important evidence reveals a steady development in the method of compilation and in the means of acquiring books, books to equip what has been aptly termed a 'literary Noah's Ark'.[17] The Franks appear to have had a sure sense of what they needed for their spiritual and intellectual formation. One way in which this manifested itself is in their libraries and the catalogues they compiled to record their contents. On what traditions were they able to draw for the compilation of these lists of books? Why were the catalogues, and, presumably, the books themselves, arranged in the way they were? It seems likely that there was some relationship between the order of listing and the arrangement of books in the library chest or room, but other influences can also be posited. Further, how did the Franks decide which books should go into their libraries, and which written texts were chosen? There is sufficient evolution in the Carolingian evidence itself to suggest that we are dealing with a new phase in library history which masked a fundamental development in the cultural history of the mediaeval west. That is, the libraries and their records are expressive of the intellectual inspiration and foundations of the Carolingian period in a new way.

The libraries of Fulda, Würzburg, Charlemagne and St Wandrille

The four earliest Carolingian book lists can be dated to the mid and late eighth century. Three of these, from Würzburg, Fulda and the royal library of Charlemagne, survive in contemporary manuscripts; the fourth, that of St Wandrille, is preserved in a chronicle of the abbots of St Wandrille, made in the second or third decade of the ninth century. The significance of the origins of two of the manuscript lists in insular centres in the German missionary area east of the Rhine will be considered at a later stage in this chapter.

About twenty volumes belonging to the monastery of Fulda, an English foundation established in 744, were listed on fos. 17v–18r of Basle F.III.15a, a collection of works by Isidore of Seville written on twenty-three folios, and still in its original binding, (*CLA* VII, 842). The codicological context of this list is, as we shall see below, particularly appropriate. Like the rest of the manuscript the list was written in an insular hand. Some of it has been erased and is now impossible to decipher. Lehmann was able to distinguish a collection which began with books of the Old and New

[17] H. Koeppler, '*De viris illustribus* and Isidore of Seville', *JTS* 37 (1936) 16–34, at 32.

Testament and included the apocryphal Apocalypse of Paul, followed by the Homilies of Gregory the Great on Ezekiel and on the gospels, the *Synonyma* of Isidore of Seville and then works by such early church fathers as Ambrose and Basil, miracles and lives of the saints, and the popular story of the seven sleepers of Ephesus. With the last were bound a chronicle, the Life of St Fursey, a book of sentences and the story of Alexander.[18] It can hardly be said that this was a comprehensive library, or even a well-conceived missionary collection. But its biblical books and the Homilies of Gregory, as well as a selection of saints' lives, were part of the basic equipment for an ecclesiastical establishment. It is significant that the Fulda list was apparently independent of any general ecclesiastical inventory. It, with the Würzburg list, appears to constitute a crucial stage in the enumeration of an institution's wealth, in that the books are perceived to be in a different category, even if the methods employed to record them are the same as those for itemizing plate and land. Most of the books listed are likely to have been imports and, like the *Ragyndrudis Codex* (Fulda, Bonifatianus 2, *CLA* VIII, 1197, in Luxeuil script) and a number of insular manuscripts, written elsewhere. It is only possible to trace the development of Anglo-Saxon script at Fulda from the end of the eighth century onwards with such books as Bede's Life of Cuthbert (Budapest Cod.lat. 441 *CLA* XI, 1589), and Jerome's letters (Marburg Hr 3 5a–b). Later lists from the library of Fulda, still to be edited adequately, record a great increase in the abbey's literary possessions. The portion of Vat. pal. lat. 1877, fos. 35–43, dated to the first half of the ninth century, lists books *de cella paugolfi*. It is, for the most part, a 'short title list' of books, neatly numbered, and with a new line for each title. After the missal, gospel lectionary and Bible, Jerome's and Augustine's works are listed, with a full provision of details concerning the letter collections. There are some other works noted, such as the chronicle of Eusebius and Jerome, a book of excerpts from the prophets and Lives of Paul the Hermit and Hilarion. It is very similar in the form of its entries to the first catalogue from Lorsch.[19]

An English hand of about the year 800 listed thirty-four books belonging to the cathedral library of Würzburg on fo. 236r of Oxford Bodleian Library Laud misc. 126 (*CLA* II, 252). This Würzburg list

---

[18] Paul Lehmann, 'Fuldaer Studien', *Sitzungsberichte der Bayerischen Akademie der Wissenschaften, phil.-hist. Klasse* (Munich, 1925), 48–9.

[19] On the English scribal activity at Fulda see Herrad Spilling, 'Angelsächsischen Schrift in Fulda', in A. Brall, ed., *Von der Klosterbibliothek zur Landesbibliothek* (Fulda, 1978), pp. 47–98. A later Fulda list, wrongly dated, was included in Gustav Becker, *Catalogi bibliothecarum antiqui* (Bonn, 1885), pp. 30–1. The Fulda list in Vat. pal. lat. 1877 is part of a volume containing three catalogues from Lorsch, see below, pp. 186–7.

constitutes important evidence for the state of the library at the end of the eighth century. Lowe commented that the order of the Würzburg list (headed by the Acts of the Apostles and followed by Gregory the Great's *Cura Pastoralis* and Dialogues, the Jerome commentary and Bede's ecclesiastical history, before theological works by Jerome, Augustine and Ambrose), while not altogether haphazard, was peculiar.[20] A number of books appear to have been so well known that only short titles, with no authors, are given: *dialogi* (Gregory the Great's Dialogues), *pastoralem* (Gregory the Great's *Cura Pastoralis*) *enciridion* (Augustine, *Enchiridion*), *Historia anglorum* (Bede, *Historia ecclesiastica gentis anglorum*). Lowe, furthermore, identified the *Actus apostolorum*, which heads the list, with the venerable codex Laud gr. 35. No other extant library catalogue begins with Acts and Lowe suggested that it was in recognition of the antiquity of the book and its status that it was placed at the beginning. Similarly, the list proceeds with other codices important to the English community at Würzburg, with the main writings of Gregory, the Pope most beloved of the English, an ancient uncial copy of Jerome, and their own native historian Bede. In other words, the list is not simply of the books at Würzburg, but one which tells us of the high regard for certain codices in the collection. The collection is, nevertheless, one designed to equip an evangelical bishop and his clergy with essential texts and knowledge. Of great importance, to be explored further below, is the possession of Jerome's *De viris illustribus*, a guide to Christian authors and their work.[21] Some of the books at Würzburg were those originally brought by Italian missionaries to England and exported again by the English missionaries to Germany. Others may have been brought, or sent, directly from Rome or Frankish Gaul.

The insular foundations clearly played a crucial role in the introduction of particular texts into the lands east of the Rhine. Würzburg itself disseminated texts. On the list, a later hand noted that the *commentarium*, identified with Würzburg M.p.th.q. 2, a copy of Jerome's commentary on Ecclesiastes which had belonged to the English Abbess Cuthswitha (*CLA*

---

[20] E. A. Lowe, 'An eighth-century list of books in a Bodleian manuscript from Würzburg and its possible relation to the Laudian Acts', in Bieler, ed., *Palaeographical Papers* I, pp. 239–50.

[21] The pastoral and evangelical concerns of the early English bishops in the Rhineland were elucidated by Wilhelm Levison, *England and the Continent in the Eighth Century* (Oxford, 1946), pp. 70–93, and Theodor Schieffer, *Winfrid-Bonifatius und die Christliche Grundlegung Europas* (Freiburg, 1954), pp. 156–87. New light was shed on Boniface in particular by Malcolm B. Parkes, 'The handwriting of St Boniface: a reassessment of the problems', *Beiträge zur Geschichte der deutschen Sprache und Literatur* 98 (1976) 161–79, and on Burchard of Würzburg by G. Morin, 'L'Homéliaire de Burchard de Würzburg', *RB* 13 (1896) 97–111.

IX, 1430a and b), had been lent to the monastry of Holzkirchen, and that the group at the top of the second column, *speculum, omelia s[an]c[t]i gregorii maiora pars, lib. proverbium, beatitudines.* had been borrowed by Fulda, presumably for copying.

It is undoubtedly the case that it is only possible to talk of book production in the Frankish realms east of the Rhine with the advent of the English missionaries. Study of the script at Würzburg, for example, has shown that Würzburg was producing books of its own from the time of Burchard (742–53) onwards; and that many of the earliest were in insular script of the Continental type; only a few of the Würzburg manuscripts in insular script appear actually to have been written in England, such as M.p.th.f. 79, M.p.th.q. 24 or M.p.th.f. 62 (*CLA* IX, 1426, 1433, 1417). The manuscripts extant from eighth- and early ninth-century Würzburg, together with the earliest record of its library, illustrate a fairly orthodox and narrow range of texts, suitable for instruction in the Christian faith. Their scripts and glosses in Old High German, Old Irish and Old English point to the nationalities of the scribes responsible and are an eloquent witness to the common culture created by Christianity in western Europe. They suggest, too, a very quick response to the need for books and the establishment of a canon of accepted and (for the most part) approved texts which was to burgeon and be a constant feature elsewhere in the course of the ninth century.[22]

While certain of the contents of the Würzburg lists influenced other establishments to possess the same authors, the structure and arrangement of both the Fulda and Würzburg lists are such that they can be seen to have had no discernible influence on the compilation of library catalogues elsewhere in the Frankish kingdoms. The same may be said of the list of a portion of the collection in the most famous library of all, that of the royal palace of Charlemagne. Written in an Italian hand on pp. 218–19 of a collection of poetry in Berlin Diez B. Sant. 66 (*CLA* VIII, 1044), it contains titles of many quite rare classical works which, Bischoff has argued, were in Charlemagne's library by the end of the eighth century.[23] It may represent the last portion of a larger list, for, as we shall see, the place for any classical works in an institutional library tended to be with the school books, grammars, works on metre and poetry, and listed at the end of the library catalogues. Berlin Diez B. Sant. 66 constitutes vital information

---

[22] On the Würzburg manuscripts see Bernhard Bischoff and Josef Hofmann, *Libri sancti Kyliani. Die Würzburger Schreibschule und die Dombibliothek im VIII. und IX. Jahrhundert* (Würzburg, 1952).

[23] Ed. Becker, *Catalogi*, pp. 38–41, who dates it, wrongly, to the ninth century. Compare Bischoff and Hofmann, *Libri sancti Kyliani*, pp. 113 and 151–2, who warn readers from using Becker's incompetent reproduction of a bad edition, made originally by Reuss.

concerning the riches of the royal library, but our knowledge of Carolingian libraries as a whole suggests that the collection recorded here was unusual and arcane, and only to be found in a place which could exploit many different connections and cultural contacts, and which could be expected to house scholars able to benefit from them. Even though it did provide a great many exemplars for other institutions to copy,[24] it does not appear to have been the royal library which played a key role in the formation of a canon of essential texts.

It is thought that Einhard (abbot 817–23), or, more probably, Ansegis, abbot of St Wandrille from 823 to 833, commissioned the *Gesta abbatum Fontanellensium* which records the books given to the abbey by its abbots or written in the abbey scriptorium.[25] The list of Wando's books, therefore, may date from his time as abbot between 747 and 754, and represent an early instance of the way in which a list of books could be arranged. It may, on the other hand, be a reconstruction in the third decade of the ninth century of an earlier record, and thus have been influenced by contemporary library practice.[26] The randomness of the thirty-one items belonging to Wando and presented by him to St Wandrille, however, suggests that it is an authentic reproduction of the mid-eighth century record. The complaint that there were too many to list, on the other hand, may be the ninth-century author's reaction to the prospect of copying out the earlier list. The first book noted is a volume in 'Roman letters' containing a commentary on the Gospels of Matthew, John and Luke. Works on theology by the leading church fathers, Jerome, Augustine and Gregory, are interspersed with a volume containing the Rules of Benedict and Columbanus and a martyrology, Gennadius (*Definitio dogmatum ecclesiasticorum*), Rules of the holy fathers,[27] the Life of Felix of Nola,

---

[24] Fully documented by Bernhard Bischoff, 'Die Hofbibliothek Karls des Grossen', *MS* III, pp. 149–69.

[25] See M. Sot, *Gesta episcoporum, Gesta abbatum*, Typologie des Sources du Moyen Age Occidental, fasc. 37 (Turnhout, 1981), pp. 34–5. But compare the arguments of Philip Grierson, 'Abbot Fulco and the date of the *Gesta abbatum Fontanellensium*', *EHR* 55 (1940) 275–84, and Wilhelm Levison, 'Zur Kritik der Fontaneller Geschichtsquellen', *Neues Archiv* 25 (1899) 593–607, and his 'Zu den Gesta abbatum Fontanellensium', *RB* 46 (1934) 241–64, reprinted in his *Aus Rheinischer und Fränkischer Frühzeit* (Düsseldorf, 1948), pp. 530–50.

[26] F. Lohier and J. Laporte, eds., *Gesta sanctorum patrum Fontanellensis coenobii* (Paris and Rouen, 1936), pp. 66–8.

[27] The rules listed are in fact attributed to Serapion, Macharius, Pafnutius and another Macharius. On the possible link with Lérins for at least one of the *Regula Macarii* see Adalbert de Vogüé, *Les Règles des Saints Pères I and II*, Sources Chrétiennes 297 and 298 (Paris, 1982), I, pp. 21–39, and also his introduction, to *Les Règles monastiques anciennes (400–700)*, Typologie des Sources du Moyen Age Occidental, ed. L. Genicot, fasc. 46 (Turnhout, 1985). Compare A. A. R. Bastiaensen's review of de Vogüé's 'Les Règles des Saints Pères', *Vigiliae Christianae* 38 (1984) 400–9.

Jordanes' History of the Goths and the story of Apollonius, king of Tyre. St Wandrille, founded by the Frankish nobleman Wandregisil on 1 March 649/650 and afterwards closely linked by patronage to the Carolingian royal family, had been in existence for nearly a century before we have the information concerning its books. But it may perhaps be presumed that it already possessed a few. Wando himself had entered the monastery in 694–6, giving part of his patrimony when so doing.[28] He may well have been a young man by then, perhaps already with some education. How he acquired his books, and where they may have come from, however, is not known. The list of codices associated with Wando may thus be what it seems, the first collection of books acquired by the monastery.

The lack of any order in Wando's list may simply reflect the personal, and thus, inevitably, the miscellaneous, nature of his collection. So, too, with the next list of books recorded in the St Wandrille chronicle. This notes the books given to the church of St Peter by Abbot Gervold (787–806).[29] There has been some attempt to systematize the list, in that it starts with the Pentateuch and the minor prophets and proceeds with two works by Augustine, before giving an account of the books written under the direction of Harduin in the newly established abbey scriptorium. This event is of the utmost importance. Despite the length of time this monastery had been in existence, it appears that it was not until the end of the eighth century that a scriptorium was established within the monastery, and that scribes were trained to write books to serve the monastery's needs, as well as those of its school (also founded by Gervold and placed in Harduin's charge). The significance of the timing is inescapable. St Wandrille is a key witness to the impetus provided by the Carolingians towards the provision and production of books. The list of books provided, moreover, is very much that of basic texts for a new house rather than a record of the copying of more esoteric luxuries for a well-stocked library. Thus it is only right at the end of the eighth century that we hear of gospels, epistles, mass books, lectionaries, Homilies of Gregory, *computus*, Augustine, Bede's treatises on time, the psalter and lives of the saints of the house, Wandregisil, Ansbert and Wulframn. Whereas the other early lists are those of newly established institutions, the St Wandrille records permit us to observe a real difference between the commitment to learning of the Merovingian and the Carolingian establishment. They show us, too, how books were gradually accumulated over a number of decades through gift, inheritance, home production and possibly purchase and exchange as well.

[28] See Ferdinand Lot, *Etudes critiques sur l'abbaye de Saint-Wandrille*, Bibliothèque de l'Ecole des Hautes Etudes 204 (Paris, 1913), p. cxiii and Charter 17.

[29] Lohier and Laporte, eds., *Gesta Fontanellensis coenobii*, pp. 88, 89–90.

The library at St Wandrille was further augmented under Abbot Ansegis (823–33). There the list is roughly ordered, with biblical books preceding theological commentaries, and ending with the new Homiliary of Paul the Deacon, two volumes of *libri glossarum* and a collection of canon law.[30] Similarly, the list of books at St Germer-de-Flay of the same date begins with a selection of books of the Old and New Testament, preceded by a pandect or entire Bible. Bound in with a copy of the Book of Daniel, the Gospel of Matthew and excerpts from Ambrose's *Hexameron*, was the so-called decree of Gelasius, *De libris recipiendis et non recipiendis*. Many of the theological works by Augustine were listed, as were a number of the key exegetes – John of Constantinople on Matthew, the Homilies of Gregory on Ezekiel, Bede on Acts, the catholic epistles, the Apocalypse and the Gospel of Luke. Isidore of Seville's *Liber differentiarum*, his *Etymologiae*, Prosper (that is, Julianus Pomerius) on the active and contemplative lives, Alcuin, *De Trinitate* were added. So too were a number of the standard ecclesiastical histories, such as the *Historia Tripartita* and the *Historia ecclesiastica* of Eusebius. The Rules of Basil and Benedict were bound into the same volume, and the Lives of Jerome, Augustine, Gregory and Columba *virgo* (*sic!*) in another. Last of all was a copy of a *Gesta francorum*. This could be a reference to Gregory of Tours, or to the chronicle of Fredegar, or to one of the sets of Frankish annals. St Germer-de-Flay also possessed two sacramentaries. Generally, however, while rich in patristic theology and scripture, it has very little in the way of liturgy, saints' lives, monastic rules or school books. The overall impression is of a library of a learned community, equipped for its Lenten and daily reading.[31]

West Frankish libraries: the problems of the evidence and the example of St Riquier

Consideration of the later accessions of St Wandrille has taken us well into the ninth century. Generally the lists from St Wandrille are unsophisticated and appear to represent an early stage in the evolution of a library catalogue. Unfortunately, there are no surviving catalogues of the great west Frankish houses – Laon, St Amand, St Denis, Corbie, Auxerre, Fleury, Lyons or Rheims – from the ninth century,[32] though there are many from

---

[30] *Ibid.*, pp. 103–4.
[31] *Ibid.*, pp. 108–10.
[32] On Laon, see J. J. Contreni, 'The formation of Laon's cathedral library in the ninth century', *Studi Medievali* 13 (1972) 919–39, and *idem, The Cathedral School of Laon from 850 to 930. Its Manuscripts and Masters.* Münchener Beiträge zur Mediävistik und Renaissance Forschung 29 (Munich, 1978). On the general context see McKitterick, *Frankish Kingdoms*, pp. 200–27.

the twelfth century.[33] Although, therefore, there is ample witness in the form of surviving manuscripts, both to the quantity and quality of their book production, and to the many contacts with other houses in both the eastern and western portions of the Frankish kingdoms,[34] we can only guess at their methods of organization and the likelihood of their having compiled library catalogues. It seems reasonable to surmise, however, that the great monasteries and cathedrals of the western portion of the Carolingian realm also once had book inventories and library catalogues and that these probably took a form similar to that of the great ninth-century catalogues of Cologne, Lorsch, Murbach, Reichenau and St Gall. There is so much that is common to the organization of these five that is also to be observed in twelfth-century French catalogues that one must see the five Carolingian catalogues as a culmination of Frankish developments and the models for the later, eleventh- and twelfth-century, cataloguers to emulate.

One west Frankish library of the ninth century for which a written description does survive makes this supposition the more likely. An inventory made in 831 from the abbey of St Riquier survives in the copy of it incorporated by Hariulf into his *Gesta ecclesiae Centulensis*.[35] Unlike the other extant catalogues so far considered, this inventory was not free-standing but constitutes part of a general survey of the property of St Riquier, vestments, church plate, estates, tenants and rents received, as well as books, made at the command of the Emperor Louis the Pious. This is a timely reminder that these book lists are more than the quantification of knowledge that any one centre had at its disposal, or a check list for the custodian; they are also inventories of wealth and a demonstration of how possession of the written word could mean great wealth.

The books are divided into several large sections, a division that appears to be that of the original document rather than of Hariulf's devising. The compiler was careful to note the number and title or author of the separate works or *libri* bound together to form one *codex* or volume. Biblical books (*libri canonici*), and theology for the monks to read, were included in the first

---

[33] See, for example, those of St Amand, St Martial, Moissac, Massay, Le Puy and others in Léopold Delisle, *Le Cabinet des manuscrits de la Bibliothèque Impériale* I (Paris, 1868), pp. 307–19, 395, 105, and II (Paris, 1874), pp. 427–40 (Corbie), 440–1 (Moissac), 441–3 (Massay), 443–5 (Le Puy), 448–58 (St Amand).

[34] Jean Vézin, 'Les Relations entre Saint-Denis et d'autres scriptoria', in Peter Ganz, ed., *The Role of the Book in Medieval Culture*, Bibliologia. Elementa ad librorum studia pertinentia 3 (Turnhout, 1986), pp. 17–40.

[35] Hariulf, ed. F. Lot, *Hariulf, Chronique de l'abbaye de Saint-Riquier Ve siècle–1104* (Paris, 1894), pp. 69, 89–96. The account includes the books in the dependent cells of Forestmontier, in the *cella ... quae vocatur Incra* (Albert arr. Péronne) and in the *cellula quae vocatur Botritium* (Bourecq, Pas-de-Calais), which were primarily liturgical books.

section. St Riquier had a pandect as well as the text of another Bible divided up into about forty volumes. The theology books were fairly carefully set out with all the works by one author together, and with the principal church fathers – Jerome, Augustine, Gregory, Isidore, Origen, Hilary, John Chrysostom, Cassiodorus (on Psalms), Fulgentius, Bede (the exegesis) – represented by a number of works, and others with one or two works each, such as Julius, Eugippius, Paschasius, Primasius on the Apocalypse, Arnobius, Gregory Nazianzus and Athanasius, given in a very rough chronological order in a short section thereafter. The canon law collection included Gelasius' *De libris recipiendis et non recipiendis'*, and was followed by three volumes of a homiliary, Boethius' *De consolatione Philosophiae*, Gregory of Tours, *De gestis Francorum* (that is, the *Historiae*), Philippus' commentary on Job, and thereafter an increasingly miscellaneous list of minor works of exegesis and theology, saints' lives, monastic rules (Benedict, Augustine, Fructuosus and Isidore) the Homilies of Caesarius of Arles, Alcuin's *De fide trinitatis*, seven psalters and three different *florilegia*, including Defensor of Ligugé's *Liber Scintillarum*.

The second section of the St Riquier list comprised school books, with the grammars of Donatus and Priscian and others, including the Englishman Tatwine, Cicero's *De Rhetorica*, Vergil, a number of the late Roman Christian poets, including Fortunatus, which perhaps survives in Leningrad F.v.XIV.1,[36] a respectable and interesting group of history books and other more arcane literature, such as Josephus, Pliny, Aethicus Ister's *De mundi descriptione* (that is, presumably, the *Cosmographia*), the rare Philo Iudaeus, Jordanes, Jerome's chronicle and Eusebius' *Historia ecclesiastica*, more or less in the order in which they were written, a law book containing Roman and the Salic Frankish law and a *Passio Domini in theodisco et in latino*.[37] These were probably used in the schools associated with St Riquier.[38]

The last section listed the liturgical books used in the churches and chapels of the abbey. St Riquier possessed copies of all three types of sacramentary in use in the early ninth century in the Frankish kingdoms as well as a lectionary, antiphonary and a gospel book described as *textus evangelii IV litteris scriptis totus I*. This probably refers to the gospel book,

---

[36] And in BN lat. 7701 + 13048, *CLA* V, 570, identified by Ludwig Traube, 'O Roma nobilis', *Abhandlungen der Königlichen bayerischen Akademie der Wissenschaften, phil.-hist. Klasse* 19 (1894) 329–30; and compare E. Dekkers (trans. J. Godard), 'La Bibliothèque de Saint-Riquier au moyen âge', *Bulletin de la Société des Antiquaires de Picardie* 46 (1955–6) 157–97, especially 169 n. 51.

[37] Dekkers, 'La Bibliothèque de Saint-Riquier', 175–7, discusses the various conclusions that have been drawn from this bilingual text.

[38] See below, pp. 219–23, and McKitterick, *Frankish Kingdoms*, p. 146.

now Abbéville 4, which was given to Angilbert, lay abbot of St Riquier by Charlemagne in c. 800.[39] Two other gospel books are mentioned in the section on church plate and vestments, presumably because of their precious cases.[40]

Apart from the Abbéville Gospels, and the volume of Fortunatus' poetry in Leningrad, Traube identified a further survivor of this magnificent library in Paris BN lat. 13359, a copy of Augustine's *De doctrina Christiana*.[41] Products of St Riquier itself may be recognized in the so-called Psalter of Charlemagne,[42] while Dekkers is of the opinion that the Corbie Psalter, Amiens 18, was once in the library of St Riquier, as were BN lat. 11504–5, a pandect of the Bible, and BN lat. 45 and 93.[43] But these appear to be all that remains of the 256 codices in the library in Angilbert's day. It is likely that little escaped the disruption caused by the Vikings in 881 and the catastrophic fires of 28 August 1131 and 29 March 1719. Whether the great strength of the library is to be attributed to Angilbert alone is not clear, but it would seem that like St Wandrille, St Riquier, founded at the end of the seventh century, only rose to glory and fame as a library in the late eighth century and that it was unmistakably a Carolingian phenomenon.[44] Not until the abbacy of Angilbert, Charlemagne's *de facto* son-in-law, did the monastery achieve prosperity, largely due to the patronage of Charlemagne, who himself celebrated Easter there in 800.[45]

III THE SYSTEMATIZATION OF LIBRARY CATALOGUES: THE EAST FRANKISH EXAMPLES

The two most closely related of the five extant library catalogues from the east Frankish kingdom are those from Reichenau and St Gall.

[39] CLA VI, 704, one of the famous court school manuscripts, positively gaudy in its purple-dyed parchment and rich pigments.

[40] Hariulf, ed. Lot, *Chronique*, p. 88: *Euangelium auro scriptum unum cum capsa argentea, gemmis et lapidibus fabricata. Aliae capsae euangeliorum duae ex auro et argento paratae, faldene addito ex argento fabricatum ad opus ipsarum. I.* Other rich bindings are described on pp. 68 (*Codex eburneus auro, argento et gemmis optime paratus* I) and 69 (*Euangelium auro scriptum cum tabulis argenteis auro et lapidibus preciosis mirifice paratum. I. aliud euangelium plenarium. I.* See my comments above, pp. 147–8.

[41] Traube, 'O Roma nobilis', 329, and compare Dekkers, 'La Bibliothèque de Saint-Riquier', 170 n. 56.

[42] The 'Psalter of Charlemagne', BN lat. 13159. See M. Huglo, 'Un tonaire du Graduel de la fin du VIIIᵉ siècle', *Revue Gregorienne* 31 (1952) 176–86, 224–33, and *idem*, *Les Tonaires: inventaire, analyse, comparaison* (Paris, 1971), pp. 25–9.

[43] Dekkers, 'La Bibliothèque de Saint-Riquier', 169–71.

[44] On the early history of St Riquier, see the account of its founder Richarius by A. Poncelet, 'La Plus Ancienne Vie de S. Riquier', *Analecta Bollandiana* 22 (1903) 173–94.

[45] *Annales regni francorum* s.a.800, ed. R. Rau, *Quellen zur karolingischen Reichsgeschichte* I (Darmstadt, 1974), p. 72, Eng. trans. Bernard Scholz, *Carolingian Chronicles* (Ann Arbor, 1970), p. 78.

Reichenau

Reichenau, founded on a peninsular island at the western end of Lake Constance by the Aquitainian or Visigothic Pirmin in 724, enjoyed the patronage of the Carolingian house from the very beginning of its history.[46] To have achieved such a considerable collection of some 415 books by the second decade of the ninth century, it is likely that the monastery had been active in book production and acquisition for at least the half-century preceding the compilation of its catalogue, and that this rapid growth had much to do with the monastery's wide network of contacts with the great houses of western Francia and those of Alemannia.[47] The catalogue survives in a copy made in 1630 by Johann Egon from a now lost parchment roll.[48] The list was far more systematic in its arrangement than any yet made, and clearly owes much to the intelligence and dedication of its probable compiler, Reginbert (d.847), whose own books, copied or given by him, are listed in a separate section of the catalogue.[49] The date of the first list is carefully recorded in the heading: *Brevis librorum qui sunt in Coenobio Sindleozes Auua, facta anno VIII Hludovici imperatoris*, and the categories of book are distinguished under separate headings. The books of the Old and New Testament come first, starting with a complete Bible and followed by the separate books, more or less in the order of the accepted scriptural canon. There were eight gospel books, three copies of the Epistles of Paul, two of Acts and the Book of Revelation. Thereafter the works of Augustine, Jerome, Gregory, Leo, Cyprian, Eusebius, Hilary of Poitiers, Basil and Athanasius were detailed at length, succeeded by a section of saint's lives (including such early Carolingian ones as the Lives of Arnulf, Geneviève and Emmeram), a motley collection of books that the cataloguer appears to have had some difficulty classifying, such as the group of *collectanea* and *sententiae*, the *Liber Pontificalis*, the *Ordo Romanus*, Daretus Phrygius, Apollonius, Vitruvius, *De Architectura* and a *Mappae clavicula de efficiendo auro*. The works of Josephus then precede a

---

[46] See, for example, the foundation charter edited with commentaries by Peter Classen, ed., *Die Grundungsurkunden der Reichenau*, Vorträge und Forschungen 24 (Sigmaringen, 1977). Pirmin's career is charted by A. Angenendt, 'Pirmin und Bonifatius. Ihr Verhältnis zu Mönchtum, Bischofsamt und Adel', in Arno Borst, ed., *Mönchtum, Episkopat und Adel zur Grundungszeit des Klosters Reichenau*, Vorträge und Forschungen 20 (Sigmaringen, 1974), pp. 251–96, and Arnold Angenendt, *Monachi Peregrini: Studien zu Pirmin und den monastischen Vorstellungen des frühen Mittelalters* (Munich, 1972).

[47] For full treatment of the culture and intellectual activity at Reichenau in the Carolingian period see K. Beyerle ed., *Die Kultur der Abtei Reichenau: Erinnerungsschrift zur zwölfhundertsten Wiederkehr des Grundungsjahres des Inselklosters, 724–1924* (Munich, 1925), and Borst, ed., *Mönchtum*.

[48] Lehmann, *Mittelalterliche Bibliothekskataloge*, pp. 240–52.

[49] *Ibid.*, pp. 257–62, and see Paul Lehmann. 'Die Mittelalterliche Bibliothek', in Beyerle, *Reichenau*, pp. 645–56.

large group of law books, comprising Roman law (the Theodosian code), barbarian codes (Ripuarian, Salic, Lombard and Alemannic), and the laws of the Carolingian kings (presumably the capitulary collection made by Ansegis), the history by Gregory of Tours, some German songs, a map of the world and Einhard's Life of Charlemagne. A small collection of medical books and a very large one of liturgical books (fifty-eight sacramentaries, twelve lectionaries, ten antiphonaries, eight books of offices and fifty psalters) then precede a further selection of minor patristic and early mediaeval works, including the *collectanea* of Eugippius and Primasius, the poetry of Aldhelm and a large collection of the exegetical works of Bede, all arranged under author headings like those in the first part of the catalogue, and with composite volumes clearly indicated. These authors, moreover, are for the most part in chronological order from Ambrose to Alcuin. They are succeeded by sections on canon law, sermons, monastic rules, saints' lives, glossaries, grammar and poetry.

This, then, is a subject catalogue, arranged according to the general function of the books, that is, reading and general wisdom in scripture and theology (Bible, church fathers), practical knowledge (law and medicine), ecclesiastical ritual (the liturgical books), education (the grammars and school books), ascetic discipline and the religious life (the monastic rules and saints' lives). Within these broad categories the authors are arranged very roughly into chronological order. Wild aberrations in this, such as putting Gregory the Great between Jerome and Leo may well reflect the status of the author as far as the community of Reichenau was concerned. This resembles the practice of the Würzburg catalogue, which listed its possessions in the order of their importance to the foundation itself. Gregory the Great was very early counted as one of the foremost fathers of the church with Augustine and Jerome, and this in fact was an approbation bestowed generally by the Anglo-Saxons and Franks, and not just by the Reichenau monks.[50] It would be tempting to see in this Reichenau catalogue the signs of a new order and development, and accord it the status of model or exemplar. It certainly appears to have influenced the structure of the St Gall catalogue, and could have done so directly, and at Lorsch and Murbach there are significant similarities in the layout of the lists.

[50] Gregory the Great undoubtedly owed much of his reputation in the early mediaeval west to the staunch championship on the part of the English. The English probably taught the Franks to revere this Pope, though his theological writings had begun to circulate in the Frankish kingdoms by the end of the seventh century; see, for example, the Luxeuil manuscripts Ivrea 1 (*Cura Pastoralis*), BL Add. 11878 (*Moralia in Job*), Verona XL (*Moralia in Job*), Leningrad Q.v.I.14 (Homilies on Ezekiel): *CLA* III, 300; II, 163; IV, 497; XI, 1617).

Reichenau's thoughtful systematization, however, may owe more to a developing canon of knowledge and categorization of learning which it embodied and passed on, as it were, in codified form. That is, rather than being the initiator it may represent one, surviving, instance of developments common to Carolingian monastic and cathedral libraries as a whole. These common developments will be discussed below. Other lists, therefore, could be independent reflections of this same canon of knowledge and pass on their codification of it to their own institutions and their associates.

Reichenau's list was not recast subsequently. There was little attempt to accommodate later acquisitions; lists were simply added to it. Thus there is one of the books written at Reichenau in the time of abbot Erlebald (823–38), which can be taken as the librarian's assessment of the library's needs. It comprised many works by Augustine and other patristic authors and additional school books. The liturgical books of Abbot Erlebald himself are noted, and the list contains added information in the form of indications of the scribe or donor, and, occasionally, records of to whom the books have been lent. In the case of Jerome's commentary on Ezekiel, for example, the volume had been lent to the abbey of St Denis. There is also a list of gifts presented by a number of priests (whose names in these or similar forms also occur in the Reichenau confraternity book), and two further lists of books drawn up in 838 to 842 under Abbot Ruadhelm.[51]

The first of these notes that the Institutes of Cassiodorus have been added to the library as well as treatises by such contemporary authors as Hraban Maur. A rough chronological order is also maintained in the recording of these volumes. The second is the most detailed list of all. It provides descriptions of the contents of many composite volumes written by Reginbert of Reichenau himself. He copied a selection of treatises on various prayers and creeds; another consisted of grammars; the third of historical works; a fourth, more grammar and poetry; a fifth, a collection of accounts of visions; a sixth contained hymns; another concerned heresies; and further collections were compiled of philosophical treatises, the passions and lives of saints, law, the Rule of Benedict, German songs, penitentials, antiphons, prayers and accounts of voyages to the holy land, medicine, the offices and the Christian life, history, the mass, and Bede's *De natura rerum*. It is a staggering collection and, judging from some repetitions of items in the 821 list, does not necessarily represent new additions to the library since 821. Reginbert's item 18, for example, corresponds word for word with the composite law book containing the

---

[51] Lehmann, *Mittelalterliche Bibliothekskataloge*, pp. 254–6.

capitularies of Charlemagne listed in the 821 catalogue. In other words, some of Reginbert's work had already been recorded in the earlier list.

A further Reichenau catalogue of the second half of the ninth century attests to the continuing interest in maintaining the rich resources of the library on the part of the librarians. It is primarily a list of patristic and more recent theology, though there are also a number of history books, such as Freculph's *Chronicorum tomi duo*, Paul the Deacon's *Historia langobardorum* and Bede's *Historia ecclesiastica gentis anglorum*. Significantly, too, there is the guide to Christian authors provided in Gennadius' *De viris illustribus*. More works on asceticism were added, and the school book and poetry collection was also augmented. Reichenau was quite clearly a thriving institution, with a remarkable library, and a productive scriptorium. It is a monument to the effectiveness of the Frankish promotion of literacy, learning and education. Many of its books now survive in Karlsruhe, whither they were removed in 1805. Its cultural preeminence in the Alemannian region is clear, not least because of the wealth of evidence afforded by its library catalogues, and by the activities of the more illustrious of its scholars, such as Walafrid Strabo.[52]

St Gall

St Gall, with which Reichenau had many links, was also possessed of a fine library, an active scriptorium and a famous school.[53] That the monastery which has proved to have played such an active role in the promotion of the uses of literacy and in the conduct of legal business in the community should also have been a centre of learning and book production is only fitting. It serves to stress the essential link there was between the uses of literacy in day-to-day living and the promotion of the written word and education as a vehicle for the word of God, the scriptures and the wisdom of the holy fathers.[54] As at Reichenau, the relationship between scriptorium and library can be seen very clearly in the catalogues produced in the second half of the ninth century. The oldest book list from St Gall survives

[52] Bernhard Bischoff, 'Eine Sammelhandschrift Walahfrid Strabos (cod. Sangall. 878), *MS* II, pp. 34–51, and Wesley Stevens, 'Compotistica et astronomia in the Fulda school', in M. H. King and W. M. Stevens, eds., *Saints, Scholars and Heroes. Studies in Medieval Culture in Honour of Charles W. Jones* (Collegeville, Minnesota, 1979), pp. 27–64, especially pp. 31–2.

[53] There is a wealth of literature on St Gall and its cultural and intellectual activity in the Carolingian period. Only a selection of the most recent can be provided here, but all contain ample bibliographical guidance for further study: Johannes Duft, *Abendländisches Mönchtum* (St Gall, 1980); Peter Ochsenbein, *St Galler Klosterschule* (St Gall, 1983); and J. Duft and R. Schnyder, *Die Elfenbein-Einbände der Stiftsbibliothek St Gallen* (Beuron, 1984).

[54] See above pp. 87–126.

in two redactions, the original in St Gall 728, pp. 4–21, at the beginning of a law book, and a copy of it in St Gall 267.[55] Lehmann dated the catalogue between 850 and 860, with additions dating from about 880, which note the loss of a book, books required by the library, and whether or not a book has been lent, either to an individual, or to another centre for copying, or to the school for use in the classroom. Sometimes there are descriptive notes concerning the quality of the book or the script in which it is written. There is, indeed, a whole section at the beginning on scripts *in scottice scripti*, that is, in insular script. A disillusioned reader annotated the list with various intemperate comments on the lies and falsehoods in a work, how unreadable or useless or out of date it was, and, very occasionally, added an approving remark.[56]

The insular books represent a complete miscellany of titles, with the books of the Bible, exegesis on scripture, grammar and poetry in a random selection. The full St Gall catalogue, on the other hand, is organized in an arrangement very similar to that of the first Reichenau catalogue, save that there are some differences in the sequence of authors which may or may not be significant. Of the 264 codices (395 separate works), the full Bible pandect, or *Bibliotheca*, is listed first, followed by the Heptateuch and other Old Testament and New Testament volumes. This corresponds to the Reichenau order. But then Gregory the Great precedes Jerome, Augustine, Ambrose, Prosper, Isidore, Origen, Pelagius, Cassiodorus, Eusebius and Gregory of Tours. There are then a number of *florilegia* volumes, Tichonius' commentary on the Apocalypse and that of Primasius, works by Alcuin, monastic rules, lives of the fathers, virtues and passions of the apostles, saints and martyrs, conciliar decrees, exposition of the mass, canon law, hymns and penitentials, law and more recent homilies and exegesis. School books, with grammars, treatises on spelling and metre, and poetry, are listed last. Such relegation of school books to the end was also a feature of the Reichenau catalogue, and also of the St Riquier inventory.

Extra and later lists record gifts made to the abbey by Grimalt, abbot from 841 to 872, and the books written in the abbey's scriptorium and added to the library in the time of Hartmut, abbot from 872 to 883.

---

[55] Lehmann, *Mittelalterliche Bibliothekskataloge*, pp. 66–82. The best account of the St Gall catalogues is provided by Johannes Duft, 'Die Handschriften-Katalogisierung in der Stiftsbibliothek St Gallen vom 9. bis zum 19. Jahrhundert', in B. M. von Scarpatetti, *Die Handschriften der Stiftsbibliothek St Gallen* (St Gall, 1983), pp. 9*–99*, especially 9*–28*.

[56] For example, of a commentary on the Psalms attributed to Jerome, the annotator notes that it is *inutilia* and that excerpts made from Jerome's commentary on Matthew and Mark are *mendacium*, and another set of excerpts on Matthew is of no use (*ad nihil utilia*). A copy of the *Sententiae* of Isidore of Seville is defective and full of gaps; Isidore's *Liber Differentiarum* and *De officiis* are very old and the copy of the *Etymologiae* is corrupt.

Hartmut also bequeathed his personal collection of books to the library.[57] This meant that the library acquired some duplicates, but for the most part greater riches, in every branch of learning – scripture, liturgy, theology, philosophy, history, grammar and literature – were added, as well as a few works by contemporary Carolingian scholars. In Grimalt's time, Hartmut, for example, acquired for the abbey the *Visio Wettini* of Walafrid Strabo and also the *Visio Barontii*. Generally, however, the St Gall library was remarkably conservative in its accessions policy, rarely acquiring authors later than Bede, and with a preponderance of patristic authors. If deficient in contemporary authors, on the other hand, St Gall had a notable collection of classical authors, though not quite so many as the monastery at Lorsch.[58] We have a record, moreover, only of the books in the main library of the monastery; on an analogy with St Riquier, the liturgical books for use in the abbey church may have been kept in the sacristy, and the books in constant use in the school, including the many didactic treatises of Carolingian authorship, may have been kept in the schoolroom. The lectionarium in Grimalt's library is sent *ad basilicam*. The copies of Kings, and some of the books of the Apocrypha are noted as having been borrowed for the school.[59] Thus the school or church could borrow from the main library when necessary. The libraries of Grimalt and Hartmut, therefore, may well represent additions divided among the three possible repositories of books in the monastery.

The careers of Grimalt and Hartmut do much to account for the many similarities to be observed between library organization at Reichenau and St Gall. Grimalt, born of a noble Rhineland Frankish family, had been a pupil of Alcuin, taught at Reichenau and served as chaplain at the court of Louis the Pious, as abbot of Weissenburg and finally as chancellor and archchaplain to Louis the German, second son of Louis the Pious and ruler of the east Frankish kingdom created for him by his father after the *Ordinatio Imperii* of 817. Grimalt also served as abbot of St Gall from 841 to 872, and was succeeded in the office by Hartmut, an Alemannian, who had been educated at Fulda but had made his career at St Gall as the

---

[57] Lehmann, *Mittelalterliche Bibliothekskataloge*, pp. 87–9. Grimalt's collection, according to the superscription, owed much to Hartmut's energy: *Hos libros patrauit Grimoldus abba in monasterio s[an]c[t]i Galli in dieb[us] Hludouui[ci] regis Germanie cu[m] adiutorio Hartmoti p[re]positi sui p[er] annos XXX et unum.* It consisted of fifty-three entries mentioning sixty-seven different works.

[58] For example, Vergil, Horace, Seneca, Juvenal, Apuleius, Solinus, *Dicta Catonis*, Donatus, *Dictys Cretensis*, Seruius, Vegetius, Dares Phrygius, Pompeius, Asper, Terence, Aratus, Persius, Statius, pseudo-Caper, Hermas Pastor and Diomedes; and see Heinrich Büttner and Johannes Duft, *Lorsch und St Gallen in der Frühzeit* (Constance and Stuttgart, 1965), especially pp. 37–8. See also Duft, 'Handschriften-Katalogisierung', pp. 24*–25*.

[59] Lehmann, *Mittelalterliche Bibliothekskataloge*, pp. 86–7.

protégé of Abbot Grimalt.[60] It was under Hartmut's direction that the greatest glories of the St Gall scriptorium were produced, such as the so-called Hartmut Bible, the Folchart Psalter and the Golden Psalter (St Gall 77, 78, 81, 82, 83, 23 and 22).[61] St Gall clearly owed the richness and diversity of its library, and the nature of its catalogue, to its own links with other communities and to those of its illustrious abbots. It is surely no accident that the best evidence of outstanding libraries comes from those houses most favoured by royal patronage, such as Reichenau, St Gall and Lorsch.[62]

Lorsch

Lorsch owed its origins to a Frankish noble family. It was founded by Count Chancor, one of those who assisted the Carolingian mayors in the process of the extension of Carolingian influence into Alemannia.[63] He served as count in the Thurgau in 745, after that he acted as count in the Breisgau in 758 and later on was active in the Lahn region in the Wetterau and Rheingau. Lorsch, however, was put under the authority of Chrodegang of Metz by Chancor and thus from the very beginning its fortunes were entwined with those of the newly emergent Carolingian house, its politics and its enterprise for ecclesiastical reform in the second half of the eighth century.[64] Having begun life as a family monastery or *Eigenkloster*, it thus came in due course under the aegis of the bishop of Metz and became in 772 a royal monastery. Its prosperity and importance increased rapidly thereafter. The monastery's first abbot was Gundeland (d. 778). In his time alone a staggering number of gifts were made to the abbey. Büttner estimates them as over 1,500. But well into the ninth century Lorsch was the fortunate recipient of great wealth, especially from

---

[60] Bernhard Bischoff, 'Bücher am Hofe Ludwigs des Deutschen und die Privatbibliothek des Kanzlers Grimalt', *MS* III, pp. 187–212.

[61] On the Bible see the comments in Duft, 'Handschriften-Katalogisierung', p. 19*, and his exhibition catalogue. *Die Bibel in der Stiftsbibliothek* (St Gall, 1981), p. 9. On the scriptorium of St Gall in the time of Grimald see Bruckner, *Scriptoria* III, pp. 24–42.

[62] A long series of royal diplomata conferring land, privileges and concessions on St Gall attests to the royal patronage the monastery enjoyed in the ninth and tenth centuries from Louis the Pious and his successors. See W.226, 233, 234, 263, 312, 357, 434, 435, 449, 453, 454, 477, 503, 519, 527, 569, 570, 586, 587, 588, 590, 591, 602, 604, 608, 613, 614, 623, 627, 628, 632, 642, 653, 661–4, 666, 667, 670, 674, 675, 682, 683, 685, 687, 688, 694, 695, 698, 706, 708, 716, 720, 724, 726, 730, 734, 735, 740, 741, 748, 755, 765, 767, 769.

[63] On the early history of Lorsch, see H. Büttner, 'Lorsch und St Gallen', in Buttner and Duft, *Lorsch und St Gallen*, pp. 7–20, and his references.

[64] Chrodegang's promotion of reform and the link with the Carolingians are discussed by Eugen Ewig, 'Saint Chrodegang et la réforme de l'église franque' in *Saint Chrodegang* (Metz, 1967), pp. 25–53.

members of the Carolingian royal family. It is hardly to be wondered at, nay, rather to be expected, that Lorsch should be a highly active centre of book production. And so it was. Its manuscripts fully reflect the key position the monastery occupied in Frankish culture and intellectual life, and its catalogues are, with the extant manuscripts, our best evidence of the magnificence of this library.[65]

There are four ninth-century catalogues of the Lorsch library, dated between 830 and 860. Three are in Vat. pal. lat. 1877, a manuscript unusual in that its sole contents are the three Lorsch catalogues (I: fos. 67–79; II: fos. 40–60; and III: fos. 1–34) and a catalogue of books in the library of Fulda dated to the first half of the ninth century (fos. 35–44). The fourth Lorsch catalogue, III*, is on fos. 1–7 (the first quire) of Vat. pal. lat. 57, the remaining folios of which contain the Epistles of St Paul and some homilies. Some late ninth-century additions were made to these catalogues, and the gifts of Gerward, who had been librarian at the court of Louis the Pious and who retired to Lorsch, are listed at the end of the first catalogue.

The relationship between these four catalogues was unravelled by Bernhard Bischoff.[66] The earliest catalogue numbered I, that in the last section of Vat. pal. lat. 1877, fos. 67–79, was written in a regular and attractive caroline minuscule with the title and headings in rustic capitals. Additions were made by at least five different hands, and with the exception of a few headings, Bischoff had dated this list to *c.* 830. Spaces were left between author sections, quite clearly for later acquisitions of works by the same author to be inserted. This early catalogue provided the model for the later ones. It appears to have been the librarian's copy and was used for some time. Catalogue II is incomplete. It was written by two scribes in hands not of the Lorsch type in the second quarter of the ninth century, that is, not many years after catalogue I. There are few corrections and no additions. Bischoff concluded that catalogue II was a calligraphical, that is, a fair, copy, which unlike catalogue I appears hardly to have been used. Although a very close relationship can be observed between the two lists, II is not a direct copy of I, for it lists about seventy volumes not in I. It is possible that these were overlooked when I was compiled. Catalogue II may have been a copy made for taking, or sending, elsewhere. Catalogue III is the most comprehensive catalogue of them all

---

[65] Fully analysed by Bischoff, *Lorsch*, and celebrated in 1986 in the magnificent exhibition in Heidelberg, for the bulk of the Lorsch manuscripts now form part of the Palatine collection in the Biblioteca Apostolica in the Vatican: see Elmar Mittler, ed., *Bibliotheca Palatina. Katalog der Ausstellung vom 8. Juli bis 2. November 1986 Heiliggeistkirche Heidelberg* (Heidelberg, 1986).

[66] Bischoff, *Lorsch*, pp. 8–18.

and occupies the first thirty-four folios of the manuscript. It starts with the biblical books and appended to it is the list of Gerward's books. It is headed *Breviarium librorum s[an]c[t]i Nazarii* and includes the liturgical books and monastic rules which were probably kept in the sacristy. Bischoff dated the two hands responsible for this catalogue to the third quarter of the ninth century. The books of Gerward added at the end must have been listed in about 860.

These lists thus record the activity of the Lorsch scriptorium and the zeal of the abbots and librarians in acquiring books for most of the ninth century. Essentially, the scribal activity of Lorsch in the Carolingian period is also recorded in these catalogues. The first century of the monastery's history seems to have been one of rapid expansion and growth in the library, but this eased off by about the mid-ninth century; the rate both of acquisition and copying of new manuscripts appears subsequently to have diminished. Seen in conjunction with the manuscripts extant from the Lorsch scriptorium, most of them now in the Palatine collection in the Vatican or the Laud collection in the Bodleian Library in Oxford, the catalogues reflect clearly the interdependence of scriptorium and library. It was of crucial importance that the abbot or master of the school or director of the scriptorium should be devoted to learning and should promote the activity of the scriptorium. He should also donate books to, and acquire books and exemplars from elsewhere for, the library. Such devotion has to be seen within the general context of the promotion of Christian learning and education on the part of the Carolingian rulers and scholars. Particular abbots and scholars, as we have seen in the instances from Reichenau and St Gall of Reginbert, Grimalt and Hartmut, can be credited with the activity of the monastery's scriptorium in the production of books. While no one person can be associated with the compilation of the Lorsch catalogues, it seems certain that their compilation was to serve the administration of the library. Catalogue III* is of particular interest in this respect. Bischoff has argued that it was a copy of III made in the mid-ninth century from an older exemplar of III, and that it was the 'short title' catalogue used as a check list and control of the contents of the library. Twenty titles have been crossed out, presumably because they were no longer to be found in the library. Although it occupies only a single quire, it contains most of catalogue III; it abbreviates words and titles to a drastic degree, as well as economizing on space and omitting the detailed itemization of sermons and letters in their respective volumes.

Structure of the Lorsch catalogues and its influence

The structure and organization of these catalogues is impossible to determine from the jumbled travesty of an edition provided by Angelo Mai, and reproduced, with its errors compounded, by Becker.[67] Only resort to the manuscripts can clarify Mai's pastiche, the shortcomings of which have been lucidly exposed by Bischoff.[68] Once observed in their original state, however, the Lorsch catalogues are impressive for their sophistication and detail. The order of the first catalogue, I, is as follows: without the customary preliminary biblical books the list starts with church fathers, and, unusually, with Cyprian, Athanasius and Hilary of Poitiers. Gregory Nazianzus, Basil, Fulgentius, Timothy and Eucherius complete what is primarily, apart from the Gallo-Romans Hilary and Eucherius, a section of early eastern church fathers. Following them are two Spaniards, Julian of Toledo and Isidore of Seville, and then Gregory the Great and Bede. The latter's ecclesiastical history is listed before his biblical exegesis. Thereafter come the commoner patristic authors: Origen, Augustine, Eugippius and Jerome succeeded by John of Constantinople, Irenaeus of Lyon, Prosper, Jacobus, and Gregory Nazianzus. Works thereafter tend to be single items but some are by all of the authors already listed. Last of all come the grammars, monastic rules, letter collections, medical books, hymns, poetry, passions of saints and the *De locis sanctis* of Adomnan, bound into the same volume as Isidore of Seville's *De ordine creaturarum*. Finally, there is a volume of epitaphs. Great care was taken in the recording of these titles, and much detail is supplied, especially in the itemization of the sermons and letters in the Augustine and Hieronymian collections.

Catalogue II is set out more systematically than catalogue I. All the author sections have spaces left between them and the list begins with various collections of homilies and *sententiae* before starting the author list with Origen, Ambrose, Augustine and Prosper, an order which is at least chronological.

Catalogue III, on the other hand, is presented in an order close to that of the Reichenau and St Gall catalogues. The first folio lists gospel books, homilies, monastic rules and liturgical books. An *Evangelium scriptum cum auro pictum habens tabulas eburneas* heads the catalogue, and it is possible that this can be identified with the famous Lorsch Gospels, product of the

---

[67] Becker, *Catalogi*, No. 37, pp. 82–125, from (with some adjustments) Angelo Mai, *Spicilegii Romani* V (Rome, 1841), pp. 161–200.

[68] A new edition is being prepared by Gunter Berndt for the series *Mittelalterliche-bibliothekskataloge Deutschlands und der Schweiz*, now under the general editorship of Bernhard Bischoff.

court school of Charlemagne. The separation of this portion of the catalogue from the rest by a blank leaf, one side of which was subsequently filled up with notes concerning books of biblical exegesis, including a number of volumes of the contemporary author Hraban Maur of Fulda, suggests that it may refer to books kept in a different part of the monastery. The main hand resumes on folio 3r, and records the books of the Old and New Testament, though without the gospels. The new section is full of history books – Eusebius, Josephus, Orosius, Bede, the *Liber Pontificalis*, Gregory of Tours, Jordanes, Pompeius Trogus, and the *Historia Tripartita*, an Epitome of Livy, Hydatius and Solinus. Subsequent entries are organized under authors, with very full descriptions of the contents of each volume of *Quaestiones*, *Epistolae* and *Homiliae*. Augustine leads followed by Jerome, Bede, Ambrose, Origen, Cassiodorus, Isidore, Hilary, Alcuin, John Chrysostom and other early church fathers. Among Jerome's works is listed a composite volume containing guides to Christian authors: *De inlustribus viris et Gennadii et liber institutionum divinarum scripturarum Cassiodori et de historiis Christianis in uno codice*. There is a section devoted to minor exegesis and theological controversy, another to letter collections, and a major portion of the catalogue is devoted to classical authors, school books, grammars, works on metre, poetry and the works of Cicero. It includes, however, some more practical volumes in the shape of Vegetius' *De re militari* and copies of the Visigothic, Salic and Ripuarian law codes. The final lines are devoted to saints' lives, among whom appear the Lives of the Merovingian saints Vedast and Medard, and the English missionaries Willibrord and Boniface.

Gerward's books, listed separately, show a devotion to the work of Augustine, even to a copy of his Life. He also owned Bede's *De templi aedificatione*, his commentary on Luke, *De orthographia* and *Hexameron*, Jerome *De actibus virorum* and Cassiodorus' *De institutione divinarum lectionum*, Orosius and a copy of the Song of Songs bound with Bede's commentary on it, as well as his own copies of some of the books of the Old Testament – Job, Tobit, Judith, Esdras, Esther and Maccabees, the Prophets – and Acts, Homilies by Gregory the Great, Hilary's *De trinitate* and, revealingly, his own copy of the poetry of Virgil. Bischoff has identified some of these twenty-seven volumes among extant manuscripts.[69] Gerward had been taught at Lorsch in the second decade of the ninth century but was afterwards transferred to the palace, perhaps through the agency of the Abbot Adalung, who was high in favour at the court of Louis

[69] Gerward's books and his career are discussed by Bischoff, *Lorsch*, pp. 54–7. See also Heinz Lowe, 'Studien zu den Annales Xantenses', *Deutsches Archiv für die Erforschung des Mittelalters* 8 (1950) 59–99.

the Pious. There Gerward acted as librarian to Louis and did much to rehabilitate the royal library.[70] With Walafrid Strabo he was a member of the group of scholars who enjoyed the patronage of the Empress Judith.[71] Gerward later retired to Gannita (Ghent) near Nijmegen, which his family had also endowed, and there was responsible for writing the Xanten Annals until 860, the probable year of his death.

The essential agents for the growth of a Carolingian library, a series of zealous and well-educated abbots and librarians, were not lacking at Lorsch. Indeed, Lorsch was closely linked with the royal court as well as such centres as Fulda, Reichenau and St Vaast. Like Reichenau and Weissenburg, it is possible that Lorsch sent promising boys to the great school at Fulda, widely renowned in its heyday under the direction of Hraban Maur and Rudolf. A succession of abbots who had been taught by the leading scholars of the day ensured the importance of Lorsch. Abbot Ricbod (784–804), had been a student of Alcuin's and later was elevated to the see of Trier. Himself the author of a commentary on the Rule of Benedict, the *Adunatio regulae*, and with links with the royal palace, he probably contributed much to the development of the scriptorium, as did Abbot Adalung (804–37), who was also connected with the court and from 808 onwards abbot of St Vaast, an appointment which undoubtedly enhanced Lorsch's connections with the main cultural centres of northern Francia. The likelihood that the Lorsch catalogue II was intended for the north-east Frankish monastery, possibly for St Vaast itself, is an indication of the way in which Lorsch influence could extend itself. Samuel, abbot from 837 to 856, a friend and former school-fellow of Hraban Maur, also appears to have presided over a great increase in the library's possessions (despite later Lorsch traditions to the contrary), while under Abbot Engilbert (856–64) there was the last great period of growth of the library and output of the scriptorium.[72]

For much of the ninth century, therefore, Lorsch maintained a position of importance and influence within the Carolingian political and intellectual world. Owing much throughout its existence to Carolingian patronage, in many ways it exemplifies the systematic cultivation of knowledge, production of books and encouragement of learning we have learned to associate with the great Carolingian houses. The close links with Fulda in particular, moreover, evinced not least in the presence of the Fulda library catalogue in the Lorsch collection, as well as with Reichenau,

---

[70] Bernhard Bischoff, 'Die Hofbibliothek unter Ludwig dem Frommen', *MS* III, pp. 170–86.

[71] Friedrich von Bezold, 'Kaiserin Judith und ihre Dichter Walahfrid Strabo', *Historische Zeitschrift* 130 (1924) 375–439.

[72] Bischoff, *Lorsch*, pp. 52–61.

the royal court and St Vaast, make it necessary to acknowledge Lorsch as one of the principal disseminators of the canon of texts and knowledge elaborated by its catalogue. Both the exemplars it provided for other houses and the catalogue itself, as we will see, can be recognized as the means by which this propagation and dissemination were achieved.

Cologne

A close link with the royal court can also be postulated for the cathedral library of Cologne in the time of Archbishop Hildebald, Charlemagne's archchaplain (785–819). Written in the year 833 in a slightly ragged caroline minuscule, and thus some years after Hildebald's death, the catalogue of Cologne's cathedral library represents a tribute to the energy with which Hildebald assembled books and encouraged his own, and other, scriptoria to write them for his cathedral library.[73] The surviving list was entered on the four flyleaves of a *Liber Ferrandi diaconi ad reginum comitem*, a volume itself identifiable with item 93 in the list it contains, though it is possible that these leaves were bound into the volume at a later stage. Dekker, the catalogue's editor, thought the *capitalis rustica* inscription on fo. 1 referred to the whole list and thus that all the books listed were those sent by Pope Leo to Charlemagne, but this has been convincingly refuted by Lehmann.[74] Many of the items in this catalogue were identified by Dekker with books of eighth- and ninth- century date in the *Dombibliothek* at Cologne, many of which bear the inscription *Codex s[an]c[t]i Petri sub pio patre Hildebaldo scriptus*.

The catalogue as a whole conforms to the arrangement observed in the others so far discussed. A *bibliotheca* (Bible) precedes separate volumes of the Old and New Testament Books, and is followed by a rich selection of liturgical codices. These may have included liturgical books in use in the church. Among them, however, is recorded an illustrated Apocalypse in addition to the copy of the Book of Revelation listed in its proper place. Thereafter each author is listed in turn, with every entry on a new line and, usually, a space of between one and four lines left between each author or section, presumably to accommodate any later additions. Thus Augustine, Athanasius, Augustine (again), Bede, Jerome, Gregory, *Collectanea* by various authors, Isidore, John Chrysostom and Ambrose and

---

[73] On book production for Hildebald, see Bernhard Bischoff, 'Die Kölner Nonnen-handschriften und das Skriptorium von Chelles', *MS* I, pp. 16–34.

[74] A. Dekker, 'Die Hildebold'sche Manuskriptensammlung des Kölner Domes', in *Festschrift der drei und vierzigsten Versammlung deutscher Philologen und Schulmänner dargeboten von den höheren Lehranstalten Kölns* (Bonn, 1895), pp. 215–51. Compare the comments on it by Paul Lehmann, 'Erzbischof Hildebald und die Dombibliothek von Köln', in *Erforschung des Mittelalters* II, pp. 139–44, and L. W. Jones, *The Script of Cologne from Hildebald to Hermann* (Cambridge, Mass., 1983).

Alcuin are succeeded by canon law, saints' lives (in which a goodly number of the lives of local saints are preserved), *computus* texts, treatises on different aspects of asceticism, penitentials, an ancient medical codex, some secular law codes (Roman, Salic and Ripuarian) and some poetry (Vergil, Sedulius and Iuvencus). Last of all are the grammatical works, treatises on orthography and glossaries, a manual for instructing pagans and rustics, and the Prayers of Gregory the Great. It is an unpretentious library, admirably reflecting the various preoccupations of the scriptorium's production, assisting the diocesan clergy in their daily ministry and augmenting the Christian learning of the abler canons and, no doubt, the archbishop himself. It is likely that there was also a school at Cologne, and that it maintained its tradition of instruction, assisted by the books in its library, throughout the ninth and tenth centuries. The library also served the needs of the community apart from the priests and canons of the cathedral and diocese. A list of borrowers at the back of the same manuscript in which the catalogue of 833 is preserved, records loans to a number of laymen and laywomen who presumably had some personal connection with the cathedral.[75]

The acquisition of books: the example of Murbach

Some interesting questions with regard to the methods and principles for acquiring books are raised by the catalogue from the abbey of Murbach.[76] It was compiled in the mid-ninth century but survives only in a copy made on paper by Sigismund Meisterlin in 1464, now Colmar, Archives Départementales du Haut-Rhin, Cartulaire Abbaye Murbach No. 1, pp. 86–96 (fos. 44v–49v). It is from the third quarter of the ninth century and contains after the main catalogue a shorter list of books belonging to Abbot Iskar. This lists books not in the library when the first catalogue was made. The monastery was another of Pirmin's foundations, established by him in 728, though as early as 730 Romanus had been installed as abbot. It is likely that all the foundations of Pirmin – Reichenau, Murbach, Hornbach in the diocese of Metz, and the smaller houses which came into his sphere of influence such as Schuttern, Gengenbach, Maursmünster and Neuweiler – maintained links with each other. Thus some influence from Reichenau as far as the library and its organization are concerned is likely, likelihood that grows to certainty when it is recalled that Geneva

---

[75] See below, pp. 261–6.
[76] W. Milde, ed. with commentary, *Der Bibliothekskataloge des Klosters Murbach aus dem 9. Jahrhundert. Ausgabe und Untersuchung von Beziehungen zu Cassiodors 'Institutiones', Beiheft* to *Euphorion. Zeitschrift für Literaturgeschichte* 4 (Heidelberg, 1968).

21, a ninth-century copy of the Reichenau library catalogue, was actually sent to Murbach.[77]

The main catalogue is organized like those of Lorsch, St Gall, Reichenau and St Riquier according to author and, loosely, subject, but omits all reference to biblical or liturgical books. The authors are listed as follows: Cyprian, Hilary of Poitiers, Ambrose, Jerome, Augustine, in strict chronological order, followed by Origen, Basil, John Chrysostom, Gregory I, Isidore of Seville, Bede, Cassiodorus, Cassian, Prosper, Primasius, Julian of Toledo and Gregory Nazianzus, where the chronological order is somewhat awry. All these works are expositions on books of scripture, or theology, sermons and letters, though Bede's ecclesiastical history is included in the list of his works rather than in the later section on history books. Thereafter the catalogue is devoted to school books or the works of contemporary authors. After two entries for Apponius' commentary on the Song of Songs and Pelagius on the Epistles of Paul, there is a section for the works of Boethius, then books of excerpts from the works of Gregory by Taio of Saragossa and Paterius, and Junilius' *De diversis librorum regulis*. A large collection of the didactic treatises of Alcuin and of Hraban Maur follows, between which are listed some minor works, mostly *collectanea* such as that of Eugippius. Thereafter the catalogue becomes a subject catalogue with separate headings for history, Christian poetry, the prose of classical antiquity (Livy, Cicero and grammars), classical poetry (in which Vitruvius' *De Architectura* is included!) and a short list of medical books. Last of all is a *liber notarum*. Milde felt unable to identify this, but it could be a dictionary of tironian notes like the one written at St Amand at the end of the eighth century and now Kassel, philol. fol. 2.

Of great interest are the long lists of *desiderata*. The compiler of the Murbach catalogue listed fourteen works by Cyprian and noted that the other books by this author were wanted (*Reliquos eius libros adhuc quaerimus*). Similarly, after Ambrose's fourteen works is a list of a further eight the library did not have. The abbey possessed twenty-six works by Jerome and knew of a further five that it wanted and sought. At the end of different sections of the lists of Augustine's treatises, but before the itemization of his sermons, no less than thirty-nine books by Augustine are enumerated as *desiderata*. Lists of wanted books are also inserted after the sections on Prosper, Primasius and Bede. Murbach was very well stocked with the English historian and exegete's works, but with the comment,

---

[77] Lehmann, *Mittelalterliche Bibliothekskataloge*, p. 224, and compare Walter Berschin and K. E. Geith, 'Die Bibliothekskataloge des Klosters Murbach aus dem IX. Jahrhundert', *Zeitschrift für Kirchengeschichte* 83 (1972) 61–87, especially 62 n. 4.

sequentes libros non habentes, the librarian listed a further twenty he wished to acquire. Occasionally there are notes on the lack of parts of a work already possessed, such as the remaining books of Jerome's commentary on Jeremiah.

How did this cataloguer at ninth-century Murbach know about the existence of the books he wanted for the abbey library? Whence came his desire to provide his monastery with the works of these authors? The *desiderata* lists suggest a store of knowledge concerning the potential ideal library. The cataloguer knew what he should possess if only he could obtain it. This knowledge came partly, no doubt, from an accumulated familiarity with the output of the leading theologians of the Christian church and the school texts. More particularly, however, it was based on a number of bibliographies available in the early middle ages. The cataloguer himself twice mentioned that the *Retractationes* of Augustine, in which Augustine listed most of his works, apart from his letters and sermons, down to the year 427, was a source for his Augustinian *desiderata*. Milde has suggested that Bede's *Historia ecclesiastica gentis anglorum*, in which Bede helpfully lists his own writings, was used by the cataloguer when compiling his list of Bede *desiderata*, that Augustine's *Contra Iulianum* provided the list of works by Ambrose and that Book I of the *Institutiones* of Cassiodorus supplied the references to the wanted works of Jerome, Prosper, Primasius and a few of the Ambrosian titles.[78] Indeed, Cassiodorus, who mapped out a complete course of reading in scripture, patristic exegesis and theology in the first book of his *Institutiones*, was drawn upon most often.[79] Much may be due, therefore, to the zeal for increasing the store of religious learning that Cassiodorus inspired in the librarian at Murbach. The catalogue from Reichenau could also have served as a shopping list, as well as providing a model, for the organization of Murbach's own book catalogue. It will be clear from the itemization of author headings how closely the Murbach and Reichenau catalogues correspond, but the same can be said of those from St Gall, Lorsch and St Riquier. More general influences may well be at work, and these will be discussed more fully below in order to determine the precise role of these catalogues in the dissemination of knowledge.

The catalogue of Abbot Iskar of Murbach lists the books added to the library in the next two or three decades. It is arranged in a completely random order and is a very diversified collection, fully documented by Geith and Berschin. In view of the late date of this manuscript it is

---

[78] Milde, ed., *Murbach*, pp. 62–74, 109–21; and see also his sections on the use of lists of desired books as bibliographies, pp. 99–105.

[79] Cassiodorus, ed. R. A. B. Mynors, *Cassiodori Senatoris Institutiones* (Oxford, 1937).

impossible to establish why no order was imposed. Yet we have observed above that many later additions to clearly arranged catalogues tended to be miscellaneous in their presentation, especially those representing the books of one individual. Most branches of contemporary knowledge were represented, with an abundance of school texts and a group of Carolingian authors, such as Alcuin (commentary on Genesis), Hraban Maur (on Kings), Theodulf of Orleans (poetry) and Claudius of Turin (commentary on Matthew). Iskar's copies of the works of Bede duplicate those recorded in the earlier catalogue. The books themselves include none of those referred to as *desiderata* in the earlier catalogue. Nor are there any notes on the Iskar lists concerning items still required. Nevertheless, taken together, the Murbach catalogues are an impressive witness to the richness of this Alsacian monastery, the degree of resemblance between it and the other libraries we have considered and the conformity to an apparent orthodoxy in the provision of books.

Smaller inventories of books

Such conformity is evident also in the smaller lists and fragments of inventories of books extant from a number of Carolingian monasteries and cathedrals. The Staffelsee inventory fragment of 811, for example, a remnant of Charlemagne's request for information concerning the property of the churches in his realm, begins with the Heptateuch, other Old Testament Books and New Testament volumes, a lectionary and homiliary and basic liturgical texts as well as Gregory the Great's Homilies, Jerome's commentary on Matthew and a monastic rule.[80] The recorder of Walgarius of Cysoing's bequest to the monastery compiled more miscellaneous a list, with Gregory's *Moralia in Job* succeeding a homiliary and missal, and *Vitas patrum* before Bede's commentary on the Apocalypse and on the catholic epistles, a book of offices, a glossary, a *collectaneum* and two antiphonaries. Walgarius' complete Bible headed the list. The famous collection of Wulfad of Bourges is also somewhat random in its arrangement, but it is a specialist one of primarily theological and philosophical treatises.[81] The personal libraries of the noblemen Eberhard of Friuli and Eccard of Mâcon, on the other hand, conform more closely to the standard arrangement.[82] The extant list from Freising in Clm 6399 fo. 32v appears to be only of the

---

[80] It is preserved in Wolfenbüttel Helmst. 254, fos. 9r–9v. See Bischoff, ed., *Schatz-verzeichnisse*, pp. 90–1.

[81] Becker, *Catalogi*, No. 21, p. 42, and M. Cappuyns, 'Les *Bibli Wulfadi* et Jean Scot Erigène', *Recherches de Théologie Ancienne et Médiévale* 33 (1966) 137–9.

[82] See below, pp. 245–50, where these collections and their implications are discussed more fully.

school books, for it starts with Priscian and contains classical poetry (Virgil and Homer). The compiler adds a note to the effect that the library does not contain the Histories of Josephus and Freculph, nor the works of Alcuin, Martianus Capella or Terence.[83] So, too, the lists preserved from Oviedo in the tenth century, Pfäfers, Passau, Benediktbeuren and, above all, from tenth-century Bobbio are arranged in the same way as the main ninth-century Frankish catalogues, all of them undoubtedly influenced by the process of systematization that had gone on in the great Carolingian libraries of the first half of the ninth century.[84] The book lists from the dependant churches of Rheims similarly adopt the same organizing principles used.[85] The treasure inventories, of which such a substantial number survive from the ninth and early tenth centuries, when they include books, do so in the conventional way established by the Carolingians.[86]

IV THE ORIGINS OF LIBRARY CATALOGUES AND THEIR
ARRANGEMENT

Principles of organization

If one important impulse for the compilation of library catalogues was the habit of making inventories of property encouraged by the Carolingian rulers, this still does not explain why these catalogues should be arranged and set out as they were, with the authors in a particular order, and certain subjects apparently taking precedence over others. No rules for cataloguing survive, nor does an earlier model in the form of a library

---

[83] The manuscript itself is a school book containing Bede's *De schematibus et tropis* written in a hand of the first half of the ninth century in the Tours region. The book list was entered in a Bavarian hand in the diocese of Freising in the second half of the tenth century. See Bischoff, *Schreibschulen* I, p. 148, and Natalia Daniel, *Handschriften des zehnten Jahrhunderts aus der Freisinger Dombibliothek. Studien über Schriftcharakter und Herkunft der nachkarolingischen und ottonischen Handschriften einer bayerischen Bibliothek,* Münchener Beiträge zur Mediävistik und Renaissance Forschung 11 (Munich, 1973), pp. 49–50.

[84] On Pfäfers see P. Iso Muller and Carl Pfaff, *Thesaurus Fabariensis. Die Reliquien-, Schatz- und Bücherverzeichnisse im Liber Viventium von Pfäfers* (St Gall, 1985). The lists from Oviedo, Passau, Benediktbeuren and Bobbio are reproduced in Becker, *Catalogi*, Nos. 26, 28, 30, pp. 59–73. On Bobbio, see also G. Mercati, *De fatis bibliothecae monasterii S. Columbani Bobbiensi in M. Tulli Ciceronis De re publica libri e codice rescripto Vaticano Latino 5757 phototypice expressi* (Rome, Vatican City, 1934); P. Engilbert, 'Zur frühgeschichte des Bobbio Skriptoriums', *RB* 78 (1968), 220–60; and B. Bischoff, *Paläographie des römischen Altertums und des abendländischen Mittelalters* (Berlin, 1979), pp. 239–41. Bobbio also possessed an early eighth-century copy of Jerome–Gennadius (*CLA* III; 391).

[85] And incidentally provide important evidence for the richness of the Rheims diocesan churches. See B. Guérard, *Polyptyque de l'abbaye de Saint Remi de Reims* (Paris, 1853).

[86] Bischoff, ed., *Schatzverzeichnisse.*

catalogue.[87] That a broad division by subject, into books for the church, cloister and school, was common is suggested both by the specific indications for this provided in the inventory from St Riquier and the arrangement and headings in the east Frankish catalogues. In other words, a division according to function and repository is readily understandable. Yet it still leaves the author arrangement and the presentation of an approved canon of writing in a virtually standardized form to be accounted for. We observed in the examination of the east Frankish catalogues that they were generally subject catalogues arranged according to general categories – scripture, theology, practical knowledge, liturgy, education, asceticism and the religious life. Within these, authors were arranged in roughly chronological order.

Duft comments that the order of catalogues into Bible, church fathers, profane authors is *üblich* for the 'pre-scholastic era'.[88] Quite clearly, thanks to the efforts of the Carolingians, it became so in the course of the ninth century, but how, and why? Was it usual before the end of the eighth century? On what tradition were the compilers of catalogues able to draw? Why were the catalogues arranged in the way they were? Is there any significance in the fact that two of the earliest lists of books come from insular centres?

Allusion has been made to the possibility of a common canon of knowledge and categorization of learning inherited and developed by the Carolingians. In this context a number of features may be remarked by way of summarizing the observations on the organization of the catalogues made above. Far from a random or mindless arrangement, there is in fact a distinct system to be detected. The whole Bible comes first, if the institution concerned is fortunate enough to possess one, and thereafter the separate books of the Old and New Testament canon. The usual order of these books was a long time settling, though fairly well established long before the Carolingian period.[89] This arrangement of the books therefore would have been based on that of a whole Bible or pandect and be something the Franks (and the English) learnt as they were introduced to the text of the Bible. The order of the patristic authors, on the other hand, is not so obvious a development. Alphabetical order of any kind is eschewed in these book lists. Although alphabetical *florilegia* and

---

[87] Apart from the book lists extant on papyri from Egypt, see Roger A. Pack, *The Greek and Latin Literary Texts from Greco-Roman Egypt* (Michigan, 1965).

[88] Duft, 'Handschriften-Katalogisierung', p. 17*.

[89] Hans von Campenhausen, *Die Entstehung der Christlichen Bibel* (Tübingen, 1968), trans. J. A. Baker, *The Formation of the Christian Bible* (London, 1972). For comments on the hypothesis of a link between the adoption of the codex form of the book and the development of the canon of scripture, see C. H. Roberts and T. C. Skeat, *The Birth of the Codex* (London, 1983), pp. 62–6.

gnomonologia from the late antique period are fairly numerous, and there is continuity in the use of alphabetical order in lexicography from antiquity to the middle ages, alphabetical order was not used in other contexts. The early lists of books in the Oxyrhynchus fragments are not in alphabetical order; Daly suggests that the lack of alphabetization in mediaeval library catalogues is in fact a symptom of continuity of practice in this sphere between the ancient and mediaeval periods. Alphabetical catalogues do not appear to have existed before the twelfth century.[90] But, as has been observed, the author lists are not entirely random. In the case of Fulda and Würzburg, it appears to be the importance of a work to the institution itself that was the guiding principle in the arrangement of the list. A marked absence, or only minor presence, of contemporary authors' works was to be observed in all the libraries considered. In the other catalogues considered above, however, a chronological order according to the author's life can be discerned, and, in addition to this, a fairly consistent classification according to subject, or type of work (whether *florilegium*, letter collection, or homiliary) or function (school books or liturgy). This may reflect how the books were stored, but it nevertheless needs elucidation.

The question of insular influence

In none of the early catalogues, from Würzburg, Fulda, the royal library or St Wandrille, is there an orderly arrangement. Their individuality could be due to their early date, though, as we saw, even by the time of Gervold of St Wandrille's gift to his monastery between 787 and 806, some order is emerging. The catalogue of the royal library, as remarked above, is in any case a list of only a part of the palace collection. The lists from Würzburg and Fulda at an early stage of these monasteries appear as anomalies. Is their oddity a result not so much of their date as of their geographical and historical position, away, at this stage at least, from the mainstream of Frankish development? Can the Würzburg and Fulda lists be held to represent insular ignorance of, or simple lack of compliance with, the Continental classification of the corpus of Christian literature?

Whether this is really the case, however, needs to be considered in relation to the famous praise of the library at York in Alcuin's poem, *Versus de patribus regibus et sanctis euboricensis ecclesiae*. Alcuin describes the way in which Albert, his teacher, divided his wealth, of which the books were

[90] L. W. Daly, *Contributions to a History of Alphabetization in Antiquity and the Middle Ages*, Collection Latomus 90 (Brussels, 1967), pp. 62–77, but for a Greek precedent see A. Masson, *The Pictorial Catalogue* (Oxford, 1981), pp. 1–2.

a part. Shorn of its cadences, Alcuin's praise can be reduced, with all apologies to the poet, to a prosaic list of authors strikingly similar to that of the catalogues we have considered so far. Jerome, Hilary, Ambrose, Augustine, Athanasius, Orosius, Gregory the Great, Leo, Basil, Fulgentius, Cassiodorus and John Chrysostom clearly represent the church fathers, though one does not normally encounter Orosius and Cassiodorus in these positions. Any oddities can no doubt be attributed to the exigencies of metre. Thereafter Alcuin extols the teaching of Aldhelm and Bede, before listing school books on the arts, Christian and profane poetry and grammars, mentioning the authors Victorinus, Boethius, Pompeius (Trogus), Pliny, Aristotle, Cicero, Sedulius, Iuvencus, Alcimus Avitus, Prudentius, Prosper, Paulinus, Arator, Fortunatus, Lactantius, Virgil, Statius and Lucan, and the grammarians Probus, Focas, Donatus, Priscian, Servius, Euticius, Pompeius and Cominianus.[91] Whether this list of authors really represents a catalogue of the books in the library of York has been questioned. The most recent editor of the poem, for example, has, following Riché, made the interesting proposal that the list resembles less a catalogue than a 'learned advertisement'.[92] Yet the list's relation to reality is not so much our concern here as the form this possible 'learned advertisement' took. Much hinges, therefore, on whether Alcuin wrote this poem in England in the early 780s or on the Continent in the 790s. That is, was Alcuin drawing on newly apprehended Continental traditions of the organization of knowledge? Alternatively, was he drawing on a native insular tradition, thus providing crucial evidence that England was as much aware of the cultural traditions of library organization as the rest of western Europe? Although the latter is the most likely, there are, unfortunately, no decisive arguments in favour of either the earlier or the later date for the poem. Some of Godman's own arguments seem to favour the earlier date, even though he settles for the later one.[93] As I have suggested elsewhere, the manuscript tradition provides little assistance, but raises, rather, the tantalizing possibility that the poem did not reach the Continent until the tenth century.[94]

If this be the case, and Alcuin's list in his poem represents an English tradition, then the Würzburg and Fulda lists are simply primitive check lists, and no great significance can be read into their lack of system. Nevertheless, in view of a recent argument concerning Alcuin's

---

[91] Alcuin, ed. Ludwig Traube, *MGH Poet.* I, pp. 203–4, lines 1530–61, and Eng. trans. Peter Godman, *Alcuin. The Bishops, Kings and Saints of York* Oxford Mediaeval Texts (Oxford, 1983), pp. 124–6, lines 1531–162.

[92] Godman, *Alcuin*, p. lxvi, and compare Riché, *Education et Culture*, trans. Contreni, p. 383.   [93] Godman, *Alcuin*, pp. xliii–xliv.

[94] Review of Godman, *Alcuin, Journal of Ecclesiastical History* 35 (1984) 621–2.

contribution to the development of libraries, the matter must be pursued a little further.[95] Humphreys considered the influence of the Anglo-Saxons and of Alcuin in particular, in what he regards as 'the period of revolution in the development of libraries and their organization' (that is, the Carolingian period) to be 'paramount'. He maintained that the Anglo-Saxons transmitted the ideal of a library well stocked to provide for instruction and study, and well balanced in its composition, to Carolingian Europe.[96] In his view, Alcuin's experience in the library at York and the so-called versified catalogue of its contents may have encouraged the building up and proper maintenance of these Continental libraries. It is doubtful that Alcuin should be credited with quite so much. Humphreys rightly notes the points in common between Alcuin's account of the library at York and the Reichenau list of 821, but extrapolates too far in assuming Alcuin is the model for the rest, and in judging the other lists by the degree to which they conform with Alcuin's arrangement. This is methodologically unsound, for he is attempting to attribute to one individual what has every sign of being a more generalized phenomenon of which Alcuin provides the evidence of England's participation. Any lingering notions of totally benighted Franks being led towards the light by the English should be discarded. I have argued elsewhere how emphatic the evidence is for the shared culture and purpose of the English and the Franks, united in their faith and in their learning.[97] The common sources of inspiration for the provision of books and the formation and organization of libraries are to be sought elsewhere. These we must now examine.

The role of the 'De viris illustribus', the 'De libris recipiendis' and other early mediaeval bibliographical guides

Jerome composed his *De viris illustribus* (*On illustrious men*) to show the heretics and pagans how many and how excellent were the writers among Christians. It was produced in about 392 and consisted of a bio-

[95] Kenneth Humphreys, 'The early medieval library', in Gabriel Silagi, ed., *Paläographie 1981*, Münchener Beiträge zur Mediävistik und Renaissance-Forschung 32 (Munich, 1982), pp. 59–70.

[96] The emphasis in Humphreys is rather differently placed than in the original phrasing of Bischoff on which he draws. In Bernhard Bischoff 'Scriptoria e manoscritti mediatori di civiltà del sesto secolo alla riforma di Carlo Magno', *MS* II, p. 324, the author was discussing the pre-Carolingian period and saw the Anglo-Saxons bequeathing an ideal of a library to posterity in general rather than transmitting a specific model which was adopted.

[97] R. McKitterick, 'The diffusion of insular culture in Neustria between 650 and 850: the implications of the manuscript evidence', in Hartmut Atsma, ed., *La Neustrie. Les pays au nord de la Loire, 650 à 850, Beihefte der Francia* 16/1 and 16/2 (Sigmaringen, 2 vols., 1989), vol. 16/2, pp. 395–432.

bibliography of some 135 authors.[98] It was substantially augmented by Gennadius of Marseilles in about 490, who added ninety-one fifth-century authors. It was thus an introduction to the Christian writings capable of illuminating the main theological and intellectual problems of the day. But it also provided a list of works free from heresy and full of learning which could be used for the education of the young.[99] Further additions to Jerome-Gennadius were made by Isidore of Seville. His thirty-three additional writers, many of them Spaniards, constitute a work, which, in conjunction with Jerome-Gennadius, has been seen as a reflection of Isidore's concern 'to improve the woeful state of learning in his region' and the desire to 'preserve and foster the knowledge of orthodox writers ... in Spain'.[100] A forty-six-chapter version of Isidore, with an *Appendix Africana* of thirteen additional authors, possibly to be attributed to an African author of the late sixth century, also circulated in the early middle ages.[101] Although local in its original intent, Isidore's collection was undoubtedly eminently adaptable to Frankish circumstances, and we find it in a number of Carolingian manuscripts, usually appended to Jerome–Gennadius, as in Montpellier 406.

Jerome–Gennadius was recommended as a guide to Christian authors by Isidore in his *Etymologiae*, another text widely disseminated throughout the Frankish kingdoms, and it is also recorded in a number of the Carolingian library catalogues extant. The earliest Würzburg list, for example, possessed Jerome's *De viris illustribus*, Reichenau had Jerome–Gennadius, and Lorsch possessed a bibliographical handbook which added the first book of Cassiodorus' *Institutiones*: *eiusdem [Jerome] de illustribus viris et Gennadii et liber institutionum divinarum scripturarum Cassiodori et de historiis Christianis in uno codice*.[102] None of the Lorsch manuscripts extant can be identified with this item. Of the twenty-three

[98]   E. C. Richardson, *Hieronymus, Liber de viris inlustribus. Gennadius De viris inlustribus* (Leipzig, 1896), provides details of the manuscript transmission, but some of the dates and origins of the earlier manuscripts in his list need amending. See also C. A. Bernoulli, ed., *Hieronymus und Gennadius, De Viris Inlustribus* (Freiburg-im-Breisgau and Leipzig, 1895). Jerome's preface states his purpose, Richardson, *Hieronymus*, pp. 1–2.

[99]   Gennadius, preface, ed. Richardson *Hieronymus*, p. 57.

[100] Isidore, *PL* 83, cols. 1081–106. See also H. Koeppler, '*De viris illustribus* and Isidore of Seville', *JTS* 37 (1936) 16–34. The interpretation is that of Richard H. Rouse and Mary A. Rouse. 'Bibliography before print: the medieval *De viris illustribus*', in Ganz, ed., *The Role of the Book*, pp. 133–54.

[101] The author may have fled from the Vandal kingdom on the arrival of the armies of Belisarius. Procopius, for example, in his *Gothic Wars*, ed., with Eng. trans., H. B. Dewing (London and Cambridge, Mass., 1914–40), 3.24.10–12, attests to trade and possibly diplomatic relations between Vandal Carthage and Visigothic Spain.

[102] Würzburg, ed. Lowe, 'An eighth-century list of books', item 30, p. 242; Reichenau, ed. Lehmann, *Mittelalterliche Bibliothekskataloge*, lines 4–5, pp. 246; Lorsch, ed. Becker, *Catalogi*, item 210, p. 95.

manuscripts dating from the late seventh to the tenth centuries containing Jerome–Gennadius, almost all of which are of Frankish origin, the late seventh- or early eighth-century copy in BN lat. 12161, a palimpsest from Corbie, is of particular interest.[103] The text is written in a cursive minuscule and adds the Lives of Jerome, Sidonius, Honoratus of Marseilles and Caesarius of Arles, not found in other copies of the text, and references directing the reader to refutations of some of the heresies mentioned in the text. David Ganz has noted the use of the *require* sign beside the titles of works by Apollonius, Origen, Macharius, Evagrius, Serapion and Cassian, and has suggested that the volume was used as a guide for acquisitions for the library of Corbie, just as the librarian at Murbach used Cassiodorus' *Institutiones*, Augustine's *Retractationes* and Bede's *Historia ecclesiastica*.[104] Unfortunately, the *require* signs cannot be precisely dated, though the possibility is strong that they were made by the Carolingian librarians of Corbie. This manuscript is all the more tantalizing in the absence of a ninth-century catalogue of Corbie's magnificent library.

Montpellier 406, Hereford O.III.2, and many others, enhanced their usefulness as bibliographical handbooks with their inclusion of the so-called 'Gelasian Decretum', *De libris recipiendis et non recipiendis*, a definition and tabulation of orthodox and approved writers and their works.[105] It appears to have had nothing to do with Gelasius, but instead may be a product of Frankish Gaul. Certainly its earliest manuscript witness, Brussels 9850–2, was produced *c.* 700 in the Corbie region, possibly in Soissons itself, and given to the abbey of St Médard at Soissons by Abbot Nomedius.[106] The earliest surviving manuscript copy of the full text is Fulda, Bonifatianus 2, written either at Luxeuil itself or by a Luxeuil-trained scribe elsewhere.[107] It should be remembered that both Abbot Nomedius and Corbie itself were connected with the monastic zeal of Queen Balthild, and that Corbie's first community included monks from Luxeuil.[108] As the manuscript transmission attests, *De libris recipiendis* was

---

[103] *CLA* V, 624.   [104] Ganz, 'Merovingian library', pp. 153–72, especially p. 154.

[105] E. von Dobschutz, *Das Decretum Gelasianum de libris recipiendis in kritischem Text*, Texte und Untersuchungen zur Geschichte der altchristlichen Literatur 3 Reihe, 8.Band, Heft 4 (Leipzig, 1912).

[106] In Delisle's opinion, the title and first line of this text on fo. 139v, all that remains of this manuscript, were once accompanied by the rest of the text, for he thought that in quire 19 (fos. 139–147), where the text occurs, leaves 2, 3 and 4 had been cut out, and replaced by four leaves in 'a–b' script adding supplementary text to the Homilies of Caesarius of Arles: Leopold Delisle, 'Notice sur un manuscrit mérovingien de la Bibliothèque royale de Belgique, 9850–9852', *Notices et extraits des Manuscrits de la Bibliothèque Nationale et autres Bibliothèques* 31 (1884) 33–48.   [107] *CLA* VIII, 1197.

[108] *Vita Balthildis* c. 7, *MGH SS rer. merov.* II, pp. 475–508, at pp. 489–91.

disseminated with quite astounding speed and efficiency throughout the Frankish realm, even into north Italy. It was, moreover, adapted by individual compilers and scribes in the many different centres and incorporated into various types of handbook. Its commonest associations in its subsequent transmission are with canon law, particularly the *Dionysio-Hadriana* collection (Lucca 490, Vat. pal. lat. 493, BN lat. 3838B and 3837) or *Anselmo dedicata* collection (Bamberg can. 5 (P.I.12)), with introductions to the books of the Bible by such authors as Junilius, Cassiodorus and Eucherius (Clm 14469) or with patristic and literary texts, especially precisely those bibliographical guides we have identified as so popular with the Franks (Montpellier 406, Hereford O.III.2, Vercelli CLXXXIII(3)) or in volumes of Jerome's exegesis (Albi 29, *CLA* VI, 705) or with works of Isidore of Seville (Fulda, Bonifatianus 2) or in liturgical manuscripts (Wolfenbüttel Weissenburg 91). In nearly every case its codicological context is that of coherent and deliberate miscellanies of texts which provide guides to orthodox and approved Christian writings. The Fulda codex, for example, contains two letters of Pope Leo on dogma, treatises against Arianism by Cerealis, Agnellus and Faustus of Riez, three creeds, the *De libris recipiendis et non recipiendis*, Ambrose's *De bono mortis* and Isidore of Seville's *Synonyma*. It has rightly been described as a collection of texts against heretics,[109] but it reflects, too, a late Merovingian and early Carolingian preoccupation with authority, orthodoxy and correctness that was to become the prevailing characteristic of Carolingian scholarship. Ganz's observations on the possible status of early eighth-century Corbie as a repository of approved texts and home of authority are highly pertinent when one considers the palaeographical associations of the earliest representatives of this prime definition of the orthodox, the *De libris recipiendis et non recipiendis*, namely Brussels 9850–2 and Fulda, Bonifatianus 2. Both codices were produced within the Luxeuil-Corbie-Soissons sphere of influence. Given the subsequent transmission of the text *De libris recipiendis* in the Frankish kingdoms and the historical context of the development of bibliographical guidance provided above, it would be appropriate to posit the production of this famous text to a north Frankish or north Burgundian centre at the turn of the seventh century. That this coincides with the upsurge of interest in canon law, embodied in the *Vetus Gallica* collection is no mere coincidence.[110] *De libris recipiendis et non*

---

[109] Ganz, 'Merovingian library', p. 161.
[110] Hubert Mordek, *Kirchenrecht und Reform im Frankenreich* (Berlin, 1975), and see also R. McKitterick, 'Knowledge of canon law in the Frankish kingdoms before 789: the manuscript evidence', *JTS* 36 (1985) 97–117.

recipiendis was a vital Frankish contribution to the definition of orthodox knowledge and one that was widely influential in the Carolingian world.

It had, too, with other bibliographical guides – Jerome–Gennadius–Isidore, Augustine's *Retractationes* and Cassiodorus' *Institutiones* – a crucial role to play in the organization of library catalogues.[111] The entries in Jerome–Gennadius–Isidore conform to a simple format, with the scheme: A, bishop (or deacon or priest) of B wrote famous books entitled C, D, and E, in chronological sequence. Whereas Jerome and Gennadius were fairly systematic in their arrangement of their subjects in chronological order, Isidore did it more by association; the chronological order of his chapters is thus not always maintained. The approved authors in the *De libris recipiendis* are listed in the following order: Old and New Testament Books of the Bible, Cyprian, Basil, Theophilus, Hilary of Poitiers, Ambrose of Milan, Augustine, Jerome, Prosper, Cyril of Alexander, Leo, Flavianus, Gregory the Great, saints' lives, *Vitas Patrum, Actus beati Silvestris*, Rufinus, Origen, Eusebius (chronicle and history), Orosius, Sedulius (*Carmen Paschale*), Iuvencus and so on. It will be readily recognized that these authors are, for the most part, arranged in chronological order. This was undoubtedly derived from the example of the bio-bibliography of Jerome–Gennadius.

Another text which reflects the influence of the Jerome–Gennadius compilation is the *Versus Isidori*, written by the third continuator of the *De viris illustribus* himself. The verses, or *tituli*, were possibly intended to be painted on the cupboards or walls of the book room in the bishop's palace in Seville. There are verses first of all for the Bible, and then a series for the church fathers Origen, Hilary, Ambrose, Augustine, Jerome, John Chrysostom, and Cyprian; for the Christian poets Prudentius, Avitus, Iuvencus and Sedulius; for the church historians Eusebius and Orosius; and for Isidore's contemporaries, Gregory the Great and Leander of Seville. There followed some for the Roman law codes and commentaries of Theodosius, Paul and Gaius, and a selection for the medical books and for the herbs and medicines in the dispensary. Although some have sought to

---

[111] Some of these bibliographies are discussed by Rouse and Rouse, 'Bibliography'. Humphreys, 'Early medieval library', also mentions these bibliographies, but only in terms of their function as guides to acquisition. Rouse and Rouse largely follow Paul Lehmann, 'Literaturgeschichte im Mittelalter', in *Erforschung des Mittelalters* I, pp. 82–113 (a survey of a wide variety of mediaeval bibliographies, book lists and accessus literature), in their exposition, yet Rouse and Rouse, while acknowledging the creation by the Carolingians of a 'new bibliographic genre', the library catalogue, did not make the essential connection made here between the bibliographies and the catalogues.

dispute the authorship,[112] Ortega has championed it.[113] He drew parallels between the ideas of 'illustrating' the walls of a library with appropriate inscriptions suggested by the *Versus Isidori* and the *Ditocheum* or *Tituli historiarum* of Prudentius, also intended to illustrate the wall paintings of a church.[114] Verbal echoes of Isidore's verses detected by specialists in early mediaeval Latin poetry and prose as well as the diffusion of this text into Francia by the ninth century (the copy in Vat. pal. lat. 276, for example, is of the first half of the ninth century, of Weissenburg origin and Lorsch provenance) suggests that it might also have had a role in disseminating the accepted arrangement of a library.

It was above all, however, the *De viris illustribus* and the *De libris recipiendis* together which provided a clear, authoritative and influential guide not only to the most desirable contents of a library but also to the organization of the library catalogues. In these composite guides, therefore, popular and widely disseminated throughout the Frankish kingdoms, we have the obvious context in which to place the arrangement of the Carolingian library catalogues. It may not be the case that the catalogues always followed Jerome–Gennadius–Isidore or *De libris recipiendis* as slavishly as they would a model; what these late antique and early Carolingian guides did was to create a habit of mind and a customary framework of reference within which to organize knowledge. Catalogue compilers could come to the ordering of their libraries with an historical understanding of the successive contributions to Christian learning of their contents. Creators of libraries and directors of scriptoria could have a clear and inherited sense of what the well-equipped library should contain. Important corroboration of the status of these guides is evident from a distinctive Carolingian compilation, the bibliographical handbook.

---

[112] Godman, *Alcuin*, commentary on lines 1541–4, p. 122. Compare Jocelyn Hillgarth, 'The position of Isidorean Studies: a critical review of the literature 1936–1975', *Studi Medievali* 24 (1983) 817–905, at [25] [35] and [46] n. 86 (= 839, 849 and 860) who also supports the authenticity of these poems.

[113] See A. Ortega, 'Los "Versus Isidori"', *Helmantica* 12 (1961) 261–99, with an edition of the text. I am very grateful to Jocelyn Hillgarth for sending me a copy of the article and to the late Tom McKitterick for his help with the translation of the Spanish. Compare C. H. Beeson, *Isidor-Studien* (Munich, 1913), pp. 135–73, who offers an edition of the text, details of manuscript transmission and commentary. The text is extant in two redactions: a shorter one in manuscripts of Spanish origin and a longer one in a number of Frankish manuscripts such as BL Harley 2686, 3941 and Vat. lat 7803 and Vat. pal. lat. 276, and Italian manuscripts such as Milan Ambrosiana C 74.

[114] C. I. Rodriguez, *Introduction a la Obras Completas de Prudencio* (Madrid, 1950), p. 63.

Carolingian bibliographical handbooks

A number of manuscripts which can be described as bibliographical handbooks, compiled for that purpose by the Carolingian scholars, provide the key to what these sources of inspiration and knowledge were. Montpellier 406, of the early ninth century, for example, contains the standard guide to Christian writings which, in its three portions, came to be regarded as a composite work and treated as a unit. The ninth-century note inserted into this manuscript actually provides a direction for future copying to this effect. *Iste liber est Hieronimi virorum illustrum. In proximo isto debet scribi liber Genadii. In tertio loco Ysidore et debent esse toti tres in uno volumine* ('This is Jerome's *De viris illustribus*. Next to it should be written Gennadius' book and in the third position Isidore's and all three should be in one volume'). A further note at the end of the manuscript refers to Carloman and Charlemagne, the sons of Pippin III, as still ruling jointly. This would suggest a late eighth-century date for the manuscript, belied by the script. It is possible that Montpellier 406 is a copy of an earlier, similar, compilation, and that the scribe has taken over an earlier colophon. It could on the other hand reflect the compiler's use of an earlier text of the *De libris recipiendis* alone (here attributed to Pope Hormidas) to which this colophon had been appended.[115]

A similar argument concerning a compiler's use of texts of different origin and age to make up a new bibliographical collection can be mounted for the important codex, Hereford O.III.2. It was written by two accomplished Carolingian hands of the late ninth century, possibly at Rheims, and contains Jerome–Gennadius–Isidore, the *De libris recipiendis*, Augustine's *Retractationes*, Cassiodorus' *Institutiones* Book I, Isidore's *Prohemia* (including extracts from his *De ecclesiasticis officiis*), *De ortu et obitu sanctorum patrum*, *Allegoriae*, and selections from the grammarian Terence. Mynors thought the whole manuscript was descended from a manuscript in insular minuscule.[116] But the insular abbreviations for *autem* and *per*,

---

[115] Little has been published about Montpellier 406. It is undoubtedly a Frankish manuscript, and came into the library of the Ecole de médécine with the other manuscripts in the Bouhier collection in 1804. See *Catalogue générale des manuscrits des bibliothèques publiques des départements* I (Paris 1849), p. 447, and on the history of the Montpellier collection: Charles Samaran and Robert Marichal, eds., *Catalogue des manuscrits en écriture latine portant des indications de date, de lieu ou de copiste* VI Bourgogne, centre, sud-est et sud-ouest de la France (Paris, 1968), pp. xvii–xviii.

[116] On Hereford O.III.2 see the discussion by Mynors, ed., *Cassiodori Institutiones*, pp. xv–xvi. See also Helmut Gneuss, 'Manuscripts written or owned in England up to 1100', *Anglo-Saxon England* 9 (1981), item 263, and A. T. Bannister, *A Descriptive Catalogue of the Manuscripts in the Hereford Cathedral Library* (Hereford, 1927). Mynors commented, *Cassiodori Institutiones*, p. xvi, 'Somewhere on the Continent not later than the eleventh century and no doubt very much earlier, there must have existed a manuscript which

and the two Irish glosses taken over and misunderstood from the exemplar by the copyist cited by him, occur only in the first text, Jerome's *De viris illustribus*. We should regard this manuscript as an independent compilation for bibliographical and educational purposes, made in the Rheims area possibly at the very time when the Rheims school was having a revival under Archbishop Fulk, Remigius of Auxerre and Hucbald of St Amand. The Jerome text's exemplar is thus possibly from a centre under insular influence rather than the whole manuscript being dependent on an insular compilation. There is a sufficient number of other, similar, Carolingian bibliographical handbooks, some of which are detailed below, extant from the Carolingian period to make such an independent compilation likely. Indeed, their existence is a manifestation of the general initiative to organize knowledge and provide guides to authors and their writings. This is not to say that individual compilations could not serve as exemplars for others to reproduce. Hereford O.III.2., for example, was in England by the end of the eleventh century and a copy of it was made then at Salisbury (now BL Cotton Vespasian A XIII). It may also have been the direct parent of Oxford, Bodley 391 (2222); if so, Hereford O.III.2. could have been used at Canterbury in about 1100.

Other independent bibliographical handbooks which can be cited are the ninth-century portions of St Gall 191, written at St Gall in about 830. As well as Jerome–Gennadius it contains the account of the council of Rome in the time of Pope Damasus and its *De explanatione fidei*, and a text entitled *De ordo Vet. Testamen.*, which is none other than the *De libris recipiendis*. Thereafter is a treatise dealing with the definition of the Old and New Testament canon and the elements of the Catholic faith.[117] A similar text is to be found in a manuscript from Reichenau.

A mid-ninth-century codex from Weissenburg, now Wolfenbüttel Weissenburg 79, offers a different selection of bibliographical guides, for it adds Cassiodorus' *Institutiones* Book I to Jerome–Gennadius.[118] Vercelli CLXXXIII (fos. 3–104), on the other hand, offers Jerome–Gennadius, Augustine's *Retractationes*, Cassiodorus' *Institutiones* Book I and the *De libris recipiendis*. It is written in a rapid cursive minuscule Lowe described as 'doubtless north Italian'. The headings, usually the authors' names, are

perhaps contained Jerome–Gennadius–Isidore, *De viris illustribus* and the *De XII scriptoribus* ascribed to Jerome [other manuscripts credit other writers with this text: BN lat. 1856, a tenth-century French codex, for example, ascribes it to Bede] which had a text of *Inst. div. litt.* closely akin to H [Hereford O.III.2] though independent of it and divided into two books before c.xxiv.' Mynors, in other words, was suggesting the existence of another bibliographical handbook.

117 Described in Gustave Scherrer, *Verzeichnis der Handschriften der Stiftsbibliothek von St Gallen* (Halle, 1875), pp. 69–70.

118 H. Butzmann, *Die Weissenburger Handschriften* (Frankfurt, 1964), pp. 240–1.

distinguished with uncial script. The use of a whole line of uncial letters for the beginning of the entry on Eusebius of Vercelli in Jerome–Gennadius *De viris illustribus* led Richardson to suggest a Vercelli diocese provenance, though he was inclined to a Frankish origin for the manuscript.[119] Whether Frankish or north Italian, this compilation points to the extension of the Carolingian interest in compiling bibliographical handbooks to Carolingian Lombardy. In the tenth-century catalogue of the library of Bobbio, moreover, reference is made to what could be another bibliographical handbook: as well as Eugippius' excerpts from the works of Augustine, a volume listed there contained Cassiodorus' *Institutiones* Book I, Jerome's *De viris illustribus*, the soliloquies of Augustine and Alcuin's exposition of the Book of Genesis.[120]

The first book of the *Institutiones* of Cassiodorus (on divine letters), in which he discusses the great patristic authors and their work, appears to have been that portion of Cassiodorus' guide most usually combined with such texts as Jerome–Gennadius–Isidore, the *Retractationes* of Augustine and the *De libris recipiendis*, to form bibliographical handbooks in the Carolingian period. Thus in Kassel, theol. fol. 29, a mid-ninth-century volume from Fulda, the *Institutiones* are included with the *Retractationes* of Augustine. In Clm 14469, fos. 145–175, excerpts from Cassiodorus' *Institutiones* Book I are combined with the *De libris recipiendis*.[121]

The second book of the *Institutiones*, on the other hand, a discussion of works on the seven liberal arts, tended to be combined with introductions to Latin grammar or treatises on metre, or on rhetoric and other didactic texts. It appears to have had a transmission largely independent of Book I.[122] St Gall 855, for example, much worn by use, is a Carolingian school book made up of Donatus, Alcuin's *De Rhetorica*, Cassiodorus' *Institutiones* Book II, Mallius Theodorus' *De metris*, Sisibut's poem *Carmen de eclipsi lunae* and a *Capitula de diversa miracula quae sunt super terra* (put together from Gregory of Tour's *De cursu stellarum* and Isidore's *De natura rerum*). BL Harley 2637, a late ninth-century Lotharingian codex, contains a list of verbs and Smaragdus' treatise on verbs, a letter of Helisachar to Nidibrius, archbishop of Narbonne, about an antiphonary the latter had requested and Cassiodorus' *Institutiones* Book II. A similar collection is to be found in

---

[119] Vercelli CLXXXIII, fos. 3–104 (*CLA* IV, 469).
[120] Becker, *Catalogi*, No. 32, item 492, p. 70.
[121] Bischoff, *Schreibschulen* I, p. 245.
[122] Mynors, ed., *Cassiodori Institutiones*, pp. xviii–xxxix, has a full discussion of the complex transmission of this text. In many instances Book I, on 'divine letters', was transmitted separately. Book I is preserved in many copies of ninth- to eleventh-century date; Book II, either with Book I, or in an interpolated version of the Carolingian period, produced in two successive stages and expanded with material largely extracted from the works of Boethius in order to provide a guide to the *artes liberales*.

the Reichenau manuscript, Karlsruhe Aug. 241. The compiler of the ninth-century Frankish volume Berlin 176, from Fleury, put together Augustine's *De dialectica*, the *Catagoriae*, Alcuin's *De Rhetorica and De dialectica* and Cassiodorus' *Institutiones* Book II. Chartres 130 of the early tenth century (from St Père de Chartres) combined the guide with the two treatises on music, the *Institutio Harmonica* of Hucbald of St Amand, and the *Scholia Enchiridis*.

In its turn, Jerome–Gennadius spawned a number of miscellanies of related texts which can perhaps be regarded as school compilations on Christian knowledge, if not necessarily as bibliographical handbooks. Pursuit of the manuscript transmissions of all these works may well yield further examples of Carolingian bibliographical aids.

As well as their own bibliographical handbooks, the Carolingians were thus able to transmit to their contemporaries and successors models of an appropriately stocked library by means of the library catalogues themselves. The immediate use of these catalogues may have been simply to act as check lists for the custodian of the books. But the catalogues also came to serve other important functions. Their debt to the inventories of treasure and property was expressed in their quantification of the intellectual wealth of a centre. They were also the means by which knowledge could be shared with other centres and increased. I have commented briefly elsewhere how the number of exchanges of texts and manuscripts between one centre and another suggests a wide network of communications. I suggested, too, that what was in another centre's or individual's library and the availability and whereabouts of certain exemplars may well have been derived from the circulation of the library catalogues between centres. A copy of the Reichenau catalogue was made for Murbach, Lorsch catalogue II may have been prepared for St Vaast, another Reichenau list appears to have been made for Constance, and the Lorsch catalogue collection in Vat. pal. lat. 1877 included the ninth-century holdings of Fulda. Wulfad of Bourges may well have let his friends become acquainted with the volumes in his collection by circulating the list among them. Lupus asked for a list of the books at St Germain-des-Prés and had a copy of the list of books belonging to Einhard.[123]

The library catalogues not only record the possession of knowledge, therefore, but themselves constitute bibliographical guides to book

---

[123] Lupus, Ep. 1, and see McKitterick, *Frankish Kingdoms*, pp. 212–13. The work of Bernhard Bischoff is replete with examples of communication and exchange. For some recent comments of his on the nature of 'influence' in script consequent upon the network of communication see his 'Die Rolle von Einflüssen in der Schriftgeschichte', in Silagi, ed., *Paläographie 1981*, pp. 93–105.

accessions and the acquisition of knowledge. The conventions and rules of compilation evolved by the Carolingian *bibliothecarii* as a cooperative, rather than as an isolated, endeavour were to become established as the proper method of embarking upon the creation and organization of libraries throughout the middle ages. They represent, in other words, a systematization of the written word, and an organization of knowledge, with far-reaching consequences. For one thing, they effectively defined the intellectual framework within which literate skills were to be exercised. It was an intellectual framework within which the Bible and the need to understand the Christian faith were paramount, and for which the great fathers of the church acted as the main supports. Although provided by scholars, this definition, with its determination of particular written texts, also had significant repercussions for the laity, both in the character and expression of their piety, and in the channelling of their intelligence in specific directions. These will be discussed in the following chapter.

6 ❄ *The literacy of the laity*

What is the material evidence for the acquisition of literate skills on the part of the laity? Was literacy really confined to a clerical elite or learned class? Were legislative and judicial activities and the reception of the written word in Frankish society really things in which lay Franks had no part? I have argued in the earlier chapters of this book that pragmatic literacy, and even professional 'mandarin' literacy, were widespread in Carolingian society. It is the purpose of this chapter to explore some of the ways in which the laity was educated and how laymen and laywomen used and enjoyed the literate skills they acquired. This is not a straightforward matter of totting up the numbers of educated laymen and laywomen, of which instances can be excavated from the sources, however telling the cumulative effect of such quantitative investigation might be. Rather, I wish to provide a qualitative evaluation of the material available, and to explore the kind of transformations in lay culture effected by the stress on literacy in the Carolingian realm. This chapter will thus consider the question of the continuity of a literate lay culture from the Merovingian period into the ninth century, and examine the information concerning the education of the laity. It will confront the problem of audience of many different kinds of Carolingian text, and discuss the implications of the ownership of books and the impressive bulk of manuscript evidence with lay associations of one kind or another. The implications of the type of text owned and used by laymen and laywomen in the Carolingian period, especially as far as their religious observance is concerned, are examined in the final section. It is here that the most significant consequences of literacy can be observed.

It must be acknowledged that most of the evidence invoked in what follows concerns the 'nobility', in the sense that the relevant texts refer to individuals as 'noble'. Nobility itself is hard to define, for its use can indicate 'notable', or 'able' as well as 'well-born'. There appears, in any case, to have been a fair degree of social mobility in the Carolingian period, in the sense that elevation in status or accretion in power and wealth was the reward for the able and the energetic in the military and administrative spheres, if not in the ecclesiastical one as well.[1] Nobility, in other words, was a somewhat elastic attribute that could be acquired. One was not necessarily born into it as one might be born into a rigid social caste. I have, therefore, assumed that 'nobles' comprised that class of freemen eligible for, or likely to hold, some public office. That the 'nobility' so defined, who figure so prominently in the texts and manuscripts discussed in the course of this chapter, does not include all Carolingian laymen is self-evident. One should nevertheless be wary of making the mistake of jumping to the conclusion that one is therefore dealing with an elitist culture. It has to be understood that such transformations of attitude, thinking or faith, as one can posit for those among the upper ranks of society whom one can document, are likely to have filtered further down the social scale. It is too easy to dismiss a body of evidence as pertaining to an elite without taking into account the repercussions of the activities of that elite, and the framework of assumptions they provide concerning the function of the written word for the whole of society.

I THE EDUCATION OF THE LAITY

Continuity from the Merovingian into the Carolingian period

To become literate, a layman or laywoman must be educated. Our knowledge of the continuity of some of the Gallo-Roman aristocratic families into the Carolingian period,[2] as well as the initial rapid assimilation of the Franks into Roman Gaul, make it reasonable to suppose that some of the old aristocratic values expressed by diehards like Sidonius Apollinaris – of service to the people, official duty and a modicum of education – may have endured.[3] Indeed, there are shreds of evidence concerning the continuity of late Roman aristocratic education into the Merovingian period.[4] As we shall see, moreover, the tradition of the educated noble appears to be preserved into the Carolingian period.

For the Merovingian period, the findings of both Pirenne and Riché have

---

[1] Stuart Airlie, 'Bonds of power and bonds of association in the court circle of Louis the Pious', in Roger Collins and Peter Godman, eds., *Charlemagne's Heir: New Perspectives on the Reign of Louis the Pious 814–840* (Oxford, 1990), pp. 191–204.

[2] Karl-Ferdinand Werner, 'Bedeutende Adelsfamilien im Reich Karls des Grossen', in Wolfgang Braunfels, *Karl der Grosse. Lebenswerk und Nachleben* I *Persönlichkeit und Geschichte* (Düsseldorf, 1965), pp. 83–142, Eng. trans. in Timothy Reuter, ed., *The Medieval Nobility* (Amsterdam, New York and Oxford, 1978), pp. 137–202.

[3] Sidonius Apollinaris, ed. W. B. Anderson, *Sidonius, Poems and Letters*, Loeb edition (London and Cambridge, Mass., 2 vols., 1965), especially VIII.2,4 and 8.

[4] Gathered together by P. Riché, *Education et culture dans l'Occident Barbare VIᵉ–VIIIᵉ siècles* (Paris, 1962), Eng. trans. J. J. Contreni (Columbia, South Carolina, 1976), pp. 177–245.

lent weight to the supposition of continuity, though both inclined to a 'Pirenne thesis' about the survival of lay education and argued that it died out by the eighth century.[5] But both Wood and Bergmann are demonstrating a considerable degree of Merovingian literacy in pragmatic terms as well as cultural ones, and it is their work which should be consulted for a detailed exposition of the evidence.[6] It is becoming increasingly clear that the essential foundation for Carolingian literacy was Merovingian literacy, and that there was no dramatic break between the Merovingian and Carolingian periods. Nor was there decline in lay culture by the eighth century. Yet here, interpretation of the evidence for the seventh and eighth centuries would appear to be largely a matter of perspective. Pirenne, Riché and others thereafter interpreted sympathetically for the Merovingian period, both in quality and quantity, precisely the same kind of evidence they dismissed as inconclusive, exceptional or too sparse to be significant for the Carolingian period. Riché's own work has contradicted his own conclusions implicitly, and, in his brief survey of the education and culture of aristocrats, even explicitly, but it does not seem yet to have changed current perceptions of Merovingian and Carolingian literacy as a whole.[7] The Carolingian material, far greater and less ambiguous than that of the Merovingian period, is ripe for more sympathetic and positive assessment. A beginning therefore is made in this chapter; it builds on the foundations laid by Riché, though much of it is necessarily speculative.

What, then, is the evidence that Carolingian laymen possessed literate skills and the means of acquiring them? Was the gradual assimilation of Christian literate culture by Frankish aristocrats of the Merovingian period continued into the eighth and ninth centuries? If so, was it a general phenomenon rather than being an occasional occurrence?

Let us first summarize the principal characteristics of Merovingian lay education. First of all, both Pirenne and Riché commented on the lay aristocrats still celebrated for their education in the late antique tradition in the pages of Gregory of Tours.[8] The public schools ceased to exist but

---

[5] Henri Pirenne, 'De l'état de l'instruction des laïques à l'époque mérovingienne', *RB* 46 (1934) 165–77; Pierre Riché, 'L'Instruction des laïcs en Gaule mérovingienne au VIIᵉ siècle', *Settimane* 5 (1958) 873–88; and *idem*, 'L'Enseignement et la culture des laïcs dans l'occident pré-Carolingien', *Settimane* 19 (1972) 231–53.

[6] Work in progress. The basis for all such considerations remains Riché, *Education et Culture*.

[7] Pierre Riché, *Ecoles et enseignement dans le Haut Moyen Age de la fin du Vᵉ siècle au milieu du XIᵉ siècle* (Paris, 1979), pp. 287–313.

[8] See also the examples furnished by V. M. O. Denk, *Geschichte des Gallo-Fränkischen Unterrichts- und Bildungswesens von den ältesten Zeiten bis auf Karl den Grossen* (Mainz, 1892). Both Gregory of Tours' *Historiae* and his *Life of the Fathers* are full of examples.

their place in some *civitates* at least was gradually taken by ecclesiastical schools open to the nobility. The evidence suggests that education also continued on a private basis within the family. Sons of less wealthy families were not taught by their parents or a private tutor but may well have been taught in a boys' school of some kind.[9] The example of Patroclus may indicate that freemen's families may have had to make difficult decisions about which of their offspring were to receive the benefits of an education. He was at ten years old put to train as a shepherd while his brother Antonius went to a boys' school. Goaded by his brother's taunts, however, Patroclus sped to the school himself, learnt readily, and did so well that he was recommended for employment to Nunnio, a man with the reputation for influence at the court of Childebert of Paris (*c.* 511–58).[10] That the outcome of Patroclus' schooling, by implication, was a place at court, is indicative of the role of the royal court and the needs of administration in the career structure of freemen in the Frankish kingdoms.[11] The court appears to have acted as an alternative source of instruction outside the family or as the secondary stage after basic schooling. The lives of the sprigs of nobility inspired by the ascetic Columbanus have many telling observations about the education and careers on the part of Frankish aristocrats. Dado and Faro, for example, educated their children themselves.[12] Leading magnates sent their sons to court and the young Merovingian princes were confided to teachers, who were generally the mayors of the palace.[13] The context of the references to

such as Asteriolus and Secundinus, described as well-educated men trained in rhetorical studies (*retoricis inbutus litteris*), Parthenius the tax collector, Sulpicius of senatorial rank who 'was extremely learned in literature and rhetoric, and second to none as a poet' (*in litteris bene eruditus, rethoricis in metricis uero artibus nulli secundus*): Gregory of Tours, *Historiarum Libri Decem*, ed. R. Buchner (Darmstadt, 1977), and Eng. trans. Lewis Thorpe (Harmondsworth, 1974), III, 33, 36; VI, 39. In addition, the Life of Bonitus, referendary to King Sigibert, describes him before his elevation to the see of Clermont as a man learned in literature and the Roman law (*grammaticorum inbutus initiis necnon Theodosii edoctus decretis a sophistis*): *Vita Boniti, MGH SS rer. merov.* vi, p. 119.

[9] See, for example, the *Vita Leobardi* c. 1, by Gregory of Tours, *MGH SS rer. merov.* I, p. 741, Eng. trans. Edward James, *Gregory of Tours, Life of the Fathers* (Liverpool, 1985), p. 131. He was of free birth though not of senatorial rank and was sent with the other children to school.

[10] *Vita Patrocli* c. 1, *MGH SS rer. merov.* I, p. 702, trans. James, *Gregory of Tours*, pp. 78–9: Antonius told his brother 'You herd sheep, while I study letters; the care of such a task ennobles me, while you are made common through your work.'

[11] Summarized by Riché, *Education et Culture*, trans. Contreni, pp. 210–46, and compare Martin Heinzelmann, *Bischofsherrschaft in Gallien. Zur Kontinuität römischer Führungschichten vom 4. bis zum 7. Jahrhundert. Soziale, prosopographische und bildungsgeschichtliche Aspekte* (Munich, 1976).

[12] Jonas, *Vita Columbani* I, 26, and II,7, *MGH SS rer. merov.* IV, pp. 99 and 120.

[13] See, for example, the *Vita Arnulfi* c. 3, *MGH SS rer. merov.* II, p. 433, the Carolingian *Vita Ragneberti, AA SS*, June II, col. 695, and Fredegar, IV.86, ed. J. M. Wallace-Hadrill, *The Fourth Book of the Chronicle of Fredegar and its Continuations* (London, 1960), p. 72.

these young men suggests that they would have been given appropriate administrative training, learning the business of the notariat as well as military skills.[14] Sources such as the *Vita Arnulfi* or *Vita Wandregisili* indicate that Merovingian noble families educated their own children either personally or by employing a tutor; Arnulf, ancestor of the Carolingians, was entrusted to a *preceptor*, and Wandregisil, founder of the monastery called after him in Neustria, was taught by his parents.[15] Wandregisil was trained in the military and courtly discipline at the court of Dagobert I, was married, and served as an administrator in the king's service before founding the abbey to which he gave his name. Apart from the actual process of education, that Venantius Fortunatus still found an audience at the Frankish court has important implications for the aspirations of Frankish nobles and their willingness in the sixth century to emulate their Gallo-Roman peers in a taste for public poetry.[16] It was a willingness that went beyond the ability to sit through the recital of elaborate panegyric; it was one consequence of the acquisition and exploitation of a literate culture. While our knowledge of the content and nature of aristocratic literate culture in the Merovingian period is lamentably imprecise, and our understanding of the degree to which Merovingian officials exercised pragmatic literate skills is hardly less so, the general purport of the scraps of evidence extant is that education – within households and at schools – continued, that it was primarily practical in its aims, that the old Roman rhetorical tradition had disappeared, but that occasionally there were instances of aristocrats with more intellectual interests than their peers. Information about the kings themselves, largely derived from an infuriatingly ambiguous passage in Gregory of Tours, cannot justify any firm conclusion concerning the customary education of kings in the sixth century, and tells us nothing about the later Merovingian rulers.[17] It would, however, be an unusual society if its kings did not seek

[14] See the discussion by Riché, *Education et Culture*, trans. Contreni, pp. 236–46, especially pp. 239–40, and the references there assembled.
[15] *Vita Arnulfi* c. 3, *MGH SS rer. merov.* II, p. 433, and the account of Wandrille in F. Lohier and J. Laporte, eds., *Gesta sanctorum patrum Fontanellensis coenobii* (Paris and Rouen, 1936), pp. 2–3, and compare the *Vita sancti Wandregisili abbatis, MGH SS rer. merov.* V, p. 13.
[16] Richard Collins, 'Some observations on the form, language and public of the prose biographies of Venantius Fortunatus in the hagiography of Merovingian Gaul', in H. Clarke and M. Brennan, eds., *Columbanus and Merovingian Monasticism* (Oxford, 1981), pp. 105–31, and Riché, *Education et Culture*, trans. Contreni, p. 221; compare the discussion by Peter Godman, *Poets and Emperors. Frankish Politics and Carolingian Poetry* (Oxford, 1987), pp. 1–37.
[17] The Latin text reads as follows: *Hic cum natus esset in Galliis et diligenti cura nutritus ut regum istorum mos est, crinium flagellis per terga dimissis litteris eruditus.* Gregory of Tours, *Historiae* VI.24. The emphasis both the English and the German translators have provided

to be better than its nobles in every respect or the nobles seek to emulate the kings. The role of the court itself throughout the Merovingian period suggests that the rulers themselves possessed literate skills.

Merovingian and Carolingian education: the evidence of the saints' lives

Much of the information about the education of the laity in the Merovingian period is derived from hagiographical sources. Saints' lives are fraught with hazards as far as credibility is concerned.[18] The hagiographer tends either to make a dramatic story about the conversion, or devotion to the clerical life, of someone hitherto destined for a worldly career, or he avers that the boy concerned was destined for the holy life from or before birth and his education designed accordingly.[19] In the case of Nicetius of Trier, for example, as a baby he looked as if he had a tonsure: 'Because of that his parents brought him up with great care, instructed him in letters and sent him to the abbot of a monastery.'[20] This may well be the hagiographer's projection of the later achievement back on an earlier norm in order to account for it. That is, he suggests that the

for this passage is that it was the custom of the Frankish kings to wear their hair long. Thorpe, for example, rendered the passage thus: 'Gundovald was born in Gaul and educated with great care. He wore his hair long and down his back, as is the custom of the Frankish kings. He was taught to read and write.' Pirenne, 'Instruction des laïques', chose to relate the phrase *ut mos est* to the phrases *et diligenti cura* and *litteris eruditus*, and argue that not only was Gundovald taught to read and write but that it was the Merovingian custom to educate their kings. Riché, *Education et Culture*, trans. Contreni, p. 220 n. 272, on the other hand, was quite definite that Pirenne had misunderstood this passage in Gregory and that *ut mos est* referred to the long hair. The Latin, as can be seen, is one sentence rather than the two or three translators tend to make of it. Its structure, however, is sufficiently ambiguous in its placing of the *ut mos est* clause to support Pirenne's interpretation. If one reads the passage without prejudice, it would seem that the *ut* clause qualifies what has gone before, not what follows. That is, Gundovald was brought up with extreme care as is the custom with these kings. The reference to being taught to read might then be understood as implied by the phrase 'being brought up with great care' or else it might be something peculiar to Gundovald. If the *ut* clause were to qualify the *flagellis...dimissis* phrase, one would expect a connective before *ut*. It is unlikely that *ut mos est* refers only to long hair, and I doubt whether it refers to the hair at all. It may well be that the stress in recent historiography, seduced by the description of the Merovingian kings in Einhard's *Vita Karoli* c. 1, has unduly influenced interpreters of this passage.

[18] The discussion by Hippolyte Delehaye, *Les Légendes hagiographiques* (Brussels, 1955), is seminal. See also the papers in Pierre Riché, *L'Hagiographie, cultures et sociétés* (Paris, 1981), and B. de Gaiffier, *Etudes critiques d'hagiographie et d'iconologie* (Paris, 1967), and idem, 'Mentalité de l'hagiographie médiévale d'après quelques travaux récents', *Analecta Bollandiana* 86 (1968) 391–9.

[19] For example, Venantius, who decided on a clerical life even after he had begun to love the girl to whom his parents had betrothed him, or Brachio, a servant to a Frankish count, or Gregory of Langres who was senator and count of Autun, and married with sons, before finally being consecrated bishop after the death of his wife Armentaria: Gregory of Tours, *Vita patrum* XVI, XII and VII, *MGH SS rer. merov.* I, pp. 724–5, 712 and 687, trans. James, *Gregory of Tours*, pp. 109–10, 92 and 60.

[20] Gregory of Tours, *Vita patrum* XVII, XVII, trans. James, *Gregory of Tours*, p. 114.

education had only been given the child because of divinely-given foreknowledge of the subsequent fate, sainthood, of the child. It could, on the other hand, simply have been the usual course for a child of that class, provided with an edifying explanation by the hagiographer for his own purposes. There is thus in the saints' lives a tension between the dictates of the genre's conventions and the actual historical record.

We find exactly the same problem in the contemporary or near contemporary lives of Carolingian men and women who were accorded the status of saint. Here too the details are provided and interpreted in the light of subsequent sainthood. The details themselves, however, are incidental to the main edificatory purpose of the relevant life as a whole, and therefore deserve serious consideration. They are not to be dismissed as mere hagiographical topoi. The subject is known to have achieved not merely sanctity, but high position in a particular church or see, or in relation to a particular monastery. The references to his early education are always a preliminary to his spiritual career, and it is assumed by both author and modern reader that the clerical career was inevitable from the outset. Careful reading of these lives shows, however, that in a great many cases what we have is the account of the education of a young boy who at a particular stage elected to follow a religious life. The lives thus constitute crucial evidence for a more general provision of basic education for the young sons of freemen by parents as a matter of course, within the context either of a cathedral or monastic school, or at home from a private tutor.

Odo of Cluny's Life of Gerald of Aurillac, written between 909 and 942 about a man who died in 909, for example, contains the following information:

By the grace of divine providence [Gerald] applied himself to the study of letters, but by the will of his parents only to the extent of going through his Psalter; after that he was instructed in the worldly exercises customary for the sons of the nobility; to ride to hounds, become an archer, learn to fly falcons, and hawks, in the proper manner. But lest the time suitable for learning letters should pass without profit in being given to useless pursuits, the divine will ordained that he should be ill for a long time, though with such a sickness that he should be withdrawn from the worldly pursuits but not hindered in his application to learning. And for a long time he was so covered with small pimples that it was not thought he would be cured. For this reason his father and mother decided that he should be put more closely to the study of letters, so that if he should prove unsuited for worldly pursuits he might be fitted for the ecclesiastical state. So it came about that he not only learnt the chant but also something of grammar... Even when he became strong he continued to study for he had developed a taste for Scripture and reading it.[21]

---

[21] *PL* 133, cols. 639–704, at col. 645, trans. Gerard Sitwell, *St Odo of Cluny* (London, 1958) p. 97.

On the face of it, this account would appear to support the prejudices of those who believe the lay nobility received no instruction in reading, for only when some affliction, perhaps dreadful acne, made his parents fear that he would have to be diverted towards an ecclesiastical career, was the boy Gerald permitted to pursue his studies. This is to miss the significance of the account of Gerald's earliest instruction. He was only permitted to go through his psalter. This could simply be a reference to Gerald's ability to recite the psalter by heart. It may be the outcome of purely oral instruction and he may not even have been able to read. But the text does say he studied letters and that he subsequently learnt grammar, which in a Carolingian context appears to have meant learning to analyse a language already known.[22] The Latin psalter is in any case a demanding compilation of figurative and evocative poetry. It may have served as a primer, but it was a primer that provided a key to and a means of expression of faith in God[23] in an idiom that was the foundation of much of Carolingian Latin prose. It seems clear that Gerald received a standard basic education, and only extended it to more advanced learning when it appeared that he might be unfit for a martial career. This accords with the impression provided in the Merovingian sources of the content of the basic instruction of freemen, that is, a grounding in the fundamental Christian texts.

That other nobles shared the experience of basic instruction but were able to attain rather more is evident from such accounts as John of Salerno's description, derived from Odo himself, of Odo of Cluny's father, Abbo, reporting Odo's words: 'My father knew by heart the ancient histories and the novella of Justinian. In his conversation there was always to be found something of the Gospel.'[24] Odo himself, when old enough, was handed over to a certain priest who dwelt in a remote place to be educated and introduced to the study of letters. Again there is the hint that further learning is only permitted if a military life seemed impracticable: 'As time went on my father began to withdraw me from the ecclesiastical life and sent me to military exercises, and with this purpose he sent me to serve as page in the household of Duke William.'[25] Thus a basic education was received by boys at a tender age before being removed from a tutor's care to continue their education in the physical skills required of the noble warrior class. It may be that the phrase *vita ecclesiastica* is here used as a

[22] Above, pp. 7–22.
[23] Pierre Riché, 'Le Livre Psautier, livre de lecture élémentaire', *Etudes Mérovingiennes. Actes des Journées de Poitiers 1952* (Paris, 1953), pp. 253–6, and Bernhard Bischoff, 'Elementarunterricht und Probationes Pennae in der ersten Halfte des Mittelalters', *MS* I, pp. 74–87.
[24] *PL* 133, cols. 43–86, at cols. 45–6, trans. Sitwell, *Odo of Cluny*, pp. 7–8.
[25] *Ibid.*, col. 47, trans. Sitwell, *Odo of Cluny*, p. 9.

synonym for scholarly life, or the life of a *clericus*, which involved learning to read and learning things associated with the Christian faith and the church.

Benedict of Aniane, too, before he turned to the monastic life, was, as a layman, learned in unusual studies, but he gave up all those things in which human weakness is accustomed to take pride.[26] The Old Latin Life of Gerard of Vienne records, for what it is worth, that he was well versed in law as well as being a good warrior, well educated and active in the royal administration.[27] As Riché reminds us, the Lives of Landeric, Clodulf, Paul, Gerald and Poppo tell of the saints when young being entrusted to clerics, not to be made into clerics in their turn, but to be given the literary instruction suitable for a noble.[28] Other lives, such as those of Gerald of Aurillac, John of Gorze, Bernard of Menthon and Theodoric of Andage, describe the children of the nobles being instructed at home.[29] Girls were not necessarily excluded from this. Liutberga of Halberstadt is said to have taught girls the psalmody and to let them go home after their lessons or elsewhere as they wished.[30] That is, she was clearly not simply instructing novices destined for an enclosed life in a religious community, but teaching within a region in a 'public' school.

We can add to this hint from the *Vita Liutbergae* as to the existence of schools. Another is recorded in the *Vita Liudgeri*. This describes how the saint, as soon as he could walk and talk, began to collect bits of animal skin and bark and sew them together to make little books for himself with which he and the other children would play. He then began to write books and read them for himself, and swore that God had been his teacher. Thereafter he asked his parents to entrust him to some man of God for instruction. He was sent to Gregory of Utrecht in whose school were educated other 'noble and wise fellow pupils' some of whom became bishops and others 'in lower orders' became teachers in churches.[31] The structure of the passages concerning Liudger gives the distinct impression that the education came first and that only subsequently did he put aside

[26] Ardo, *Vita Benedicti* c. 1, *MGH SS* XV, pp. 200–20, at p. 201.
[27] See Bernard de Gaiffier, 'Un dossier hagiographique réuni pour Girart de Vienne', *Analecta Bollandiana* 88 (1970) 285–8.
[28] Riché, *Ecoles et enseignements*, pp 382–93; *Vita Landerici, AA SS* April II, 489; *Vita Clodulfi, Acta Sanctorum Ordinis Sancti Benedicti*, ed. L. d'Achery and J. Mabillon (Paris, 1668–1701), II.10; *Vita Pauli, AA SS* Feb. II, 175; *Vita Geraldi, MGH SS* VIII, p. 643; and *Vita Popponis, MGH SS* XI, p. 293.
[29] *Vita Geraldi, PL* 133, col. 645; John of Gorze, *Vita Iohanni, MGH SS* IV, p. 340; *Vita Bernardi, AA SS* June III, 1074, *Vita Theoderici, MGH SS* II, p. 39.
[30] *Vita Liutbergae* c.35, *MGH SS* IV, pp. 158–64, at p. 64, and see O. Menzel, 'Die heilige Liutberg', *Deutsches Archiv für die Erforschung des Mittelalters* 2 (1938) 189–93, and compare the account of her life in Gisela's household, p. 160.
[31] *Vita Liudgeri* c.8, *MGH SS* II, pp. 403–19, at p. 406.

the lay habit and enter the monastery of Utrecht. Further indications of the existence of schools is to be found in the Life of St Valery, written in the ninth century. According to this account the saint in his early youth came to the place where the children of nobles were being instructed and demanded of his teacher that an alphabet be written for him and that he be taught to read.[32] He himself, by implication, was not of noble birth. Other children of noblemen or *potentiores*, or even of kings, such as Einhard, Abbo of Fleury, Hugh (bastard son of Charlemagne), Jerome (bastard son of Charles Martel), Pippin III and the twin sons of Charles the Bald, were educated in monastic schools.[33]

There were clearly some schools in the Carolingian realm open to laymen. The chronicle of St Riquier by Hariulf, furthermore, preserves the famous description by Abbot Angilbert of a liturgical procession in which boys of the lay school and boys from the abbey school took part.[34] Angilbert did not make it clear whether one had to belong to a particular social group or intend to join the church to go to one or the other school, but it is possible that the lay school was the place for elementary instruction before one decided, one's parents decided, or particular aptitude made it appropriate, to pursue a clerical career. In other words, a local monastery could provide basic education for lay boys. The *Admonitio Generalis* of 789 had decreed that schools were to be set up for boys in every station of life, but in 817 Louis the Pious' conciliar decisions at Aachen included the statement that only those intending to be monks should be taught in monastic schools.[35] He may here have been making a distinction between monastic schools for aspiring clergy and lay schools for others, though he does not mention the latter. As the decrees were concerned wholly with monastic reform this is perhaps not surprising. It remains a possibility, however, that Louis' measure was the first step

[32] *Vita Valerii, MGH SS rer. merov.* IV, p. 160. It is of the greatest significance that education is understood in terms of learning the alphabet and to read. Apart from the references to schools, when a child is taught at home in these saints' lives, more often than not it is the mother rather than the father who is charged with the preliminary instruction.

[33] On Einhard see Walahfrid Strabo's prologue to Einhard's *Vita Karoli*, ed. G. Waitz (after G. H. Pertz), *MGH SS i.u.s.* (1911), pp. xxviii–xxix. On Abbo's education see *PL* 139, col. 389; on Hugh see J. van der Straeten, ed., '*Vita Hugonis*', *Analecta Bollandiana* 87 (1969) 233. Pippin III was educated at St Denis: see Pierre Riché, 'Le Renouveau culturel à la cour de Pepin III', *Francia* 2 (1974) 59–70. Jerome and the twin sons of Charles the Bald were educated at St Amand: BN lat. 5327 from St Amand records the name of Jerome, and the epitaph of the twin boys by Milo of St Amand is preserved in *MGH Poet* III, pp. 677–8.

[34] I discuss the schools more fully in McKitterick, *Frankish Kingdoms*, pp. 146–7. The *Gesta abbatum Lobbiensis* c.23, *MGH SS* XXI, p. 327, refers to an external school at Lobbes. See also Riché, *Ecoles et enseignements*, pp. 137–214.

[35] *Admonitio Generalis* c.72, *MGH Cap.* I, No. 22, p. 60; 817 decrees, *MGH Cap.* I, No. 170, c.45, p. 346.

towards the exclusion of the laity from monastic education unless they intended to continue within the cloister. A stricter interpretation of the Rule of Benedict encouraged by the reform decrees, moreover, may have meant the withdrawal of some of the customary services to the community on the part of the monastery. But much of this, given the meagre evidence, must remain conjecture. Louis' decree, on the other hand, might have been a protest against the number of lay boys attending monastic schools and an attempt to limit or stop the practice out of fear for the undesirable worldly interests and influences thereby brought within the cloister. It may also have had behind it a wish to persuade parents to find an alternative means of educating their sons if an ecclesiastical career were not envisaged for them.

The St Gall Plan's provision for two schools, an external school a little removed from the main cluster of monastic buildings and an inner school or novitiate east of the abbey church, may be an implementation of Louis the Pious's decrees. I have suggested elsewhere, building on a remark of Walter Horn's, that the external school of St Gall, like the abbey school of St Riquier, may have been the elementary school where every student would be taught basic education – reading, some grammar, the Latin psalter – regardless of his eventual vocation. The internal school, on the other hand, offered a more advanced education for those who had decided, or whose parents had decided for them, to withdraw from the world.[36] Ekkehard of St Gall records that Tuotilo taught music to the sons of nobles in a place designated by the abbot and that Notker Balbulus, author of the *Gesta Karoli Magni*, educated boys who were to succeed to their fathers' property as well as those who were to enter the church.[37] There is no hint in the brief reference we have to cathedral schools that laymen were necessarily excluded.[38] Even if they were excluded, there must have been some who dropped out, either through changes in the family fortunes, such as the death of an elder brother, greater acquisition of wealth, the exigencies of war, recovery of health, or simple recognition of a lack of vocation, among those who had originally or provisionally been intended for a clerical career. Not everyone can have suffered as much as Gottschalk for his change of mind.

[36] McKitterick, *Frankish Kingdoms*, p. 147, and see Walter Horn, 'On the author of the Plan of St Gall and the relation of the Plan to the monastic reform movement', in Johannes Duft, ed., *Studien zum St Galler Klosterplan* (St Gall, 1962), pp. 103–27.

[37] Ekkehard, *Casus Sancti Galli* c.34, ed. Hans F. Haefele, *Ekkehard IV, Casus Sancti Galli* (Darmstadt, 1980), p. 78, and E. Lechner, *Vita Notkeri Balbuli. Geistesgeschichtlicher Standort und historische Kritik*, Mitteilungen zur Vaterländische Geschichte 47 (St Gall, 1972). See, too, Eberhard Url, *Das mittelalterliche Geschichtswerk 'Casus sancti Galli'* (St Gall, 1969).

[38] Council of Paris (829) c.30, *MGH Conc.* II.2, p. 632.

Although most of the evidence about schools relates to the training of the regular and secular clergy, it would be a mistake to assume that education and learning were confined to clerics. Some laymen clearly did go to school, but how much they learnt, and whether their education was separate from those intending to enter, or who had already entered, the church cannot at present be established. Notker Balbulus' story from his *Gesta Karoli* is relevant in this respect. Notker describes Charlemagne's anger at finding the sons of his lay magnates slothful at their studies. The king had entrusted boys of noble parents, *mediocres* (boys of the middle class), and poor boys to Clement the Irishman for instruction. The compositions and poems of the noble boys were weak and full of errors. They were scolded for their neglect of the pursuit of learning. The good boys, that is, the *mediocres* and the *infimi*, were to be rewarded with bishoprics and monasteries.[39] An *infimus* who had especially distinguished himself was transferred to the palace chapel. The castigation of the sons of the nobility can be understood as a warning that they would never receive honours and offices from Charlemagne unless they acquired a respect for and knowledge of those things Charlemagne wished to promote. Whether it was Charlemagne or his successors who emphasized the value of education in quite this way cannot be established. The story, nevertheless, is important in so far as it indicates the opportunities that were envisaged as emanating from the patronage of the royal court, and that it was accepted that even those not necessarily destined for an ecclesiastical career would be expected to acquire some Latin learning. They needed it to qualify for administrative office.

It is possible that laymen were only trained to be functional in the administration. That is, Notker's story of the sloth and arrogance of the noble boys with regard to their letters (what need did they have to rely solely on their wits to get on in the world?) may preserve some sense of most nobles' lack of enthusiasm for learning. Nobles evidently rarely became learned, but they were taught enough to read laws and royal legislation and to make use of charters in the conduct of their own business. They attained pragmatic literacy. Some, more intelligent, presented with more opportunities, or simply more interested (having acquired, like Gerald of Aurillac, a taste for study), attained rather higher levels of learning.[40]

This was the case whether boys went to schools or were educated

---

[39] Notker Balbulus, *Gesta Karoli Magni* c.3, ed. R. Rau, *Quellen zur karolingischen Reichsgeschichte* III (Darmstadt, 1975), pp. 324–6, Eng. trans. Lewis Thorpe, *Two Lives of Charlemagne* (Harmondsworth, 1969), pp. 95–6.

[40] See the examples given below, pp. 245–52.

privately. As recounted above, there is a small body of material, mostly in the saints' lives, attesting to the existence of private education in the Carolingian period. References to the process, place or means of instruction for young boys and girls before they achieved fame are few, but sufficient to suggest a variety of accepted places for instruction and training, whether from the local priest, in the local monastery, at a comital, ducal or royal court, or within the household. In the last named, it appears to have been the women who were all-important.

The role of women in Carolingian education

A number of sources give prominence in the instruction of the young within the family to the mother. Hugh, half-brother of Charles Martel, for example, who eventually rose to become abbot of St Wandrille and archbishop of Rouen, was brought up by his grandmother, Ansfledis, by all accounts a redoubtable old lady.[41] It was she who fostered in Hugh both a love of sacred learning and spiritual devotion, and who urged him towards a clerical career. She may well have considered this her grandson's safest bet in the context of family politics. (Hugh in fact became a staunch ally of Charles Martel in his efforts to win Neustria to his rule.) Hugh's actual instruction in Latin grammar and reading may have been provided by a tutor, though none is mentioned. It seems to have been Ansfledis herself who taught Hugh what he needed for a public career in the church. The abilities and activities of a later abbot of St Wandrille, Gervold, suggest that he had received a secular training as well as a more strictly clerical education, but, though of noble birth, no hint is provided in the account of his career of who taught him.[42] This is a common failing in our sources. More often than not they present instances of accomplishment rather than details of how skills were acquired. The most obvious instance of this is William of Septimania, but here at least, the role of his mother is clear.

On his departure, at sixteen years old, to serve Charles the Bald, Dhuoda presented her son William with a manual of good conduct, from the reading of which he was clearly intended to derive benefit.[43] He was, furthermore, going to serve at a court where he can hardly have been the odd man out, or eccentric, in being possessed of the ability to read. It may well have been Dhuoda who taught her son. Whatever the case, she herself was adequately educated and believed with all her heart that it was

[41] Lohier and Laporte, eds., *Gesta Fontanellensis coenobii* IV.1, p. 39.
[42] *Ibid.*, XII, 1 and 2, pp. 84–7.
[43] Dhuoda, *Liber Manualis*, ed. Pierre Riché, *Manuel pour mon fils*, Sources Chrétiennes 225 (Paris, 1975).

from the written word that her dear son would derive the most benefit. She urged William to acquire more books to add to the little one she had written for him:

Knowing that most women in the world have the joy of living with their children, and seeing that I, Dhuoda, am withheld from you, my son William, and am far away – as one anxious because of this and full of longing to be useful, I am sending you this little work of mine, copied for you to read, a work that is formative in a mirror-like way. I should be happy if, since I am not physically present, the presence of this little book call to your mind, as you read it, what you should do for my sake... I want you, when you are weighed down by hosts of worldly and temporal activities, to read this little book I have sent you... Even if, more and more, you acquire books, many volumes, may it please you still to read frequently this little work of mine – may you have the strength to grasp it profitably, with the help of almighty God... I urge you William, my handsome, lovable son, amid the worldly preoccupations of your life, not to be slow in acquiring many books where, through most holy teachers, you should discover and learn something about God the Creator – more things and greater than are written here. My son, you will have teachers who will give you more lessons, and more valuable ones – yet not in the same way, with the heart burning within, as I with mine, my first-born one.[44]

It is a heartfelt appeal, from a desolate mother whose children have been taken from her by a harsh and ambitious husband. Dhuoda hopes that through her writing she can still influence her boy. Through his reading of her book, and of the writings of others, William may be kept to the path of honour and truth and this wisdom may thereby be with him in the worldly concerns of politics at the Frankish court. Dhuoda expresses the ethos of a great house, where one may learn from one's peers and betters, if one wishes: 'humility, charity, chastity, patience, gentleness, modesty, sobriety, astuteness, and other virtues, together with the eagerness to do good'.[45]

What of Dhuoda herself? She wrote her *Liber Manualis* between 840 and 843 in her home in Septimania. It was a moral treatise, full of both the aristocratic ideals of honour and fidelity to one's lord and Christian moral teaching. Dhuoda does not usually cite her sources, except for Donatus, Isidore's *Synonyma* and Gregory the Great's *Cura Pastoralis*, but she does say she wrote from books in her own possession. Some of her sources have been identified. They include the *Liber Cathemerinon* of Prudentius, Augustine's *Enchiridion*, the *Tractatus in Iohannem*, various homilies and the *Moralia in Job* of Gregory the Great. She had also read some saints' lives and books on virtues and vices, including those by Alcuin and Ambrosius Autpert. She knew her Bible well, especially the Gospel of St Matthew,

---

[44] *Ibid.*, pp. 72 and 80, Eng. trans. Peter Dronke, *Women Writers of the Middle Ages* (Cambridge, 1984), p. 40.
[45] *Ibid.*, p. 170, trans. *ibid.*, p. 44.

Paul's Epistles and the psalter.[46] Some of Dhuoda's knowledge of the patristic authors may well have been gained from collections of extracts. Many such *florilegia* were compiled in the ninth century, some specifically for members of the nobility.[47] Even so, her learning and her skill in Latin composition are impressive. Although somewhat unorthodox and with some errors, Dhuoda's Latin prose and verse nevertheless reveal a fine intelligence and sensitivity and an understanding of what she has read that needs to be fully appreciated. Dronke, for example, has drawn attention to Dhuoda's awareness of the context of Ovid's limning of the flesh, the inner conflict of man and the spirit in the *Amores*, and of St Paul's insistence of the essential opposition between them, and Dhuoda's attempt to project a harmony of these elements of man's nature.[48] Her Latin suggests some influence of Germanic rhythmic patterns, with two dominant stresses in each half-line of her verses.

How exceptional was Dhuoda? Is she the model of a noblewoman, or a rare instance of a Carolingian bluestocking, bound in marriage for the sake of her family and beholden to her husband for support thereafter? Her name is thought by most scholars to suggest a north Frankish origin rather than membership of a family in the region of Uzés where her husband's property lay, and to which he bid her retire at some stage after 826. Dhuoda had been married to Bernard in the palace chapel at Aachen on 29 June 824, but this is more likely to reflect her husband's position in relation to Louis the Pious than that of her own family.[49] She was, therefore, an educated woman of a Frankish aristocratic family, well read, and with a high sense of duty and loyalty. If she is a random example of the educational attainments of a Frankish noblewoman (in the sense that chance survival has preserved her treatise for posterity) is it justifiable to think in terms of her being representative of her class? Of course one should like to think so. Fragments of other evidence extant, in the form of works dedicated to or commissioned by laywomen, books owned by them, borrowed or given to them, indeed, make an assessment of Dhuoda as one well-documented instance of a general phenomenon more than mere wishful thinking.

Prudentius of Troyes (d. 861), for example, wrote a short introduction to the Bible for an aristocratic, unnamed lady.[50] Two monks, Richer and

---

[46] *Ibid.*, pp. 33–7.
[47] McKitterick, *Frankish Church*, pp. 155–83.
[48] Dronke, *Women Writers*, p. 46.
[49] See, for example, the *Annales regni francorum* s.a.829, ed. R. Rau, *Quellen zur karolingischen Reichsgeschichte* I (Darmstadt, 1974) p. 154, Eng. trans. B. Scholz, *Carolingian Chronicles* (Ann Arbor, 1970) p. 124. See also Riché, ed, *Manuel*, pp. 17–24.
[50] PL 115, cols. 1449–56.

Ratelm, composed in the ninth century a commentary on the psalter for a Countess Hoda.[51] John Contreni has gathered together the references to the number of 'emperors, kings, queens, archbishops, bishops, abbots, nuns, priests and occasional laymen and laywomen who commissioned biblical expositions', in his study of how the greatest book of them all, the *bibliotheca*, or Bible, was introduced and expounded to the Carolingian people.[52] Wicbod's *Quaestiones in Octateuchum* is typical of this genre,[53] and the Emperor Lothar requested a 'literal commentary on Genesis, a spiritual commentary on Jeremiah and an anagogic commentary on Ezekiel' of Hraban Maur.[54] Female members of the royal family are consistently recorded as educated. Gisela and Rotrud, for example, sister and daughter of Charlemagne respectively, begged Alcuin to write them a commentary on the Gospels of St John.[55] The daughters of Eberhard of Friuli – Judith, Hadwig or Heiliwich, and Engeldrud – as we shall see below, received their complement of books from their parents, and women are recorded among the borrowers' lists from Cologne and Weissenburg.[56]

Educated noblewomen of high rank were thus, on the basis of these scraps of information, not unusual in the Carolingian period. To counter that they must be exceptions is to avoid acknowledging the climate of social acceptability surrounding such manifestations of learned interest. These ladies may be exceptional in the quality of their learning, but it would be justifiable to conclude that a general level of basic literacy and instruction prevailed among the nobility, that educated noblewomen were not unusual in the Carolingian period and that they may well have customarily played a part in the instruction of their children. The female members of the household, therefore, may have acted as the principal conduits for an educational and cultural tradition within the ranks of the nobility. The easy assurance and confidence with which Dhuoda entrusts her son with the treatise she has composed for him are expressive,

[51] See Henry Stevenson, *Codices Palatini latini Bibliothecae Vaticanae* (Rome, 1886), p. 2 n. 14: *Richerii* [sic] *et Ratelmi monachorum Adnotatio de psalteriis decantatis pro Hodane comitissa.* Ludwig Traube, *Karolingische Dichtungen* (Berlin, 1888), p. 140, thought this Hoda should be identified with Dhuoda.

[52] John J. Contreni, 'Carolingian biblical studies', in Uta-Renate Blumenthal, ed., *Carolingian Essays*, Andrew W. Mellon Lectures in Early Christian Studies (Washington, 1983), pp. 71–98.

[53] *PL* 96, cols. 1105–68 (= *PL* 93, cols. 233–85), *PL* 93, cols. 285–456. On Wicbod see Michael Gorman, 'The Encyclopedic Commentary on Genesis prepared for Charlemagne by Wigbod', *Récherches Augustiniennes* 17 (1982) 173–201, and Contreni, 'Biblical studies', p. 85.

[54] *MGH Epp.* V, p. 475.

[55] MGH Epp IV, p. 324, and see Contreni, 'Biblical studies', pp. 90–1.

[56] See below, pp. 246–7 and 261–6.

moreover, of the abilities properly brought up noble sons could be assumed to possess. They provide an additional response to the implications of the legal material, namely, that there existed an educated class of administrators and officials and their families. In none of the references to schools or education is basic instruction in reading Latin absent.

I am well aware of the dangers of maximalist interpretations, but it seems to me that the evidence for the education of the laity, though hardly substantial or overwhelming, does point to a far stronger possibility of the widespread provision of basic instruction, at least among the *nobiles* and *potentes*, if not the *mediocres* and fortunate *pauperes* or *infimi*, than has hitherto been acknowledged. There are too many 'exceptions' for the 'rules' to which they were once related to hold any longer. The 'rules' themselves must be changed to allow for the acceptance of the existence of the wider spread of basic literacy which provided the necessary foundation for administrative careers, for the conduct of judicial business dependent on the use of the written word and for the practice of the Christian faith.

II LAY CULTURE AND THE QUESTION OF AUDIENCE

The elevation of the status of the written word and the promotion of literacy had crucial consequences for the moral emphases and the material and ethical values of lay culture. We find increasing written witness to it, and are thus able to essay some remarks as to its nature and the role of the written word and of particular texts in determining its character. The evidence is too meagre to be conclusive, but read against the background of the preceding chapters it is powerfully suggestive. I have, moreover, only scraped the surface of this potentially rich lode, so that my comments perforce are of a preliminary kind, are often conjectural and will need to be substantiated, or contradicted, by further investigation.

The audience for Carolingian Latin poetry

Let us first consider the question of audience. For whom were the texts extant from the Carolingian period written? There are many Latin literary texts, for example, which it would be possible to assign to a clerical milieu if one were bent on doing so, but which make better sense if considered as intended for a lay patron or audience, and thus with something to tell us of the secular world. The *Waltharius* poem is one obvious example. Its date has been much disputed, with some preferring an early ninth-century and some a late tenth-century date, and ascription to a number of different poets, for none of whom are the arguments conclusive.[57] The date perhaps does not matter as far as the aristocratic ethos it portrays is concerned; it is as relevant for the early as for the late Carolingian period. But it is crucial if one reflects on the language of the poem and its possible audience in the context of the vitality of Latin as a vernacular and the ability of its audience to understand it. It is easier to imagine this poem being understood by the lay audience for whom it was apparently intended in the early ninth century, whereas by the late tenth century the rift between spoken Romance and written Latin would have made the poem's likely audience a more restricted one. Later vernacular versions of the poem, in Provençal, and other mediaeval languages, may point to the solutions resorted to in order to make the poem accessible to its most appropriate audience.[58]

The *Waltharius* can hardly have been intended for a clerical audience, though one should not discount the possibility that Carolingian monks and priests enjoyed heroic lays and fostered their production.[59] But the poem's idealization of heroic deeds and noble prowess was designed to strike a chord in the hearts of its hearers and readers as a larger-than-life realization of their own fantasies. It was about heroes of their own class moving in a world of battles, revenge, cunning and valour, to which they could relate. Written in a language much indebted to both Roman and Christian Latin poetry, the context is nevertheless Germanic and heroic. Nor is it a pervasively Christian text, in that God does not direct the course of events or determine their outcome. It can be understood as fit for recitation as well as for private reading in the same way that twelfth-century German vernacular poetry, such as that of Wolfram von Eschenbach, was received in aristocratic circles. The chief protagonists, Walter and Hagen, embody an ideal image of a nobleman. Their learning

---

[57] On the various arguments concerning the *Waltharius* see A. K. Bate, *Waltharius of Gaeraldus*, Mediaeval and Renaissance Latin Texts (Reading, 1978); Ursula and Peter Dronke, *Barbara et antiquissima carmina* (Barcelona, 1977), pp. 27–79; Rudolf Schieffer, 'Silius Italicus in Sankt Gallen – ein Hinweis zur Lokalisierung der "Waltharius"', *Mittellateinisches Jarhbuch* 10 (1975) 7–19; Karl Langosch, *Waltharius: die Dichtung und die Forschung* (Darmstadt, 1979); and Dieter Schaller, 'Ist der Waltharius früh-karolingisch', *Mittellateinisches Jahrbuch* 18 (1983) 63–83. The poem was translated into English by H. M. Smyser and F. P. Magoun Jnr, *Survivals in Old Norwegian of Medieval English, French, and German Literature, together with the Latin Versions of the Heroic Legend of Walter of Aquitaine* (Baltimore, 1941), pp. 11–45, and also by Dennis M. Kratz, *Waltharius and Ruodlieb* (New York, 1984). The standard edition is that of Karl Strecker, *MGH Poet.* VI, pp. 1–85.

[58] Discussed by Dronke and Dronke, *Barbara carmina*.

[59] Both Alcuin and Otfrid of Weissenburg, however, disapproved of such frivolity. Compare Alcuin, *MGH Epp.* IV, No. 124, p. 183, and Otfrid, ed. Oskar Erdmann, *Otfrids Evangelienbuch* (Tübingen, 1973), p. 5, and see the Eng. trans. F. P. Magoun, 'Otfrid's Ad Liutpertum', *Publications of the Modern Language Association* 58 (1943) 869–90.

and their training in martial pursuits were those of the true hero who excels in all fields, with a clear implication that they were literate.

The linguistic and imaginative subtlety of the *Waltharius*, if indeed designed for a lay comital or royal courtly audience, could tell us much of the poet's hopes from his audience. In other words, an attempt should be made to read these poems with the audience in mind and thus for what they can tell us of the poet's hopes and expectations (not necessarily the same thing) as far as his audience's sensibilities and comprehension is concerned. For whom, for example, were the Vergilian echoes intended? Would such a passage as Hagen's attempt to save Walter's life by trying to force his nephew to see his love of fame as cupidity, with its deliberate Vergilian quotation, have been recognized by the audience generally, and would they have appreciated the connotations of the original quotation?[60] It may be more realistic to suppose that the poem was appreciated at a number of different levels depending on the sophistication and intellectual training of the hearers, much as highly allusive poets, such as the Metaphysicals, Browning or T. S. Eliot, are enjoyed today. Nevertheless, if literary allusions were lost on the audience, the rich fabric of the poem's story, its vigour, its emotional energy and the purity of its language would have the effect for which the poet aimed on most of his audience. It is conceivable that the poem was recited in several sittings at feasts in a lord's hall. It could also have been read by an individual to himself.

Other literary works from the ninth century are more readily understood if a lay audience be envisaged, even though many had their counterparts in clerical milieux and even liturgical contexts. The genre of *planctus*, laments on the death of particular personages or to mark particular events, for example, included a number that could have been commissioned by the surviving relatives. They do not have the character of an unsolicited response by a poet to the death of a local notable or patron intended for clerical consumption. The *planctus*, probably sung, may have assumed some prominence in aristocratic and secular funeral rites. It was certainly a widespread genre, with surviving examples in Latin, Provençal, English, French, German, Italian, Catalan and Galician Portugese from the eighth to the fifteenth centuries.[61] The best known Carolingian example is the lament on the death of Charlemagne: *A solis ortu usque ad occidua*, probably

---

[60] *Waltharius* lines 876–7, ed. Strecker, *MGH Poet.* VI, p. 60, and compare Dronke and Dronke, *Barbara carmina*, p. 79. I am grateful to Peter Dronke for his discussion in conversation on this particular point.

[61] On the genre of *planctus* see Janthia Yearley, 'A bibliography of *planctus* in Latin, Provençal, French, German, English, Catalan and Galician Portuguese from the time of Bede to the early fifteenth century', *Journal of the Plainsong and Medieval Music Society* 4 (1981) 12–52.

by Columbanus of St Trond,[62] and there are others for Carolingian lay notables, such as that for Adalhard, count of Paris, *Ecce Iudas uelut olim saluatoris tradidit,*[63] the lament on the death of Eric, count of Friuli by Paulinus of Aquileia,[64] or the *planctus*: *Cordas tange melos pange* composed on the death of William of Aquitaine,[65] quite apart from those composed for prominent ecclesiastics. For Charlemagne's illegitimate son Hugh, abbot of St Quentin, and archchancellor to Louis the Pious, for example, was written the fine *Hug dulce nomen*. It appears to have been composed after Hugh was killed in his attempted coup d'état in 844, when he raised an army against his nephew, Charles the Bald. It is skilfully structured with an irregularly recurring refrain, and represents a fusion of native and learned elements, very unlike the formal *planctus*. It expresses to the full the pity of kindred at war (and uses the pluperfect subjunctive to suggest how different it all might have been). The surge of compassion at the sight of Hugh's naked corpse, the rueful sorrow with which a suitable burial place is determined and the reproach underlying the introductory stanzas all suggest that this is a lament on the part of Charles the Bald's entourage, sung to mourn the passing of a good man led astray.[66]

Other poems may have formed the centrepiece of victory celebrations and feasts. The vigorous rhythmical poem celebrating Pippin's victory over the Avars, for example, is full of circumstantial detail likely to have been appreciated by those taking part in the expedition.[67] The language of the poem has been interpreted as an attempt on the author's part to write at a different level of language from the learned Latin verse which forms the characteristic product of the poets of the court circle. Thus the 'vulgarisms' which stud the text are not 'marks of ignorance but the sign of a cultivated author's conscious attempt to compose a Latin intelligible to fellow clerics'.[68] Why should this poem have been addressed to fellow-clerics? Do not the 'vulgarisms' of this victory poem or of the verses in praise of Verona, and the very sense that the poet is writing down to his audience, suggest that a lay audience is envisaged?[69] These apparently provincial

---

[62] *MGH Poet.* I, pp. 435–6, Eng. trans. Peter Godman, *Poetry of the Carolingian Renaissance* (London, 1985), pp. 207–11. With musical setting in the tenth-century BN lat. 1154, fo. 132r.

[63] Text in BN lat. 2683 (s.ix/x) unpublished. See Bischoff, *MS* II, p. 28.

[64] *MGH Poet.* I, p. 131. With musical setting in the tenth-century BN lat. 1154, fo. 116r.

[65] Karl Strecker, ed., *Carmina Cantabrigiensia* (Berlin, 1926), p. 101 (extant in the Cambridge Songs manuscript, Cambridge University Library, Gg.5.35, fo. 441v, of the mid-eleventh century).

[66] *MGH Poet.* II, pp. 139–40. With musical setting in the tenth-century BN lat. 1154, fo. 113r.   [67] *MGH Poet.* I, pp. 116–17, Eng. trans. Godman, *Poetry,* pp. 187–191.

[68] The advocate of the clerical audience is Godman, *Poetry,* p. 31.

[69] *MGH Poet.* I, pp. 120–2, Eng. trans. Godman, *Poetry,* pp. 181–7 and compare *ibid.,* pp. 31–2.

efforts at composition of less learned and more 'colloquial' poetry among the many assuredly clerical effusions extant may well be the slim remainder of aristocratic 'courtly' or secular literature from the ninth century.

The *Versus de bella quae fuit acta Fontaneto*, for instance, has strong secular elements, and is a world away from classical verse forms and preoccupations.[70] It is powerful rhythmic verse designed for recitation and it is significant that one of its surviving manuscripts retains Latin forms that are still less classical than in the printed version.[71] This is not the verse of a poet writing in an acquired language. Angelbert, its author, was a follower of Lothar, and his poem may be the one response from the lay nobles who followed Lothar that we can identify (comparable to the public and private history of the quarrel between the sons of Louis the Pious by Charles the Bald's supporter Nithard). It has the character of a 'lay of the last survivor' and was composed by a man well versed in the Bible as well as in the *planctus* tradition.

Concentration on the learned tradition behind such poems is, of course, valuable for the insight into the exploitation and availability of sources it provides, but it leaves too little room for the poetry's social context and the important questions it raises concerning levels of Latin literacy in the Carolingian world.

Who composed the audience, for example, of the political poems of Charlemagne's court? A poem of Theodulf of Orleans indicates a process of passing poems at court from hand to hand among members of the royal family.[72] A poem in praise of poetry by *Hibernicus exul*, moreover, sees poetry, or, at least, public panegyric, as the particular offering to the king for those who, unlike the *proceres mundi*, do not deliver tribute in the form of gold, silver and precious gems, but in words.[73] The effectiveness of these verbal tributes, poetic epistles and public panegyrics is only conceivable if there were an audience sufficiently educated to understand and appreciate them.

A reading of these poems suggests that there were, no doubt, many subtle allusions missed or misunderstood, and many of the poets' best jibes and thrusts were so blanketed with poetic verbiage and literary artifice as to miss their target; but the existence of an elaborate genre of this kind seems hardly credible without a coterie of scholars and statesmen to receive it. These poems were designed to be admired, whether as literary

[70] *MGH Poet*. II, p. 138, Eng. trans. Godman, *Poetry*, pp. 263–5. I am grateful to Peter Dronke for his discussion in conversation on this poem.
[71] Compare for example, readings in BN lat. 1154 (s.x.) and Pfäfers Mbr.4 in the Stiftsarchiv St Gall (s.ix).
[72] *MGH Poet*. I. pp. 483–9, at lines 9–12 on p. 483, Eng. trans. Godman, *Poetry*, p. 151.
[73] *MGH Poet*. I. pp. 396–7, Eng. trans. Godman, *Poetry*, pp. 175–9.

tours de force, panegyric or lament. The description of this body of poetry as one 'which drew upon traditions both sacred and profane and was equal to adapting its style and register to the varying requirements of public recitation and private exchange' is crucial in its implications.[74] There was an audience for these verses. They were the equivalent of the 'heroic panegyric' created to foster the illusion of success that we will observe (below) in the vernacular *Ludwigslied*. The audience was by no means an exclusively clerical audience, or a pettifogging scholarly one. It was a courtly audience of magnates, clerics and laymen, anxious to get on in a world whose leaders had made the written word more than the vehicle of the Christian faith. The poems constitute a bold affirmation of the relevance of letters in political life. Indeed, many of the poems' authors were themselves lay magnates forging a career for themselves in the brutal realities of Carolingian politics. Einhard and Angilbert, for example, prominent courtiers both, made distinctive contributions to the genre.

The audience for written German poetry

It is not only Latin literacy that must be considered in the context of potential audience, but also the evidence of the meagre remains of German literature. Much of it was clearly confined to a clerical milieu, for its purposes were ecclesiastical and didactic. The bulk of it, moreover, survives in the form of translations of Latin Christian writings. Apart from the Old French *Eulalia Sequence* of the late ninth century, there is nothing at all in the way of literature in Romance or proto-French from the ninth century. In Old High German, however, there are a few fragments of secular poetry, such as the *Hildebrandslied* and the *Muspilli* fragment, as well as longer works which may have had a secular audience, such as one copy of Otfrid of Weissenburg's *Evangelienbuch* dedicated to Louis the German.[75] These represent both works actually composed and conceived in written form, and poems possibly originally transmitted orally and recorded in writing only subsequently, presumably on the Latin model.

One such transcription has engendered much excitement and controversy, not least arising from the provenance of the written copy. It merits consideration in some detail for some light can be thrown on its intended audience thereby. The Old High German *Ludwigslied*, in a dialect

---

[74] Godman, *Poetry*, p. 33, though the question of audience is not addressed.
[75] See Berhard Bischoff, 'Bücher am Hofe Ludwigs des Deutschen und die Privatbibliothek des Kanzlers Grimalt', *MS* III, pp. 187–212, at p. 191, and compare Erdmann, *Otfrids Evangelienbuch*, pp. 1–3, with the text of Otfrid's dedicatory poem to Louis in Old High German.

essentially Franconian though with some Low German and Middle Franconian forms, was copied onto three scraps of parchment bound into Valenciennes 150 after the last quire (quire 18) of the volume.[76] It is preceded by the Old French *Eulalia Sequence* and the text of that actually starts on the last page of quire 18, fo. 140v. The main manuscript contains the *Apologeticum* of Gregory Nazianzus written in an unidentified centre on the left bank of the Rhine or lower Lotharingian region. The entire volume is only securely located from the twelfth century at St Amand, for it was then listed in the St Amand library catalogue, now BN lat. 1850.[77] Although the binding is a later mediaeval one, of the type categorized by Knaus as a *Koperteinband*,[78] the leaves containing the *Eulalia Sequence* and the *Ludwigslied* appear to have been attached to the book since they were copied into it. No fewer than three different hands were responsible for these additions, one each for the Latin Sequences, the *Eulalia Sequence* and *Ludwigslied*, and the Latin distichs added after the *Ludwigslied*.[79] They are late ninth-century hands but none is of the St Amand type. The scribes therefore transcribed these poems, presumably, from an interest in linguistic curiosities understandable in the frontier region in which the book was written, but it is not possible to be more precise. Two clues remarked upon by Bischoff are the 'palaeo-frankish neums' on fo. 36r, associated with St Amand until the twelfth century but also evidenced in manuscripts from Essen, Corvey and north-east France (including Corbie and Rheims), and the *Koperteinband* associated with the Essen and Cologne or lower Rhine regions.

The palaeography, the musical notation and the binding therefore suggest an origin and early provenance outside the west Frankish kingdom for the *Ludwigslied*. So does the language, Rhenish-Franconian. The dialect of the *Eulalia Sequence*, Picard-Walloon, suggests a north French or lower Rhine connection on the part of the scribe who entered that text into the manuscript. One is dealing therefore with a centre which received its members or visitors from the Rhineland region north of Speier. The *Ludwigslied* language was that of the region embracing Speier, Worms, Mainz and Frankfurt, though its Low German and Middle Franconian elements suggest contact at least with the area lower down the Rhine,

---

[76] *Ludwigslied*, ed. Wilhelm Braune, *Althochdeutsches Lesebuch*, No. XXXVI (Tübingen, 1969), pp. 136–9, Eng. trans. J. Knight Bostock, *A Handbook on Old High German* 2nd edn revised by K. C. King and D. R. McLintock (Oxford, 1976), pp. 239–41.

[77] Léopold Delisle, *Le Cabinet des manuscrits de la Bibliothèque Impériale* I (Paris, 1868), pp. 307–19, and text ed. in II (Paris, 1874), pp. 448–58, at p. 450, item 47.

[78] H. Knaus, 'Hochmittelalterliche Koperteinbände', *Zeitschrift für Bibliothekswesen und Bibliographie* 8 (1961) 326–37.

[79] Bernhard Bischoff, 'Paläographische Fragen deutscher Denkmäler der Karolingerzeit', *MS* III, pp. 73-111, at pp. 108–10.

nearer Essen perhaps.[80] So far so good, one might think, but for the accepted subject of the poem itself. It is similar to the political battle poetry in Latin of which some instances have been cited above, for it celebrates a victory of a King Louis, son of another King Louis, over the Vikings. It is a positive and rousing portrait of the ideal king, answerable to God alone, who rallies his army and leads them to a triumphant defeat of the enemy. This king has always been identified with Louis III, teenage king of the west Franks from 879 to 882, and the victory with that of the battle of Saucourt in 881. Yet it is an identification that has given rise to much puzzlement and many ingenious explanations as to why a minor success on the part of a young west Frankish king should be celebrated in an east Frankish (German) language. There is a possibility that just as the *Eulalia Sequence* in Old French, the companion piece to the *Ludwigslied* in Valenciennes 150, has the character of an experimental translation from a Latin poem, so the *Ludwigslied* may represent an Old High German version of an existing Latin poem, composed by someone alive to the differences in the language and fascinated by them. The Latin poem may have been of French origin and transmitted through any of the diverse connections which monasteries in north-east France had with houses in the Rhineland and Lotharingia. It could thus join the group of Latin political poems aimed at lay or courtly audiences discussed above.

Another, stronger, possibility, however, is that this Rhenish-Franconian poem was composed, not for a west Frankish audience at all, but as a battle victory song for the courtly audience or the army of a Rhenish-Franconian hero, namely, Louis the Younger of Germany, whose main residence was at Frankfurt, where he died after an illness in 882 (the same year as his young cousin Louis III).[81] Louis the Younger was also the son of a King Louis as the poem describes. He too had been involved in a division, with his brother Carloman, of the kingdom of his father on the latter's death in 877, though in Louis the Younger's case there had been a third party to this division, namely Charles the Fat.[82] Louis the Younger also had a victory against the Vikings in Francia: in 880 at Thiméon on the Sambre

---

[80] The linguistic characteristics are summarized by Bostock, *Handbook*, pp. 245–7.

[81] Annals of Fulda s.a.882, ed. Rau, *Quellen* III, p. 116.

[82] *Ibid.* s.a.876, p. 104. It is arguable that, like his contemporary annalists, the poet of the *Ludwigslied* regarded Charles the Fat as of no importance in political affairs north of the Alps between 876 and 882 and did not see fit to mention him. The omission of Charles' name in the poem is nevertheless one obstacle to the identification of Louis the Younger with the Louis of the poem. Another is the fact that the victorious ruler is referred to as *Kind uuarth her faterlos* (as a young man, or, in his youth, he was rendered fatherless) which is certainly the case for Louis III who lost his father Louis the Stammerer while still in his teens, whereas Louis the Younger was forty when his father, Louis the German, died. It could on the other hand be a poetic device to enhance the pathos of Louis' position that he had lost his father.

river. The Annals of Fulda record that he there fought with the Northmen and more than 5,000 Vikings were killed.[83] Louis however lost his son Hugh in the carnage. The annalist of St Vaast, not notably warm in his attitude to Louis the Younger, said that Louis the Younger gave up the fight on learning of his son's death and thus failed to achieve what might have been a notable victory.[84] Surely Louis would have been set upon revenge at the news and would have redoubled his efforts? The *Ludwigslied* itself, given the vagueness of the details it supplies about the battle, is of little assistance in deciding which victory over the Vikings this celebrates – Thiméon in 880 or Saucourt in 881. A victory celebration might have seemed in poor taste if the king's own son had been killed, but if those who have perceived a propaganda purpose in the poem are correct, then it may have been politic, or even naturally in tune with the ethos of the times, to stress the victory, rather than grief for their own dead.

What, then, can be concluded about the audience and context for this poem? Ruth Harvey, in a now classic article, concluded that

To ascribe a Rhenish-Franconian provenance [*sic* for origin] to the *Ludwigslied* is to set up multiple problems of theme, of date, of transmission, of style, of historical fact, in order to satisfy the claims of language. The assumption of a west Frankish origin for the poem overcomes all these obstacles and leaves only one — that of language — in their place.[85]

The identification of the hero Louis with the Rhenish-Franconian ruler Louis the Younger (as far as the area he ruled was concerned), and the palaeographic indications that the manuscript was not in fact of west Frankish origin, overcome the language problem, for all the indications are thereby clearly Rhenish-Franconian. Thus the all-important question of the potential original audience for this poem is settled in favour of the subjects and supporters of Louis the Younger, based at Frankfurt. The poem, in the vernacular of the late ninth-century east Frankish kingdom, speaks to us with the vigour and immediacy of the other Carolingian victory and praise poems from the west Frankish kingdom extant in Latin, and tells us as much as they did of the aristocratic culture of its hearers or readers.

[83] *Ibid.* s.a.880, p. 112.
[84] Annals of St Vaast s.a.880, ed. R. Rau *Quellen zur karolingischen Reichsgeschichte* II (Darmstadt, 1972), p. 296.
[85] Ruth Harvey, 'The provenance of the Old High German Ludwigslied', *Medium Aevum* 14 (1945) 1–20. Compare the interpretation of, for example, Rudolf Schutzeichel, 'Das Heil des Königs. Zur Interpretation volkssprachiger Dichtung der Karolingerzeit', in Herbert Backes, ed., *Festschrift für Hans Eggers zum 65. Geburtstag* (Tübingen 1972), pp. 369–91, and Paul Fouracre, 'The context of the OHG Ludwigslied', *Medium Aevum* 54 (1985) 87–103.

The audience for history

The political context of the *Ludwigslied* is one of its most suggestive features as far as positing a secular audience is concerned. This is also the case with some major pieces of Carolingian prose writing, not least the history of the sons of Louis the Pious by Nithard. Nithard's history is that of a man not only strictly contemporary with, but closely involved in, the events he describes.[86] His work is usually regarded as that of the bluff soldier. Nelson has shown, however, that it is not just a history, but an historical work composed to convey a series of interpretative judgements; it encloses a private history of Nithard himself and his reactions to his personal predicament as well as the public history his narrative purports to convey.[87] The private history is one of hope disillusioned and trust betrayed. Its first two books, written for a contemporary audience and covering the background of the events which led to the confrontation at Fontenoy in 841, and the circumstances of the battle of Fontenoy itself, provide justification of the precise series of choices made by the men who supported Charles the Bald (king of the west Franks, 840–77). The third book had the immediate propagandic purpose of stressing Charles the Bald's leadership and the crucial role of his followers; Book IV is written in a bitter tone, very different from the first three. In it, Nithard's personal perplexity and conflict of loyalties, and the losses incurred because of his fidelity to his king, are most apparent. Nithard's history is thus not just a valuable historical narrative. It actually provides a guide to contemporary values, motives and expectations. He suggests something of why the events of 840 to 843 occurred and what they meant to some of those involved.

Nithard was a layman, fruit of a union between Charlemagne's daughter Bertha and Angilbert, one of his courtiers, himself a well-educated layman given the lay abbacy of St Riquier. Thus Nithard's history provides an aristocratic or, at least, well-connected, layman's reaction to the same concatenation of intrigue, valour, fidelity, perfidy and duty that we observed in Dhuoda. She, a passive observer of the fate of her menfolk, contributed all she could in the form of exhortation to her son William, effectively a hostage to his father's good behaviour. She urged on William the same noble virtues of loyalty, integrity and honour that

---

[86] Nithard, *Historiae*, ed. R. Rau, *Quellen* I, pp. 386–461, Eng. trans. Scholz, *Carolingian Chronicles*, pp. 129–74. Also ed. with Fr. trans. P. Lauer, *Nithard, Histoire des fils de Louis le Pieux* (Paris, 1964).

[87] Janet L. Nelson, 'Public histories and private history in the work of Nithard', *Speculum* 60 (1985) 251–93, reprinted in Janet L. Nelson, *Politics and Ritual in Early Medieval Europe* (London, 1986), pp. 195–238.

Nithard strove so hard to maintain at the cost of his personal wealth, and, in the end, his life, for he was killed fighting in another battle for Charles the Bald on 14 June 844.[88]

The audience for Dhuoda's treatise was limited. It was certainly intended only for her son, and the manuscript transmission of the text sheds little light on its subsequent fate. Cordoliani Vernet's discovery of the Barcelona manuscript, Barcelona 569, fos. 57–88, might permit us to conjecture that William's own copy of his mother's treatise was left by him in his quarters in Barcelona after he had captured that city in 848 and, due to his execution for treason a year later, was never recovered by him, but survived to be copied, and the copy was used as a correcting text, in the first half of the fourteenth century; the exemplar of the Barcelona manuscript appears to have been a Catalan manuscript.[89]

The audience for Nithard's history, on the other hand, merits further investigation. What was the possible audience for political polemic and history in the ninth century? Is it not precisely these genres which would appeal to and be aimed at the ruling magnates, whether clerical or lay? Nelson suggests precisely such a contemporary audience for Nithard's work, or at least the first three books of it, among the followers of Charles the Bald in 841–2.[90] The manuscript transmission is of no assistance in determining the intended audience. Only one copy of the work survives, in BN lat. 9768, dated to the end of the ninth century (an incomplete copy of it made in the fifteenth century is now BN lat. 14663). Its provenance is the abbey of St Médard of Soissons. It is accompanied by a copy of the Annals of Flodoard, presumably bound in at a later stage by someone either tidy-minded or genuinely interested in the history of the west Frankish kingdom in the ninth century. Whether this copy was made from an autograph of Nithard is impossible now to establish. Lauer thought such an autograph could have been at St Riquier, no doubt because Nithard succeeded to his father's position as lay abbot of that monastery.[91] The book, which its author may have decided to keep to himself rather than follow his original, more public, intentions, may have been sent to St Riquier after his death on the battlefield near Angoulême in 844. The manuscript transmission thus suggests the treatise was never seen or heard by those for whom it was written, but it does not stop us from appreciating the levels of literacy implied by Nithard's authorship and his intended audience.

[88] I here follow Nelson, 'Nithard', Appendix 2, pp. 291–3/235–7.
[89] Riché, *Manuel*, p. 49.
[90] Nelson, 'Nithard', p. 256/200.
[91] Lauer, *Nithard*, pp. xiv–xvii. After the disastrous negotiations with Lothar and the loss of Nithard's lands, the lay-abbacy was all he had left.

The work of Nithard, a Carolingian, belongs in a sense to that genre of aristocratic or royal 'house history' of which we have so many examples and which are far from being only a later mediaeval phenomenon.[92] A famous early example is the continuations of the chronicle of Fredegar, written up to chapter 34 under the auspices of Count Childebrand, uncle of Pippin III, and thereafter 'by authority of the illustrious Count Nibelung, Childebrand's son'.[93] The continuations are family history, an account of a noble house whose self-conscious high estimation of its prowess and importance seemed to be sufficient for its deeds to be recorded. In the event, the confidence of Childebrand was justified, for his nephew became king of the Franks. The work was presumably originally intended for a lay aristocratic household. There is no hint in the text that it was a work designed exclusively for clerics, or even that the author was necessarily a cleric himself. But it is not only of importance that this work should have been designed with a noble and literate audience in mind, but also that the deeds of this illustrious family (on its own reckoning) should have been set down in writing. The written word was exploited to preserve the past and persuade the future of its worth. The written word in this case, moreover, was a Latin in which the development towards 'Romance' is clearly evident, that is, this history was written in the vernacular. By association with the first four books of the chronicle of Fredegar, and the deliberate element of continuity woven into the fabric of narrative, the new ruling family of the Carolingians was making its assertions of rank and dominance in the form of written narrative history, that is, in a genre of writing that was, by definition, edifying as well as entertaining.

Lay ownership of history books and historical miscellanies

In this context the manuscript copies of the continuations are of great interest. The earliest manuscript of the chronicle proper, BN lat. 10910, is not the parent manuscript of any other copy of the chronicle. Wallace-Hadrill, the text's most recent editor, concluded that all copies of the fourth book and the continuations must have been copies of an 'official Carolingian text', that is, a version of its rise to power that the family consciously promoted by means of the written word.[94] Unfortunately we know far too little about the provenance of the ninth-century copies of the

[92] See the discussion by Karl Hauck, 'Haus und sippengebundene Literatur mittelalterlicher Adelsgeschlechter von Adelssatiren des 11. und 12. Jahrhunderts her erlautert', *MIÖG* 62 (1954) 121–45, Eng. trans. 'The literature of house and kindred associated with medieval noble families, illustrated from eleventh- and twelfth-century satires on the nobility', in Timothy Reuter, ed., *The Medieval Nobility* (Amsterdam, New York and Oxford, 1978), pp. 61–85.
[93] Fredegar, ed. Wallace-Hadrill, Continuations c.34, pp. 102–3.
[94] *Ibid.*, pp. xlvii–l.

continuations and Book IV of the chronicle, many of which are in historical compilations all to do with different phases of the history of the Carolingians. It would be misguided to interpret these compilations as being of interest only to monastic centres.[95] The interest of some Carolingian ecclesiastics, notably Hincmar, archbishop of Rheims, in history and its fabrication is well attested,[96] but more research is needed on the aristocratic sense of the past and the great deeds of noble forebears, and the number of them who chose to have their names immortalized in this way. The political propaganda implicit in the continuations to Fredegar's chronicle was aimed at an audience. Its transmission is linked at an early stage with Metz, one of the strongholds of the Carolingians. Even the earliest text of all in BN lat. 10910 could quite conceivably have been prepared for a lay patron. The text of Gregory of Tours, for instance, is one whose transmission has lay associations. The earliest manuscript, BN lat. 17655, is written in Luxeuil minuscule and uncial and has some Corbie cursive minuscule script in it as well. It contains the first six books of Gregory's *Historiae* omitting many of the miracle stories relating to Tours. A similar abridgement occurs in two other north Frankish manuscripts. The suggestion has been made that this tribute to the glories of the Merovingian past may derive from the Neustrian court, and thus be a reflection of lay interest in history.[97] Certainly Eccard of Mâcon (d. 876) possessed a copy and bequeathed it to one of his friends, and Eberhard of Friuli (d. 867) had a copy of a *Gesta Francorum* which could have been a known, or an independent, Frankish history.[98] The *Vita Karoli* was a text whose audience was evidently envisaged as the royal circle and appears to have been in the royal library itself as part of a collection of historical texts. Leningrad F.v.IV.4 of the eleventh century, perhaps from the Soissons area, is a copy of a collection that may have been put together for Charles the Bald himself.[99] As well as Einhard it contains the *Annales regni francorum* and the *Liber Historiae Francorum*. Fredegar's chronicle and its continuations also enjoyed a wide circulation, as is clear from their manuscript tradition.[100]

---

[95] That is, it is important to regard surviving copies of historical works not just as witnesses to a text but as historical artefacts that in their very existence, make up and content, and in the questions they raise about who used them, have crucial implications for our understanding of their historical context. See above for a similar emphasis on the importance of copies of the laws, pp. 46–57.

[96] J. M. Wallace-Hadrill, 'History in the mind of Archbishop Hincmar', in R. H. C. Davis and J. M. Wallace-Hadrill, eds., *The Writing of History in the Middle Ages. Essays presented to R. W. Southern* (Oxford, 1981), pp. 43–70.

[97] *CLA* V, 671, and see David Ganz, 'The Merovingian library of Corbie', in Clarke and Brennan, eds., *Merovingian Monasticism*, pp. 153–72, at p. 156, with facsimile of fo. 3v in Plate 8.II, p. 157.   [98] See below, pp. 245–50.

[99] R. McKitterick, 'Charles the Bald (823–877) and his library: the patronage of learning', *EHR* 95 (1980) 28–47, at 32.   [100] Wallace-Hadrill, ed., *Fredegar*, pp. xlvii–lvi.

It is not impossible that some of the original owners or commissioners of such manuscripts as Leiden Voss lat. Q. 5 and Vat. reg. lat. 713, a late eighth-century codex written in the St Gall–Reichenau area, Montpellier 158, BL Harley 3771 or Vat. reg. lat. 213, all of the ninth century, were members of the educated noble class. Vat. reg. lat. 213, indeed, may be classified as an historical compilation, for, besides the chronicle of Fredegar and its continuations it contains the *Annales regni francorum* from 759 to 806 and the so-called *Annales Laurissenses maiores*, and was probably produced in the Rheims area in the late ninth century. Original ownership is one of the most difficult things to establish as far as the manuscript evidence is concerned, but with the question of the likely function and destination of a particular collection in mind, the notion of a secular interest in such books has to be entertained, especially when we find precisely this kind of text in the aristocratic libraries known from the ninth century, discussed below. Collections of historical and hagiographical texts such as Montpellier 360 of the late ninth century, for example, which includes Eusebius and Gregory of Tours, Einhard's *Vita Karoli*, Sallust and a number of passions of saints, could have been such as to have been of interest to educated laymen and loyal supporters of the Carolingians. Vienna 473, of the ninth century, contains the *Gesta pontificum Romanorum* attributed to Anastasius *bibliothecarius*, the continuations of Fredegar, the *Annales Laurissenses*, Einhard's *Vita Karoli* and the revised version of the *Annales regni francorum*, the *Genealogia Sancti Arnulfi* and the *Historia francorum epitomata ab origine gentis ad Ludovicum Pium*. A more thorough promotion of the Carolingians in the form of such an historical compilation would be hard to imagine, and it is tempting to think of it in the possession, and satisfying the historical interests as well as the political loyalties, of some magnate in the Worms area. Similarly one detects secular interests in the production of Vienna lat. 510, which combines Einhard's *Vita Karoli* and the 'Astronomer's' Life of Louis the Pious. Aristocratic possession and knowledge of both books would be highly appropriate. So it would too for BL Arundel 375, a small volume containing some of Fredegar's chronicle to enhance the story *De excidio Troiae* and the account of the career of Pippin II, son of Ansegisel, or BL Harley 3771, which precedes its text of Fredegar with Quintus Julius Hilarionis' *De cursu temporum*.[101]

---

[101] The difficulty of determining function from content is exemplified by such codices as these. Vienna 473, for example, also contains Bede, Alcuin and Isidore on orthography, which may point to use in a school rather than a book designed for private study. On the other hand, such texts might have been copied in to aid the owner in the reading of these histories. The whole function of history, historical writing and the development of historical consciousness, and the manifestation of a sense of the past in the Carolingian period is in need of a comprehensive treatment, but there have been a number of specific

If one can indeed envisage the audience for history as extending beyond the confines of the cloister, as these manuscripts with possible lay associations suggest, it uncovers an attitude to the written word and the recording of the past on the part of those who read or heard these histories; it exposes too the power of written history. History is only effective propaganda if it reaches the audience it was trying to persuade to accept the particular version of the past it provides. To recognize the propaganda value of such texts as Einhard, Notker's *Gesta Karoli*, the continuations to Fredegar's chronicle or the Lives of Louis the Pious is to accept that these works were not simply written for an aloof posterity, but as works of immediate purport, with a vital message for the living and those with power. We should look at the transmission of these texts with the crucial consideration of their contemporary significance and impact in mind. The manuscripts in this context have the potential to deliver up many secrets.

The audience for hagiography

As important as history for our understanding of the magnates and *potentes* is the celebration of family and local saints. This too appears to have been affected by lay patronage. The impulse to compose saints' lives can often be intimately related to the laity's self-interest as well as to their piety. Continuing family interest on the part of descendants of an aristocratic founder of a monastery may have contributed to his or her being subsequently venerated. It is possible that the composition of a *Vita* could actually assist this process, and further study on the lines suggested by de Gaiffier and others on the authorship, patron or commissioner, and audience of many of the early mediaeval saints' lives and the circumstances of becoming a saint would repay further investigation.[102] Local politics,

---

studies of importance, notably Heinz Lowe, 'Regino von Prüm und das historische Weltbild der Karolingerzeit', *Rheinische Vierteljahrsblätter* 17 (1952) 151–79; the articles by Labande, Gautier and Ganshof in *Settimane* 17 (1970); H. Lowe, 'Das Karlsbuch Notkers von St Gallen und sein zeitgeschichtliche Hintergrund', *Schweizerische Zeitschrift für Geschichte* 20 (1970) 269–302; Irene Haselbach, *Aufstieg und Herrschaft der Karlinger in der Darstellung der sogenannten Annales Mettenses priores; ein Beitrag zur Geschichte der politischen Ideen im Reiche Karls des Grossen*, Historische Studien (Lübeck, 1970); Hans-Werner Goetz, *Strukturen der spätkarolingischen Epoche im Spiegel der Vorstellungen eines Zeitgenössichen Mönchs* (Bonn, 1981).

[102] De Gaiffier, *Etudes critiques*, and *idem*, 'De l'usage et de la lecture du martyrologie. Témoignages antérieures au XIe siècle', *Analecta Bollandiana* 79 (1961) 40–59, in which he discusses the implications of the requirement in the 817 decrees from Aachen: *Ut ad capitulum primitus martyrologium legatur et dicatur*, MGH Cap. I, No. 379, p. 347. See also G. Phillippart, *Les Légendiers latins et autres manuscrits hagiographiques*, Typologie des Sources du Moyen Age Occidental, fasc. 24/25 (Turnhout, 1977).

rivalries and hopes for the status of a particular religious site or cult could have had the ironic result that a text, now regarded as a conventional piece of hagiography, was, when originally composed, a far from disinterested contribution to a carefully nuanced campaign on the part of a particular church or family to enhance its prestige. The extraordinary *Translatio sancti Alexandri*, commissioned from Fulda by Count Waltbrecht, grandson of Duke Widukind of Saxony, in the mid-ninth century, serves as an example.[103] Hauck has suggested that the count's relic gathering at Rome recounted in the *Translatio* became part of the family tradition and constituted a proclamation of family piety.[104] Another example is the *Translatio sanctorum Eusebii et Pontiani* commissioned by Count Girard and his wife and preserved in a late ninth-century codex, Brussels 1791–4.[105] This codex gathers together a number of texts relating to Girard and his obtaining of relics from Rome for Vezelay and Poitiers. An account of the translation of relics to Ghent in 944 was addressed to a local lay lord,[106] and one can speculate as to the motives, other than pious ones, which prompted the lady Angildruth to commission Eigil to write his Life of Sturm.[107] A possible aristocratic interest on the part of descendants of Sindleoz, a founder of the monastery of Reichenau, is the collection of saints' lives, now St Gall 577, written between 872 and 883.[108] It includes the Life of the Alemannian saint Meginrad in which Sindleoz's foundation of Reichenau is celebrated, as well as the *Vita Pirminii* in which Sindleoz figures again. Together, these lives present a particular version of the monastery's foundation, its early history and its political patrons, and it is tempting to think in terms of family encouragement for the composition of the lives themselves and a receptive patron for the collection.

The competition for relics so vividly portrayed in Einhard's *Translatio* of the relics of the saints Marcellinus and Petrus or the *Translatio sancti Liborii*, the claims of families to be patrons of particular houses and the jostling for preeminence in sanctity reveals not simply an extra dimension to the status of a cult and the many interests centred upon it, but also the potentially decisive role played by the written *Translatio*, *Miracula* or *Vita*.

---

[103] B. Krusch, 'Die Übertragung des heiligen Alexander von Rom nach Widelhausen durch den Enkel Widukinds 851', *Nachrichten von der Gesellschaft der Wissenschaft zu Göttingen, phil. hist. Klasse* (1933) 405–36.

[104] Hauck, 'Haus und sippengebundene Literatur'. 133.

[105] Ed., anon., '*Translatio SS. Eusebii et Pontiani in Galliam*', *Analecta Bollandiana* 2 (1883) 368–77.

[106] N. Huyghebaert, 'Une translation de réliques à Gand en 944. Le sermo de Adventu Sanctorum Wandregisili, Ansberti et Vulramni in Blandinium', in *Recueil de textes pour servir à l'étude de l'histoire de Belgique* (Brussels, 1978).

[107] Eigil, *Vita Sturmi*, ed., MGH SS II, pp. 366–77, c.1 at p. 36.

[108] Theodor Kluppel, *Reichenauer Hagiographie zwischen Walahfrid und Berno* (Sigmaringen, 1980).

More research is needed on the role of the written word, as against oral tradition, in the promotion of the cult of the saint.

Apart from the ecclesiastical and political arena, the saints' lives, their commissioners and possible audience need to be considered for their religious role in fostering and expressing lay piety. Yet the question of audience, despite Heinzelmann's plea, remains little explored.[109] Their local relevance, and the multiple function of the texts relating to a saint, deserve attention. Count Girard and his wife undoubtedly had impeccable religious motives as well as worldly ones for the promotion of the relics of Eusebius and Pontianus, as did the sons of Eberhard of Friuli for their acknowledgement of the translation account of the relics of St Calixtus of Cysoing, a monastery in which the Unruoching family had an interest.[110] The edificatory function of a saint's *Vita* stressed by Gregory of Tours remained of fundamental importance.[111] It is for this reason that we find evidence of the possession of saints' *Vitae* by many of the lay aristocrats about whose books we know, especially the collection owned by Eccard of Mâcon, the passions of the saints in the Unruoching library, or the martyrology presented to King Charles the Bald.[112] It was no doubt for private devotional purposes that Lanbertus *laicus* commissioned from a Breton scribe the copy of the life of Winwaloë, now in BN lat. 5610. Again, more work on manuscript collections of saints' lives, such as St Gall 577, or single volumes containing the life of one saint, such as the little volume of the Life of Mary of Egypt,[113] and the possibility of lay ownership needs to be explored. The great majority of Carolingian saints' lives and reworking of older Merovingian and early Christian lives can, no doubt, be seen in an entirely ecclesiastical context. Yet the few that do seem to offer lay connections and to support secular aristocratic interests should be sufficient to make us aware of the potential of this kind of written evidence for documenting one consequence of literacy in the cultivation, exploitation and patronage of religion.

---

[109] Martin Heinzelmann, *Translationsberichte und andere Quellen des Reliquienkultes*, Typologie des Sources du Moyen Age Occidental, fasc. 33 (Turnhout, 1979), especially p. 116. Heinzelmann provides the best starting point in terms of survey of past research and potentially productive texts for anyone embarking on this kind of work. See, too, J. Poulin, *L'Idéal de saintété dans l'Aquitaine carolingienne* (Quebec, 1975).

[110] *Translatio sancti Calixti Cisonium*, MGH SS XV.1, p. 418.

[111] Gregory of Tours, *Vita Patrum*, preface, MGH SS rer. merov. I, pp. 662–3. Eng. trans. James, *Gregory of Tours*, p. 27.

[112] See below, pp. 245–50, and McKitterick, 'Charles the Bald', 34.

[113] McKitterick, 'Charles the Bald', 35, though I now think that this manuscript may have been a count's copy rather than the king's. For stimulating comments on some of the Merovingian saints' lives, see Friedrich Prinz, 'Heiligenkult und Adelsherrschaft im Spiegel merowingischer Hagiographie', *Historisches Zeitschrift* 204 (1967) 529–44. See, too, François Dolbeau, 'Anciens possesseurs des manuscrits hagiographiques latins conservés à la Bibliothèque Nationale de Paris', *Revue d'Histoire des Textes* 9 (1979) 183–238.

Lay use of practical texts

The aristocratic libraries and contents which included practical handbooks on agriculture and related matters should alert us, too, to the transmission of some of the practical manuals of the early middle ages. Consider, for example, the *Agrimensores* and related gromatic, geometrical and surveying texts. Their transmission indicates successive adaptation of the text to suit different requirements, and the surviving manuscripts from the ninth century in particular represent a number of different compilations and sequences of texts. Although some can be securely related to the needs of a landowning monastery or to scholarly interest, such as the compilations made at Corbie in the time of Hadoard of Corbie (Naples V.A.13, Wolfenbüttel Gudianus 105), others, such as Clm 13084 from the Freising area, Florence Laurenziana 29.32 from west Germany (possibly Murbach), the north Italian *Corpus Agrimensorum* in Berlin lat. fol. 641 of the late ninth century, or the compilation made by Gisemundus in north Spain at the end of the ninth century, now in Ripoll (Archivo de la Corona de Aragon 106), could conceivably have been compiled for the steward or bailiff of the estates of a secular magnate. It was not only the church which owned land in the early middle ages, and the need for such practical texts as these was not confined to monks. Why, therefore, should surviving copies necessarily be those only of former monastic owners and users, or of scholars interested in classical civilization?[114]

III LAY PATRONAGE AND THE OWNERSHIP OF BOOKS

Introduction

The extension of patronage to authors need not indicate an interest in, or knowledge about, a work's content on the part of the recipient or dedicatee. Studies of the relationship between client and patron in the literary world of the sixteenth, seventeenth and eighteenth centuries, for example, have been wary of positing a cultured and enthusiastic patron unless corroborative evidence could be found. Indeed, they have been as cynical in the matter as Jonathan Swift who thought:

> For patrons never pay so well
> As when they scarce have learned to spell.[115]

---

[114] I question here the assumptions made by the compilers of the otherwise excellent L. D. Reynolds, ed., *Texts and Transmission. A Survey of the Latin Classics* (Oxford, 1983), especially p. 5.

[115] Jonathan Swift, 'Directions for making a Birth-Day Song' (1729), in *The Poetical Works of Jonathan Swift* II (London, 1883), pp. 168–77, at p. 171.

Aspiring and anxious authors may well importune potential patrons, whose only eligibility for their role is their wealth. Yet while the erudition of an early modern patron may well be in doubt, no slur has been cast on his literacy. In the ninth century, too, while the fulsome dedications to laymen and laywomen in praise of great learning of the recipients are no doubt exaggerated, it remains indisputable that a book, a written treatise, and not simply some rich present, was considered appropriate for the person in question. Such was the expense of book production and the status accorded possession of books that it is inconceivable that an author would waste precious parchment and labour on a gift for someone who could not even read. Patronage was sought from likely and potentially fruitful sources. Not only can a few laymen and laywomen who received treatises of various kinds be identified, they are representative of their class. The treatises offered and the books owned and borrowed reveal an important characteristic of lay culture. In many cases, moreover, works extant record in their prefaces that they were written at the express request of the recipient for such a work. Jonas of Orleans' moral exhortation *De institutione laicali*, for example, was addressed to and requested by Count Matfrid of Orleans;[116] Paulinus of Aquileia's *florilegium* was addressed to Count Henry of Friuli;[117] and Alcuin's *De Virtutibus et Vitiis* was written for Count Wido of Nantes.[118] As mentioned above, a number of educated laymen and laywomen commissioned or were given guides to the Bible by scholars and monks.[119]

These books were required for study and moral improvement. They instructed those who asked for and read them, and aided their understanding of the Christian faith. I shall return to the implications of these treatises later in the chapter.

Lay libraries: the examples of Eberhard of Friuli and Eccard of Mâcon

The books owned and borrowed by the lay nobility suggest that the laity offered literary patronage from an interest in reading beyond the normal everyday requirements of their positions. One of the best documented instances of lay book ownership is the Unruoching library.[120] The

---

[116] *PL* 106, cols. 121–278, and compare the *De institutione regia*, ed. J. Reviron, *Les Idées politico-religieuses d'un évêque du IXe siècle. Jonas d'Orléans et son 'De institutione regia'* (Paris, 1930).

[117] *Liber Exhortationis ad Henricum Forojuliensi*, *PL* 99, cols. 197–282.

[118] *PL* 101, cols. 613–38.   [119] See above, pp. 225–6.

[120] I. de Coussemaker, ed., *Cartulaire de l'abbaye de Cysoing et de ses dépendances* (Lille, 1885), and reprinted from Dehaisnes' edition in P. E. Schramm and F. Mütherich, *Denkmale der deutschen Könige und Kaiser* I (Munich, 1981, 2nd edn), pp. 93–4, and see the discussion by Pierre Riché, 'Les Bibliothèques de trois aristocrates laïcs carolingiens', *MA* 69 (1963) 87–104.

Unruochings possessed large tracts of land north of the Seine. The head of the family, Eberhard, had been appointed to the strategically important office of marcher lord of Friuli. This office has sometimes misled the unwary into assuming Eberhard himself was Italian. Eberhard married Gisela, the daughter of Louis the Pious and his second wife Judith. Eberhard's and Gisela's will is dated 867 and is preserved in the cartulary of Cysoing. It provides precise details about the family properties north of the Seine and elsewhere which they wished to bequeath to each of their seven children. Unruoch, the eldest son, received family lands in Lombardy and Alemannia; Berengar, the second son, was granted the formerly royal estate of Annapes, and other properties in Hasbaye and the Conde. Adalhard, the third son, was given the residences at Cysoing, *Canfinia* and *Grecina* (he was also to benefit from the patronage of his uncle King Charles the Bald and enjoy for a time the abbacy of St Amand). Ralph, the fourth son, as well as inheriting family properties at Vitry, Mestucha and elsewhere, became abbot of the rich monasteries of St Bertin and St Vaast in 883. The three girls, Engeldrud, Judith and Heiliwich were also bequeathed estates in the north of Francia. Each child was allotted some of the family treasure – gold, silver, jewellery – from both the household store and Eberhard's private chapel. This treasure included some liturgical books, such as a gospel book with ivory covers, a lectionary, missal and commentary, and an antiphonary with ivory covers.

A separate section of the will divided the books in the chapel library between the seven children, and a small gift was also made to Gisela. Thus Unruoch acquired a psalter, a Bible, the *De uerbis domini* of St Augustine, a collection of barbarian laws, Vegetius' *De Re Militari*, a book of sermons, a penitential, a collection of royal edicts (possibly the capitulary collection of Ansegis), the *Synonyma* of Isidore of Seville, a tract on the four cardinal virtues (presumably similar to the one written by Alcuin for Count Wido), a gospel book, a bestiary and the Cosmography of Aethicus Ister. This is not the sort of collection one would give to an illiterate. Unruoch was provided with a practical set of texts necessary for the exercise of his duties as a member of the nobility; his law book, for example, contained the Salic, Ripuarian, Lombard, Alemannian and Bavarian laws and is possibly the very one Lupus of Ferrières had prepared for Eberhard.[121] The Bible, gospel book and psalter were fittingly resplendent books for someone of Unruoch's rank to possess, but they also, with the book of sermons and the penitential, served as guides for the exercise of the Christian faith. The guides to morality and religion, indeed, are what one might expect from an aristocratic library. Less expected are the bestiary and Cosmography,

---

[121] Compare below, pp. 260–7, on a copy of this book now in Modena O.I.2.

though there are other instances of lay interest in the latter. King Aldfrith of Northumbria, for example, gave 7 hides of land to the monastery of Jarrow for his copy of this book.[122]

As with the lands and the treasure, Unruoch as the eldest son got the lion's share. But the character of his portion, combining practical functional texts but serving also personal piety and more general interest, is reflected to some degree in the books appropriately distributed among his siblings. Berengar was given Eberhard's other (the second best?) psalter, Augustine's *De Civitate Dei* and *De verbis domini*, a history of the Popes (possibly the *Liber pontificalis*), a *Gesta Francorum*, works by Isidore, Fulgentius and Martin, the 'book of Ephrem', the *Synonyma* of Isidore, *et librum Glosarum et Explanationis et Dierum*. Adalhard was provided with the third psalter, a commentary on the Epistles of St Paul, Augustine's *De verbis domini* and his commentary on Ezekiel, an epistle and gospel lectionary written in letters of gold, a Life of St Martin, a *librum Aniani*, Orosius' *Historiarum adversum paganos libri septem* and an item entitled *librum sancti Augustini, Hieronymi presbiteri, de hic quod Jacobus ait Qui totam legem seruauit et in uno offenderit factus est omnium reus*. Eberhard wished his son Ralph to have the psalter and commentary which Gisela had used for her private devotions, a work by Smaragdus (either the *De diadema monachorum* or, more likely, the *De via regia*), a *Collectaneum*, Fulgentius, the missal in constant use in the comital chapel, a Life of St Martin, the *Physionomia Loxi medici* and an *Ordo priorum principum*. Each of the three girls was bequeathed a much smaller collection of books, designed primarily to assist in her private devotions and provide religious instruction. Thus the eldest daughter Engeldrud received the *Vitas patrum*, the *Liber de doctrina sancti Basilidis*, Apollonius' story of the kings of Tyre and yet another copy of Isidore's *Synonyma*. Judith now gained her own missal, a book which began with Augustine's sermon on drunkenness, the Lombard law code and a copy of Alcuin's treatise on the virtues and vices written originally for Count Wido. Heiliwich, the only one of the sisters to marry, appears to have been both literate and devout. She received from her parents, in addition to her estates, a missal, a book of passions of the saints, a psalter with prayers, and a little prayer book. The latter was probably similar in content to the personal prayer book of Charles the Bald discussed below. But Judith's portion is in some ways the most striking. What use would she have had for the Lombard law code? It may be that she also inherited estates in northern Italy and needed to know the law of her tenants and agents. The book cannot be construed as an indirect gift

---

[122] Bede, *Historia Abbatum* c.15, ed. Charles Plummer, *Venerabilis Baedae Opera Historica* I (Oxford, 1896), p. 393.

to her husband, for she is not known to have married. To Gisela herself, Eberhard allotted a book on the four cardinal virtues and the *Enchiridion* of Augustine.

Eberhard and his family witness to a high degree of literacy in at least one household. This is the most commonsense interpretation of the evidence of possession of a wide variety of books, though firm proof that all members of the family could actually read the books they owned is lacking, apart from the reference to the volumes of psalter and commentary that Gisela used in her own devotions. To insist on the existence of total illiteracy in a ninth-century context of book ownership would, however, be perverse. These books were an outward symbol of skills acquired and public functions performed, and there is much similar evidence to suggest that the Unruochings were not alone in being able to read and in possession of their own books.

The beneficiaries of Eccard of Mâcon's will, for example, and Eccard himself, suggest that members of his class were educated and able to read.[123] Eccard was also related to the Carolingian house, in that he was a descendant of that same Childebrand who had commissioned the continuations of Fredegar's chronicle.[124] Neither of his wives, Albegundis and Richildis, had borne children, and by the time he came to make his will his two brothers, Theodoric and Bernard, were dead. His beneficiaries included both lay and ecclesiastical magnates, his sister Ada and his second wife Richildis. For use in her private chapel Eccard bequeathed his wife a missal with gospels and epistles for the mass and two antiphonaries. These gifts do not attest to Richildis' literacy necessarily as they could have been solely for the use of her private chaplain. To his sister, Ada, who had entered the convent of Faremoutiers, Eccard left a little psalter and a prayer book containing some psalms, while to Bertrada the abbess he gave his copy of the gospels in German and Life of St Antony. To Theutberga, the long-suffering wife of Lothar II of Lotharingia, he left a medical book. The laymen among the beneficiaries included his namesake Heccard, son of another Eccard. He received two dogs, a sparrow hawk, horn tablets (implying some secretarial or notarial use) and a volume of the *Lex Salica*. To Gebrard (or Gerbald) was given a book on the military art (probably Vegetius) and the *Lex Burgundionum*. Eccard's copy of Roman law

---

[123] M. Prou and A. Vidier, eds., *Recueil des chartes de l'abbaye de Saint-Benoît-sur-Loire* Documents publiés par la Société historique et archéologique du Gatinais V (Paris, 2 vols., 1900–7), I, pp. 65–6. See the illuminating discussion by Edmund Bishop, 'A Benedictine confrater of the ninth century', *Downside Review* (1892), reprinted in Bishop's *Liturgica Historica* (Oxford, 1918), pp. 362–9.

[124] Léon Levillain, 'Les Nibelungs historiques', *Annales du Midi* 49 (1937) 337–407 and 50 (1938) 5–66, and above, n. 93.

(presumably either the Breviary of Alaric or the *Lex Romana Burgundionum*) was left to Walter, bishop of Orleans, and a work on agriculture (Columella or Palladius) to Raganfrid, bishop of Meaux, together with two books 'of Prognostics'. To another clerical crony, Wala, bishop of Auxerre, Eccard willed a small book by Isidore of Seville (the *Synonyma?*), the *Cura Pastoralis* of Gregory the Great and Ambrose's *De ministeriis*, and Lives of St Gregory and St Laurence. Ansegis, archbishop of Sens, got Paul the Deacon's *Historia Langobardorum* and Gregory of Tours' *Historiarum libri decem*. Eccard bequeathed his Bible to the church at Sigy near Mâcon, his own family church, and conceivably an *Eigenkirche*. He possessed, too, a penitential and a collection of canon law which he left to the church of St Martin of Tours. To another lay friend, Odowrico, was given a seal ring and the Life of Mary of Egypt. In the disposition of all his plate, jewellery and weapons, Eccard left one intriguing item to his wife Richildis, a *furcella argentea*. If this was really a reference to a fork it is rather more than a century before Peter Damian's famous castigation of a lady for excessive fastidiousness in using a fork![125]

Eccard kept a modest collection of books in his chapel: a missal with a gospel and epistle lectionary, a gospel book, an antiphonary and a gradual. His other books indicate that he took his occupation as landowner, count and administrator of justice seriously, and that his library had that same mixture of practical texts, devotional works and a small selection of more general interest, mostly history, that we noted in the Unruoching library.

Fifteen executors for Eccard's will were chosen from among his own tenants and dependants. Eccard referred them to a paper of instructions so that they were to understand how to proceed on his death. He stated that he had made detailed stipulations and drawn them up in duplicate. One copy remained in his own hands and was to be passed to his executors on his death. The other he deposited for security with his sister at the monastery of Faremoutiers. He disposed of all things for the salvation of his soul.

Eberhard and Eccard thus had much in common. As well as books to assist their private devotions and those of their families and dependants, they equipped their private chapels with the necessary liturgical texts and had them bound in gold, ivory and precious gems. Further, they possessed the essential handbooks for men of their class – law books and tracts on war and agriculture. Both too possessed books designed to deepen their understanding of scripture. Riché, indeed, went so far as to conclude that these libraries represented 'le type de la bibliothèque de fonctionnaires

[125] See Bishop, 'Benedictine confrater', p. 366.

carolingiens, soldats, grands propriétaires, et chrétiens'.[126] It could hardly be better expressed, but too little attention has been paid to this definition, nor did Riché himself draw out the implications of his conclusions. In light of Eberhard's own family, all of them literate, Eccard's wide circle of friends and beneficiaries and the written instructions he leaves behind for them, it is unlikely that the educated noble was exceptional. Eberhard, Eccard and Dhuoda, too, may be exceptional in the range and richness of their personal libraries, but it is inconceivable that they were exceptional in their literacy or in their book ownership. The social transformations that made possible such spectacular examples as these three mean that the distinction between them and other members of their class may be one of rank and wealth rather than of skills or levels of literacy.[127]

Intellectual and practical interests, cultivated to such a marked degree by the kings themselves, are amply attested to by their celebrated libraries,[128] which clearly served not only as a centre from which texts were disseminated to other centres in the Frankish kingdom, but also as a model for emulation on the part of the Carolingian nobility.[129] This is suggested not only by the aristocratic libraries discussed above, and by the private libraries of *potentes* at court, but also by the number of eighth- and ninth-century manuscripts with contemporary lay associations which survive.

Courtiers' libraries

The laymen and clerics who served at court and proceeded from thence to plum lay abbacies, such as Angilbert or Einhard, or else retired altogether, like Gerung the *ostiarius* who became a monk at Prüm, or Gerward the palace librarian who spent his last years in a monastery, were at the heart of the royal administration.[130] They received and exercised patronage, and literate skills were essential. Not only was the dispensing of justice a

---

[126] Riché, 'Les Bibliothèques', 103.

[127] The investment in literacy on the part of the wealthy was discussed above, pp. 157–64. The wealth of Eberhard and Eccard in particular is the main subject of Pierre Riché, 'Trésors et collections d'aristocrates laïcs carolingiens', *Cahiers Archéologiques* 22 (1972) 39–46.

[128] Fully documented by Bernhard Bischoff, 'Die Hofbibliothek Karls des Grossen', 'Die Hofbibliothek unter Ludwig dem Frommen', 'Bücher am Hofe Ludwigs des Deutschen und die Privatbibliothek des Kanzlers Grimalt', *MS* III, pp. 149–212; Wilhelm Koehler and Florentine Mütherich, *Karolingische Miniaturen* IV *Die Hofschule Lothars* (Berlin, 1971), and McKitterick, 'Charles the Bald', 28–47.

[129] For parallels, see R. McKitterick, 'The study of Frankish history in France and Germany in the sixteenth and seventeenth centuries', *Francia* 8 (1980) 556–72, especially 568–70.

[130] Airlie 'Bonds of power'.

necessary activity, but these *potentes* or *nobiles* were also participants in the intellectual life of the royal household of which we get some inkling in the court poetry. As I have suggested above, to envisage the counts of the palace as part of the audience for these poems is to assume a high level of literacy, and even learning. In a few cases at least there is evidence for it in the form of the courtiers' libraries, the most obvious and best documented of which are those of Einhard and Gerward.

Einhard's own career and the *Vita Karoli* he wrote for courtly consumption are well known. Less so is his library. Born in the Maingau, he was sent by his parents to be educated at Fulda before pursuing his fortunes at court. He is undoubtedly an illustration of the way in which a layman of intelligence and education could follow his predilections and interests. His library is mentioned in a letter from Lupus of Ferrières to him, dated 826.[131] Lupus, then studying at Fulda, ventured to write to Einhard, as the celebrated author of a work he much admired, in order to ask for the loan of some of his books, including Cicero's *De Inventione* and *De Oratore*, four books on rhetoric addressed to Herennius (once attributed to Cicero), a commentary on the books of Cicero and the *Noctes Attici* of Aulus Gellius. It was from a catalogue or *brevis* listing these books, which Lupus had seen at Fulda, that he had learnt of Einhard's possession of these volumes, and Lupus stated that he should like to borrow others on the list after he had finished with the first batch, in order to make copies of them. As this *brevis* no longer survives, it is idle to speculate further as to what Lupus may have found among Einhard's books to appease his appetite for classical texts.

In the case of Gerward, however, the list of his books is still extant, preserved in Vat. pal. lat. 1877, fos. 33v–34r as part of the Lorsch library catalogue.[132] Gerward, member of a family of aristocratic patrons of Lorsch, had been trained at Lorsch before being sent to the court of Louis the Pious by his abbot. He served there as palace librarian and director of the palace scriptorium and then retired to Gannita near Nijmegen where he was responsible for the Xanten Annals, probably until his death *c.* 860. He left his library of twenty-seven volumes to Lorsch, and some of these still survive, such as the collection of twenty-five minor works by Augustine and two tracts by Nicetias of Remesiana in Vat. pal. lat. 210, and Augustine's *De doctrina Christiana* in Vat. pal. lat. 189.[133] Owing to Lupus of Ferrières' preoccupation, we have the impression of a

---

[131] Lupus of Ferrières, ed. Léon Levillain, *Loup de Ferrières. Correspondance* (Paris, 1964), p. 8.

[132] G. Becker, *Catalogi bibliothecarum antiqui*, (Bonn, 1885), pp. 118–19, but compare above, pp. 189–90.

[133] Bischoff, *Lorsch*, pp. 13–14 and 54–7.

predominantly classical content to Einhard's library. With Gerward's books, on the other hand, the principal patristic writers and early mediaeval exegetes were represented, with Augustine's *De Civitate Dei*, his expositions on the Psalms and Genesis, Eugippius' excerpts from Augustine, Jerome's commentaries on Isaiah and the Minor Prophets and the *De viris illustribus*, Gregory the Great's Homilies, and Bede's commentaries on the Song of Songs and on the Gospel of St Luke as well as his *De Templi Aedificatione*. Gerward also possessed Cassiodorus' *Institutiones* Book I, Orosius and other historical works, Hilary of Poitiers' *De Trinitate* and some books of the Bible. His sole classical work was a copy of Vergil.

A further witness to the culture of a Carolingian court is the library of Grimalt, archchancellor to Louis the German and abbot of St Gall.[134] It is a collection of liturgical, theological and ascetic works, with a number of saints' lives, gathered together from the writing centres of Regensburg, south-west Germany, Lorsch, Fulda and east France, as well as some apparently copied in his own hand. As colleague and intellectual companion of the Carolingian ruler, Grimalt throws light on the king's and the court's culture generally.

Manuscripts with lay associations

The evidence of manuscripts with lay associations detracts significantly from the solitary distinction of these aristocratic libraries and makes it possible to think in more general terms of noble book ownership. Nevertheless, this kind of evidence presents its own problems. Many codices, among them the law books discussed above in chapter 2, can only be inferred to be books used by laymen because of their content. The sheer sumptuousness of others, such as the Douce, Utrecht or Stuttgart Psalters, BN lat. 323 and the host of magnificent codices attributed to the palace libraries of Charlemagne, Louis the Pious, Lothar, Louis the German and Charles the Bald, Odo, Arnulf of Carinthia or Otto III suggests, especially in the light of the discussion in chapter 4, that they belonged to royalty or wealthy high nobility.[135]

Another category of book is the sumptuous codex whose content appears to have been designed for secular consumption. An example is the Montpellier Psalter, Montpellier 409, a Roman psalter with interpretations

---

[134] Bischoff, 'Bücher am Hofe Ludwigs des Deutschen'.
[135] See above, n. 128, and Florentine Mütherich, 'The library of Otto III', in Peter Ganz ed., *The Role of the Book in Medieval Culture*, Bibliologia, Elementa ad librorum studia pertinentia 4 (Turnhout, 1986), pp. 11–25.

or commentary interspersed throughout the text. Its appearance is rich and distinctive. It has titles in lines of silver and gold capitals or green and red uncials, and many fine initials with fish, leaf, zig-zag and plait motifs coloured in gold, silver, red, yellow and green, as well as two full-page miniatures of David and Christ. The decoration is of the type reminiscent of Anglo-Saxon ornament produced in southern Germany in the second half of the eighth century and the script is a south-east German minuscule.[136] The manuscript was probably written at Mondsee towards the end of the eighth century. At a later stage, between 783 and 794, *Laudes* and canticles were added in two separate quires at the end of the original text. The *Laudes* commemorate many members of the Carolingian royal family, Charlemagne and his sons Pippin, Charles and Louis, Pope Hadrian (d. 795) and Queen Fastrada (wife of Charlemagne from 783 until her death in 794), as well as a number of saints, including the saints in the diocese of Soissons – Bantaridus and Drausicus (fourteenth and twenty-second bishops of Soissons), Medresmis, Vodoalus and Leodardus – which enable the book to be located to Soissons after 783, and these additions to be dated between 783 and 794.[137] Remigius, patron saint of the metropolitan province to which Soissons belonged, is also invoked, as are the three angels Orihel, Raguhel and Tobihel that the Roman synod of 745 had classified as demons.[138] The invocations also included phrases in a 'Romance vernacular' regularly in the text – *tu lo iuua* (*tu illum adiuuo*), *tu los iuuo* (*tu illos adiuuo*), and *ora pro nos* (*ora pro nobis*). In a later hand of the first quarter of the ninth century a prayer was added after the *Laudes* and canticles. It invokes the Virgin, Apostles and all saints, asks for peace, joy, life, health, protection against enemies, propitious times and remission of sins for a 'sister Rotrud'. Still later additions indicate that by the second half of the ninth century the manuscript was at Auxerre. The murder of Bernegaudus by pagans on the 25th of October is recorded, and he has been identified with the Bernegaudus of Ferrières sent by Lupus of Ferrières to Auxerre to perfect his studies *c*. 860–2.[139] He was probably killed in one of the raids soon after 862.

There are a number of features of the later additions to this codex, therefore, to connect the manuscript with a Carolingian house. Quite apart

---

[136] *CLA* VI, 795. Probably from the same centre is the *Codex Millenaris*, Kremsmünster Cim. 1, and see the discussion of the Mondsee school in Bischoff, *Schreibschulen* II, pp. 9–26, especially pp. 16–18.

[137] Philippe Lauer, 'Le Psautier carolingien du Président Bouhier, Montpellier Univ. H 409', *Mélanges d'histoire du Moyen Age offerts à Ferdinand Lot par ses amis et ses élèves* (Paris, 1925), pp. 359–83.

[138] R. Rau, ed., *Bonifatii Epistulae Willibaldi vita Bonifatii* (Darmstadt, 1968), p. 408.

[139] Lauer, 'Le Psautier carolingien', p. 381.

from the *Laudes*, the eleven canticles are (except for the last one, the *Te deum laudamus* or *Hymnus Sancti Ambrosii et Augustini*) set in the same order as those in the Dagulf Psalter of the Ada school group of manuscripts associated with the court of Charlemagne. The prayer for Rotrud may be for Rotrud daughter of Charlemagne who retired to Notre Dame at Soissons, and died in 810. Charlemagne's sister Gisela was abbess of Chelles and of Notre Dame at Soissons. The manuscript would appear thus to have come into the possession of the royal monasteries of either Chelles or Soissons, or to have been the personal property of a member of the Carolingian royal family such as Gisela or Rotrud herself. But how did this book, written in Bavaria and decorated in a style reminiscent of the 'German-Northumbrian' style of the Tassilo Chalice or the Lindau Gospels book cover, come to be in northern France so soon after its completion?[140]

One possibility is that it was commissioned by a Carolingian from Bavaria soon after 788, or even before, which, given Carolingian connections and interests in Bavaria before the final annexation of the region and Tassilo's renunciation of his duchy in 788, is not impossible.[141] Another, stronger, possibility is indicated by the centre, Mondsee, where it is likely that the psalter was written. If the manuscript had been commissioned by a Carolingian, then the *Laudes* and canticles would surely have been included in the order. As it is, they have every appearance of having been added by a second owner. Mondsee and its abbot Hunric in the late 780s would in any case have been unlikely to be willing to do work for Charlemagne, for they were staunch supporters of Tassilo; Hunric was one of those who, with Archbishop Arno of Salzburg, besought the Pope in 787 to act as intermediary between Tassilo and Charlemagne.[142] This fine psalter, therefore, could have been produced at Mondsee for a member of the Agilolfing family in Bavaria. It may then have been among the possessions of Tassilo, his son, wife or daughters, who were confined to west Frankish monasteries after Tassilo relinquished his claim to Bavaria in 788. Cotani, one of Tassilo's daughters, is said to have been sent to Chelles, presided over by Gisela, abbess of that convent and also of Notre Dame of Soissons, while Hroddrud was sent to Notre Dame at Laon where one of Charlemagne's cousins, Theodrada, presided.[143] It may not be necessary to postulate that this book was actually confiscated but that it

---

[140] On the Tassilo chalice, see J. Hubert, J. Porcher and W. Volbach, *Carolingian Art* (London, 1970), pp. 209–13.

[141] Alain Stoclet, 'Gisèle, Kisyla, Chelles, Benediktbeuren et Kochel. Scriptoria, bibliothèques et politique à l'époque carolingienne. Une mise au point', *RB* 96 (1986) 250–70.

[142] McKitterick, *Frankish Kingdoms*, pp. 65–7.

[143] See J. F. Böhmer and Engelbert Mühlbacher, *Register Imperii* I (Innsbruck, 1908), p. 122.

was a possession which one of Tassilo's daughters took with her to her prison. The circumstances of the change in ownership cannot now be fully unravelled, but the range of historical alternatives all point to the likelihood of original lay ownership.

The character of the psalter itself, and of its *Interpretationes*, reinforces this possibility. The *Interpretationes* are an unusual feature of a psalter text, midway between a formal commentary and a summary one, and constitute a straightforward, uncomplicated commentary on the Psalms which differs from all others known from this period.[144] It was obviously designed for private study, with the *Interpretationes* interspersed between the verses and clearly indicated with marginal titles. Given the importance of the psalter in the education of the literate noble, or indeed any schoolchild, the function of this book as an aid to private devotion and instruction is unmistakable.

It would be possible to discuss at length the claims of lay ownership in relation to many Carolingian manuscripts for which definite proof is lacking, but here is not the place for it. Much of such a discussion would be, perforce, highly speculative in nature. Instead, therefore, I here confine myself to those manuscripts which contain colophons, inscriptions or other explicit clues of lay associations. Some were written for laymen, others were commissioned by or for them, or given or owned by them.

Most studies of Carolingian book production assume that it was an exclusively ecclesiastical affair. Undoubtedly the main centres of book production were the great monastic and cathedral scriptoria. It was they who developed their distinctive house styles of script, who trained great numbers of scribes and who built up the library resources of the institutions of which they were a part. There remains room, however, for the existence of professional scribes, notaries, secretaries and chaplains who may or may not have been in clerical orders, and who exercised their writing skills outside the cloister or cathedral close. Was Einsiedeln 375, a tenth-century collection of sermons and written *in scriniis*, the product of a notary writing outside a monastery for a lay or ecclesiastical patron, or was the term *scrinium* one a scribe might use of a monastic scriptorium? Even within a monastic scriptorium, the writing lecterns may not necessarily have been reserved for monks. The Bremen Stadtbibliothek copy of the *Pericopes* of Henry III, written at Echternach between 1039 and 1040, depicts the scribes of the book as a monk and a layman working together.[145] This is a late example, but may well be relevant for the ninth

---

[144] Lauer, 'Le Psautier carolingien', p. 369.
[145] Fo. 124v. Illustrated in Adolph Goldschmidt, *German Illumination* II (Florence and Paris, 1928), Plate 52A.

and tenth centuries as well. So little is known about the scribes who recorded their names in the books they copied that firm conclusions with regard to their status are simply not possible. Who, for example, was the Alitramnus who wrote *Alitramnus scripsit* in tironian notes in BN lat. 7730 fo. 85v in the ninth century? Was he a notary (as his knowledge of tironian notes might suggest), the owner or the scribe of the book or merely an idle doodler? Was Adam, son of Haynhard at Worms who wrote BN lat. 7494 (the grammar of Diomedes) for Charlemagne in about 780, a lay boy aspiring to be one of the group Notker describes in his *Gesta Karoli*, a young cleric similarly desirous of patronage or a monk secure in a monastic scriptorium?[146] Was Commoneus, who wrote Oxford Bodleian Library Auct.F.4.32, fos. 19–35, for his 'father and master' (*pater et dominus*) between 817 and 835, an oblate writing for his abbot or a boy demonstrating new skills to his parent? Was Sigilaus, scribe of BN lat. 266 for Lothar in the mid-ninth century, actually a monk of Tours or was he someone else trained in the Tours scriptorium who so excelled at his craft that he was in receipt of prestigious commissions? Where did Ademar, copyist of Zurich 523, function as a scribe? We are probably justified in thinking that Agilulfus *peccator*, who wrote Valenciennes 247 in west Frankish script of the early ninth century for Abbot Remigius, was a monk. So was Agambertus, scribe of the commentaries of Jerome in Valenciennes 59, possibly in the Fleury region, who copied the text for an Abbess Theotildis or Hlottildis at an average of eleven pages per day between 1 July and 4 August 806. But can the same be said of Droadus *peccator*, scribe of Chartres 21? And what of Winidhar *peccator*, who copied the commentary on the Romans in Vienna 743 *c.* 760–9? Baldo *magister Salisburgensis*, who wrote Graz 790 with several other scribes, was based in the scriptorium at Salzburg, as seems evident from his activity; and so was Lantrih, who copied the Pseudo-Augustinian *Sermo de Symbolo contra Iudaeos* for Liuphramnus of Salzburg (now Clm 19815). But in neither case have we any certainty that they were monks or secular clergy. Do the runes in Clm 6250 spelling the name *Cunradus* refer to the scribe, an owner or a random scribbler? Whether Gundohinus, scribe of the famous gospels in Autun 3, was a layman or a cleric is not known, nor can we now determine the status of Faustinus, copyist at the palace of Chasseneuil near Poitiers of Claudius of Turin's commentary on Genesis in 811 (BN lat. 9575). For whom did the bald scribe Secundus, responsible for Wolfenbüttel 579 (Helmst. 532, fos. 2–54), work? Were Regnardus, son of Helvidius who copied BN lat. 5237, or Gundoinus, scribe of BN lat.

---

[146] Notker, *Gesta Karoli* c.3, ed. Rau, *Quellen* III, p. 324; Eng. trans. Thorpe, *Two Lives of Charlemagne*, p. 95.

11683, non-monastic or monastic scribes? Were Berengar and Liutward, scribes of the *Hofschule* of Charles the Bald, professional itinerant craftsmen or cloistered monks?[147]

Such examples of unanswerable questions about scribes and their work are legion. The major problem of our evidence is that while the palaeography of a manuscript can tell one where the scribe was trained, it cannot settle the question of his lay or his clerical status or whether or not he was working within or without a monastic scriptorium. Other pieces of information, such as the availability of a particular text, presence of the hand in another manuscript indisputably ascribed to a monastic scriptorium for external reasons, the recording of a scribe's name among the brethren in a monastic confraternity book, or clear evidence of the scribe's training and subsequent activity in manuscripts of a centre over an appreciable period, such as the scribes of some of the south-east German scriptoria identified by Bischoff, render it unduly sceptical to suggest other than a monastic or ecclesiastical origin. Nevertheless, there remains some doubt about so categorizing all our extant codices. While the great majority of the scribes of the eighth, ninth and tenth centuries are anonymous, those who do provide their names raise many questions concerning their status and function which, as can be seen from the sample provided above, cannot be settled. Very occasionally more information than the ambiguous *peccator* or *indignus* is provided. Norbertus *acolitus*, for example, wrote Vat. lat. 316, Dominicus *grammaticus* was scribe of Novara 14.XLII in northern Italy in the ninth century, Engilricus *subdiaconus* copied Karlsruhe Aug. 108 at the beginning of the ninth century and Amalricus *magister scolare* at Tours was one scribe of BN lat. 1. Names apparently belonging to members of religious communities are, after all, so much easier at first sight to account for. Thus Dulcia, scribe of Laon 423,[148] the women at Chelles who wrote so many books for the bishop of Cologne,[149] the women at Jouarre who may have been doing the same for the bishops of Meaux and Paris[150] or Ada, sister of Charlemagne, associated with the Rylands Psalter and the Trier Gospels,[151] give rise to few

---

[147] There is much to be said in favour of their being the former: see McKitterick, 'Charles the Bald', especially 39–40, and Wilhelm Koehler and Florentine Mütherich, *Karolingische Miniaturen V Die Hofschule Karls des Kahlen* (Berlin, 1982).

[148] See Bischoff, 'Die Kölner Nonnenhandschriften und das Skriptorium von Chelles', *MS* I, pp. 16–34, at p. 32.

[149] *Ibid.* especially pp. 16–28.

[150] See R. McKitterick, 'The diffusion of insular culture in Neustria between 650 and 850: the implications of the manuscript evidence', in Hartmut Atsma, ed., *La Neustrie. Les pays au nord de la Loire, 650 à 850*, Beihefte der Francia 16/1 and 16/2 (Sigmaringen, 2 vols., 1988), vol. 16/2, pp. 395–432, at pp. 406–12.

[151] Manchester John Rylands Library 116 (Ada is referred to in the obits) and Trier 22.

problems as long as one does not start to question how, when or where they learnt to write and at what age they entered the religious community in which they died. Certainly the greater proportion of those named and unnamed can be located to the great monasteries, such as the host of scribes at Tours, St Gall, Rheims, St Amand, Lorsch or Corbie.[152] Few actually describe themselves as *laici*. Nevertheless, it is they who must prompt us to preserve an open mind regarding the status and affiliations of a scribe in Carolingian society.

Ragambertus, for example, was a layman, and a bearded one at that. He completed his copy of Seneca's letters, now BN lat. 8658A, in the second half of the ninth century and wrote in a neat and compact caroline minuscule. An inscription on folio 128 in ornate rustic capitals reads: *Ragambertus quamvis indignus laicus barbatus hunc codicem scripsit.* There is no reason to suppose that this rustic capital inscription was written by anyone other than the scribe of the rest of the manuscript. The letter forms are entirely in keeping with its character as a colophon and are sufficiently like the capitals in the rest of the manuscript, especially in the case of the 'H', to make it plausible to identify the scribe of text and colophon.[153] It would be open to the sceptic to maintain that the inscription was slavishly copied from the exemplar, but he would still have to reckon with a Germanic layman Ragambertus *laicus* who wrote that exemplar. Whether Ragambertus was writing for himself or for some other patron cannot now be determined. Robertus *laicus*, on the other hand, who copied the Histories of Josephus, now Berne 183, 'in honour of St Benedict and at the request of the reverend father Abbo' at the end of the tenth century, probably did so for Abbo, abbot of Fleury 988–1010. Cuissard identified this Robert with Robert the Pious, later king of France, but it could well have been a less exalted lay pupil in the Fleury region.[154]

The collection of saints' lives written by someone on a military expedition against the Avars, now Brussels 8216–18, in about 818,

---

[152] See, for example, E. K. Rand, *A Survey of the Manuscripts of Tours* (Cambridge, Mass., 1929); Bruckner, *Scriptoria* II and III; F. L. Carey, 'The scriptorium of Rheims during the archbishopric of Hincmar', in L. W. Jones, ed., *Classical and Medieval Studies in Honor of Edward Kenneth Rand* (New York, 1938), pp. 41–60; and Bischoff, *Lorsch*.

[153] Compare E. Chatelain, *Paléographie des classiques Latins* II (Paris, 1892), p. 22 and Plate CLXX, and C. Samaran and R. Marichal, eds., *Catalogue des manuscrits en écriture latine portant des indications de date, de lieu ou de copiste* III *Bibliothèque Nationale fond latin (suite)* (Paris, 1974), p. 727. The authors do not identify the scribe of the manuscript and of the colophon as I do.

[154] Cited by A. Vidier, *L'Historiographie à Saint-Benoît-sur-Loire et les miracles de Saint Benoît* (Paris, 1965), p. 40 n. 93. References to the scribes mentioned by name in the colophons of their books may be pursued in the work of the Bénédictins du Bouveret, *Colophons des manuscrits occidentaux des origines au XVIe siècle* (Freiburg, 1965).

although he does not state explicitly that he is a layman and he could have been one of the clerics who accompanied the army, seems more likely to have been the work of a literate soldier than otherwise. The appropriateness of the text as matter for copying will be discussed below in the final section of this chapter.

As one might have expected, the books that can be ascribed to lay ownership are primarily those of a devotional or practical character similar to the type in the libraries of Eberhard, Eccard or Dhuoda. A copy of Augustine's *Enarrationes in Psalmos* from southern France or northern Spain, for example, was annotated by one Honemundus 718–31, but later in the eighth century appears to have come into lay ownership.[155] The Ragyndrudis codex and the Gundohinus Gospels both have associations with eighth-century noblewomen. The Ragyndrudis codex contains the *Synonyma* of Isidore of Seville, and is now in Fulda (Bonifatianus 2). It was written on the orders of Ragyndrudis according to the inscription on folio 2v: *in honore dni nostri ihu xpi ego ragyndrudis ordinaui librum istum*. Various attempts have been made to identify this woman. Schulung thought she was the sister of Adela, abbess of Pfalzel.[156] A Ragyndrudis is mentioned in charters from Echternach and Lorsch dated between 751–68 and 771–2 respectively, as well as in Adela's will. Whether this is the same Ragyndrudis who was wife of the Waldbertus who had links with the monastery of St Omer is not clear. Sources cited by scholars in relation to the Ragyndrudis question mention her as married to three different men: Waldbertus 660–98, Milo 751–68 and Amanolc 774. The only fact that seems clear is that she was a laywoman of some wealth and education. The date and script type of the manuscript, late seventh- or early eighth-century Luxeuil minuscule, make identification with the wife of Waldbertus the most likely.[157] The Gundohinus Gospels were completed in 754 or 757, and commissioned from the scribe Gundohinus.[158] He records on fo. 186 that he wrote the book from beginning to end at Vosevio in July 'in the third year of King Pippin' at the request of Fausta and the monk Fulculph of the monastery of St Mary and St John. The whereabouts of Vosevio and whether this manuscript is Frankish or Lombard is disputed. Merlette's view was that the monastery of St Mary and St John is to be identified with that at Laon, founded by Salaberga, daughter of another

---

[155] *CLA* VI, 729 (Autun 107 (S.129) +BN n.a.lat. 1629 (fos. 15–16) and in a Carolingian binding).

[156] *CLA* VIII, 1197; Hermann Schulung, 'Die Handbibliothek des Bonifatius', *Archiv für Geschichte des Buchwesens* 4 (1961–3) cols. 285–346.

[157] Compare my discussion of this manuscript in McKitterick, 'The diffusion of insular culture', p. 21.   [158] *CLA* VI, 716 (Autun 3 (S.2)).

Gundohinus and brother of another Fulculph in about 650. The names Gundohinus and Fulculphus appear to be family names of the foundress and if these names were used in subsequent generations, then the scribe Gundohinus and one of the commissioners, the monk Fulculphus, were members of the same family, still based in the Laon region. The Laon connection has been questioned by Nees, but the precise origin – whether Burgundy or Laon – remains uncertain.[159] Wherever she lived in Francia, Fausta appears as a moderately wealthy patroness or commissioner of a gospel book either for her own use and that of her chaplain from a lay scribe, Gundohinus. Madalberta of Meaux may well be another such small-scale patroness, for her name appears in Cambrai 300 (282), a copy of Augustine's *De Trinitate*, written at the end of the eighth century.[160] A further instance of a patroness is the Adeldrudis who commissioned BN lat. 10865 in honour of Bishop Arnulf of Metz.[161]

From the ninth century there are a number of books extant which can be associated with counts. The famous Gauzlin Gospels in Nancy cathedral, for example, have been suggested as the work of Adalbald of Tours for Count Arnaldus, great-uncle of Bishop Arnaldus of Toul.[162] Count Arnald's son Arnulf was himself educated at Tours and preceded his nephew in the see of Toul. Count Hechiardus or Eccard of Angers commissioned a lectionary, but this is no longer extant.[163] The psalter written for Count Achadeus in the Rheims area between 883 and 900 by the scribe Abundius, is now Corpus Christi College, Cambridge, 272. It is an elegant volume, lavishly decorated with fine gold initials and commissioned for his private use by Achadeus himself.[164] Berengar, son of Eberhard of Friuli appears to have maintained his interest in books, for Vercelli A.Cap.A. s.4 and Trier 137, a volume containing Isidore of Seville's *Synonyma*, have now been associated with him.[165] Modena O.I.2, dated 991, moreover, appears to be a copy of a law book transcribed from the codex written for

---

[159] B. Merlette, 'Ecoles et bibliothèques à Laon du déclin de l'antiquité au developpement de l'université', *Actes du 95ᵉ congrès de sociétés savantes, Reims 1970, Sect. de phil. et d'hist. jusqu'à 1610* I (Paris, 1975), pp. 26–7, and echoed by S. Martinet, 'Sainte-Marie, Saint-Jean de Laon', *Les Dossiers de l'archéologie* 14 (1976) 26–34. Neither cites supporting evidence. Compare Laurence Nees, *The Gundohinus Gospels* (Cambridge, Mass., 1988), pp. 4–9, 213–14.

[160] *CLA* VI, 739, and see Bernhard Bischoff, 'Die Kölner Nonnenhandschriften', p. 33.

[161] George Waitz, 'Beschreibung von Handschriften welche in den Jahren 1839–42 näher untersucht worden sind', *Archiv* 11 (1858) 248–532, at 264.

[162] Suggested by Samuel Berger, *Histoire de la Vulgate pendant les premiers siècles du moyen âge* (Paris, 1893), p. 249.

[163] Recorded by Etienne Baluze, *Capitularia regum francorum* II (Paris, 1677), col. 1309. It had the inscription: *rogatu viri venerabilis Hechiardi comitis Ambianenses*, and was dated to s.ix².

[164] See below, p. 269.   [165] See *Colophons*, No. 1977 and above p. 247.

Eberhard by Lupus of Ferrières himself *c*. 832. This one, too, was no doubt for the use of some lay administrator. The Hague 43 appears to have been written for a Count Theodricus of Holland in the tenth century. One or two books which hint at the level of learning on the part of a layman can also be cited. A copy of the *Ars Minor* of Donatus was given to its early tenth-century owner, a schoolboy named Sado, by his mother.[166] Munich 8°132, a copy of the *Lex Baiuuariorum* seems to have belonged to a count in the Ingolstadt area.[167] The most interesting remnant of a nobleman's library is, however, the Quintus Curtius, now BN lat. 5716.[168] This fine volume was written for Count Conrad in the Loire region by Haimo in return for borrowing the text of Hraban Maur's *Expositio in Ecclesiastes* in order to copy it. Not only did this count have a classical work in his library, therefore, but he also seems to have been improving his understanding of the Bible with the assistance of Hraban Maur's relentless exegesis. This count may perhaps be identified with the Count Conrad who made a grant to St Colombe on 16 July 878, signed the charter recording the grant, and sealed it with his seal (*manu propria eam inscripsimus*).[169]

Lay borrowers from ecclesiastical libraries

Those who could not afford to possess their own books, or were otherwise unable to acquire them, sometimes borrowed what they needed. Eccard of Mâcon, for example, whose wealth is not in question, also borrowed books from Fleury to supplement his own collection. A clause in his will directed his executors to return the books belonging to the monastery of St Benedict at Fleury which he kept in the little casket (*in illa utica paruula*) at Sigy in the same cupboard as the Lombard box in which he kept his charters.[170] Eccard did not list the titles of the books he had borrowed, but that he was not alone in borrowing books from a nearby monastery or church, or one with which he had a special relationship, is attested by references in the library catalogues from one or two centres to men and women borrowing books, and by two surviving borrowers' lists from the ninth and tenth centuries.

Annotations inserted into the catalogue of the books of St Gall, for

---

[166] Formerly Phillipps 16308, it is now Aberystwyth 21553 C; see R. McKitterick, 'A ninth-century school book from the Loire valley: Phillipps 16308', *Scriptorium* 30 (1976) 225–31.   [167] Suggested by Bischoff, *Schreibschulen* I, pp. 249–50.

[168] Illustrated in Chatelain, *Paléographie* II, Plate CLXXVIII.2°, p. 26.

[169] Maximilien Quantin, *Cartulaire générale de l'Yonne. Recueil de documents authentiques pour servir à l'histoire de pays qui forment ce département* (Auxerre, 2 vols., 1854–60), I, No. LIV, pp. 104–5; he is thought by the editor of the charter (of the monastery of St Colombe) to be Conrad Count of Vermandois.

[170] Prou and Vidier, eds., *Chartes de Saint-Benoît-sur-Loire*, p. 67.

example, served as a reminder to the librarian that some of the books had been lent to outsiders: the codex containing Judith and Maccabees had been lent to the school, one of the volumes of homilies on the Gospels by Gregory the Great had been borrowed by the Emperor Charles the Fat, and his wife Richardis had Gregory's sermons on Ezekiel and Jerome's commentary on Jonah.[171] Of the four volumes of Jerome's letters possessed by St Gall, Liutward had borrowed two, as well as the collection of lives of the minor fathers. Other institutions as well as lay individuals could benefit from the availability of St Gall books; both Reichenau and Rohrbach borrowed the works of Gregory the Great, though in the case of Reichenau, St Gall was returning a copy of the Dialogues of Gregory that it had borrowed from Reichenau, but which had been recorded as a St Gall possession.

The borrowers' lists come from Weissenburg and Cologne. The Cologne list was in private possession at the end of the nineteenth century, though known to be Cologne 93, and the then owner made it available for study to Dekker, who edited the list in 1895.[172] It is most unfortunate that this manuscript has since been burnt. It was apparently a small volume bound in soft covers and containing the *Liber Ferrandi diaconi ad Reginum comitem* in a late seventh- or early eighth-century script. At the beginning of this slim, forty-four-folio codex were the four leaves containing the Cologne book list, usually dated 833, and the whole book is thought to have been part of Archbishop Hildebold's library. At the end of the list were the records of borrowers. It began with a section listing books borrowed by one Ermbaldus 'for the exercise of his ministry': a gospel book written in gold and bound in gold and precious stones, and a sacramentary of the Gregorian type written in gold and a lectionary, a book of Augustine's works (not identified more specifically), a commentary on the Book of Samuel, an antiphonary and a homiliary. From the books of Langolf (presumably a former owner of some books given to Cologne library before 833), Ermbaldus borrowed a *comes* and another sacramentary. Space was left by the compiler for the insertion of any additional loans for Ermbaldus to be recorded. A note was added recording the books the bishop of Cologne himself had taken to use in his private chapel: a gospel book, a lectionary and a copy of the Song of Songs. To Hilduin, abbot, was lent a

[171] Lehmann, *Mittelalterliche Bibliothekskataloge*, p. 72, lines 17 and 21, from St Gall 728, p. 6.
[172] A. Dekker, 'Die Hildebold'sche Manuskriptensammlung des Kölner Domes', in *Festschrift der drei und vierzigsten Versammlung deutscher Philologen und Schulmänner dargeboten von den höheren Lehranstalten Kölns* (Bonn, 1895), and see Paul Lehmann, 'Erzbischof Hildebold und die Dombibliothek von Koln', *Zentralblatt für Bibliothekswesen* 25 (1908) 153–8, who dates the list 833.

lectionary. A further note of another gospel book and lectionary borrowed by Ermbaldus is then added after a space. The compiler then noted that the bishop of Cologne had given a sacramentary and lectionary and an antiphonary to his sister, and to his sister's son he had given a psalter. Count Egilolf had been lent a lectionary and a volume of sermons by Gregory the Great, as well as a sacramentary and lectionary, probably for use in his private chapel. Someone called Voso had a lectionary and a Bishop Baldericus (possibly a *chorepiscopus*) had a missal and lectionary in one volume. Hildiswint had borrowed a copy of the Wisdom of Solomon, Baldrih had been lent Julianus Pomerius' *De Vita activa et contemplativa*, Osman had a missal, lectionary and lives of the fathers, possibly in one volume, and Suebrat had a gospel lectionary. Ratleih, rather than the liturgical and devotional books favoured by other borrowers from the Cologne library, took out Pompeius Trogus. Of the entire list of borrowers he is the only one to borrow a secular text. Wadolf, on the other hand, borrowed the *Apologeticum* of Gregory Nazianzus, Thetmar had Gregory's *Moralia in Job*, Heimbrat, brother of the bishop, had a lectionary and an antiphonary, Folcar a missal and lectionary and Redolf a missal. A later hand noted that Engilhelm had borrowed the Book of Kings, that the wife of one Werinbald had been lent a lectionary, that Gundolf had taken out a homiliary, and Hartgar a sacramentary.

The inclusion of the names of relatives of the bishop in this list, as well as that of the wife of Werinbald, and Count Egilolf himself, suggests that, like Fleury for Count Eccard, Cologne cathedral library was available for those with a special relationship either to the church or to the incumbent of the see. A local count, other local landowners and loyal supporters of the faith in the Cologne region were able to draw on the resources of the cathedral library to assist their private devotions and meditation. Most used the books they borrowed for the conduct of their liturgical observance, but the occasional instance of a more demanding theological commentary or collection of sermons being borrowed indicates greater efforts on the part of the individual to enrich and deepen his or her understanding of the Christian faith. One is not justified in assuming that all these names are those of laymen, but nor is there any justification for assuming that they are all the names of clerics unless it is explicitly so recorded. General usage, on the contrary, both in this and in the Weissenburg list, and in ninth-century library catalogues, suggests that it is usual for a man's clerical status to be noted.[173] One would, in short, expect the appellation of *presbyter*, *diaconus* or *monachus* if the names in the list were those of clerics. Given the analogous use Count Eccard made of Fleury library, and the

---

[173] See above, chapter 3.

Count Egilolf recorded as a user of Cologne's library, there seems no reason to doubt that in this Cologne list the names indeed represent those of some of the pious laity of the diocese. It should not be forgotten, moreover, that Cologne is in a German-speaking area, and thus that these borrowers of Latin theology and liturgy for private study were, in all likelihood, native German speakers. This is also the case in the list of borrowers from Weissenburg.

The Weissenburg lending list survives in Wolfenbüttel Weissenburg 35, fos. 113v–114r.[174] It records books that had been lent to people both within and without the monastery, men and women, priests and laymen. There are twenty-seven lines of the list altogether, with the names crossed out once the book had been returned. The books appear to have been lent not only for use, but also for copying. The manuscript containing this list is a ninth-century copy of Hilary of Poitiers' commentary on the Gospel of Matthew. The list on folio 113v at least would appear to have been started after 880 and is dateable palaeographically to the mid-tenth century. There are many gaps in the list, but some of the names, like those in Cologne, appear to belong to laymen and laywomen. Thus, Sigihel had borrowed a rule of guidance for women desirous of the religious life; Lantfrid had been lent a missal, lectionary, antiphonary and psalter. Liturgical books, usually antiphonaries or graduals and psalters, had also been lent to 'Uuolbrant', 'Ferding', 'Rihbert', 'Reginb[e]r[t]', 'Otakar' and 'Egib[e]r[t], Thiotbald', 'V...s' and 'Geilo'. The last named also borrowed a grammar and some liturgical vestments and may have been a local or *Eigenkirch* priest borrowing what he needed for a festive occasion, or it may be that he was simply a count's agent sent to fetch things the monastery had agreed to lend to the household. Liudrih also borrowed vestments when he took out a psalter and missal. A gospel book in German was borrowed, possibly by the bishop mentioned in the line above. On the second leaf, folio 114r, a number of loans to monasteries, abbots and priests are recorded. These appear to reinforce the possibility that the first part of the list, on folio 113v, is for the laity. Nevertheless, even among the books and borrowers recorded on folio 114r, the widow of Gerold is recorded as borrowing a psalter and 'Irm.', the wife of Reinbold, had a psalter and a gradual. The lady Liutgart (*domna liutgart*) was also lent a psalter.

Many of these names can be found among the charters of Weissenburg of the later eighth and first half of the ninth centuries; some of the monks'

---

[174] See the description by Hans Butzmann, *Die Weissenburger Handschriften* (Frankfurt, 1964), pp. 146–7. The text was edited by Otto Lerche, 'Das älteste Ausleihverzeichnis einer deutschen Bibliothek', *Zentralblatt für Bibliothekswesen* 27 (1910) 441–50.

and priests' names are recorded in the Weissenburg martyrologium. Weissenburg monastery, itself originally an aristocratic foundation that never lost its close links with the lay community within which it was established, appears to have added an extra dimension to its relationship with the surrounding population by functioning as a lending library for the local gentry.

These notes of borrowers are to be distinguished from the lists of brethren within a monastic community whose names are recorded each Lent with the book they borrowed. Hildemar in his commentary on the Rule of Benedict, written *c.* 845, described the process, paraphrased here. With the assistance of the brethren, the librarian of the monastery brought all the books into the chapter house at the beginning of Lent. After the chapter business (customary each day and similar in function to a modern school assembly) was concluded, the librarian read out the name of each brother who had a book. As his name was called, the brother produced the book he had been reading, and the prior would examine him on its contents. If the brother answered satisfactorily then he might suggest another book suitable for the pursuit of his studies; whatever book he asked for was given him unless the abbot deemed it unsuitable and suggested an alternative. If, on the other hand, the said brother could not give a coherent account of his reading, he had to have the same book back again unless it were clear that his failure to understand it were due to lack of ability rather than negligence, in which case a different book would be given him. After the departure of the brothers the abbot would check that all the books on the list were present; if any were missing he would search until they were found.[175]

Although it is possible that the Weissenburg list, or part of it, is a Lenten borrowers' list, it does not detract from the significance of the presence of laymen and laywomen on it. Indeed, it raises interesting possibilities regarding the role of the monastery in fostering the Lenten devotions of its lay patrons, dependants or supporters. The Cologne and Weissenburg lists and the random notes in the St Gall catalogue, together with the use of Fleury made by Eccard of Mâcon, suggest how some of the more educated members of the laity were able to exploit their relationship with a particular monastery, no doubt one they had themselves endowed and which numbered their relatives among the brethren, to borrow from the monastic library's resources for their private religious purposes. It is

---

[175] R. Mittermüller, ed., *Vita et regula SS. P. Benedicti una cum expositione regulae a Hildemaro tradita* (Regensburg, New York and Cincinnati, 1880). The discussion by Mary Alfred Schroll, *Benedictine Monasticism as Reflected in the Warnefrid–Hildemar Commentaries on the Rule* (New York, 1941), is of some value.

another dimension of the monastery's role in the community which was outlined in relation to the charter evidence in an earlier chapter. But it is also a manifestation of lay piety in literate terms which deserves now further consideration.

IV LAY PIETY AND THE USES OF LITERACY

In the course of the ninth century a model for the ideal layman was formulated. The Christian *florilegia*, of which many examples composed by Carolingian scholars survive, were addressed, almost without exception, to laymen or laywomen and provided their addressees with definitions and expositions of the Christian ethic and the social behaviour expected in accordance with it.[176] Jonas of Orleans' *De institutione laicali*, for example, written for Matfrid, count of Orleans, sets out precepts first of general application and then specifically for married men. Thus in the first book it explains the significance and obligations of baptism, the means of gaining forgiveness for sins and the importance of understanding the faith. It extols the benefits of Lenten devotion and gives assurances that the appropriate reading can be done. It stresses the need to educate the young in the tenets of the faith, and the importance of regular prayer and repentance, and provides guidance on Christian morality. It is, in short, a guide both to the Christian faith and the proper conduct of Christian life. The section on marriage and sex in the second book is matter of fact. It stresses, too, the necessity for parents to teach their children to love God and not to instruct their children in worldly matters at the expense of the laws of God. There are many basic social precepts concerning kindness to the poor, administering justice fairly, the evils of lying, bearing false witness or being too curious, and the duties of hospitality. The third book conforms to the pattern of other Christian *florilegia* in discussing the vices and virtues and completes neatly this set of guidelines for how a layman should live.[177]

The manuscript transmission of these *florilegia*, such as the *De Virtutibus et Vitiis* by Alcuin, the *Liber de Studio Virtutum* attributed to an Adalberus or Adalgerus, Haimo's *De varietate librorum sive de amore caelestis Patriae* and Paulinus of Aquileia's *Liber Exhortationis* for Count Henry of Friuli, and the presence of, for example, Alcuin's *De Virtutibus et Vitiis*, originally written for Count Wido, in the libraries of both Eberhard of Friuli and Eccard of Mâcon, indicate that these treatises came to be regarded as

---

[176] See McKitterick, *Frankish Church*, pp. 155–83, for a definition and full discussion of these texts.
[177] *PL* 106, cols. 121–278.

being addressed generally to the laity and being of use to them in cultivating Christian discipline.[178] These texts inculcate a consciousness of sin; they propose both a public and a private morality, and offer guidance to a man seeking to satisfy the moral, devotional and emotional demands made of him by acceptance of the Christian faith. There is an obvious possibility that some among the many *florilegia* manuscripts represent compilations or copies of them made for lay patrons. The copy of Alcuin's treatise, for example, was combined with his exposition of the penitential psalms, in BN lat. 2847. A compilation in BN lat. 2328 comprised the *Sententiae* of Isidore of Seville, Alcuin's *De Virtutibus et Vitiis* and treatises on the baptism and the mass. The codex, now BN lat. 2373, contained a miscellany of texts on the vices and virtues (by Halitgar of Cambrai and Alcuin), expositions of the Lord's Prayer and creed and a *Quaestiones in Heptateuchum*, as well as short texts and prayers. All these are the sort of books that would have fitted into the aristocratic libraries about which we have information. Some of these composite manuscripts on the Christian life in the secular world also contain the *Synonyma* of Isidore of Seville, a short treatise which has been described as an introductory manual on Christian spirituality.[179] It certainly appears to have been used as such among the lay nobility; it was striking, for example, how many copies of this work were bequeathed to the Unruoching sons and daughters. We find it often elsewhere in lay ownership, such as that of the lady Ragyndrudis, and Dhuoda, and it was drawn on by compilers of the Christian *florilegia*.[180] It sometimes occurs with the accompaniment of prayers, a litany (as in BN lat. 1153 and 1154) or with saints' lives and treatises on the catholic faith (as in BN lat. 2990).

The first book of Isidore's *Synonyma* was an examination of conscience and an abasement of the Christian in lamentation and sorrow for his faults.[181] It is presented in the first person as an internal dialogue. The second book, on the other hand, is a precise and vigorous rule for the Christian life, the practical means for the triumph of virtue and the proper conduct for the *doctores* and *iudices*. Like the Carolingian *florilegia* it stresses, too, the help to be found in the scriptures, and many of its precepts are addressed to the preoccupations of secular life. Whatever its initial

---

[178] The manuscript transmission may therefore be of relevance and would merit investigation. A start was made by H. M. Rochais, 'Contributions à l'histoire des florilèges ascétiques', *RB* 63 (1953) 246–91.

[179] Jacques Fontaine, 'Isidore de Seville auteur "ascétique": les énigmes des Synonyma', *Studi Medievali* 6 (1965) 163–95.

[180] On the manuscript tradition see M. Diaz y Diaz, *Index scriptorum latinorum medii aevi hispanorum* I (Salamanca, 1958), p. 31.

[181] A new edition is being prepared by Juan Antonio Peris, but at present it still is only available in *PL* 83, cols. 827–68.

purpose, the *Synonyma* clearly gained considerable popularity among the nobility in the Frankish kingdoms.

It was this kind of guidance, in written form, which helped to determine the nature of Carolingian religious sensibility. What this was like is most clearly observable in the personal faith of the brothers Louis the German and Charles the Bald, kings of the east and the west Franks respectively. Louis' Psalter, for example, displays that same devotion to the cross so evident in the prayer book of Charles the Bald,[182] and the royal libraries of both kings reveals how they grappled with the perplexities of their faith. Besides his copy of Otfrid's *Evangelienbuch*, Louis had a commentary on the Psalms and a number of exegetical works, mostly works on books of the Bible by Hraban Maur but including a small treatise by Hincmar of Rheims on the meaning of Verse 17 of Psalm 103:

> But the merciful goodness of the Lord endureth for ever
> and ever upon them that fear him and his righteousness
> upon children's children
> When he turneth him unto the prayer of the poor
> destitute and despiseth not their desire.[183]

The most sumptuous expression of lay piety is the personal prayer book of Charles the Bald, which, with his Psalter, reveals something of the king's personal devotion to his religion.[184] The litanies in both books, for example, provide a catalogue of those saints venerated by Charles and, no doubt, his entire family. As well as Benedict, Gregory, Hilary, Ambrose, Jerome, Leo and Augustine – the intellectual and spiritual giants of the late antique period – there are a host of Merovingian saints, particularly those from the Meuse–Moselle region, and a small group of Carolingian family saints – Geneviève, Gertrude and Arnulf. The texts of the prayers and canticles, appear to have been chosen, or composed, specifically for inclusion in the royal codices. The prayer book in particular, the earliest of the *Hofschule* manuscripts and written *c.* 860, incorporates, among its supplicatory prayers at the beginning of the volume, the *Confessio* Alcuin wrote for Charlemagne. It is preceded by the prayer of Gregory the Great to be said before confession. More prayers were added both in association with the taking of communion and making confession, and for private meditation. The seven penitential Psalms are a major section of the book and are succeeded by prayers against visible and invisible enemies (how heartfelt

---

[182] See the discussion by Robert Deshman, 'The exalted servant: the ruler theology of the prayerbook of Charles the Bald', *Viator* II (1980) 385–417.

[183] Bischoff, 'Bücher am Hofe Ludwigs des Deutschen', p. 191; *PL* 125, cols. 957–62.

[184] For full details of the contents of this manuscript see Koehler and Mütherich, *Karolingische Miniaturen* V. Compare also the Emperor Lothar's Psalter, BL Add. 37768.

these were, no doubt, by the 860s!), supplications for his wife Irmindrudis and her children, as well as Psalms for the tribulations and temptations of the flesh, for the afflicted, for those in distress and need. A centrepiece is provided by the devotion to the holy cross. The prayer book is in fact the only one of Charles the Bald's books containing a royal portrait which depicts the king kneeling in an attitude of *proskynesis* before the cross rather than triumphantly enthroned. This prostration of the worshipper before the cross was a means of imitating Christ's humility when he submitted to death on the cross, a theme complemented by the inclusion of Psalm 50 (51) which according to the Hebrew Bible and Vulgate heading expresses David's remorse and repentance for his sin with Bathsheba. The king, in Deshman's words is the 'exalted servant' who supplicates Christ.[185] The iconography reinforces the association between Christ the king and Charles the king, whose power comes from God. The sense of sin, the humble abasement of soul and body before God and the awed worship of the divine, as well as the love of God, are clearly manifest in Charles the Bald's Psalter, as is a clearly defined rulership in relation to the church. These books provide a precious glimpse into the personal religion of a layman. So, too, the psalters of noblemen that can be identified suggest something of their religious devotion and piety. One example is Corpus Christi College, Cambridge, 272, the Psalter of Count Achadeus. As noted above, it was clearly designed to fulfil the count's private needs.[186] At the end of each Psalm is a collect, and a litany was added at the end of the book in fine arched and pedimented frames with marbled purple or green shafts entwined with plants and richly coloured plinths, lintels and tympana. The litany celebrates, among others, a selection of Rheims saints, including the great Remigius. The name of Columbanus is also picked out in gold. There are no specially monastic suffrages. The invocations to King Carloman, Bishop Fulco and Pope Marinus permit the book to be dated 883 4. The canticles and the addition of the *Quicunque vult*, the Lord's Prayer and the creed with the collects, and a number of short prayers at the end, make of this book a prayer book rather than simply a psalter text. There can be little doubt that it was a book such as this which was used by members of the Unruoching family, or Dhuoda, and no doubt many other noblemen and women of the Carolingian period as well.

---

[185] Deshman, 'The exalted servant', 406.
[186] A full description is to be found in M. R. James, *Catalogue of the Manuscripts in Corpus Christi College Cambridge* II (Cambridge, 1912), pp. 27–32, but is to be compared to the forthcoming volume on Rheims in the series *Karolingische Miniaturen*, edited by Florentine Mütherich.

The probable possession of guides to the Christian life and personal copies of religious and biblical texts is not only significant for the implications it has for the ability of the addressees to read these simplified moral exhortations, prayers and psalms. It is also crucial for the demonstration of the way in which the faith and emotions of the laity were channelled by the Christian faith, a religion of the book, and found both outward expression and inner guidance in relation to a specific set of texts. The written word of God's revelation in the Bible was to provide guidance for the laity as well as for the clergy; it was the Bible's precepts, as interpreted and presented by Frankish clerics, which reached the laity. Through the medium of the written word, lay devotion was shaped. Through gifts of books to churches, lay support of the church was symbolized. In the rare instances of prayer books and psalters belonging to laymen or laywomen, moreover, we can glimpse lay piety. It was a literate piety; religious observance as much for the laity as for the clergy was defined and directed by the written word.

All the emphases in Carolingian education make this the natural consequence. But this chapter has also discussed evidence which throws light, however dim or uncertain, on many aspects of lay culture. The nature of the reception and potential audience of texts such as poetry, history, saints' lives, biblical exegesis and devotional manuals are fundamental questions which need to be pursued much further than has been possible here. I have suggested, too, that the manuscript evidence itself has much to offer us, even if only in terms of the questions of ownership and use of particular books and texts that it raises. On many issues and points of detail concerning the education and culture of laity, and, indeed, the extent and proficiency of lay literacy, the sources reveal more by implication than they provide as certainties. In many respects, too, there is but meagre evidence for the consistent and habitual use of literate modes in all aspects of everyday life. Yet the evidence adduced and the hypotheses formulated in this chapter, added to the weight of the legal, charter and 'economic' evidence discussed in the preceding chapters, point not only to the high status of the written word in Carolingian lay society but also to the Carolingian perception of its relevance to the conduct of daily business, entertainment and religious expression. The Carolingian laity, for a considerable way down the social scale, was a literate laity.

Epilogue

It is against the background of the evidence presented in this book, and within the context of the divers uses and status of the written word in Carolingian society, that the developments of the tenth, eleventh and twelfth centuries, heirs to the Carolingians, have to be seen. Yet it will also be clear that I have not provided a complete, nor a comprehensive, exposition of the evidence available. Not only have I concentrated on the Frankish kingdoms, and thus, perhaps, not given due weight to developments in Visigothic or Muslim Spain, Lombard, Byzantine or Papal Italy, Anglo-Saxon England, or elsewhere, I have also had to leave for treatment or fuller discussion another time, and by others, many more kinds of evidence and other contexts and manifestations of literacy, ideological as well as practical, in the Carolingian realm itself. One obvious omission is, of course, the evidence of inscriptions. Thanks to the new project for publishing the inscriptions for mediaeval Gaul, we may soon be in a position to assess this evidence.[1] Another is the concept of Carolingian culture as a 'script culture', that is, one based on the actual form of the written word, and the meaning and implications of the phenomenon of the emergence of caroline minuscule, which has received and is receiving attention of a kind that has much to tell us about the reception and propagation of the written word in the Carolingian world.[2] Indeed, there

---

[1] Nancy Gauthier, ed., *Recueil des inscriptions chrétiennes de la Gaule antérieure à la Renaissance carolingienne* I *Première Belgique* (C.N.R.S., Paris, 1975), which constitutes a reedition and amplification of the work of Edmond le Blant, *Inscriptions chrétiennes de la Gaule* (Paris, 1856 and 1865), and idem, *Nouveau recueil des inscriptions chrétiennes de la Gaule* (Paris, 1892).

[2] All Bernhard Bischoff's work expounds this, but see also for particular theses concerning the role and significance of script or particular kinds of script Heinrich Fichtenau, *Mensch und Schrift im Mittelalter*, Veröffentlichung des Instituts für Osterreichische Geschichtsforschung 5 (Vienna, 1946); Stanley Morison, *Politics and Script. Aspects of Authority and Freedom in the Development of Graeco-Latin Script from the Sixth Century B.C. to the Twentieth Century A.D. The Lyell Lectures* 1957 (Oxford, 1972); David Ganz, 'The preconditions for caroline minuscule', *Viator* 18 (1987) 23–44; and R. McKitterick, 'Manuscripts and scriptoria in the reign of Charles the Bald, 840–877', in E. Menesto and C. Leonardi (eds.), *Giovanni Scoto nel suo tempo. L'organizzazione del sapere in eta' Carolingia* (Todi and Perugia, 1989).

271

are many more functions and manifestations of literacy, not least the development of written musical notation, than it has been possible to deal with in the compass of one book, but those I have discussed provide at least some inkling of the great diversity in uses of the written word and the many levels on which literacy and literate skills must be assessed.

That religious observance among both clergy and laity should be shaped and given expression by the written word is an obvious consequence of the acceptance and promotion of Christianity – a religion of the Book. Education also was largely provided by *clerici* or by people brought up within a clerical (or at least Christian) milieu who imparted a Christian education. Yet a clear-cut distinction between 'orders' in society cannot be envisaged, and certainly not in the Carolingian period. Lay culture is not to be seen in opposition to clerical. Enough has been said in the preceding chapters to warn against any attribution of literate skills, or even an appreciation of the potential of literacy and the written word, to the clergy alone. For one thing, the church and the clergy worked among, with and for the people. The Christian faith was the focus of devotion for both laity and clergy, and everyone participated in its ritual. The people as much as the clergy, their kinsmen, acknowledged Christianity as the religion of the Book, the Word made flesh, the Gospels as holy object and transmitter of revealed Truth. Christianity, as we have seen, lent a new complexion to lay culture, with a new ideal of the Christian nobleman and warrior, with knowledge of the Bible and of the law, and zealous in the administration of justice. Indeed, the most obvious evidence, apart from that discussed in this book, for the respect commanded by the Christian church and all it represented, including its vital association with the written word, its learning and its uses of literacy, is that men and women continued to enter the church, to support it with a proportion of their wealth, to endow it with land and to found churches and monasteries, to seek its intercession and its blessing, and to vow their children to God.

. Frankish society was far from being illiterate; a Christian society cannot be a wholly illiterate society. It has already made a crucial step towards being literate in its acknowledgement of the written law of God and Christ's teaching. The literate and the learned were respected; learning and literacy were aspired to, and became, in the Carolingian world at least, a means of social advancement as well as of religious expression.

Yet it was not just Christianity that provided the Franks with so many potential uses for literacy. I have argued above, with reference to Carolingian royal administration, the import of the written law and the extensive charter evidence recording legal transactions, that the heritage of Roman administrative methods and assumptions concerning the role of the written word in the legal process and secular life as a whole made a vital and remarkable contribution to the fabric of Frankish society. The written word, moreover, was used by the Carolingians on an apparently larger scale than ever before in the barbarian kingdoms of western Europe. Books themselves were accorded a new status and that new status had repercussions on how this kind of wealth was safeguarded, replenished, augmented and distributed. To the Franks in the eighth and ninth centuries, and to their successors, literacy, and the Latin culture that went with it, were essential elements of a civilized Christian society. Carolingian society was thus not simply one where rather more people than used to be thought were literate to some degree, even if not necessarily learned. It was a society to which the written word was central. The written word was used, moreover, in such a way as to indicate that it was not just a tool, a weapon or a means of communication, but was also a resource, a guide, a key and an inspiration.

Index of manuscripts

General index

A solis ortu, 229
Aachen decrees of 816, 34
Abbo of Fleury, 220
Abraham, 127
Achadeus, count of Rheims, 260, 269
Acts of the Apostles, 171
Ada, sister of Charlemagne, 248, 257
Adalelm of Laon, 156
Adalgoz, 103
Adalhard, abbot of Corbie, 139; statues of, 151
Adalhard, count of Paris, planctus for, 230
Adalhard, son of Eberhard of Friuli, 148, 246
Adalung, abbot of Lorsch, 190
Adam, scribe, 256
Adela, abbess of Pfalzel, 259
Adeldrudis, patroness, 260
Ademar, scribe, 256
Admonitio Generalis (789), 20, 36, 220
Aeneid, cost of, 137
Aethelstan, 156 n. 86, 160–1 n. 105
Agambertus, scribe, 256
Agilolfing family, 254
Agilulfus, scribe, 256
Agobard, bishop of Lyons, 156
Agrimensores, 244
Albrih, scribe, 96, 112
Albuin, 105
Alcuin, 18, 150, 152, 193, 195, 196, 208, 268; on books, 151; De Orthographia, 11, 12; De Virtutibus et Vitiis, 245, 247, 266, 267; pupils of, 190; York poem (Versus de patribus regibus et sanctis euboricensis ecclesiae), 198
Aldfrith, king of Northumbria, 247
Alemannian laws, see Lex Alemannorum
Alemannian minuscule, see minuscule
Alemans, 82; Christianity of, 83
Alitramnus, scribe, 256
alphabet, learning of, 220 n. 32
alphabetical order, 197–8
Alphart, scribe, 114
Amalger, scribe, 94, 100, 112

Amalricus, scribe of Tours, 257
Ammianus Marcellinus, 65
Anastasius, bibliothecarius, 240
Andreas, local scribe, 109–11, 122, 126
Angelbert, 231
Angers, Formulary of, 69
Angilbert, abbot of St Riquier, 16, 178, 220, 236, 250
Angildruth, 242
Annals of St Vaast, 235
Ansegis, abbot of St Wandrille, 35, 46, 173, 175; capitulary collection of, 46, 47, 51–53 Table A, 246
Ansfledis, 223
antiquity, 152–5
Apocalypse, 4, 191
Arbon, 82
archives, efficiency of, 35
aristocratic literature, 230–2
army, mobilization of, 30
Arnaldus, count, 260
Arnulf, education of, 215
Ars Asporii, 15
Ars Bonifacii, 16, 17
Ars Tatuini, 16, 17
Ascrichus, ostiarius of Fulda, 129
Asger, scribe, 129
assembly, records of, 30–1
Astronomer, Life of Louis the Pious, 240
Athala, 64
Atto, clericus, 92
audience, 227–44; for German poetry, 232–5; for hagiography, 241–3; for history, 236–41; for Latin poetry, 227–32; for practical manuals, 244
Audo, clericus, 87
Augustine: Contra Iulianum, 194; Retractiones, 194, 202, 207
Aurelian, cancellarius, 130
autograph signatures, 92
Autramnus, lay scribe, 47, 51 Table A, 60
Autun, scribes of, 131
Auxerre, 175
Avars, 230, 258

Stammheim, 104, 105
Stancliffe, Clare, 167
Starcho, local scribe, 103
Steinach, 115
Strasbourg oaths (842), 9
Sturm, Life of, 242
Stuttgart Psalter, 252
subject catalogue, 180
subscriptio, 93, 109
Suzzo, scribe, 112, 123
Swift, Jonathan, 244
Synonyma, see Isidore of Seville

tabularius, 70
Tänikon, 105
Tassilo, duke of Bavaria, 154; daughters of, 254–5
Tassilo Chalice, 254
Tatto of Reichenau, 86
tax register, 160
Terence, 154
texts, collation of, 152
textual communities, 56 n. 76
Thannkirchen, 162
Theodoric of Andage, 219
Theodrada, 254
Theodricus, count of Holland, 261
Theodulf of Orleans, 150, 151, 152, 231
Theophilus, *De diversis artibus*, 143, 146
Theotmar of Fulda, *cancellarius*, 128, 129
Theotpert, *cancellarius*, 116
Theutberga, queen, 248
Thimeon, battle of, 234, 235
Thiothart, scribe, 100, 112
tironian notes, 58, 90, 193
tournesol, 143
Tours, 144, 149, 157, 162, 166; charters of, 130; Formulary of, 69; scribes of, 130 n. 130
Tours Bibles, 140
tractoria, 26
traditor, 160
Translatio sancti Alexandri, 242
Translatio sancti Eusebii et Pontiani, 242
Translatio sancti Liborii, 242
Tuotilo of St Gall, 221

ultramarine blue, use of, in manuscripts, 144
Umbertus, *cancellarius*, 111
Unruoch, 39, 246–7
Unruoching library, 245–8
Unruochings, 269
Uozo, 112
Urlau, 124
Uster, 104

Utrecht Psalter, 252
Uuinibaldus: 127
Uznach, 94, 104, 111–12, 123; scribes at, 111 n. 58; witnesses at, 98–101

Valerius, local scribe, 109, 110, 126
van Uytfanghe, Marc, 12
Venantius Fortunatus, 215
Vercelli, 85
verdigris, use of, in manuscripts, 145
vermilion, use of, in manuscripts, 145
Verona, poem in praise of, 230
Versus Isidori, 204, 205
Victor, bishop of Chur, 83
Vigilius, local scribe, 109, 110, 126
Vikings, 135, 159, 162, 163, 178, 234, 235, 253; as book thieves, 136
Vinomna, *see* Rankweil
Virgil, 153, 189
Virgilius, scribe of Echternach, 132
Virgilius Romanus, 153
Virgilius Palatinus, 189
Visigothic laws, 189
Vita Karoli, 239
Vita sancti Columbani, 83
Vita sancti Galli, 83
Vodalrichus, scribe, 128
Vunolf, 117, 127

Walafrid Strabo, 18, 182, 184, 190, 220 n. 33
Walgarius of Cysoing, books of, 159, 195
Wallace-Hadrill, J. M., 238
Waltbrecht, count, 242
Waltharius, 227–9
Walthere, 112
Waltram, 102–3, 123, 124
Wandalgarius, 43, 46
Wando, abbot of St Wandrille, 153, 156; library of: 173
Wandregisil, 174, 215
Wängi, 104
Wanilo, 122
Wasserburg, 104, 121, 124
Weissenburg, 190, 207; borrowers' list of, 204, 226, 262, 264–6; charters of, 133
Wenilo of Sens, 163
Werdo, local scribe, 111
Weringis, local scribe and *cancellarius*, 87, 111, 117, 121
Wetzikon, 122
white, use of, in manuscripts, 145
white lead, use of, in manuscripts, 144
Wido, count of Nantes, 245, 247, 260
William of Aquitaine, *planctus* for, 230
William of Septimania, 223, 236